Adobe® Dreamweaver® CS5

ILLUSTRATED

Sherry Bishop

COURSE TECHNOLOGY
CENGAGE Learning

Australia • Brazil • Japan • Korea • Mexico • Singapore • Spain • United Kingdom • United States

COURSE TECHNOLOGY
CENGAGE Learning™

Adobe® Dreamweaver® CS5—Illustrated

Sherry Bishop

Vice President, Publisher: Nicole Jones Pinard

Executive Editor: Marjorie Hunt

Associate Acquisitions Editor: Brandi Shailer

Senior Product Manager: Christina Kling Garrett

Product Manager: Karen Stevens

Associate Product Manager: Michelle Camisa

Editorial Assistant: Kim Klasner

Director of Marketing: Cheryl Costantini

Senior Marketing Manager: Ryan DeGrote

Marketing Coordinator: Kristen Panciocco

Developmental Editor: Janice Jutras

Content Project Manager: Jennifer Feltri

Art Director: GEX Publishing Services

Print buyer: Fola Orekoya

Cover Designer: GEX Publishing Services

Cover Artist: Mark Hunt

Text Designer: GEX Publishing Services

Copy Editor: Andrew Therriault

Proofreader: Camille Kiolbasa

QA Manuscript Reviewers: Jeff Schwartz, Danielle Shaw, Susan Whalen, Ashlee Welz Smith

Composition: GEX Publishing Services

For product information and technology assistance, contact us at
Cengage Learning Customer & Sales Support, 1-800-354-9706
For permission to use material from this text or product, submit all requests online at **www.cengage.com/permissions**
Further permissions questions can be emailed to
permissionrequest@cengage.com

Library of Congress Control Number: 2010930070

ISBN-13: 978-0-538-47869-4
ISBN-10: 0-538-47869-1

Course Technology
20 Channel Center Street
Boston, MA 02210
USA

Cengage Learning is a leading provider of customized learning solutions with office locations around the globe, including Singapore, the United Kingdom, Australia, Mexico, Brazil, and Japan. Locate your local office at: international.cengage.com/region

Cengage Learning products are represented in Canada by Nelson Education, Ltd.

To learn more about Course Technology, visit www.cengage.com/coursetechnology

To learn more about Cengage Learning, visit www.cengage.com

Purchase any of our products at your local college store or at our preferred online store www.cengagebrain.com

Adobe product screen shot(s) reprinted with permission from Adobe Systems.

CREDITS: Fig B-20 www.nea.gov; Fig C-1 www.ffbh.com; Fig C-30 © 2009 Snapfish by HP; Fig D-30 www.loc.gov; Fig E-21 www.usa.gov; Fig E-22 & E-23 www.loc.gov; Fig E-28 Used with permission by www.ushorse.biz; Fig F-34 www.nih.gov; Fig G-31 Used with permission by James at the Mill; Fig H-24 Used with permission from Waterfield Designs; Fig I-1 www.ssa.gov; Fig I-2 www.fbi.gov; Fig I-24 www.irs.gov; Fig J-1 www.nasa.gov; Fig J-15 www.peacecorps.gov; Fig J-21 www.navy.mil; Fig 2-1 www.navy.mil; Fig 2-2 www.whitehouse.gov; Fig 2-4 & 2-6 Adobe product screen shot reprinted with permission from Adobe Systems Incorporated

Printed in the United States of America
1 2 3 4 5 6 7 16 15 14 13 12 11 10

Brief Contents

Contents

Preface

Welcome to *Adobe® Dreamweaver® CS5—Illustrated.* The unique page design of the book makes it a great learning tool for both new and experienced users. Each skill is presented on two facing pages so that you don't have to turn the page to find a screen shot or finish a paragraph. See the illustration on the right to learn more about the pedagogical and design elements of a typical lesson.

This book is an ideal learning tool for a wide range of learners—the "rookies" will find the clean design easy to follow and focused with only essential information presented, and the "hotshots" will appreciate being able to move quickly through the lessons to find the information they need without reading a lot of text. The design also makes this a great reference after the course is over!

Coverage

Ten units offer thorough coverage of basic to intermediate skills for working with Adobe Dreamweaver, including setting up a Web site, using CSS for page layout, inserting media objects, using Live view, and publishing a Web site. Best practices covered include designing accessible Web sites, using CSS to separate content from presentation, and managing Web site files.

New features of this book include:

- New coverage of Web 2.0 tools
- New chapter on Adding Media and Interactivity
- Expanded appendix coverage of Using Templates and Presenting and Publishing a Web Site
- Resigned and updated Data Files—HTML files, text files, images, Flash content, and video content—are included with the text to engage students and give them the tools they need to develop Web sites from start to finish

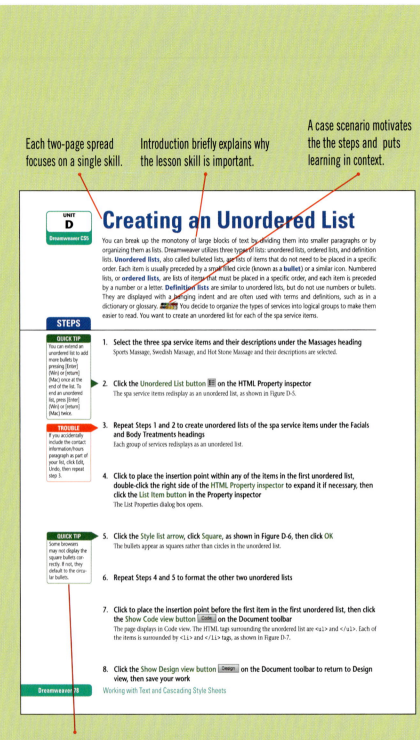

Each two-page spread focuses on a single skill.

Introduction briefly explains why the lesson skill is important.

A case scenario motivates the the steps and puts learning in context.

Tips and troubleshooting advice, right where you need it–next to the step itself.

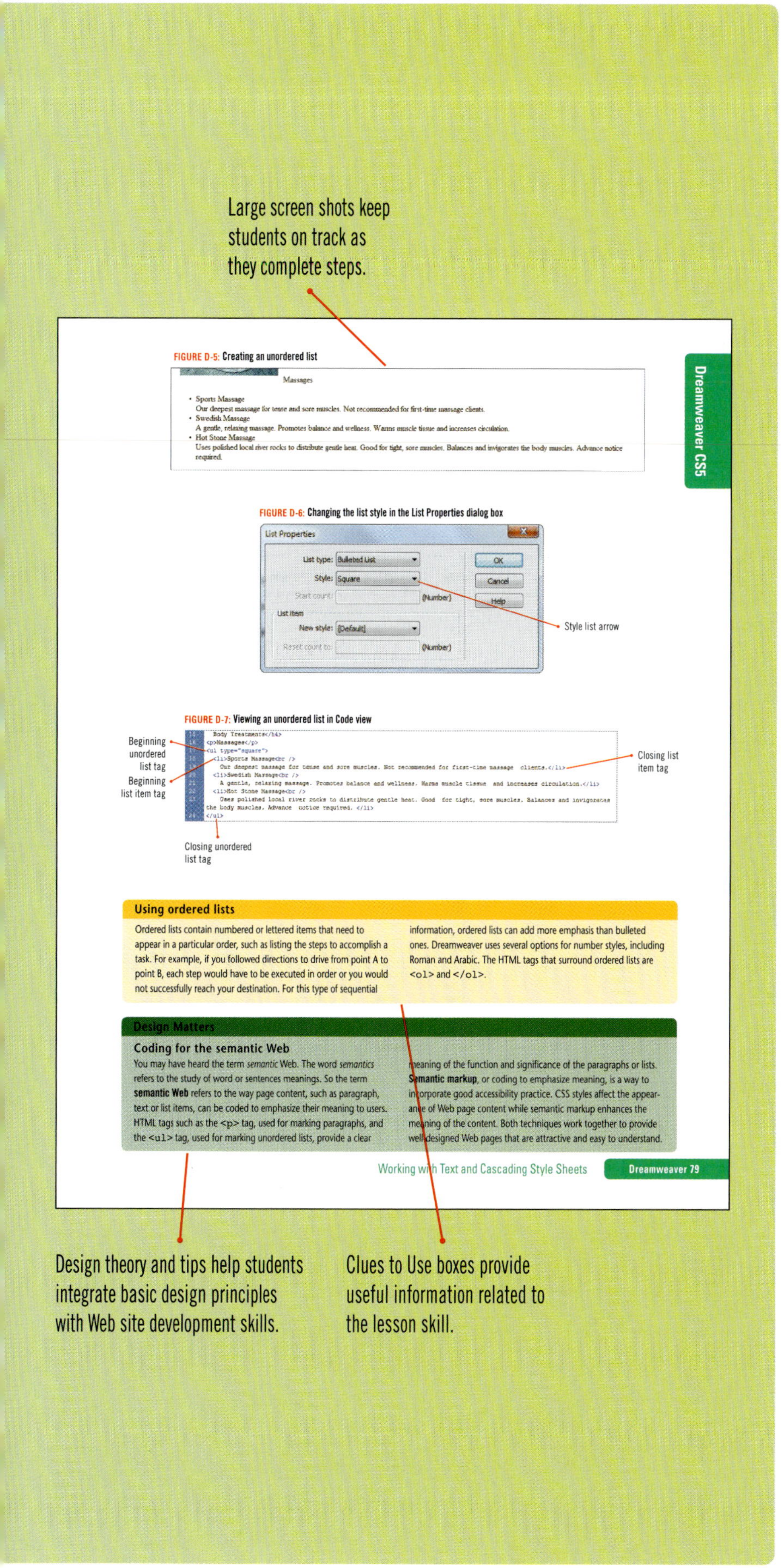

Large screen shots keep students on track as they complete steps.

FIGURE D-5: Creating an unordered list

Massages

- Sports Massage
  Our deepest massage for tense and sore muscles. Not recommended for first-time massage clients.
- Swedish Massage
  A gentle, relaxing massage. Promotes balance and wellness. Warms muscle tissue and increases circulation.
- Hot Stone Massage
  Uses polished local river rocks to distribute gentle heat. Good for tight, sore muscles. Balances and invigorates the body muscles. Advance notice required.

FIGURE D-6: Changing the list style in the List Properties dialog box

List Properties
List type: Bulleted List
Style: Square
Start count: (Number)
List item
New style: [Default]
Reset count to: (Number)
OK
Cancel
Help

Style list arrow

FIGURE D-7: Viewing an unordered list in Code view

Beginning unordered list tag
Beginning list item tag

Closing list item tag

Closing unordered list tag

```
Body Treatments</h4>
<p>Massages</p>
<ul type="square">
  <li>Sports Massage<br />
  Our deepest massage for tense and sore muscles. Not recommended for first-time massage  clients.</li>
  <li>Swedish Massage<br />
  A gentle, relaxing massage. Promotes balance and wellness. Warms muscle tissue  and increases circulation.</li>
  <li>Hot Stone Massage<br />
  Uses polished local river rocks to distribute gentle heat. Good  for tight, sore muscles. Balances and invigorates the body muscles. Advance  notice required.</li>
</ul>
```

Using ordered lists

Ordered lists contain numbered or lettered items that need to appear in a particular order, such as listing the steps to accomplish a task. For example, if you followed directions to drive from point A to point B, each step would have to be executed in order or you would not successfully reach your destination. For this type of sequential information, ordered lists can add more emphasis than bulleted ones. Dreamweaver uses several options for number styles, including Roman and Arabic. The HTML tags that surround ordered lists are <ol> and </ol>.

Design Matters

Coding for the semantic Web

You may have heard the term *semantic* Web. The word *semantics* refers to the study of word or sentences meanings. So the term **semantic Web** refers to the way page content, such as paragraph, text or list items, can be coded to emphasize their meaning to users. HTML tags such as the <p> tag, used for marking paragraphs, and the <ul> tag, used for marking unordered lists, provide a clear meaning of the function and significance of the paragraphs or lists. **Semantic markup**, or coding to emphasize meaning, is a way to incorporate good accessibility practice. CSS styles affect the appearance of Web page content while semantic markup enhances the meaning of the content. Both techniques work together to provide well-designed Web pages that are attractive and easy to understand.

Working with Text and Cascading Style Sheets   Dreamweaver 79

Design theory and tips help students integrate basic design principles with Web site development skills.

Clues to Use boxes provide useful information related to the lesson skill.

Written by Sherry Bishop, a digital media instructor at North Arkansas College in Harrison, Arkansas, Dreamweaver CS5 Illustrated offers a real-world perspective with exercises designed to develop the practical skills and techniques necessary to work effectively in a professional Web development environment.

Assignments

The lessons use The Striped Umbrella, a beach resort in Florida, as the case study. The assignments on the light purple pages at the end of each unit increase in difficulty. Additional case studies provide a variety of interesting and relevant exercises for students to practice skills.

Assignments include:

- **Concepts Reviews** consist of multiple choice, matching, and screen identification questions.

- **Skills Reviews** provide additional hands-on, step-by-step reinforcement.

- **Independent Challenges** are case projects requiring critical thinking and application of the unit skills.

- **Design Quest Independent Challenges** direct students to the Internet to critique selected Web sites with regard to the features and design principles learned in each unit.

- **Real Life Independent Challenges** are practical exercises to help students with their everyday lives by creating a personal Web site of their own design. Students maintain and update this site using the skills they learn in each unit.

- **Advanced Challenge Exercises** set within the Independent Challenges provide optional steps for more advanced students.

- **Visual Workshops** are practical, self-graded capstone projects that require independent problem solving.

Assessment & Training

SAM 2010: SKILLS ASSESSMENT MANAGER SÁM

SAM 2010 is designed to help bring students from the classroom to the real world. It allows students to train and test on important computer skills in an active, hands-on environment.

SAM's easy-to-use system includes powerful interactive exams, training and projects on the most commonly used Microsoft® Office applications. SAM simulates the Office 2010 application environment, allowing students to demonstrate their knowledge and think through the skills by performing real-world tasks such as bolding word text or setting up slide transitions. Add in live-in-the-application projects and students are on their way to truly learning and applying skills to business-centric document.

Designed to be used with the Illustrated Series, SAM includes handy page references, so students can print helpful study guides that match the Illustrated Series textbooks used in class. For instructors, SAM also includes robust scheduling and reporting features.

STUDENT EDITION LABS

Our Web-based interactive labs help students master hundreds of computer concepts, including input and output devices, file management and desktop applications, computer ethics, virus protection, and much more. Featuring up-to-the-minute content, eye-popping graphics, and rich animation, the highly interactive Student Edition Labs offer students an alternative way to learn through dynamic observation, step-by-step practice, and challenging review questions.

COURSENOTES

Course Technology's CourseNotes are six-panel quick reference cards that reinforce the most important and widely used features of a software application in a visual and user-friendly format. CourseNotes serve as a great reference tool during and after the student completes the course. CourseNotes for Microsoft Office 2010, Word 2010, Excel 2010, Access 2010, PowerPoint 2010, Windows 7, and more are available now!

COURSECASTS   Learning on the Go. Always Available...Always Relevant.

Our fast-paced world is driven by technology. You know because you are an active participant—always on the go, always keeping up with technological trends, and always learning new ways to embrace technology to power your life. Let CourseCasts, hosted by Ken Baldauf of Florida State University, be your guide into weekly updates in this ever-changing space. These timely, relevant podcasts are produced weekly and are available for download at http://coursecasts.course.com or directly from iTunes (search by CourseCasts). CourseCasts are a perfect solution to getting students (and even instructors) to learn on the go!

Instructor Resources

The Instructor Resources CD is Course Technology's way of putting the resources and information needed to teach and learn effectively into your hands. With an integrated array of teaching and learning tools that offer you and your students a broad range of technology-based instructional options, we believe this CD represents the highest quality and most cutting edge resources available to instructors today. The resources available with this book are:

• **Instructor's Manual**—Available as an electronic file, the Instructor's Manual includes detailed lecture topics with teaching tips for each unit.

• **Sample Syllabus**—Prepare and customize your course easily using this sample course outline.

• **PowerPoint Presentations**—Each unit has a corresponding PowerPoint presentation that you can use in lecture, distribute to your students, or customize to suit your course.

• **Figure Files**—The figures in the text are provided on the Instructor Resources CD to help you illustrate key topics or concepts. You can create traditional overhead transparencies by printing the figure files. Or you can create electronic slide shows by using the figures in a presentation program such as PowerPoint.

• **Solutions to Exercises**—Solutions to Exercises contains every file students are asked to create or modify in the lessons and end-of-unit material. Also provided in this section, there is a document outlining the solutions for the end-of-unit Concepts Review, Skills Review, and Independent Challenges.

• **Data Files for Students**—To complete most of the units in this book, your students will need Data Files. You can post the Data Files on a file server for students to copy. The Data Files available on the Instructor Resources CD are also included on a CD located at the front of the textbook.

Instruct students to use the Data Files List included on the CD found at the front of the book and the Instructor Resources CD. This list gives instructions on copying and organizing files.

• **ExamView**—ExamView is a powerful testing software package that allows you to create and administer printed, computer (LAN-based), and Internet exams. ExamView includes hundreds of questions that correspond to the topics covered in this text, enabling students to generate detailed study guides that include page references for further review. The computer-based and Internet testing components allow students to take exams at their computers, and also saves you time by grading each exam automatically.

Read This Before You Begin

Frequently Asked Questions

What are Data Files?

A Data File is a partially completed Web page, Web site, image, or other type of file that you use to complete the steps in the units and exercises to create the final document that you submit to your instructor. The Data Files that you need for each unit are listed in the back of the book.

Where are the Data Files?

Your instructor will provide the Data Files to you or direct you to a location on a network drive from which you can download them. The Data Files are also included on a CD located at the front of the textbook. As you download the files, select where to store them, such as a hard drive, a network server, or a USB storage device. The instructions in the lessons refer to "the drive and folder where your Data Files are stored" when referring to the Data Files for the book.

What software was used to write and test this book?

This book was written and tested on a computer with a typical installation of Microsoft Windows 7. The browsers used for any steps that require a browser are Mozilla Firefox and Internet Explorer 8. If you are using this book on Windows Vista, your dialog box title bars will look slightly different, but will work essentially the same.

This book is written for the Windows version and the Macintosh version of Adobe Dreamweaver CS5. The two versions of the software are virtually the same, but there are a few platform differences. When there are differences between the two versions of the software, steps written specifically for the Windows version end with the notation (Win) and steps for the Macintosh version end with the notation (Mac). In instances when the lessons are split between the two operating systems, a line divides the page and is accompanied by Mac and Win icons.

Also, in this book, Macintosh commands instruct users to press the [return] key to enter information. On some newer Macintosh keyboards, this key may be named [enter] or the keyboard may include both [return] and [enter]. On the newest Mac OS X, the F-keys are assigned to system functions: F1=monitor brightness and F4=widgets. You can change this in your system preferences. Newer keyboards have an "FN" or "fn" key that can be used in conjunction with the F-keys so that they function "normally."

Do I need to be connected to the Internet to complete the steps and exercises in this book?

Some of the exercises in this book assume that your computer is connected to the Internet. If you are not connected to the Internet, see your instructor for information on how to complete the exercises.

What do I do if my screen is different from the figures shown in this book?

This book was written and tested on computers with monitors set at a resolution of 1280 × 1024. If your screen shows more or less information than the figures in the book, your monitor is probably set at a higher or lower resolution. If you don't see something on your screen, you might have to scroll down or up to see the object identified in the figures. In some cases, the figures will not match your screen because the Dreamweaver windows have been resized or cropped in an effort to make the figures as easy to read as possible. The Application bar (Win) or Menu bar (Mac) may be displayed as two bars when a lower resolution is used or when the application window is sized down.

How do I create Web sites that have not been built through previous consecutive units? (Windows)

If you begin an assignment that requires a Web site that you did not create or maintain earlier in the text, you must perform the following steps:

1. Copy the Solution Files folder from the preceding unit for the Web site you wish to create onto the hard drive or USB storage device. For example, if you are working on Unit E, you need the Solution Files folder from Unit D. Your instructor will furnish this folder to you.
2. Start Dreamweaver.
3. Click **Site** on the Application bar, then click **Manage Sites**.
4. Click **New**.
5. Type the name you want to use for your Web site in the Site Name text box. Spaces and uppercase letters are allowed in the Site name.
6. Click the **Browse for folder icon** next to the Local Site Folder text box.
7. Navigate to the location of the drive and folder of your newly copied folder to set the local site root folder. The local site root folder contains the name of the Web site you are working on. For example, the local site root folder for The Striped Umbrella Web site is called striped_umbrella.
8. Double-click the local site root folder, then click **Select**.
9. Click **Advanced Settings** in the category list in the Site Setup dialog box, click the **Browse for folder icon** next to the Default Images folder text box. A message appears stating that the site cache is being updated. This scans the files in your site and starts tracking links as you change them.
10. Double-click the assets folder in your site root folder, then click **Select**.
11. Verify that the **Links relative to: Document option** is checked.
12. Click **Save** to close the Site Setup dialog box.
13. Click **Done** to close the Manage Sites dialog box.

How do I create Web sites that have not been built through previous consecutive units? (Macintosh)

If you begin an assignment that requires a Web site that you did not create or maintain before this unit, you must perform the following steps:

1. Copy the Solution Files folder from the preceding unit for the Web site you wish to create onto the hard drive, or USB storage device. For example, if you are working on Unit E, you need the Solution Files folder from Unit D. Your instructor will furnish this folder to you.
2. Start Dreamweaver, click **Site** on the Menu bar, then click **New Site**.
3. Click **Site** in the category list in the Site Setup dialog box (if necessary).
4. Type the name you want to use for your Web site in the Site name text box.
5. Click the **Browse for folder icon** next to the Local Site Folder text box, and then navigate to the location of the drive and folder of your newly copied folder to set the local site root folder.
6. Click the local site root folder, then click **Choose**.
7. Click **Advanced Settings** in the category list in the Site Setup dialog box, then click **Local Info** if necessary.
8. Click the Browse for folder icon next to the Default Images folder text box. If necessary, click the drive and folder of your newly copied folder to locate the assets folder.
9. Click the assets folder, click **Choose**, then click **Save** to close the Site Setup dialog box.
10. Click **Done** to close the Manage Sites dialog box.

How do I use Dreamweaver on multiple computers?

If you are using Dreamweaver on multiple computers, such as one in the classroom and one at home or in a lab, you must set up each Web site on each computer before you can access your Web site files on each computer. You only have to do this once for each Web site, but the site root folder must be accessible from both machines. For instance, if you are storing your Web sites on a USB storage device and using it on a computer in a lab and your computer at home, you must set up the Web site on each machine. Once you tell Dreamweaver where to find the files (the USB drive), it will find them automatically from that point forward.

What if I can't find some of the information in the exercises on the Internet?

This book uses the Internet to provide real-life examples in the lessons and end-of-unit exercises. Because the Internet is constantly changing to display current information, some of the links used and described in the book may be deleted or modified before the book is even published. If this happens, searching the referenced Web sites will usually locate similar information in a slightly modified form. In some cases, entire Web sites may move. Technical problems with Web servers may also prevent access to Web sites or Web pages temporarily. Patience, critical thinking, and creativity are necessary whenever the Internet is being used in the classroom.

What if my icons look different?

Symbols for icons, buttons, and pointers are shown in the steps each time they are used. Icons may look different in the Files panel depending on the file association settings on your computer.

What if my screen fonts look different?

Your screen fonts may be larger or smaller than they appear in figures. The figures were captured using the default Windows display setting of Smaller - 100% (default). Use the Control Panel to compare your settings in the Appearance and Personalization, Display window.

What if I can't see my file extensions?

The learning process will be easier if you can see the file extensions for the files you will use in the lessons. To do this in Windows, open Windows Explorer, click Organize, click Folder and Search Options, click the View tab, then uncheck the box Hide Extensions for Known File Types. To do this on a Macintosh, go to the Finder, click the Finder menu, then click Preferences. Click the Advanced tab, then select the Show all file extensions check box.

What if I can't see Flash content in my browser?

To view objects such as Flash movies, you must set a preference in your browser to allow active content to run. Otherwise, you will not be able to view objects such as Flash buttons. To set this preference in Internet Explorer, click Tools, click Internet Options, click the Advanced tab, then check the box Allow active content to run in files on My computer (under Security). Your browser settings may be slightly different, but look for similar wording. When using Windows Internet Explorer 7, you can also click the information bar when prompted to allow blocked content.

What do I do if I see a Server Busy dialog box?

You may see a message that says "This action cannot be completed because the other program is busy. Choose 'Switch To' to activate the busy program and correct the problem." when you are attempting to import Word content. This is probably a memory problem. If it happens, click Word when the Start menu opens. Repeat again if necessary, then switch back to Dreamweaver. You should see the imported text.

Other Adobe® CS5 Titles

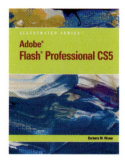

Adobe® Flash® Professional CS5—Illustrated
Barbara M. Waxer (053847789X)

Eight units provide essential training on using Adobe Flash Professional CS5 including creating graphics and text, using the Timeline, creating animation, creating buttons and using media, adding interactivity, and integrating with other programs.

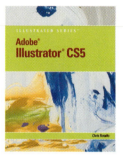

Adobe® Illustrator CS5—Illustrated
Chris Botello (1111221960)

Eight units cover essential skills for working with Adobe Illustrator CS5 including drawing basic and complex shapes, using the Pen tool, working with blends, compound paths and clipping masks, creating pattern fills and gradient fills for objects, and designing stunning 3D effects.

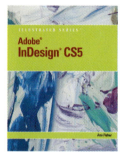

Adobe® InDesign® CS5—Illustrated
Ann Fisher (0538477873)

Eight units provide essential training on using Adobe InDesign CS5 for designing simple layouts, combining text, graphics, and color, as well as multi-page documents, layered documents, tables, and InDesign libraries.

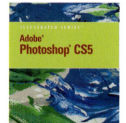

Adobe® Photoshop® CS5—Illustrated
Chris Botello (0538477814)

Eight units offer thorough coverage of essential skills for working with Adobe Photoshop from both the design and production perspective, including creating and managing layer masks, creating color effects and improving images with adjustment layers, working with text and combining text and imagery, and using filters and layer styles to create eye-popping special effects.

For more information on the Illustrated Series, please visit:
www.cengage.com/ct/illustrated

Acknowledgements

Author Acknowledgements

It is so difficult to fully express my appreciation to the many dedicated members of the Illustrated team. Nicole Pinard, Vice President and Editorial Director of Course Technology, Cengage Learning, and Marjorie Hunt, Executive Editor, are always at the top of my list for giving me the opportunity to work with Course Technology many years ago. Karen Stevens, the Senior Product Manager, is a gifted leader and wonderful encourager to all of us who work with her. It is always an honor to work with her on a project.

This was my first time working with Janice Jutras, our Developmental Editor. Her unique perspective brought many fresh ideas to the table. Thank you, Janice! Jennifer Feltri, the Content Product Manager, and Louise Capulli, the Project Manager, moved the units along smoothly, ensuring that this book would be ready for each of you. We thank them for keeping up with the many details and deadlines. Joe Villanova redesigned the Web site banners and logos to give each site a fresh look. The work is beautiful. I am always so appreciative of the work so many do to ensure that the book is technically accurate: Andrew Therriault, our Copy Editor; Camille Kiolbasa, our Proofreader; and Jeff Schwartz, Danielle Shaw, Susan Whalen, and Ashlee Welz Smith, QA Manuscript Reviewers.

Thank you, Adobe, for giving us this outstanding Web development tool. It is an exciting program that is easy to use whether you are a professional Web developer or a beginning design student. I hope each of you enjoy exploring its many exciting features.

On a personal note, I have watched the Deepwater Horizon environmental disaster in the Gulf of Mexico unfold with a heavy heart. I have a special connection to this area—the Beach Club in Gulf Shores, Alabama, provided the inspiration for The Striped Umbrella Web site. The Beach Club management has graciously allowed us to use photographs of their beautiful property in our data files and figures. I am confident that the people, wildlife, beaches, and Gulf of Mexico itself will overcome the extreme challenges this tragedy has brought. Gulf Shores is our regular family vacation destination and I cannot imagine that ever changing. I plan to donate a portion of the royalties from this book to The Nature Conservancy in honor of The Beach Club as a small gesture of support to those out there on the front line in the massive recovery effort. Our best wishes to all of you.

Lastly, thank you to my favorite beach bum, my husband Don.

UNIT A
Dreamweaver CS5

Getting Started with Adobe Dreamweaver CS5

Adobe Dreamweaver CS5 is a Web design program used to create media-rich Web pages and Web sites. Its easy-to-use tools let you incorporate sophisticated features, such as animations and interactive forms. In this unit, you learn to start Dreamweaver and examine the workspace. Next, you open a Web page and learn how to use the Help feature. Finally, you close the Web page and exit the program. You have recently been hired as a manager at The Striped Umbrella, a beach resort in Florida. One of your main responsibilities is to develop the resort's Web site using Dreamweaver. You begin by familiarizing yourself with the Dreamweaver program.

OBJECTIVES

Define Web design software

Start Adobe Dreamweaver CS5

View the Dreamweaver workspace

Work with views and panels

Open a Web page

View Web page elements

Get help

View a Web page in a browser window

Close a Web page and exit Dreamweaver

Defining Web Design Software

Adobe Dreamweaver CS5 is a powerful **Web design program** that lets you create interactive Web pages with text, images, animation, sounds, and video. You can create Web page objects in Dreamweaver as well as import objects created using other programs. Although you can create several different types of files with Dreamweaver, you will be saving files with the .html file extension throughout this book. **HTML** is the acronym for **Hypertext Markup Language**, the language Web developers use to create Web pages. You need to learn some basic Dreamweaver features for your new position.

DETAILS

Using Dreamweaver you can:

- ### Create Web pages or Web sites
  Dreamweaver lets you create individual Web pages or entire Web sites, depending on your project needs. **Web pages** are pages of text in HTML format combined with images in various image formats. **Web sites** are collections of related Web pages. Web sites are stored on **servers**, which are computers connected to the Internet. Users can view Web sites using a **Web browser**, which is software used to display pages in a Web site; some of the most popular browsers are Internet Explorer, Mozilla Firefox, Google Chrome, Opera, and Safari. You can also import Web pages created in other programs, edit them in Dreamweaver, and then incorporate them into an existing Web site. Dreamweaver provides predefined page layouts called **templates** that you can apply to existing pages or use as a basis for designing new ones.

- ### Add text, images, tables, and media files
  You can add text, images, tables, and media files to a Dreamweaver Web page by using the Insert panel. The **Insert panel** (sometimes referred to as the **Insert bar**) contains buttons for creating or inserting objects, such as tables, images, forms, and videos. Using the Insert panel, you can also insert objects made with other Adobe software programs, including Fireworks, Flash, and Photoshop. Table A-1 describes Insert panel categories and their corresponding buttons.

- ### Display Web pages as they will appear to users
  Dreamweaver is a **WYSIWYG** ("What You See Is What You Get") program. As you design a Web page in Dreamweaver, you see the page exactly as it will appear in a browser window.

- ### Use the Property inspector to view and edit page elements
  The **Property inspector** (also referred to as the **Properties panel**) is a panel that displays the characteristics of a page's currently selected object. Figure A-1 shows a Web page open in Dreamweaver. Note that the properties of the selected text appear in the Property inspector. The Property inspector changes depending upon the type of page object selected. For example, when an image is selected, the Property inspector displays image properties. When text is selected, the Property inspector displays text properties with either the HTML Property inspector or the CSS Property inspector.

- ### Use Roundtrip HTML
  Because Dreamweaver utilizes **Roundtrip HTML**, HTML files created in other programs can be opened with no additional coding. Conversely, you can open and edit a file created in Dreamweaver in other software programs, such as Microsoft Expression Web. Your HTML code can "travel" between programs without coding problems. HTML tags will not be rewritten when pages that were written with other Web editors are opened in Dreamweaver.

- ### Manage Web sites
  Dreamweaver lets you manage Web site pages to ensure that all the **links**, or connections among the pages, work properly. The importance of proper site management increases as new pages are added to a Web site. Part of managing a Web site involves identifying problems or challenges as content is added and the site becomes more complex. There are several types of reports that you can run to check for problems across the Web site. Dreamweaver also has special tools that help you manage a site when you are working as part of a team on a project.

FIGURE A-1: Web page open in Dreamweaver

Tabs display filenames of open files (Mac users will not see tabs unless multiple pages are open)

Web page

Property inspector showing properties for selected text

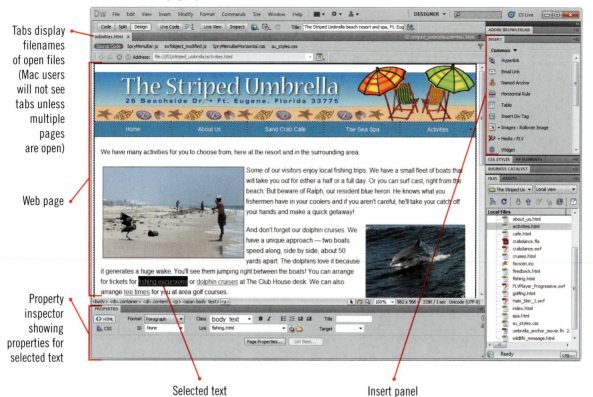

Selected text

Insert panel

TABLE A-1: Insert panel categories and corresponding buttons

category	buttons
Common	Commonly used buttons, such as images, media, and hyperlinks
Layout	Buttons for inserting divs, tables, Spry objects, and frames
Forms	Buttons for inserting form objects, such as check boxes and radio buttons
Data	Buttons for inserting Tabular Data, Dynamic Data, and Recordsets
Spry	Buttons for inserting Spry data sets, Spry validations, and Spry panels
InContext Editing	Buttons for creating editable regions to allow others to add content
Text	Buttons for formatting text; for example, strong, headings, and lists
Favorites	Buttons you can customize; Dreamweaver will add those you use most frequently

Starting Adobe Dreamweaver CS5

There are many ways to start Dreamweaver, depending on the type of computer you are using and the type of installation you have. Although the steps below start the program using the Start menu (Win) or the hard drive icon (Mac), the fastest way to start Dreamweaver is to place a shortcut (Win) or an alias (Mac) for Adobe Dreamweaver CS5 on your desktop or add it to the Quick Launch toolbar (Win) or Dock (Mac). **Shortcuts** and **aliases** are icons that represent a software program stored on your computer system. When you double-click a shortcut (Win) or an alias (Mac), you do not need to use the Start menu (Win) or open submenus (Mac) to find your program. When you initially open Dreamweaver, the Welcome Screen appears. The Welcome Screen provides shortcuts you can click to open files or to create new files or Web sites. You are given your first Web related assignment and need to begin by starting Dreamweaver.

STEPS

WIN

QUICK TIP
Your Start button may look different, depending on your version of Windows and your Windows settings.

1. **Click the Start button 🌐 on the Windows taskbar**
   The Start menu opens, which lists the names of the software programs installed on your computer.

2. **Point to All Programs, click Adobe Web Premium CS5 or Adobe Design Premium CS5 (if you have one of these suites of Adobe products), then click Adobe Dreamweaver CS5**
   Dreamweaver opens and the Welcome Screen appears, as shown in Figure A-2.

3. **Click HTML in the Create New column on the Dreamweaver Welcome Screen**
   A new blank HTML document named Untitled-1 opens.

MAC

TROUBLE
Your Adobe Dreamweaver folder may be in a folder other than Applications. See your instructor or technical support person if you have trouble locating Dreamweaver.

1. **Click Finder in the Dock, then click Applications**

2. **Click the Adobe Dreamweaver CS5 folder, then double-click the Adobe Dreamweaver CS5 program**
   Dreamweaver opens, and the Welcome Screen appears, as shown in Figure A-2.

3. **Click HTML in the Create New column on the Dreamweaver Welcome Screen**
   A blank document named Untitled-1 opens.

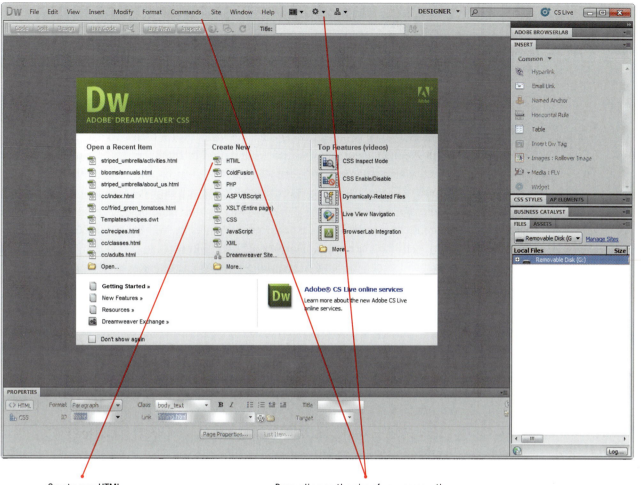

Create new HTML

Depending on the size of your screen, the Application bar (Win) or Menu bar (Mac) may appear as two different bars, one above the other

Using Dreamweaver layouts

Dreamweaver has several pre-set layouts that you can choose between. In the **Designer layout**, the panels are docked on the right side of the screen, and Design view is the default view. In the **Coder layout**, the panels are docked on the left side of the screen, and Code view is the default view. The **Dual Screen layout** is used with two monitors: one for the document window and Property inspector and one for the panels. Other layouts include App Developer, App Developer Plus, Classic, Coder, Coder Plus, and

Designer Compact. You can change the workspace layout by using a feature called the **Workspace switcher**. The Workspace switcher allows you to quickly change between different pre-set workspace screen arrangements. You can also create and name your own custom layout with the New Workspace command on the Workspace switcher menu. You can also reset your workspace back to the pre-set Designer layout after you have moved, opened, or closed panels with the 'Reset Designer' command.

Viewing the Dreamweaver Workspace

The Dreamweaver **workspace**, shown in Figure A-3, consists of the Document window, the Application bar (Win) or Menu bar (Mac), toolbars, Property inspector, and panels. The default layout in Dreamweaver is called the Designer layout. Other layouts include the Coder and Dual Screen layouts. The Designer and Coder layouts are built with an integrated workspace using the **Multiple Document Interface (MDI)**. This means that all document windows and panels are positioned within one large application window. **Panel Groups** are sets of related panels that are grouped together. **The Property inspector** is a panel that changes to display the properties of the currently selected Web page object. It contains text boxes, shortcut menus, and buttons that allow you to make formatting changes without having to open menus. Its contents vary according to the object currently selected. In order to continue with your Web site project, you want to spend some time familiarizing yourself with the Dreamweaver workspace.

DETAILS

Use Figure A-3 to find many of the elements detailed below.

- When a document is open, the filename, path, and document type appear in the **Browser Navigation toolbar**, a new toolbar in Dreamweaver CS5. This toolbar, located directly above the document window, contains navigation buttons you use when following links on your pages in Live view. **Live view** displays an open document with its interactive elements active and functioning, as if you were viewing the document in an actual browser window.

- The **Application bar** (Win) or **Menu bar** (Mac), located at the top of the Dreamweaver workspace, includes menu names, a Workspace switcher, and other program commands. The Application bar (Win) or Menu bar (Mac) appears as one bar or two bars, depending on your screen size and resolution. You use commands by using shortcut keys or by clicking corresponding buttons on the various panels.

TROUBLE
If you don't see the Insert panel, click Window on the Application bar (Win) or Menu bar (Mac), then click Insert.

- The **Insert panel** contains buttons that allow you to insert objects, such as images, tables, and horizontal rules. The buttons on the Insert panel change depending on the category you select using a drop-down menu. Each category contains buttons relating to a specific task. When you insert an object using one of the buttons, a dialog box opens, letting you choose the object's characteristics. The last button selected becomes the default button for that category. The Insert panel's drop-down menu also has an option to show the program icons in color.

TROUBLE
To see hidden toolbars, click View on the Application bar (Win) or Menu bar (Mac), point to Toolbars, then click the toolbar name. The Standard and Style Rendering toolbars do not appear by default.

- The **Document toolbar** contains buttons for changing the current Web page view, previewing and debugging Web pages, and managing files. The document toolbar buttons are listed in Table A-2.

- The **Standard toolbar** contains buttons for some frequently used commands on the File and Edit menus, such as the Copy and Paste commands.

- The **Style Rendering toolbar** contains buttons that can be used to display different media types.

- The **Coding toolbar** is useful when you are working with HTML code; it can only be accessed in Code view.

- The **Related Files toolbar** displays files related to an open and active file.

- The **Document window** is the large area under the Document toolbar that encompasses most of the Dreamweaver workspace. Web pages that you open in Dreamweaver appear in this area.

- The **Status bar** appears under the Document window. The left side displays the **tag selector**, which shows the HTML tags being used at the insertion point location. The right side displays window size data and page download time estimates.

QUICK TIP
To make an open panel active and display its contents, click the panel tab. To expand or collapse a panel, double-click the panel tab.

- **Panels** are small windows containing program controls. Related panels appear together in **panel groups**, such as the CSS Styles panel and the Files panel. You display a panel by choosing its name from the Window menu. You can dock panel groups to the right side of the screen, or undock them by dragging the panel tab. When two or more panels are docked together, you can access the panel you want by clicking its name tab to display its contents.

Getting Started with Adobe Dreamweaver CS5

FIGURE A-3: The Dreamweaver CS5 workspace

Application bar (Win) or Menu bar (Mac)
Document toolbar
File tab with file name
Browser Navigation toolbar

Document window

Status bar
Property inspector

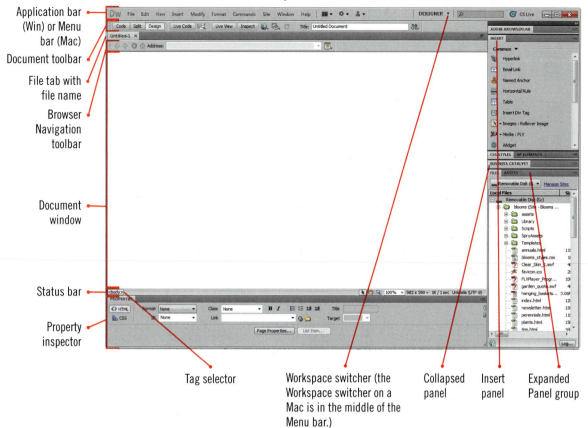

Tag selector

Workspace switcher (the Workspace switcher on a Mac is in the middle of the Menu bar.)

Collapsed panel

Insert panel

Expanded Panel group

TABLE A-2: Document toolbar buttons

button	name	function
Code	Show Code view	Displays only the Code view in the Document window
Split	Show Code and Design views	Displays both the Code and Design views in the Document window
Design	Show Design view	Displays only the Design view in the Document window
Live Code	Shows the Live View source in Code view	Displays the source code for the interactive content
	Check browser compatibility	Displays information about potential problems when the site is viewed with various browsers
Live View	Switch Design View to Live View	Displays the page with interactive elements active and functioning
Inspect	Turn on Live View and Inspect Mode	Activates the page in Live View in Inspect Mode
	Preview/Debug in browser	Activates the browser for viewing
	Visual Aids	Displays options for visual display of information
	Refresh Design view	Reloads the page to reflect any changes made in Code view
	File management	Displays file management options

Getting Started with Adobe Dreamweaver CS5

Working with Views and Panels

Dreamweaver has three ways you can view your Web pages. **Design view** shows a page within the entire document window and is primarily used when designing and creating a Web page. **Code view** fills the document window with the underlying HTML code for the page and is primarily used when reading or directly editing the code. **Code and Design views** is a combination of Code view and Design view; each layout displays in a separate window within the Document window. This view is primarily used for debugging or correcting errors, because you can see both the Design and Code views simultaneously. No matter which view you are using, panels and panel groups appear on the right side of the screen by default in the Designer workspace, although you can move them and use them as "floating panels." Panels are individual windows that display information on a particular topic, such as Reference or History. Panel groups, sometimes referred to as Tab groups, are sets of related panels that are grouped together. Panels are listed by groups on the Window menu and are separated by horizontal lines. As part of your Dreamweaver exploration, you want to learn how to work with views and organize your screen by opening and closing panels.

1. **In the Dreamweaver workspace, click the Show Code view button** `Code` **on the Document toolbar**

   The HTML code for the untitled, blank document appears, as shown in Figure A-4. The code for a blank, untitled page is very limited since the page has no content. As content is added, the number of lines of code will increase as well. Notice in the first line of code that this is an XHTML document type, although the file extension is .html. **XHTML** is the most recent standard for HTML files and has slightly different tags and rules. Although XHTML files are more updated versions of HTML files, they still use the same file extension, and you still refer to the code as "HTML code."

2. **Click the Show Code and Design views button** `Split` **on the Document toolbar**

   A split screen appears. The left side displays the HTML code, while the right side displays the open page. The page area is blank because the current document, Unitled-1, doesn't have any content.

3. **Click the Show Design view button** `Design` **on the Document toolbar**

   A blank page appears again because there is no page content to view.

4. **Double-click the CSS Styles panel tab, if necessary, to expand the panel group**

   The CSS panel group expands and displays two panel tabs: CSS Styles and AP Elements. The CSS Styles panel is the active panel in the default Designer workspace when the program is opened initially. An **active panel** is displayed as the front panel in an expanded panel group with the panel options displayed. Panels open in the position they held when the program was last closed. The CSS Styles panel contains two buttons, All and Current, which are used to view specific information in the panel.

5. **Click the AP Elements panel tab on the CSS Styles panel group**

   The AP Elements becomes the active panel with the panel contents displayed. As you click each panel tab, the panel tab changes color and the panel contents are displayed. See Figure A-5.

6. **Click the CSS Styles panel tab to display it, then double-click the CSS Styles panel tab**

   The panel group collapses. When a panel is collapsed, you double-click the panel tab or the panel group title bar to expand it. If a panel group is expanded, you simply click the panel tab to make the panel active.

7. **Click File on the Application bar (Win) or Menu bar (Mac), click Close to close the untitled document, then click No if necessary if you are asked about saving the untitled page**

   The page closes and the Welcome Screen reappears.

FIGURE A-4: Code view for a blank document

Show Design view button

Show Code view button

Show Code and Design views button

Code for blank document

Document type code

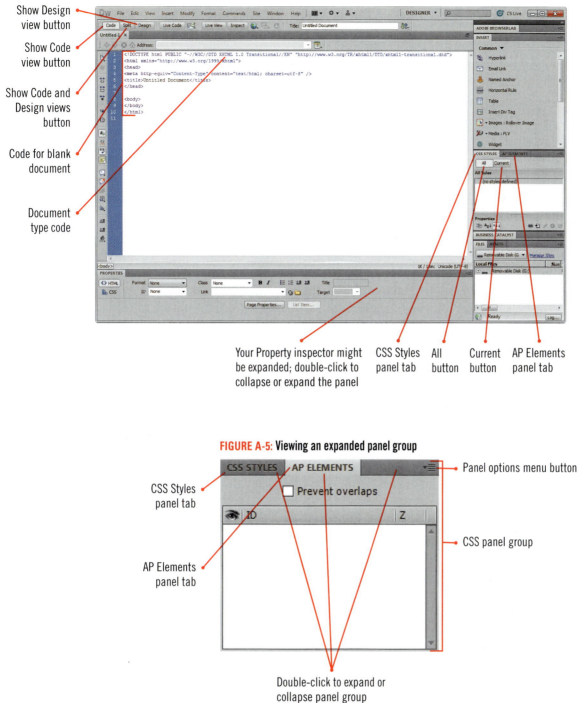

Your Property inspector might be expanded; double-click to collapse or expand the panel

CSS Styles panel tab

All button

Current button

AP Elements panel tab

FIGURE A-5: Viewing an expanded panel group

CSS Styles panel tab

AP Elements panel tab

Panel options menu button

CSS panel group

Double-click to expand or collapse panel group

Using panel groups

By default, the Insert panel, the Adobe BrowserLab, the CSS Styles and Files panel groups, and the Business Catalyst panel open when you first start Dreamweaver in Windows. (The Business Catalyst panel is a new panel in Dreamweaver CS5.) The panels will retain their arrangement from one session to the next. For instance, if you open the Files panel and do not close it before exiting Dreamweaver, it will be open the next time you start Dreamweaver. To close a panel group, right-click (Win) or [control]-click (Mac) its title bar, then click Close Tab Group. The **panel group title bar** is the dark gray bar at the top of each panel group. The Panel options menu button lets you choose commands related to the currently displayed panel. You can also rearrange the workspace using your own choices for panel placement and save the workspace with a unique name using the "New Workspace" and "Manage Workspaces" commands on the Workspace switcher.

Opening a Web Page

After opening Dreamweaver, you can create a new Web site or page, or open an existing Web site or page. The first Web page that appears when you access a Web site is called the **home page**. The home page sets the look and tone of the Web site and contains a navigation structure that directs the viewer to the rest of the pages in the Web site. The resort's marketing firm has designed a new banner for The Striped Umbrella. You begin by opening The Striped Umbrella home page to view the new banner.

STEPS

TROUBLE
If you do not have your preferences set to show file extensions, you will not see the file extensions for each file. To show file extensions, open Windows Explorer, click Organize, click Folder and search options, click the View tab, then uncheck Hide extensions for known file types.

1. Click File on the Application bar (Win) or Menu bar (Mac), then click Open
   The Open dialog box opens.

2. Click the Look in list arrow ▼ (Win) or click the Current file location list arrow ↕ (Mac), navigate to the drive and folder where you store your Data Files, then double-click (Win) or click (Mac) the unit_a folder
   The list of the data files in the unit_a folder, along with an assets folder where the image files for this unit are stored, appear in the Name column See Figure A-6.

QUICK TIP
You can also double-click a file in the Open dialog box to open it. Or click File on the Application bar (Win) or Menu bar (Mac) then click one of the recently opened files listed in the Open Recent submenu.

3. Click the dwa_1.html file, then click Open
   The document named dwa_1.html opens in the document window in Design view. Since you are in Design view, all of the page elements appear as if you were viewing the page in a Web browser.

4. If necessary, click the Maximize button ▢ on the Document window title bar

5. Click the Show Code view button Code on the Document toolbar
   The HTML code for the page appears.

6. Scroll through the code, click the Show Design view button Design on the Document toolbar to return to Design view, then, if necessary, scroll to display the top of the page

Design Matters

Opening or creating different document types with Dreamweaver

You can use either the Welcome Screen or the New command on the File menu to open or create several types of files. For example, you can create HTML documents, XML documents, style sheets, and text files. You can create new documents from scratch, or base them on existing pages. The predesigned CSS page layouts make it easy to design Web pages based on Cascading Style Sheets without

an advanced level of expertise in writing HTML code. Predesigned templates save you time and promote consistency across a Web site. As you learn more about Dreamweaver, you will find it worthwhile to explore each category to understand what is available to you as a designer.

FIGURE A-6: Open dialog box (Windows and Mac)

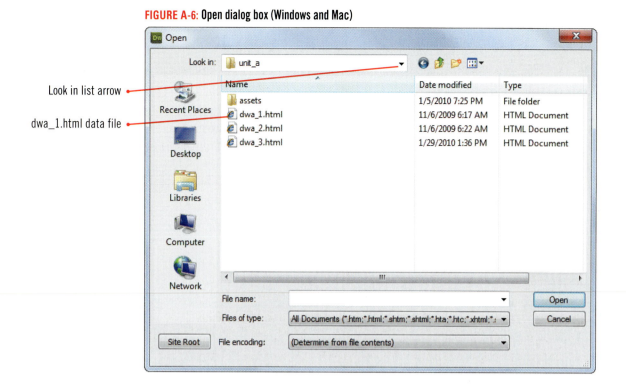

Look in list arrow

dwa_1.html data file

Current file location list arrow

File dwa_1.html

Displaying and docking panel groups

You can move panel groups to a different area on the screen by dragging the panel group title bar. To dock a panel group, drag the panel group to the right side of the screen. A heavy blue bar indicates the position it will take when you release the mouse button. This position is called the **drop zone**. You can also minimize all panels to icons by clicking the Collapse to Icons button ▸▸ in the top right corner of the top panel. You can hide and show all panels by pressing the F4 key (Win).

Viewing Web Page Elements

There are many elements that make up Web pages. Web pages can be very simple, designed primarily with text, or they can be media-rich with lots of text, images, sound, and videos. You can use the programs shown in Table A-3 to create many of the more common Web page elements. Web page elements can be placed directly on the page, or pages can be designed with elements placed in table cells or specially defined areas called **divs** to format and position page elements. Differences in monitor size and settings affect the size of the program and document windows so your screen may show a larger or smaller area of the document than the figures in this book. To familiarize yourself with Web page elements, you examine the various elements on the Striped Umbrella page.

DETAILS

Compare your screen to Figure A-7 as you examine the following:

- **Text**

    Text is the most basic element on a Web page. Most information is presented with text. You type or import text onto a Web page and then format it with the Property inspector so it is easy to read. Text should be short and to the point so that users can easily skim through it as they browse through Web sites.

- **Images**

    Images add visual interest to a Web page. However, the adage "less is more" is certainly true with images. Too many images cause the page to load too slowly and discourage users from waiting. Many Web pages contain **banners**, images that appear across the top of the screen. Banners can incorporate information, such as a company's logo and contact information.

- **Hyperlinks**

    Hyperlinks, also known as **links**, are graphic or text elements on a Web page that users click to display another location on the page, another Web page within the same Web site, or a Web page in a different Web site.

- **Tables**

    Tables, grids of rows and columns, can be used to hold tabular data on a Web page. Some Web sites still use them for placing all content, but tables are not the preferred method for page layout. When used as a design tool, the edges of the table (table borders) can be made invisible to the viewer. Elements are then placed in table cells to control the placement of each element on the page.

- **Divs and AP Divs**

    Divs and AP divs are important page layout options because they allow you to "draw" or insert blocks of content on a page. These "content containers" can then be used to hold page elements, such as text or images. Because AP divs can "float" over any page element, they are easier to reposition than table cells and are more flexible tools that can be programmed to display according to set criteria. Many designers use a combination of tables, divs, and AP divs for page design.

- **Flash movies**

    Flash movies are low-bandwidth animations and interactive elements created using Adobe Flash. These animations use a series of vector-based graphics that load quickly and merge with other graphics and sounds to create short movies. Some Web sites are built entirely by using Flash, while others may have Flash content in defined areas on individual pages. Most current browsers include Flash player as part of the software. **Flash player** is an Adobe program that is free to download and use. It is required to play Flash animations.

- **Flash video**

    Flash videos are videos that have been converted from a digital video file format to an .flv file using Adobe Flash. The big advantage to Flash videos is that they can be **streamed**, which means that they begin playing before the entire file has been downloaded.

FIGURE A-7: Viewing Web page elements

Banner

Links to
other pages
in the
Web site

Text

Image

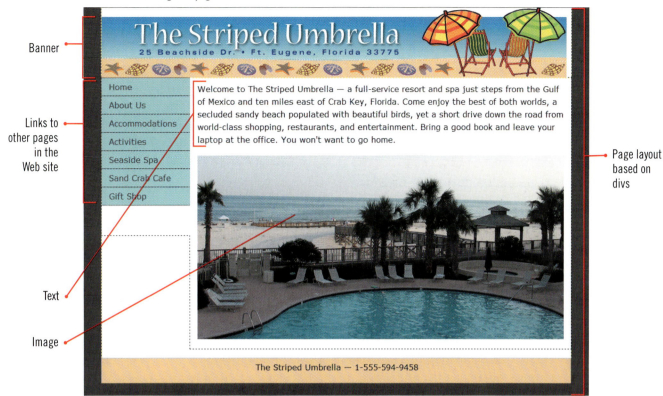

Page layout
based on
divs

TABLE A-3: Programs used to create Web page elements

source program	elements created
Adobe Illustrator	Used to create and edit vector graphics
Adobe Fireworks	Used to create and optimize images for the Web
Adobe Flash	Used to create animation and vector graphics
Adobe Photoshop	Used to edit and enhance bitmap images
Java	Used to create small applications (applets) that can be embedded on a Web page

Getting Help

Dreamweaver has an excellent Help feature that is comprehensive and easy to use. When questions or problems arise, you can use the Adobe Community Help window. This window contains two tools that you can use to search for answers in different ways: the View Help PDF link and a Search box. Clicking the View Help PDF link opens the Dreamweaver Help PDF file that is saved locally on your computer and that contains a list of topics and subtopics by category. The Search box at the top-left corner of the window enables you to enter a keyword to search for a specific topic. You can see context-specific help by clicking the Help button in the Property inspector (Win). You decide to access the Help feature to learn more about Dreamweaver.

STEPS

1. **Click Help on the Application bar (Win) or Menu bar (Mac)**
   The Help menu appears, displaying the Help categories. See Figure A-8.

2. **Click Dreamweaver Help**
   The Adobe Community Help window opens.

3. **Type Workspace switcher in the search box in the Search pane, then press [Tab] or [Enter]**
   The search pane is populated with a list of topics related to the Workspace switcher.

4. **Click the first topic listed in the Results pane, then read the information in the Content pane**
   The content pane displays information about saving and switching workspaces, as shown in Figure A-9.

5. **Click the View Help PDF button in the top-right corner of the Content pane**
   The Help PDF file that is saved locally on your computer opens, as shown in Figure A-10.

6. **Scroll through and read some of the information, then close the Adobe Community Help window**

FIGURE A-8: Help menu

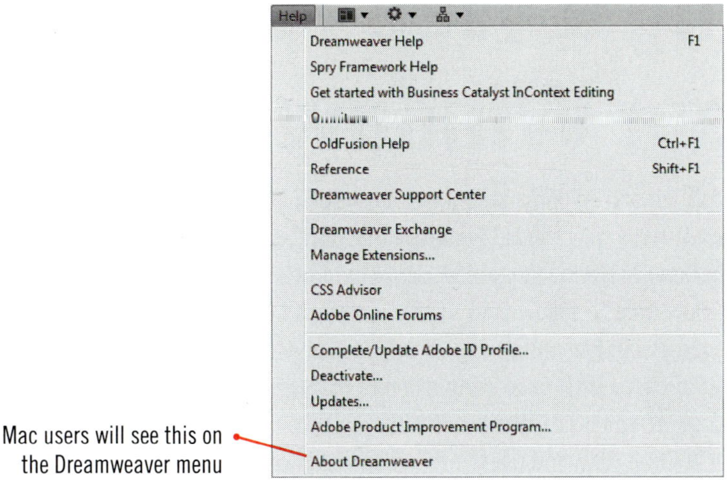

Mac users will see this on
the Dreamweaver menu

FIGURE A-9: Displaying Help content

Search text box

View Help
PDF link

Results pane

Content pane

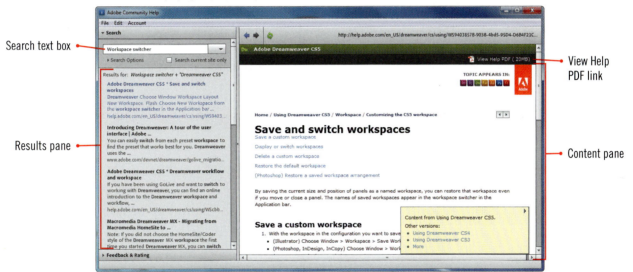

FIGURE A-10: Viewing the Adobe Help PDF file

Help PDF
opens in
Content pane

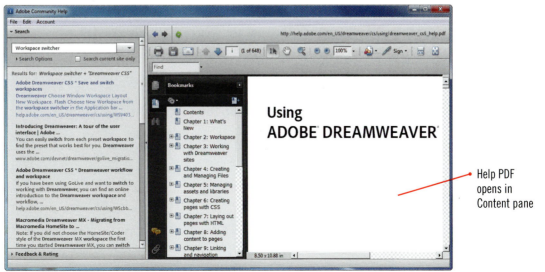

Viewing a Web Page in a Browser Window

During the process of creating and editing a Web page, it is helpful to frequently view the page in a Web browser window. Dreamweaver also has a view called **Live view** that displays the page as if it were being viewed using a browser. In Live view, the Browser Navigation toolbar above the Document window becomes active. The **Browser Navigation toolbar** allows you to follow links in Live view as if you were viewing the pages in the browser. Viewing the page in a browser window provides visual feedback of what the page will look like when it is published on the Internet. It is best to view a Web page using different browsers, screen sizes, and resolutions to ensure the best view based upon your computer's capabilities. It is important to remember that you cannot print a Web page in Dreamweaver except in Code view. You use the Print command on your browser toolbar or menu to print the page. You decide to view The Striped Umbrella home page in your default browser window.

STEPS

> **TROUBLE**
> If the status bar is out of view, then resize and reposition the document window as necessary for it to be visible. Drag a corner to resize the window and drag the title bar to reposition it.

1. **In Design view, click the Restore Down button 🗗 (Win) on the Document title bar, then click the Window Size pop-up menu on the right side of the status bar**

   The Window Size pop-up menu appears, as shown in Figure A-11. The Window Size pop-up menu lists several options for simulating commonly used screen sizes. You may need to double-click the right side of the Property inspector to collapse it in order to see the Window Size pop-up menu.

> **TROUBLE**
> If you are using a Windows computer, your menu options will be dimmed if your document window is maximized. Click the Restore Down button to restore down the document window.

2. **Click 955 × 600 (1024 × 768, Maximized)**

   The screen size is set to 955 × 600, which translates to a monitor set at a 1024 × 768 screen resolution. When you choose your screen size, it is important to consider the equipment your users may have when they view your page in their browser window. The most common screen size that viewers use today is 1024 × 768, so view your pages using that setting to check to see that the content fits well in the window. See Table A-4 for window size options.

> **TROUBLE**
> If you are using Internet Explorer 7, the menu bar might not appear. To display it, right-click any other toolbar displayed, then click Menu bar. You can also press the Alt key to temporarily display or hide the menu bar.

3. **Click the Preview/Debug in browser button 🌐. on the Document toolbar, then click Preview in [browser name]**

   The browser window opens, and the Striped Umbrella Web page previews in the browser window, as shown in Figure A-12. If you are using Internet Explorer and a security message appears when the page opens, simply click the Information bar when prompted, then click Allow Blocked Content.

4. **Click File on the browser menu bar, then click Print**

   The Print dialog box opens.

5. **Click Print**

   A copy of the Web page prints. The black background that appears on the Web page will not print unless you have selected the Print background colors and images option in your printer settings.

FIGURE A-11: Window size pop-up menu

Maximize button
indicates the
document window
is restored down

Current Window
size dimensions

Window size
pop-up menu

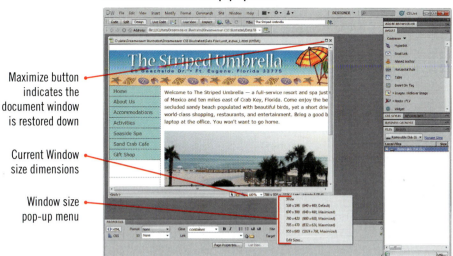

FIGURE A-12: Web page previewed in a browser window

Your path
might differ

TABLE A-4: Window size options

window size (inside dimensions of browser window without borders)	corresponding resolution
592w	(Fixed width, variable height)
536 × 196	640 × 480, Default
600 × 300	640 × 480, Maximized
760 × 420	800 × 600, Maximized
795 × 470	832 × 624, Maximized
955 × 600	1024 × 768, Maximized

Design Matters

Choosing a window size

The 800 × 600 window setting is used on some older monitors which are 17-inch or smaller. Most consumers today use a 1024 × 768 or higher screen size, but some viewers restore down individual program windows to a size comparable to 800 × 600 to be able to have more windows open simultaneously on their screen. People use their "screen real estate" according to their personal work style. When possible, it is a good idea to make your designs appear acceptable when viewed in windows smaller than 1024 × 768.

Closing a Web Page and Exiting Dreamweaver

When you are ready to stop working with a file in Dreamweaver, it is a good idea to close the current page or pages you are working on and exit the program. This should prevent data loss if power is interrupted; in some cases, power outages can corrupt an open file and make it unusable. You are finished working for the day so you want to close the Web page and exit Dreamweaver.

STEPS

1. **In the browser window, click File on the Menu bar, then click Exit (Win), or click [Browser name] on the Menu bar, then click Quit [Browser name] (Mac)**

   The browser window closes, and The Striped Umbrella Web page reappears in the Dreamweaver window, as shown in Figure A-13. In this book, screen shots of finished projects feature enlarged windows to display as much content as possible. You may have to scroll to see the same amount of content.

   > **QUICK TIP**
   > You may need to click the Dreamweaver CS5 title bar to activate the program.

2. **In the Dreamweaver workspace, click File on the Application bar, then click Exit (Win) or click Dreamweaver on the Menu bar, then click Quit Dreamweaver (Mac)**

   Dreamweaver closes.

Saving and closing Dreamweaver files

It is wise to save a file as soon as you begin creating it and to save frequently as you work. A quick glance at the title bar shows whether you have saved your file. If you haven't saved the file initially, the file-name shows "Untitled" rather than a filename. This does not refer to the page title, but the actual filename. After you save the file and make a change to it, an asterisk appears at the end of the filename until you save it again. It is always wise to save and close a page on which you are not actively working. Keeping multiple files open can cause confusion, especially when you are working with multiple Web sites which have similarly named pages. Each open page has a tab at the top of the page with the filename listed. You use these tabs to switch between each open page to make it the active page. You can also press [Ctrl] [Tab] (Win) or [command][tab] (Mac) to move between open documents.

Using Adobe Community Help

When you access the Help feature in Dreamweaver, you have a choice of using offline help (which is similar to searching in a Dreamweaver manual) or using online help. The online help feature is called Adobe Community Help. **Adobe Community Help** is a collection of materials such as tutorials, published articles, or blogs, in addition to the regular help content. All content is monitored and approved by the Adobe Community Expert program.

Practice

For current SAM information, including versions and content details, visit SAM Central (http://www.cengage.com/samcentral). If you have a SAM user profile, you may have access to hands-on instruction, practice, and assessment of the skills covered in this unit. Since various versions of SAM are supported throughout the life of this text, check with your instructor for the correct instructions and URL/Web site for accessing assignments.

Concepts Review

Label each element in the Dreamweaver window as shown in Figure A-14.

FIGURE A-14

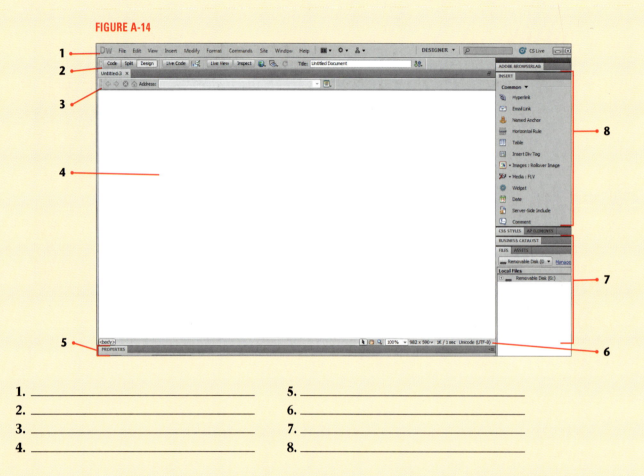

1. _____   5. _____
2. _____   6. _____
3. _____   7. _____
4. _____   8. _____

Match each of the following terms with the statement that best describes its function.

9. **Standard toolbar**

10. **Document toolbar**

11. **Code view**

12. **Tag selector**

13. **Workspace**

14. **Design view**

15. **Insert panel**

16. **Application bar**

a. The Document window, the application bar, toolbars, inspectors, and panels

b. Allows you to choose program commands

c. Shows the page layout

d. Contains buttons that allow you to insert objects, such as images

e. Contains buttons for some of the more commonly used options under the File and Edit menus

f. Shows the HTML code

g. Contains buttons for changing the current Dreamweaver view

h. Shows the HTML tags being used at the current insertion point

Select the best answer from the list of choices.

17. You display panels using the _____ menu.
    a. Window
    b. Edit
    c. Panel
    d. View

18. The tool that allows you to show the properties of a selected page element is called the:
    a. Tool inspector.
    b. Element inspector.
    c. Insert panel.
    d. Property inspector.

19. Most information on a Web page is presented in the form of:
    a. text.
    b. images.
    c. links.
    d. video.

20. The view that is best for designing and creating a Web page is:
    a. Code view.
    b. Design view.
    c. a combination of both Code and Design views.
    d. any of the above.

21. On a Windows computer, which of the following is one of the Dreamweaver default panel groups?
    a. History
    b. Design
    c. Application
    d. Files

Skills Review

1. **Define Web design software.**
   a. Write a short paragraph describing at least three features of Dreamweaver.
   b. Add another paragraph describing three views that are available in Dreamweaver, then describe when you would use each view.

2. **Start Adobe Dreamweaver CS5.**
   a. Start Dreamweaver.
   b. Write a list of the panels that currently appear on the screen.

3. **View the Dreamweaver workspace.**
   a. Locate the title bar.
   b. Locate the Application bar (Win) or Menu bar (Mac).
   c. Locate the Document toolbar.
   d. Locate the Insert panel.
   e. Locate the Property inspector.

4. **Work with views and panels.**
   a. Switch to Code view.
   b. Switch to Code and Design views.
   c. Switch to Design view.
   d. Expand the CSS Styles panel group.
   e. Collapse the CSS Styles panel group.

5. **Open a Web page.**
   a. Open dwa_2.html from the drive and folder where you store your Data Files. Maximize the window, if necessary. Your screen should resemble Figure A-15. (*Hint*: The file will open in the window size last selected. You can change it by using the Window Size menu.)
   b. Display the page in Code view.
   c. Display the page in Design view.

6. **View Web page elements.**
   a. Locate a banner.
   b. Locate text.
   c. Locate an image.

Skills Review (continued)

7. Get Help.

  a. Use the Dreamweaver Help to search for topics relating to the Assets panel.

  b. Display Help information on one of the topics.

  c. Print the topic information.

  d. Close the Help window.

8. View a Web page in a browser window.

  a. Note the window size that is currently selected in Dreamweaver.

  b. Change the window size to a different setting.

  c. Preview the page in your Web browser window. If you are using Internet Explorer 7 and a security message appears when the page opens, click the Information bar when prompted, then click Allow Blocked Content.

  d. Print the page.

  e. Close the browser window.

9. Close a Web page and exit Dreamweaver.

  a. Close the Web page file.

  b. Exit the Dreamweaver program.

FIGURE A-15

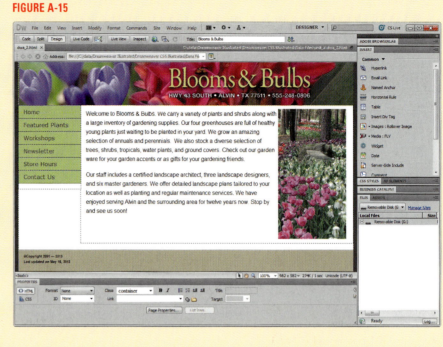

Independent Challenge 1

You have recently purchased Adobe Dreamweaver CS5 and are eager to learn to use it. You open a Web page and view it using Dreamweaver.

  a. Start Dreamweaver.

  b. Open the file dwa_3.html from the drive and folder where you store your Unit A Data Files. Your screen should resemble Figure A-16. (*Hint*: The file will open in the window size last selected. You can change it by using the Window Size menu.)

  c. Change to Code view.

  d. Change back to Design view.

  e. Collapse the Files panel group.

  f. Expand the Files panel group.

  g. Change the window size, then preview the page in your browser window.

  h. Close the browser window, close the file, then exit Dreamweaver.

FIGURE A-16

Independent Challenge 2

When you work in Dreamweaver, it is important to organize your panels so that you have the information you need where you can access it quickly.

a. Start Dreamweaver.

b. Use Dreamweaver Help to locate information on how to collapse or expand panel groups.

c. Read the information, using the Previous and Next buttons in the top right corner of the Help window to advance or back up within the screens.

d. Print the information.

e. Close the Help window, then exit the Dreamweaver program.

Independent Challenge 3

The Adobe Web site has a feature called Customer Showcase, which includes links to Web sites that were created using Adobe software such as Dreamweaver, Flash, and Fireworks. The Customer Showcase feature includes the Site of the Day and Customer Showcase Features. The Customer Showcase Features links provide information about spotlighted companies, the challenges that were presented to the design team, the solution, and the resulting benefits to the companies. You visit the Adobe Web site to look at some of the featured Web sites to get a feel for what constitutes good page design.

a. Connect to the Internet, then go to the Adobe Web site at www.adobe.com.

b. Point to the Company link near the top of the screen, then click Customer Showcase. Scroll down and click one of the companies listed under Customer Showcase Features.

c. Read the information about the company, then print the page from the browser window.

d. Close your browser window.

e. Using a word processing program or paper, write a short summary (two paragraphs) of the Web site you visited, then list three things that you learned about the Adobe software used to create the site. For example: "I learned that Flash animation files can be inserted into Dreamweaver."

Real Life Independent Challenge

You are about to begin work on an original Web site. This site can be about anything you are interested in developing. It can be about you and your family, a hobby, a business, or a fictitious Web site. There will be no data files supplied. This site will build from unit to unit, so you must do each Real Life Independent Challenge to complete your Web site.

a. Decide what type of Web site you would like to build.

b. Find sites on the Internet that are similar to the one you would like to design to gather some ideas.

c. Evaluate what works on these sites and what doesn't work.

d. Write down at least three ideas for your new site.

e. Write down the screen resolution you will use for designing your pages.

Visual Workshop

Open Dreamweaver, create a new HTML file using the Welcome screen, then use the Window menu to open the panels and document, as shown in Figure A-17. If necessary, collapse or expand the panels into the position on the screen shown in Figure A-17. Exit (Win) or Quit (Mac) the Dreamweaver program.

FIGURE A-17

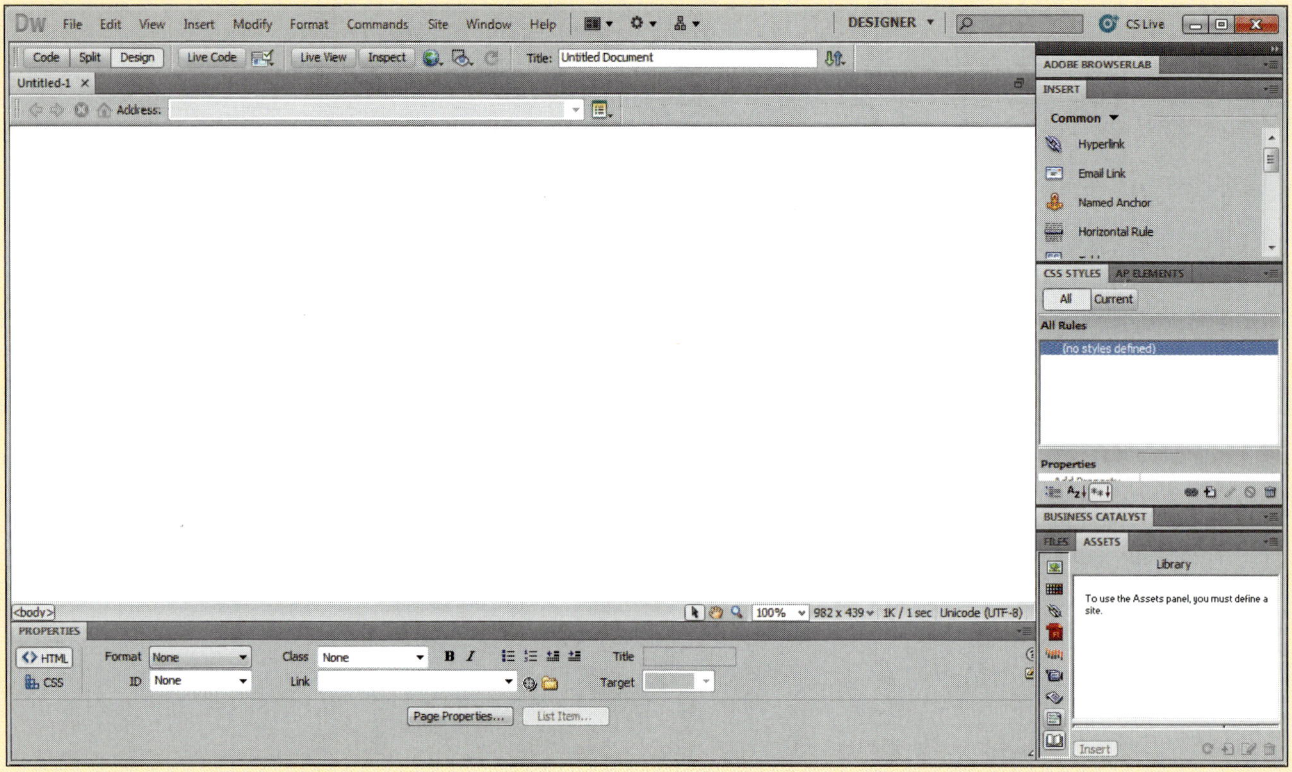

Getting Started with Adobe Dreamweaver CS5

Creating a Web Site

Creating a Web site requires lots of thought and careful planning. Dreamweaver CS5 has many tools to help you plan, create, and manage your sites. In this unit, you use these tools to plan and design a new Web site.  The owners of The Striped Umbrella meet with you to discuss their ideas for a new and improved Web site. You assure them that you can create a great site for them, using Dreamweaver.

OBJECTIVES

Plan a Web site

Create a folder for Web site management

Set up a Web site

Add a folder to a Web site

Save a Web page

Copy a new image to a Web site

Add new pages to a Web site

Planning a Web Site

Developing a Web site is a process that begins with careful planning and research. You should plan all development phases before you begin. Figure B-1 illustrates the steps involved in Web site planning. Your plan should include how you will organize and implement your site. It should also encompass testing your pages on different types of computers and modifying the pages to handle challenges such as page elements appearing inconsistently in different browsers. Careful planning of your Web site may prevent mistakes that would be costly and time-consuming to correct. After consulting with the lead member of the Web development team, you review the steps described below to help you create a plan for The Striped Umbrella site.

DETAILS

- ### Research site goals and needs

  When you research your Web site, you determine the site's purpose and requirements. Create a checklist of questions and answer them before you begin. For example: "What are the company's or client's goals for the Web site? What software will I need to construct the site? Will the site require media files? If so, who will create them?" The more questions that you can answer about the site, the more prepared you will be to begin development. Once you have gone through your checklist, create a timeline and a budget for the site.

QUICK TIP

You can easily create a simple wireframe using a software program such as Microsoft PowerPoint, Adobe Illustrator, or Adobe Fireworks. To create a more detailed wireframe that simulates site navigation and user interaction, use a high-fidelity wireframe program such as OverSite, ProtoShare, Microsoft Visio, or Adobe Flash Catalyst.

- ### Create a wireframe

  A **wireframe** can range from a small sketch that represents the relationship between every page of a Web site to a complex prototype of each page's content on a Web site, including filenames, navigation, images, text, and link information. Like a flowchart or storyboard, a wireframe shows the relationship of each page to the other pages on the site. Wireframes are used throughout the development process. Consult your wireframe before beginning work on a new page to use as your "blueprint" and compare each completed page to its prototype to make sure you met the specifications. The wireframe example shown in Figure B-2 is helpful during the planning process as it allows you to visualize how each page on the site is linked to the others.

- ### Create folders

  Before you create your Web site, you should create a system of folders for all of the elements you will use in the site. Decide where on your computer you will store your site. Start by creating a folder for the Web site with a descriptive name, such as the name of the company. Then create a subfolder to store all of the files that are not Web pages—for example, images, audio files, and video clips. An organized folder system makes it easier to find files quickly as you develop and edit your Web site. Figure B-3 shows the folder structure of the Striped Umbrella site.

- ### Collect the page content and create the Web pages

  This is the fun part! After studying your wireframe, gather the files you need to create the pages—for example, text, images, buttons, videos, and animations. Some of these elements will be imported from other software programs, and some will be created in Dreamweaver. For instance, you can create text either directly in Dreamweaver or in a word processing program and then import it into Dreamweaver.

- ### Test and modify the pages

  It is important to test your Web pages using a variety of Web browsers. The four most common browsers are Microsoft Internet Explorer, Apple Safari, Google Chrome, and Mozilla Firefox. You should also test your Web site using different versions of each browser, a variety of screen resolutions (as discussed in Unit A), and various connection speeds (dial-up modems are considerably slower than cable or DSLs (Digital Subscriber Lines). Your Web pages will need to be updated on a regular basis as new information is released and older information becomes outdated. Each time you modify a Web site element, it is wise to test the site again.

- ### Publish the site

  To publish a Web site means to make it available for viewing on the Internet or on an **intranet**, an internal Web site without public access. Many companies have intranets to enable them to share information within their organizations. You publish a Web site to a **Web server**, a computer that is connected to the Internet with an IP (Internet Protocol) address and has software that enables it to make files accessible to anyone on the internet or an intranet. Until a Web site is published, you can only view the site if you have the files stored on a hard drive, USB drive, or other storage device connected to your computer.

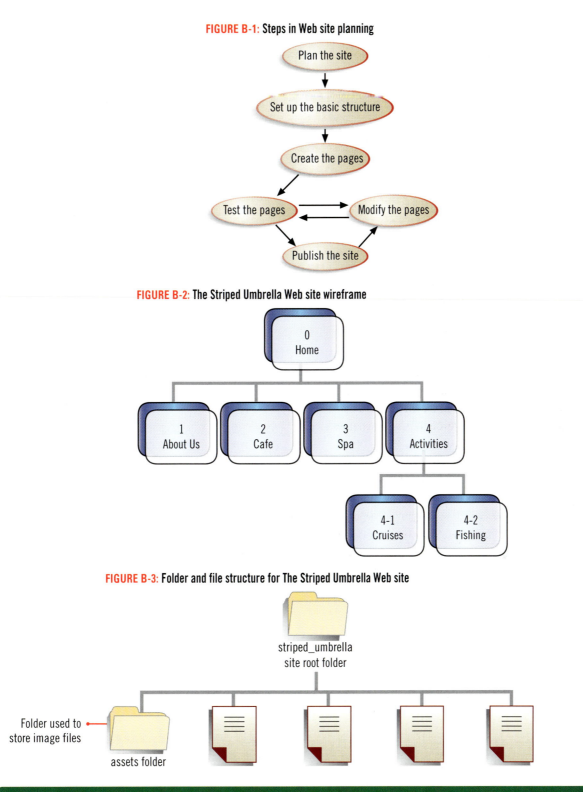

FIGURE B-1: Steps in Web site planning

Plan the site

Set up the basic structure

Create the pages

Test the pages ⇄ Modify the pages

Publish the site

FIGURE B-2: The Striped Umbrella Web site wireframe

0
Home

1
About Us

2
Cafe

3
Spa

4
Activities

4-1
Cruises

4-2
Fishing

FIGURE B-3: Folder and file structure for The Striped Umbrella Web site

striped_umbrella
site root folder

Folder used to
store image files

assets folder

Design Matters

IP addresses and domain names

To make a Web site accessible over the Internet, you must publish it to a Web server with a permanent IP (Internet Protocol) address. An **IP address** is an assigned series of four numbers, each between 0 and 255 and separated by periods, that indicates the address of a specific computer or other piece of hardware on the Internet or an internal computer network. To access a Web page, you enter either an IP address or a domain name in the address box of your browser window. A **domain name** is expressed in letters instead of numbers, and usually reflects the name of the business, individual, or other organization represented by the Web site. For example the domain name for the Adobe Web site is www.adobe.com, but the IP address (at the time of this writing) is 192.150.18.200. Because domain names use descriptive text instead of numbers, they are much easier to remember.

Creating a Folder for Web Site Management

After composing your checklist, creating wireframes, and gathering the files and resources you need for your Web site, you then set up the site's folder structure. The first folder you create for the Web site is called a local site folder, sometimes referred to as the **root** folder. A **local site folder** is a folder on your hard drive, USB drive, or network drive that contains all the files and folders for a Web site. You can create this folder using Windows Explorer (Win), the Finder (Mac), or the Files panel in Dreamweaver. The **Files panel** is a file management tool similar to Windows Explorer (Win) or Finder (Mac), where Dreamweaver stores and manages your Web site files and folders. Avoid using spaces, special characters, or uppercase characters when naming files or folders to prevent problems when you publish your Web site. When you publish the Web site, you transfer a copy of the site folder contents to a remote computer, usually hosted by an Internet Service Provider (ISP). You want to create the local site folder (root folder) for The Striped Umbrella Web site and name it striped_umbrella.

STEPS

1. **Start Dreamweaver**

   The Dreamweaver Welcome Screen opens. If you don't want the Dreamweaver Welcome Screen to open each time you start Dreamweaver, click the "Don't show again" check box on the Welcome Screen. If you change your mind later, select the Show Welcome Screen check box in the General category of the Preferences dialog box.

QUICK TIP

Determine the location where you will store your new folders and files. Check with your instructor or technical support person if you need assistance.

2. **Click the Files panel tab or expand the Files panel, if necessary, to view its contents**

   The Files panel displays a list of the drives and folders on your computer.

▶ 3. **Click the Files panel Site list arrow**

   The drop-down menu displays the list of drives on your computer. See Figure B-4.

TROUBLE

If you see a drive or folder in the list box in the drop-down menu, you do not have a Web site open.

4. **Click to select the drive, folder, or subfolder in the list where you want your local site root folder to reside**

   The name of the selected drive or folder appears in the Files panel list box. Dreamweaver will store all of the folders and files you create for your Web sites in this drive or folder.

5. **Right-click (Win) or control-click (Mac) the drive, folder, or subfolder that you selected in Step 4, then click New Folder**

6. **Type striped_umbrella, then press [Enter] (Win) or [return] (Mac)**

   The local site root folder is renamed striped_umbrella, as shown in Figure B-5. All of the folders and files for The Striped Umbrella Web site will be saved in this folder.

FIGURE B-4: Selecting a drive in the Files panel

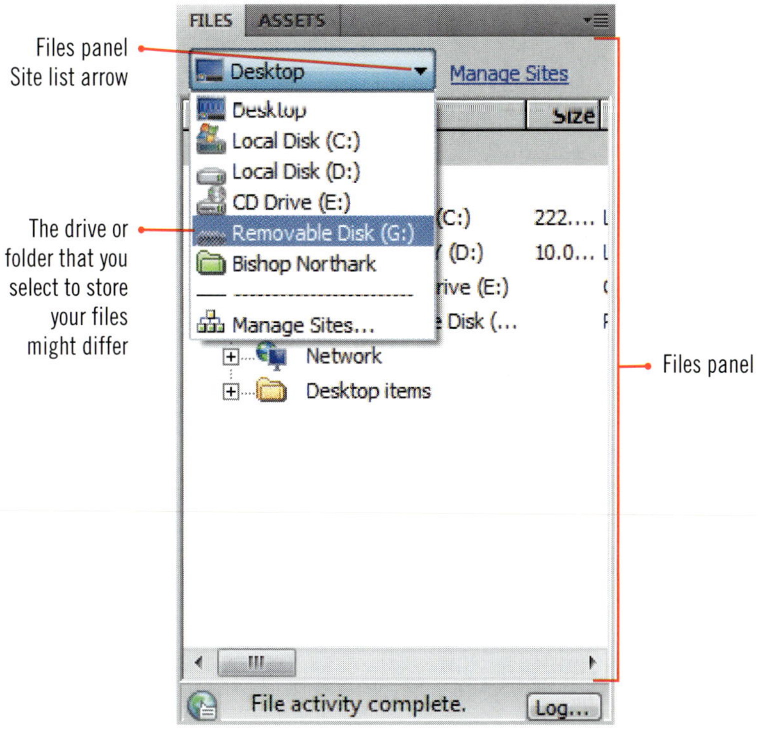

Files panel
Site list arrow

The drive or
folder that you
select to store
your files
might differ

Files panel

FILES	ASSETS

Desktop · Manage Sites

- Desktop
- Local Disk (C:)
- Local Disk (D:)
- CD Drive (E:)
- Removable Disk (G:)
- Bishop Northark
- ----------------
- Manage Sites...

Network
Desktop items

(C:) 222.... l
(D:) 10.0... l
rive (E:) 0
e Disk (... F

File activity complete. Log...

FIGURE B-5: Creating a root folder using the Files panel

striped_umbrella root
folder; the file folder is
yellow because you
have not created
a Web site yet (the
folder will be blue on
a Mac)

FILES	ASSETS

Removable Disk (G ▾ Manage Sites

Local Files	Size	Type
⊟ Removable Disk (...		Remova.
striped_umbr...		Folder

G: Log...

Design Matters

Managing files

It is imperative that you understand the basics of good file management before you can master Dreamweaver. You should be able to create new folders and new files in a specified location. You should also learn the basic file naming conventions for Web content. To ensure that your files are available to all users regardless of their operating system, do not use uppercase letters or spaces in filenames.

Although files with uppercase letters or spaces in their names may look fine on your screen, they might not when they are published on a Web server and might appear as broken links. If you do not have a basic understanding of file management, a quick review on how to use your operating system will pay big dividends and shorten your Dreamweaver learning curve.

Setting Up a Web Site

After you create a local site folder, the next step is to define, or set up your Web site. When you **set up** a Web site, you specify the site's local site root folder location to help Dreamweaver keep track of the links among your Web pages and supporting files. After you set up the site, the program displays the local site root folder in the Files panel. The Files panel commands also help you publish your Web site to a remote computer. See Appendix 2 for more information on publishing your site. You want to define The Striped Umbrella site.

STEPS

1. **Click Site on the Application bar (Win) or Menu bar (Mac), then click New Site**
   The Site Setup dialog box opens, as shown in Figure B-6.

2. **Type The Striped Umbrella in the Site Name text box**
   The site is renamed The Striped Umbrella.

3. **Click the Browse for folder icon 📁 to the right of the Local Site Folder text box, click the Select list arrow ▼ (Win) or the Current file location list arrow ▮ (Mac) in the Choose Root Folder dialog box, navigate to the drive and folder where you created your Local Site Folder, double-click (Win) or click (Mac) the striped_umbrella folder, then click Select (Win) or Choose (Mac)**
   The Choose Root Folder dialog box closes and the Site Setup dialog box reappears with "The Striped Umbrella" as the new name, confirming that you have defined The Striped Umbrella Web site with the name "The Striped Umbrella". The local site folder, striped_umbrella, is designated as the location for the Web site files and folders. See Figure B-7.

4. **Click Save in the Site Setup dialog box**
   The Site Setup dialog box closes. Your Files panel should resemble Figure B-8. You can use the Site Setup dialog box at any time to edit your settings. Notice that the striped_umbrella folder is green. In Dreamweaver, this indicates that it is a Web site folder. Other types of folders are displayed in yellow.

Design Matters

Using the Web as your classroom

Throughout this book, you are asked to evaluate real Web sites. You learn basic design principles parallel to the new skills you learn using Dreamweaver. Learning a new skill, such as inserting an image, will not be very useful if you do not understand how to use images efficiently and effectively on a page. The best way to learn is to examine how live Web sites use page elements such as images to convey information. Therefore, you are encouraged to complete the Design Quest Independent Challenges to gain a practical understanding of the skills you learn.

FIGURE B-6: Site Setup dialog box

Your default
Site number
might differ

Default name for a new site that
has not yet been named

FIGURE B-7: Site Setup for The Striped Umbrella dialog box

Site Name

The Striped
Umbrella local
site folder (your
path might differ)

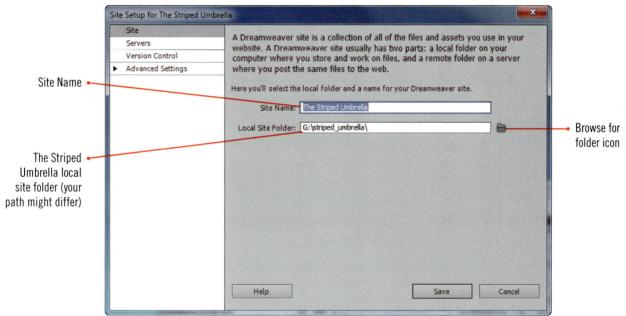

Browse for
folder icon

FIGURE B-8: Files panel

The Striped Umbrella local root folder—
your path might differ—the file folder is
now green, rather than yellow, indicating
that a Web site has been created

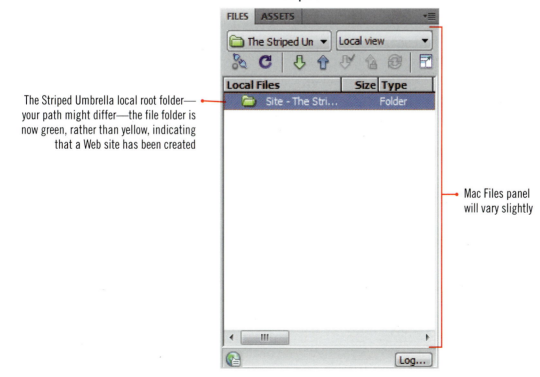

Mac Files panel
will vary slightly

Adding a Folder to a Web Site

After defining your Web site, you need to create folders to contain the non-HTML files that will add content to the site. Creating a folder called "assets" or "images" is a good beginning. Complex Web sites with many types of media or text files may have organizing subfolders within this folder—for example, separate folders for text files, image files, sound files, and video clips. It is better to create these folders in Dreamweaver rather than in Windows Explorer or Macintosh Finder; once you have defined a site, it is much easier to avoid errors if you let Dreamweaver perform all of the file management tasks. You want to create a folder called assets for The Striped Umbrella Web site and set this as the default folder for the images you save in the Web site.

1. If necessary, click the Files panel tab to expand the Files panel, then click the striped_umbrella folder in the Files panel if necessary

   The striped_umbrella folder is highlighted, indicating that the site is selected.

2. Click the Panel options button ▾☰ on the Files panel, then point to File

   See Figure B-9

3. Click New Folder, as shown in Figure B-9

   A new untitled folder appears beneath the striped_umbrella folder in the Files panel.

TROUBLE

If you are using a Mac, you may not see the new folder if the striped_umbrella folder is collapsed. To expand it, click the triangle to the left of the striped_ umbrella folder.

4. Type assets in the folder text box, then press [Enter] (Win) or [return] (Mac)

   The Files panel displays the assets sub-folder indented under the site root folder, as shown in Figure B-10. You will use the assets folder to store images and other elements used in the Web site. But first the assets folder has to be set as the default folder.

5. Click Site on the Application bar (Win) or Menu bar (Mac), click Manage Sites, then click Edit in the Manage Sites dialog box

   The Site Setup for The Striped Umbrella dialog box opens with The Striped Umbrella Web site selected.

6. Click Advanced Settings from the category list in the left column, click the Browse for folder icon 📁 next to the Default Images folder text box, then click the Select list arrow ▾ (Win) or the Current file location list arrow ↕ (Mac) if necessary to display the striped_umbrella folder in the Select text box

7. Click the assets folder, then click Open, if necessary

   The Choose Image Folder dialog box opens with the assets folder listed in the Select text box.

8. Click Select (Win) or Choose (Mac), click Save in the Site Setup for The Striped Umbrella dialog box, then click Done in the Manage Sites dialog box

   The new folder called "assets" for The Striped Umbrella Web site is created and established as the default location for saving all images. This will save steps when you copy image files to the Web site because you will not have to browse to the assets folder each time you save an image. Dreamweaver will save all images automatically in the assets folder.

Design Matters

Why name the folder "assets"?

There is no particular significance to the word *assets* for the name of the folder you will use to store non-HTML files in your Web sites. Many Web designers use the term *images* instead. You can name the folder anything you want, but the term *assets* is a good descriptive word for a folder that can be used to store other types of graphic or media files besides images for your site, such as sound files. The main idea is to organize your files by separating the HTML files from the non-HTML files by using a folder structure with appropriately-named folder names to reflect the content that they store.

FIGURE B-9: Creating a new folder in the Files panel

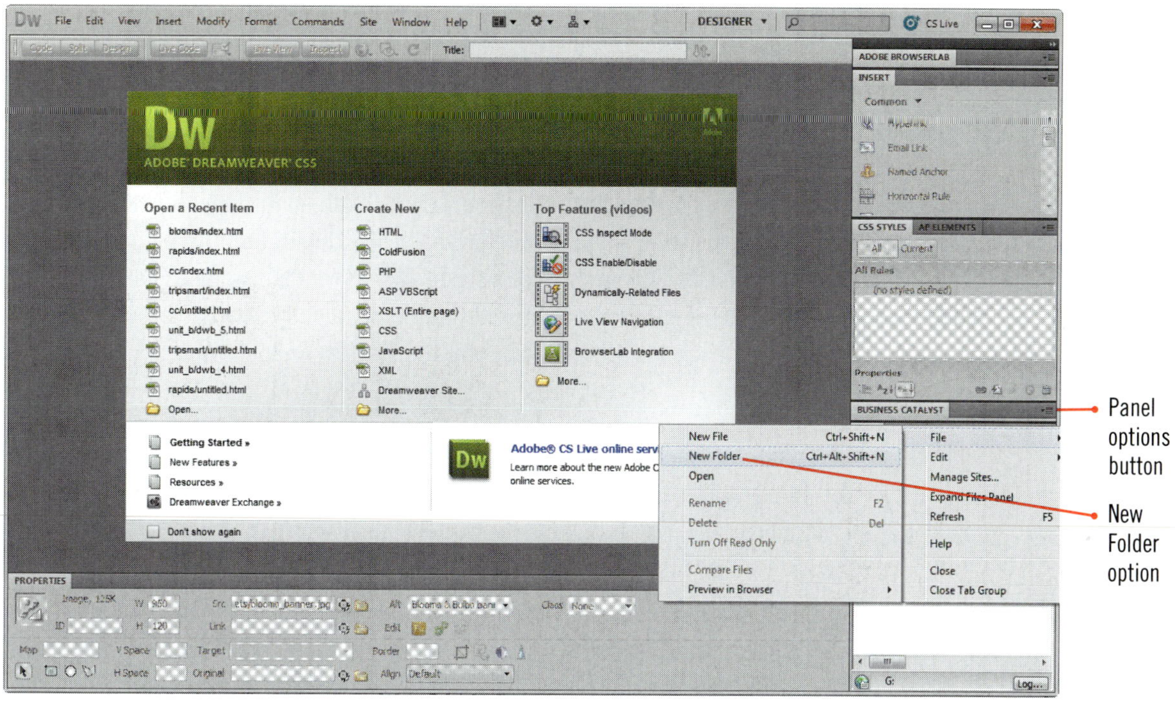

Panel
options
button

New
Folder
option

FIGURE B-10: The Striped Umbrella Site window with assets folder created

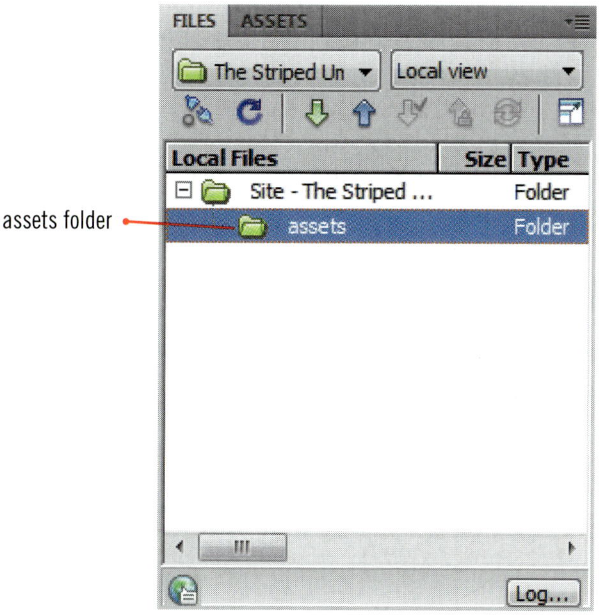

assets folder

Using the Files panel for file management

You can use the Files panel to add, delete, move, or rename files and folders in a Web site. *It is very important that you perform these file maintenance tasks in the Files panel rather than in Windows Explorer (Win) or the Finder (Mac). If you make changes to the folder structure outside the Files panel, you may experience problems.* If you move or copy the site root folder to a new location, you must define the Web site again in Dreamweaver, as you did in the lesson on defining a Web site.

Creating a Web Site   **Dreamweaver 33**

Saving a Web Page

It is wise to save your work frequently. A good practice is to save every five or ten minutes, before you attempt a difficult step, and after you successfully complete a step. This ensures that you do not lose any work in the event of a power outage or computer problem. In this book, you are instructed to use the Save As command after you open each Data File. The Save As command duplicates the open document and allows you to assign the new document a different name. By duplicating the Data Files, you can repeat an exercise or start a lesson over if you make a mistake. You are ready to create the first draft of the home page. You want to open a copy of the existing home page from a folder outside the new Web site, rename it, and then save it in the site root folder for the Striped Umbrella Web site.

STEPS

1. **Click File on the Application bar (Win) or Menu bar (Mac), click Open, navigate to the drive and folder where you store your Data Files, then double-click dwb_1.html**

   The Striped Umbrella home page opens in the Document window in Design View. This is the home page that users will see when they first visit The Striped Umbrella Web site.

   > **QUICK TIP**
   > The file extension php stands for PHP: Hypertext Preprocessor. It is a server-side scripting language.

2. **Click File on the Application bar (Win) or Menu bar (Mac), click Save As, click the Save in list arrow ▼ (Win) or the Current file location list arrow ↕ (Mac) to navigate to the striped_umbrella root folder, then double-click (Win) or click (Mac) the striped_umbrella folder**

   The home page will be saved in the Striped Umbrella Web site root folder, striped_umbrella. Because it will be the home page for your site, you save the file using the name "index.html", the conventional name for a site's home page. Web servers are programmed to search for files named "index.html" or "default.html" to display as the initial page that opens in a Web site, as well as other file types such as index.php.

   > **QUICK TIP**
   > You can just type the filename "index"; the program automatically adds the .html file extension to the filename after you click Save As.

3. **Click in the File name text box (Win) or Save As text box (Mac) if necessary, select the existing file name (dwb_1.html), type index.html, as shown in Figure B-11, click Save, click No in the Update Links dialog box, maximize the document window if necessary, then click the Show Design view button** `Design`

   The Striped Umbrella home page displays in the document window, as shown in Figure B-12. If you are not viewing the page in a separate window (Win), the path to the site root folder and the filename is displayed to the right of the document tab. If you are viewing the page in a separate window, this information appears on the document title bar (Mac). The drive designator, folder name, subfolder names, and filename is called the **path**, or location of the open file in relation to any folders in the Web site. The page banner does not appear and is replaced by a gray box, indicating the link is broken. This means the program cannot link to the image, which currently resides in the Data Files folder. In the next lesson you will repair the link so that the image appears.

   > **TROUBLE**
   > If you don't see the index.html file listed in the Files panel, click the Refresh button ↻.

4. **Click the dwb_1.html file tab to make it active, then click the Close button ☒ on the dwb_1.html file tab**

   The dwb_1.html page closes. You leave the index.html page open to correct the link to the banner image.

Design Matters

Choosing filenames

When you name a file, you should use a descriptive name that reflects the file's contents. For example, if the page is about a company's products, you could name it "products." You must also follow some general rules for naming Web pages. For example, the home page should be named "index.html" or "default.html". You can also use the file extension "htm" instead of "html." Do not use spaces, special characters, regular or back slashes, or punctuation in Web page filenames or in the names of any images that will be inserted in your Web site. Another rule is not to use a number for the first character of a filename. To ensure that everything loads properly on all platforms, including UNIX, assume that filenames are case sensitive and use lowercase characters. A good practice is to limit file names to eight characters.

FIGURE B-11: The Save As dialog box (Windows and Mac)

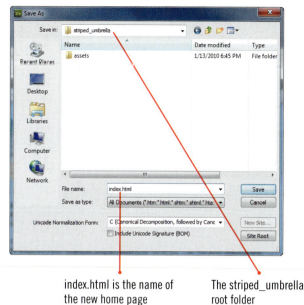

index.html is the name of
the new home page

The striped_umbrella
root folder

FIGURE B-12: The Striped Umbrella home page

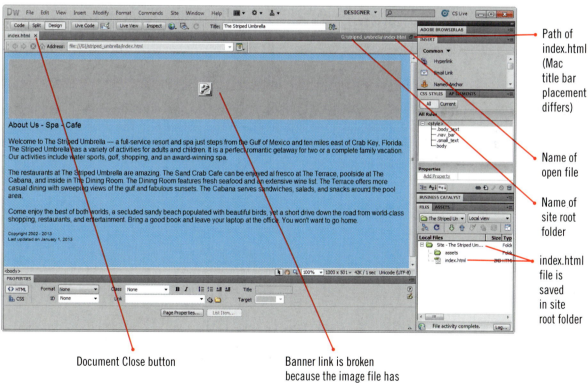

Path of
index.html
(Mac
title bar
placement
differs)

Name of
open file

Name of
site root
folder

index.html
file is
saved
in site
root folder

Document Close button

Banner link is broken
because the image file has
not been copied into the Web
site assets folder

Copying a New Image to a Web Site

When you open a Web page in one folder and then save a copy of it in a different folder, you must take care to copy each image on the page from the original folder into the new folder. If you don't do this, the links to each image will be broken when the page is published to a Web server and subsequently viewed in a Web browser. You want to identify The Striped Umbrella banner source file and copy it to the Web site's assets folder.

STEPS

TROUBLE

If your index.html page does not appear in the Files panel, click the Refresh button ⟳ on the Files panel toolbar.

TROUBLE

If the path for an image or a link begins with the word *file*, you will have linking problems. Delete all extraneous path information in the Src text box or the browser will not be able to find the image when the Web site is published. A good practice is to go to Code view and search for the word *file*. If you find *file* in your code, you must evaluate each occurrence to see if you need to remove unnecessary code.

1. **Click the gray box representing the broken image on the index page**

   Selection handles appear on the lower and right edges of the broken image and the Property inspector displays the banner's properties. The Src (Source) text box in the Property inspector displays the location: assets/su-banner.gif, but the source file is not yet copied to this location. The Striped Umbrella banner, which is the source file, currently resides in the unit_b assets folder. You navigate to the Data Files and select the source file. The concept of broken links will become clearer upon completing Unit F which explores the relationship between absolute and relative links.

2. **If necessary, double-click the right side of the Property inspector to expand it, click the Browse for File icon 🗀 next to the Src text box, click the Look in list arrow ▼ (Win) or the Current file location list arrow ⬍ (Mac) if necessary to navigate to the drive and folder where you store your Data Files, double-click the unit_b folder, double-click the assets folder, then double-click the su_banner.gif file**

   The correct source file location of the image is identified and selected, which enables Dreamweaver to automatically copy it to the Web site's assets folder. The Src text box in the Property inspector displays the path "assets/su_ banner.gif" without any extra path designation in front of it. If you see a path in front of the word *assets*, Dreamweaver is trying to link the image file to the Data Files folder.

3. **Click anywhere on the page outside of the banner, if necessary, to display the image, select the image again to display the image settings in the Property inspector, then compare your screen to Figure B-13**

   The banner now displays correctly on the page which indicates that the source file has been successfully copied to the Web site assets folder. The Property inspector displays the properties of the selected image.

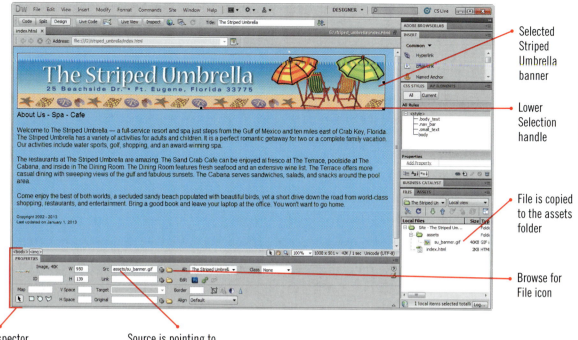

Selected
Striped
Umbrella
banner

Lower
Selection
handle

File is copied
to the assets
folder

Browse for
File icon

Property inspector
provides details about
the selected image

Source is pointing to
assets folder

Design Matters

Planning the page layout

When you begin developing the content for your Web site, you must decide what to include and how to arrange each element on each page. You must also design the content with the audience in mind. What is your audience's age group? What reading level is appropriate? Should pages be simple, containing mostly text, or rich with images and media files? To ensure that users do not get "lost" in your Web site, make sure all the pages have a consistent look and feel. This can be accomplished easily through the use of templates. **Templates** are Web pages that contain the basic layout for each page of a site. You can create original templates with the File menu in Dreamweaver or download them from the Internet. See the Appendix for more information on templates.

Dreamweaver CS5

Adding New Pages to a Web Site

Web sites may be as small as one page or contain hundreds of pages. In Dreamweaver, you can add new pages to the Web site, and then add content such as text and images. The blank pages serve as placeholders for pages that you anticipate designing. That way you can set up the navigation structure of the Web site and test the links between the pages. When you are satisfied with the overall structure, you can then create the content for the pages. You add new pages by using the Files panel. After consulting your wireframe, you decide to create new Web pages to add to The Striped Umbrella Web site. You create new pages called about_us, spa, cafe, activities, cruises, and fishing, and place them in the site folder.

STEPS

1. **Click the Refresh button** $\mathbf{C}$ **on the Files Panel, then click the plus sign (Win) or the triangle (Mac) to the left of the assets folder in the Files panel if necessary**

   The assets folder expands to display its contents, as shown in Figure B-14. The su_banner.gif file is located in the assets folder.

> **TROUBLE**
> Be careful not to delete the .html file extension when you name the file.

2. **Click the site folder under the Local Files column to select it, right-click the site folder, click New File, click in the filename text box to select untitled if necessary, type about_us, then press [Enter] (Win) or [return] (Mac)**

   The about us page is added to the Web site. You can also click the Files panel options button, point to File, then click New File to create a new file.

3. **Repeat Step 2 to add five more blank pages to The Striped Umbrella Web site, and name the new files spa.html, cafe.html, activities.html, cruises.html, and fishing.html**

   The new pages appear in the striped_umbrella root folder.

> **TROUBLE**
> If you accidentally create your new files in the assets folder rather than the site root folder, select and drag each one to the site root folder.

4. **Click the Refresh button** $\mathbf{C}$ **on the Files panel toolbar**

   The file listing is refreshed and the files are now sorted in alphabetical order, as shown in Figure B-15.

5. **Click File on the Application bar (Win) or Menu bar (Mac), click Close, click File on the Application bar, click Exit (Win) or click Dreamweaver on the Menu bar, then click Quit Dreamweaver (Mac)**

Managing a project with a team

When working with a team, it is essential that you define clear goals for the project and a list of objectives to accomplish those goals. Your plan should be finalized after conferring with both the client and team to make sure that the purpose, scope, and objectives are clear to everyone. Establish the **deliverables**, or products that will be provided to the client upon project completion, such as creation of new pages or graphic elements, and a timeline for their delivery. You should present the Web pages to both your team and client for feedback and evaluation at strategic points in the development process.

Analyze all feedback objectively, incorporating both the positive and the negative comments to help you make improvements to the site and meet everyone's expectations and goals. A common pitfall in team management is scope creep. **Scope creep** occurs when impromptu changes or additions are made to a project without accounting for corresponding increases in the schedule or budget. Proper project control and communication between team members and clients can minimize scope creep and achieve the successful and timely completion of a project.

FIGURE B-14: Files panel showing su_banner.gif in the assets folder

assets folder •

su_banner.gif file in the
assets folder

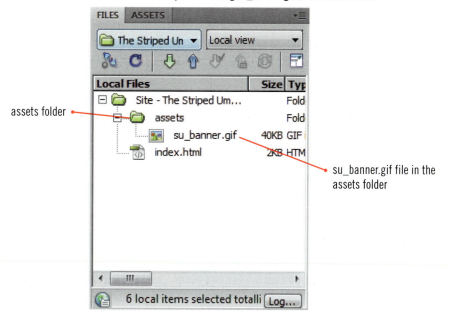

FIGURE B-15: New pages added and sorted to The Striped Umbrella Web site

Refresh icon •

Your image icon for
su_banner.gif
might differ

New pages added to the
striped_umbrella site folder
and sorted after the Files
panel is refreshed

A Mac Files panel will differ
slightly in appearance

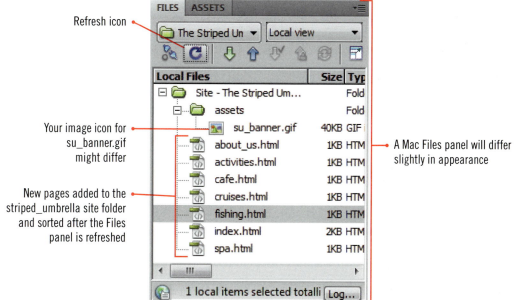

Practice

For current SAM information, including versions and content details, visit SAM Central (http://www.cengage.com/samcentral). If you have a SAM user profile, you may have access to hands-on instruction, practice, and assessment of the skills covered in this unit. Since various versions of SAM are supported throughout the life of this text, check with your instructor for the correct instructions and URL/Web site for accessing assignments.

Concepts Review

Label each element in the Site window in Figure B-16.

FIGURE B-16

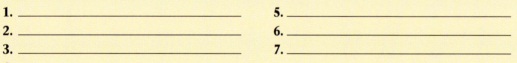

1. _____
2. _____
3. _____
4. _____

5. _____
6. _____
7. _____

Match each of the following terms with the statement that best describes its function.

8. Domain name

9. Wireframe

10. Assets

11. IP address

12. Web server

13. Local Site folder

14. Intranet

15. Home page

16. Publish a Web site

a. An address on the Web expressed in numbers

b. Computer connected to the Internet with an IP address and software that enables it to make files accessible for viewing on the Internet

c. An internal Web site without public access

d. To make a Web site available for viewing on the Internet

e. A folder that holds all the files and folders for a Web site

f. Usually the first page users see when they visit a Web site

g. A folder that contains non-HTML files

h. A diagram of a Web site's folder structure showing links and placement of main page elements

i. An address on the Web expressed in letters

Select the best answer from the following list of choices.

17. **An internal Web site without public access is called a(n):**
    a. Internet
    b. Intranet
    c. Domain
    d. Extension

18. **The first step in designing a Web site should be:**
    a. Setting up Web server access
    b. Testing the pages
    c. Planning the site
    d. Creating the pages and developing the content

19. **Which icon or button do you click to refresh the Files panel after you have changed files listed there?**
    a.
    b.
    c. Code
    d.

20. **Web pages that contain the basic layout for each page in a Web site are called:**
    a. Templates
    b. Examples
    c. Shells
    d. Forms

Skills Review

1. **Plan a Web site.**
   a. Create a wireframe with five pages for a company called Blooms & Bulbs.
   b. Name the pages **index**, **plants**, **workshops**, **newsletter**, and **tips**. (The plants, workshops, newsletter, and tips pages will be links from the index page.)

2. **Create a folder for Web site management.**
   a. Start Dreamweaver, then open or expand the Files panel if necessary.
   b. Select the drive or folder in the Site list box where you will store your Web site files.
   c. Create a new folder with the name **blooms** to store your Web site files.

3. **Define the Web site.**
   a. Create a new site using the Site, New Site command. Name the site **Blooms & Bulbs**.
   b. In the Site Setup dialog box, browse to select the root folder you created for the Web site.
   c. Save the site definition and exit the site setup.

4. **Add a folder to the Web site.**
   a. Use the Files panel to create an assets folder for the Web site.
   b. Use the Site Setup dialog box to set the assets folder as the default images folder for storing your image files.

5. **Copy a new image to a Web site.**
   a. Open dwb_2.html from the drive and folder where your Data Files are stored.
   b. Save the file as **index.html** in the Blooms & Bulbs Web site, and do not update the links.
   c. Close the dwb_2.html file.
   d. Select the gray box representing the broken banner image link on the page.
   e. Using the Browse for File icon next to the Src text box on the Property inspector, navigate to the assets folder inside the unit_b folder where you store your Data Files, then select blooms_banner.jpg.
   f. Refresh the Files panel, click on the page to deselect the banner, then verify that the banner was copied to the assets folder in your Blooms & Bulbs site.

Skills Review (continued)

6. Add new pages to a Web site.

   a. Using the Files panel, create a new page called **plants.html**.

   b. Create three more pages, called **workshops.html**, **tips.html**, and **newsletter.html**.

   c. Use the Refresh button to sort the files in alphabetical order, then compare your screen to Figure B-17.

   d. Close the index page, then exit Dreamweaver.

FIGURE B-17

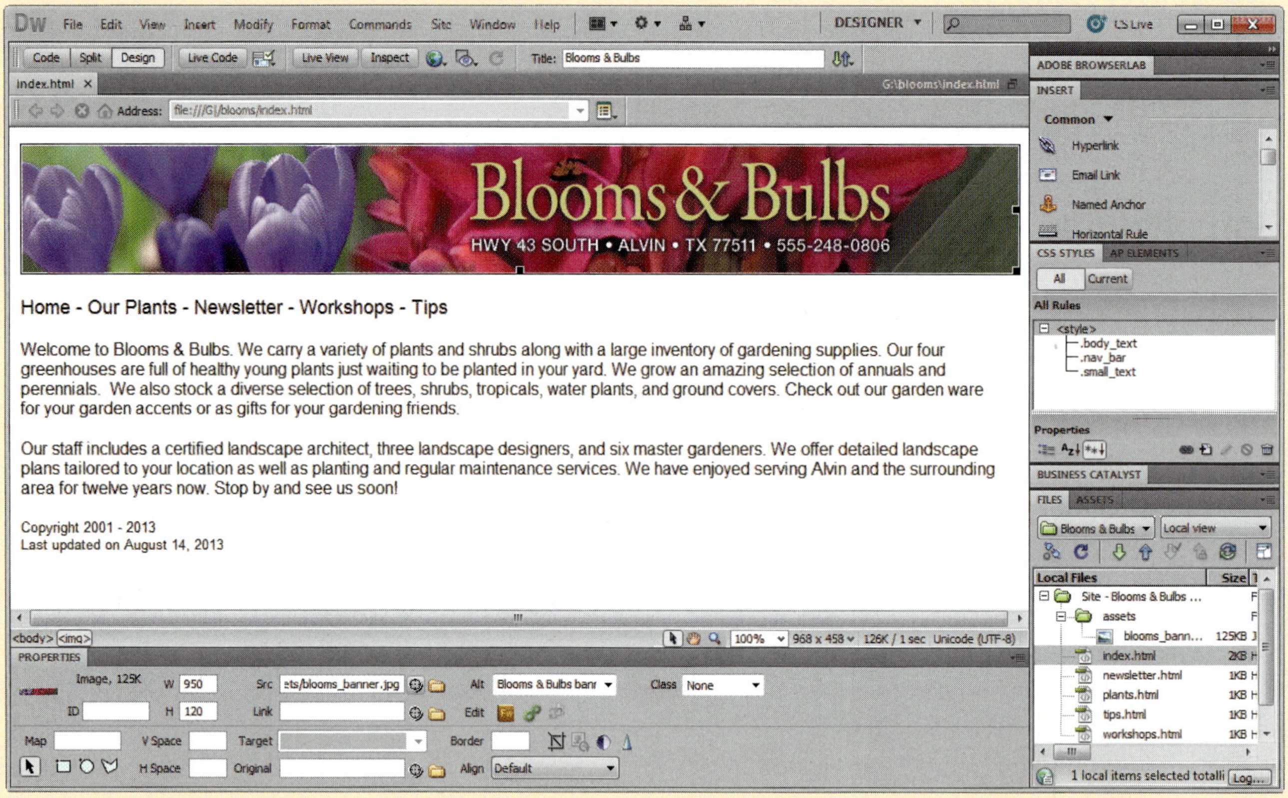

Independent Challenge 1

You have been hired to create a Web site for a river expedition company named Rapids Transit, located on the Buffalo River in Arkansas. In addition to renting canoes, kayaks, and rafts, they have several types of cabin rentals for overnight stays. River guides are available, if requested, to accompany clients on float trips. The clients range from experienced floaters to beginners. Refer to Figure B-18 as you work through the following steps:

a. Create a Web site plan and wireframe for this site.

b. Create a folder named **rapids** in the drive and folder where you save your Web site files.

c. Define the Web site with the name **Rapids Transit**, setting the rapids folder as the site root folder for the Web site.

d. Create an **assets** folder, then set it as the default images folder.

e. Open dwb_3.html from the drive and folder where you store your Data Files, then save it in the site folder as **index.html**. Do not update the links.

f. Close dwb_3.html.

g. Save the rt_banner.jpg image in the assets folder for your site. (*Hint*: Navigate to the Unit B assets folder to locate the source for the image.) Refresh the Files panel and verify that the rt_banner.jpg image was copied to the assets folder.

h. Create four additional files for the pages in your site plan, and give them the following names: **guides.html**, **rates.html**, **lodging.html**, and **before.html**. Refresh the Files panel to display the files in alphabetical order.

i. Close the index page, then exit Dreamweaver.

FIGURE B-18

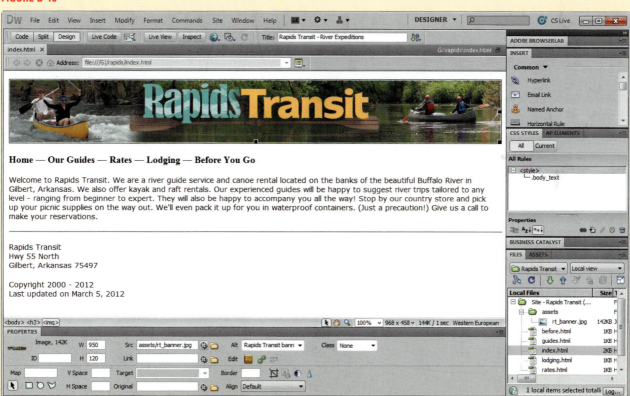

Independent Challenge 2

Your company is designing a new Web site for a travel outfitter named TripSmart. TripSmart specializes in travel products and services. In addition to selling travel products such as luggage and accessories, they sponsor trips and offer travel advice. Their clients range from college students to families to vacationing professionals. The owner, Thomas Howard, has requested a dynamic Web site that conveys the excitement of traveling. Refer to Figure B-19 as you work through the following steps:

a. Create a Web site plan and wireframe for this site to present to Thomas.

b. Create a folder named **tripsmart** in the drive and folder where you save your Web site files.

c. Define the Web site with the name **TripSmart**, then set the tripsmart folder as the site root folder for the Web site.

d. Create an assets folder, then set it as the default images folder.

e. Open the file dwb_4.html from the drive and folder where you store your Data Files, then save it in the root folder of the Web site as **index.html**. Do not update the links.

f. Close dwb_4.html.

g. Save the tripsmart_banner.jpg image in the assets folder for the site, then refresh the Files panel to display the image file in the assets folder.

h. Create four additional files for the pages in your plan, and give them the following names: **catalog.html**, **newsletter.html**, **services.html**, and **tours.html**. Refresh the Files panel to display the files in alphabetical order, then compare your screen to Figure B-19.

i. Close the index page, then exit Dreamweaver.

FIGURE B-19

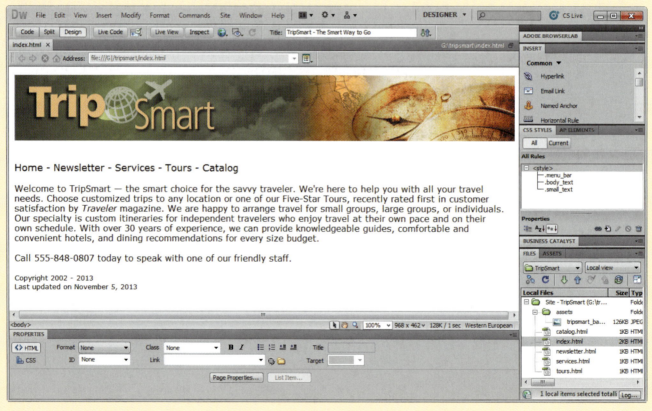

Independent Challenge 3

Patsy Broers is interested in a national program that encourages high school students to memorize and perform poetry. This program is sponsored by the National Endowment for the Arts (NEA), so she goes to the NEA Web site, shown in Figure B-20, to look for information on the program. (As this is a live site, your figure may differ due to content changes.) Record your answers to the questions below.

FIGURE B-20

a. Connect to the Internet and go to the NEA Web site at www.nea.gov.

b. Click the Site Map link at the bottom of the page. What do you think is the purpose of the site map?

c. How has the NEA organized its information to help you navigate its Web site?

d. Can you find the information that Patsy needs?

e. Did you feel that the site map helped you navigate the Web site?

f. Do you feel that the site map link is beneficial for users?

g. Close your browser.

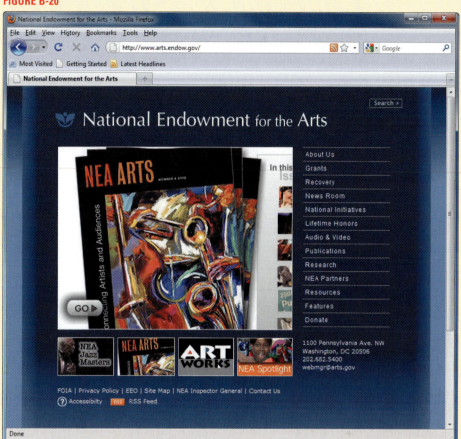

National Endowment for the Arts Web site—www.nea.gov

Real Life Independent Challenge

In this assignment, you create a personal Web site entirely on your own. There will be no Data Files supplied. These Independent Challenges will build from unit to unit, so you must do each unit's Your Site assignment to complete your Web site.

a. Decide what type of Web site you would like to build. It can be a personal Web site about you and your family, a business Web site if you have a business you would like to promote, or a fictitious Web site. Your instructor may direct your choices for this assignment.

b. Create a wireframe for your Web site and include at least four pages.

c. Create a site root folder where you store your Web site files and name it appropriately.

d. Define the Web site with an appropriate name, using the site root folder that you created.

e. Create an assets folder and set it as the default location for images.

f. Begin planning the content you would like to use for the home page and plan how you would like to organize it on the page.

g. Use the Files panel to create the pages you listed in your wireframe.

h. Collect information to use in your Web site, such as images or text. Store these in a folder (paper, not electronic) that you can bring with you to class as you develop your site.

i. Exit Dreamweaver.

Visual Workshop

Your company has been selected to design a Web site for a catering business called Carolyne's Creations. In addition to catering, Carolyne's services include cooking classes and daily specials available as take-out meals. She also has a retail shop that stocks gourmet treats and kitchen items. Create the Web site pictured in Figure B-21, using Carolyne's Creations for the site name and cc for the site root folder name. Use the files dwb_5.html for the index (home) page and cc_banner.jpg for the banner. These files are located in the drive and folder where you store your Data Files. Next, add the files catering.html, classes.html, recipes.html, and shop.html to the site root folder.

FIGURE B-21

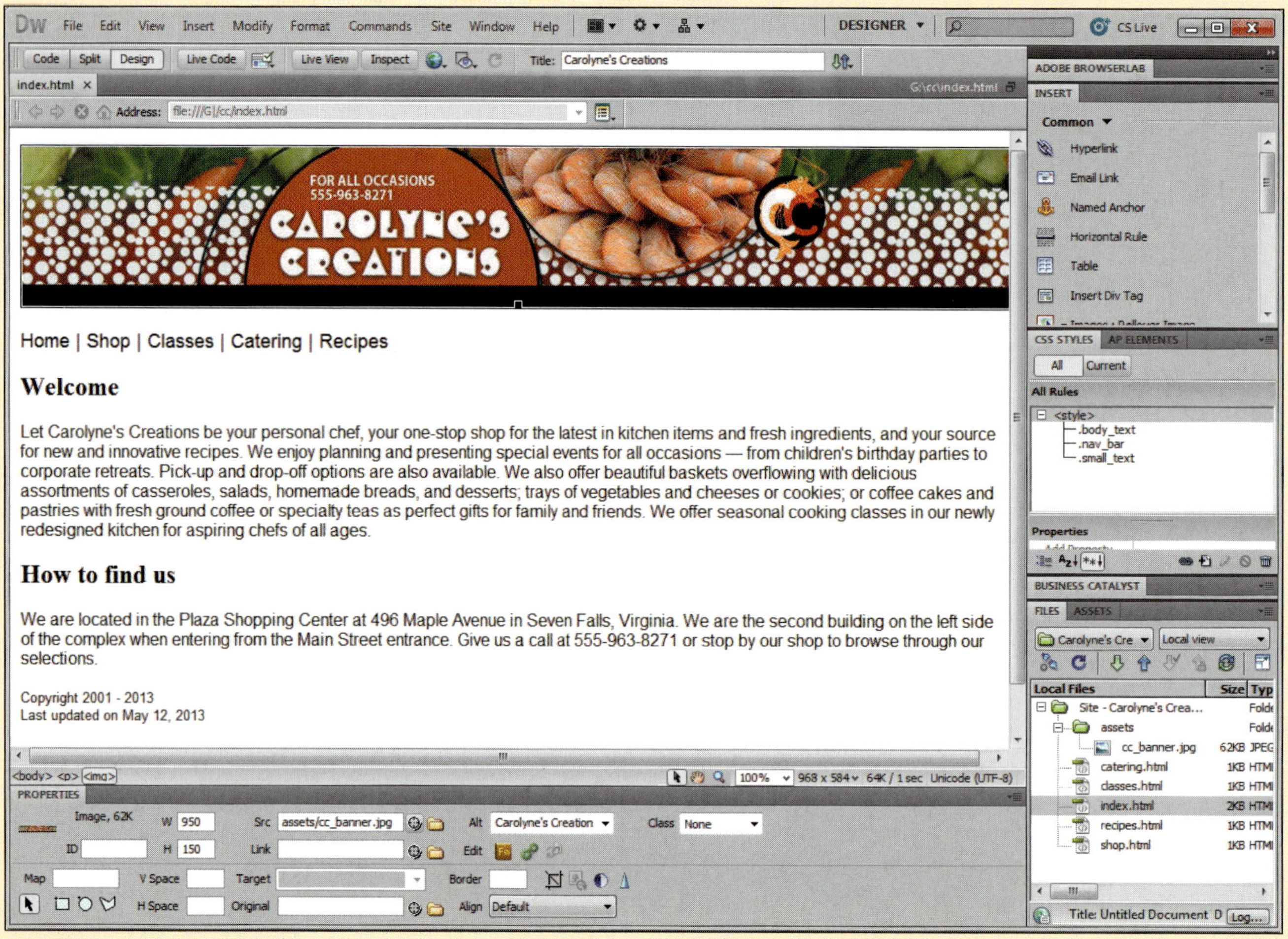

Developing a Web Page

When you begin developing Web pages, you should choose the page content with the purpose of the Web site and the target audience in mind. A Web site designed for a large professional corporation should be designed quite differently than an educational Web site for children. You can use colors, fonts, and images to set a formal or casual tone. In this unit, you learn about planning a Web site, modifying a Web page, and linking it to other pages. Finally, you'll use Code view to modify some of the page code, and test the links to make sure they work. The Striped Umbrella Web site should appeal to families, singles, and maturing baby boomers with leisure time and money to spend. You improve the design and content of the home page to attract this broad target audience.

OBJECTIVES

Plan the page layout

Create the head content

Set Web page properties

Create and format text

Add links to Web pages

Use the History panel

View HTML code

Test and modify Web pages

Planning the Page Layout

When people visit your Web site, you want them to feel at home, as if they know their way around the pages in your site. You also want to ensure that users will not get lost on the site due to layout inconsistencies. To help maintain a common look for all pages, you can use templates. **Templates** are Web pages that contain basic layouts you can apply to your Web site pages, standardizing elements, such as the location of a company logo or a menu of buttons. As you will learn in Units D and G, the use of **Cascading Style Sheets (CSS)** provides a way to easily format objects or entire pages by providing common formatting characteristics that can be applied to multiple objects. And, as you will learn in Unit H, many designers use **tables**, simple grids of cells in rows and columns, as a page layout tool to position lists of tabular data on the page easily. Before you begin working on The Striped Umbrella home page, you want to identify key concepts that govern good page layout.

DETAILS

When planning the layout of your Web pages, remember the following guidelines:

- **Keep it simple**

    Often the simplest Web sites are the most appealing. Web sites that are simple in layout and design are the easiest to create and maintain. A simple Web site that works is far superior to a complex one with errors.

- **Use white space effectively**

    Too many text blocks, links, and images can confuse users, and actually make them feel agitated. Consider leaving some white space on each page. **White space** is area on a Web page that is not filled with text or graphics. (Note that white space is not necessarily white in color.) Using white space effectively creates a harmonious balance on the page. Figure C-1 shows how white space can help emphasize strong visual page elements, yet still achieve a simple, clean look for the page.

- **Limit media objects**

    Too many media objects—such as graphics, video clips, or sounds—may result in a page that takes too long to load. Users may tire of waiting for these objects to appear and leave your site before the entire page finishes loading. Placing unnecessary media objects on your page makes your Web site seem unprofessional.

- **Use an intuitive navigation structure**

    A Web site's navigational structure should be easy to use. It can be based on text links or a combination of text and graphic links. Users should always know where they are in the Web site, and be able to find their way back to the home page easily. If users get lost on your Web site, they may leave the site rather than struggle to find their way around.

- **Apply a consistent theme using templates**

    A theme can be almost anything, from the same background color on each page to common graphics, such as buttons or icons that reflect a collective theme. Common design elements such as borders can also be considered a theme. Templates are a great way to easily incorporate consistent themes in Web sites.

- **Use tables or CSS for page layout**

    When you use tables or CSS as the basis for page layout, you can control both how the entire page appears in browser windows and how the various page elements are positioned on the page in relation to each other. This allows a page to look the same, regardless of the size of a user's screen.

- **Be conscious of accessibility issues**

    There are several techniques you can use to ensure that your Web site is accessible to individuals with disabilities. These techniques include using alternate text with images, avoiding certain colors on Web pages, and supplying text as an alternate source for information that is presented in audio files. Dreamweaver can display Accessibility dialog boxes to prompt you to insert accessibility information for the page objects, as shown in Figure C-2.

FIGURE C-1: An example of an effective Web page layout

First Federal Bank Web site — www.ffbh.com

FIGURE C-2: Accessibility attributes for page design

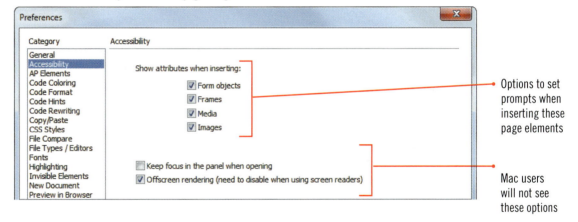

Options to set prompts when inserting these page elements

Mac users will not see these options

Design Matters

Designing for accessibility

It is extremely important to design your Web site so that individuals with disabilities can successfully navigate and read its Web pages. In fact, government Web sites must be made accessible pursuant to Section 508 of the Workforce Investment Act of 1998, based on the Americans with Disabilities Act (ADA). On May 5, 1999, the first Web Content Accessibility Guidelines were published by the World Wide Web Consortium (W3C). The levels of accessibility are grouped into three priority level checkpoints. Although all Web sites should comply with the Priority 1 checkpoints, government Web sites *must* comply with them, such as providing a text equivalent for every non-text element. For more information about priority level checkpoints, go to www.w3.org. Adobe's Accessibility Resource Center (www.adobe.com/accessibility); this site provides specific information about Web site compliance with Section 508 guidelines, such as suggestions for creating accessible Web sites, an explanation of Section 508, and information on how people with disabilities use assistive devices to navigate the Internet. These guidelines are based on four principles called the POUR principles: Web sites should be Perceivable, Operable, Understandable, and Robust. For more information about the POUR principles (Putting People at the Center of the Process) for Web site accessibility, go to www.webaim.org.

Creating the Head Content

A Web page consists of two sections: the head section and the body. The **body** contains all the page content users see in their browser window, such as text, graphics, and links. The **head section** contains the **head content**, including the page title that is displayed in the browser title bar (not to be confused with the file name which is used to save the page), as well as some very important page elements that are not visible in the browser. These items are called meta tags. **Meta tags** are HTML codes that include information about the page such as keywords and descriptions. **Keywords** are words that are representative to the content of a Web site. Search engines find Web pages by matching the title, description, and keywords in the head content of Web pages with keywords users enter in search text boxes. A **description** is a short summary of Web site content.  Before you work on page content for the home page, you modify the page title and add a description and keywords that will draw users to The Striped Umbrella Web site.

STEPS

1. Start Dreamweaver, click the Site list arrow ▼ (Win) or ⬍ (Mac) on the Files panel, then click The Striped Umbrella if it isn't already selected

   The Striped Umbrella Web site opens in the Files panel.

TROUBLE
If you don't see the index.html file listed, click the plus sign (Win) or triangle (Mac) next to the striped_umbrella folder to expand the folder contents.

2. Double-click index.html in the Files panel, make sure the Document window is maximized, click View on the Application bar (Win) or Menu bar (Mac), then if necessary click Head Content to select it

   The head content section appears at the top of The Striped Umbrella home page, as shown in Figure C-3. The head content section includes the Title icon 🔲 and the Meta tag icon 🔲.

QUICK TIP
You can also change the page title using either the Title text box on the Document toolbar or the Page Properties dialog box.

3. Click the Page title icon 🔲, place the insertion point after The Striped Umbrella in the Title text box in the Property inspector, press [spacebar], type beach resort and spa, Ft. Eugene, Florida, then press [Enter] (Win) or [return] (Mac)

   The new page title appears in the Title text box. See Figure C-4. The new title uses the words beach and resort, which potential guests may use as keywords when using a search engine.

4. Expand the Insert panel if necessary, click the Insert panel list arrow, then click the Common category (if necessary), scroll down if necessary to locate the Head object, then click the Head list arrow, as shown in Figure C-3

   Some buttons on the Insert panel include a list arrow, indicating that there is a menu of choices beneath the current button. The button that was selected last appears on the Insert panel until you select another.

QUICK TIP
Multiple keywords should always be separated by commas.

5. Click Keywords, type beach resort, spa, Ft. Eugene, Florida, Gulf of Mexico, fishing, dolphin cruises (including the commas) in the Keywords text box, as shown in Figure C-5, then click OK

   The Keywords icon 🔲 appears in the head section, indicating that keywords have been created for the page.

6. Click the Head list arrow on the Insert panel, click Description, type The Striped Umbrella is a full-service resort and spa just steps from the Gulf of Mexico in Ft. Eugene, Florida. in the Description dialog box, as shown in Figure C-6, then click OK

   The Description icon 🔲 appears selected in the head section, indicating that a description has been entered.

7. Click the Show Code view button ⬚Code⬚ on the Document toolbar, click anywhere in the code, then view the head section code, as shown in Figure C-7

   The title, keywords, and description appear in the head section of the HTML code. The title is surrounded by title tags, and the keywords and description are both surrounded by meta tags.

8. Click the Show Design view button ⬚Design⬚ on the Document toolbar, click View on the Application bar (Win) or Menu bar (Mac), then click Head Content

   The Striped Umbrella home page redisplays without the head content section visible above the document window.

FIGURE C-3: Viewing the head content section

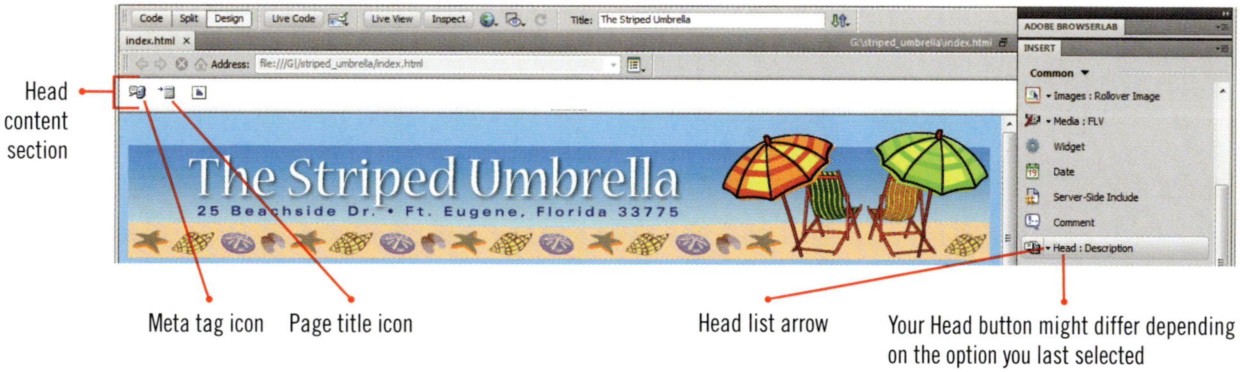

Head content section

Meta tag icon   Page title icon

Head list arrow   Your Head button might differ depending on the option you last selected

FIGURE C-4: Property inspector displaying new page title

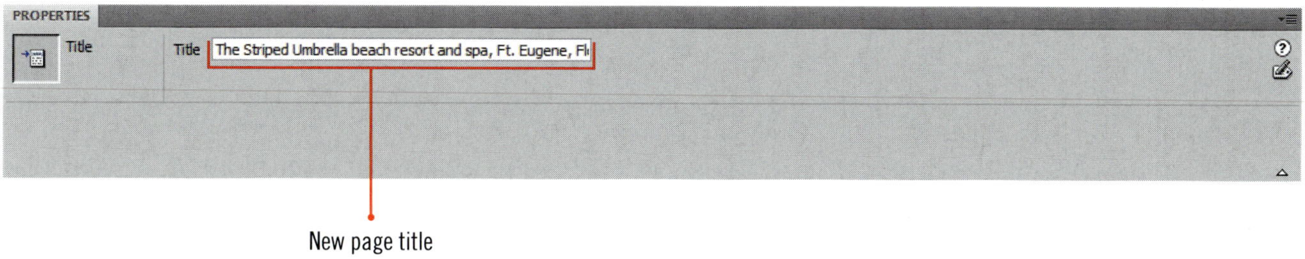

Title   Title | The Striped Umbrella beach resort and spa, Ft. Eugene, Fl|

New page title

FIGURE C-5: Keywords dialog box

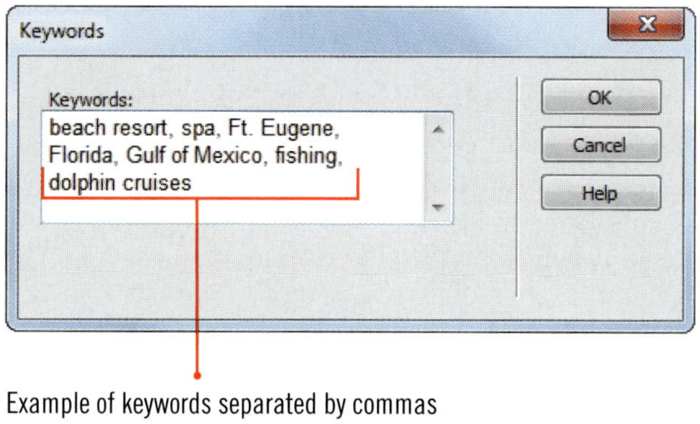

Keywords:
beach resort, spa, Ft. Eugene, Florida, Gulf of Mexico, fishing, dolphin cruises

OK   Cancel   Help

Example of keywords separated by commas

FIGURE C-6: Description dialog box

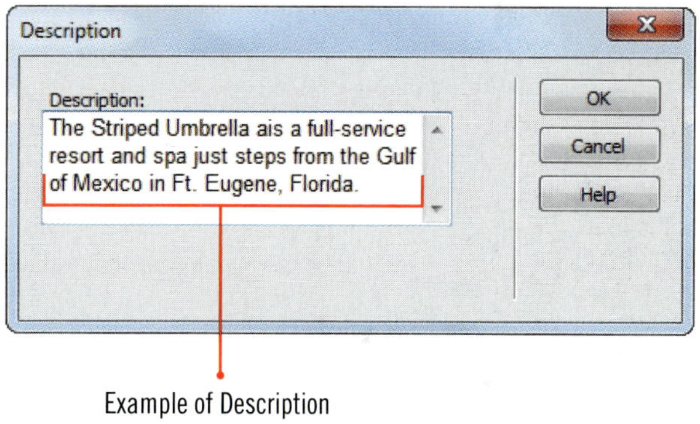

Description:
The Striped Umbrella ais a full-service resort and spa just steps from the Gulf of Mexico in Ft. Eugene, Florida.

OK   Cancel   Help

Example of Description

FIGURE C-7: Code view displaying the code for the head content

Your lines of code may appear in a slightly different order

Keywords   Description   Title   Beginning head tag

```
1  <!DOCTYPE html PUBLIC "-//W3C//DTD XHTML 1.0 Transitional//EN" "http://www.w3.org/TR/xhtml1/DTD/xhtml1-transitional.dtd">
2  <html xmlns="http://www.w3.org/1999/xhtml">
3  <head>
4  <meta http-equiv="Content-Type" content="text/html; charset=utf-8" />
5  <title>The Striped Umbrella beach resort and spa, Ft. Eugene, Florida</title>
6  <meta name="Keywords" content="beach resort, spa, Ft. Eugene, Florida, Gulf of Mexico, fishing, dolphin cruises" />
7  <meta name="Description" content="The Striped Umbrella is a full-service resort and spa just steps from the Gulf of Mexico in Ft. Eugene, Florida" />
```

Design Matters

Entering titles, keywords, and descriptions

Search engines use titles, keywords, and descriptions to find pages after the user enters search terms. It is therefore important to anticipate what your potential customers will use for search terms, and to try to include those in the keywords, description, or title. Many search engines print the page titles and descriptions when they list pages in their search results. Some search engines limit the number of keywords that they will index so again keep your keywords and description to a minimum. It is usually sufficient to enter keywords and a description only for the home page or any other page you want users to find, rather than for every page on the Web site. To choose effective keywords, many designers use focus groups to learn which words potential customers or clients might use. A **focus group** is a marketing tool that asks a group of people for feedback about a product, such as the impact of a television ad or the effectiveness of a Web site design.

Setting Web Page Properties

One of the first design decisions that you should make is the background color of your Web page. This color should complement the colors used for text, links, and images you place on the page. A strong contrast between the text and background colors makes it easier for users to read the text. You can choose a light background color and a dark text color, or a dark background color and a light text color. A white background, though not terribly exciting, is the easiest to read for most users, and provides good contrast in combination with dark text. The next decision is to choose the default text color. The **default text color** is the color the browser uses to display text when a color is not specified. Settings such as the page background color and the default text color are specified using CSS. 🎨 You want to set the background color and choose a default text color for The Striped Umbrella home page.

STEPS

QUICK TIP
You can also open the Page Properties dialog box by clicking the Page Properties button in the Property inspector.

1. **Click Modify on the Application bar (Win) or Menu bar (Mac), then click Page Properties**

   The Page Properties dialog box opens. You use this dialog box to set page properties, such as the background color and default text color.

2. **Click the Background color box 🔲 next to Background color, as shown in Figure C-8**

   The color picker opens, and the pointer changes to an eyedropper 🖋. When Dreamweaver is first installed, the Background color box appears gray, which represents the default color. This does not mean that the color gray will be applied *unless* gray has previously been selected as the default color for the selected page element. Once you select a color from the color picker, the Background color box changes accordingly.

3. **Click the blue color swatch, #9CF (the fifth color in the last row), as shown in Figure C-8**

   Each color is assigned a **hexadecimal value**, a numerical value that represents the amount of red, green, and blue in the color. For example, white, which is made of equal parts of red, green, and blue, has a hexadecimal value of FFFFFF. Each pair of numbers represents the red, green, and blue values. The hexadecimal number system is based on 16, rather than 10 as in the decimal number system. Since there aren't any digits after reaching the number 9, letters of the alphabet are then used. The letter A represents the number 10, and F represents the number 15 in the hexadecimal number system. The hexadecimal values can be entered in the code using a form of shorthand that shortens the six characters to three characters. For instance: 0066CC becomes 06C. The number value for a color is preceded by a pound sign (#) in HTML code.

4. **Click Apply in the Page Properties dialog box**

   The background color of the Web page changes to a different shade of blue while the text color remains the default color, which is black. The Apply button allows you to see changes that you have made to the page without having to close the Page Properties dialog box. The blue background does not provide the best contrast between the page background and the text.

QUICK TIP
The Background color box appears blue (the last color selected) until you click the white color swatch.

5. **Click 🔲 next to Background color, click the white color swatch (the rightmost color in the bottom row), then click Apply**

   The white page background provides a better contrast.

6. **Click the Text color box 🔲 next to Text color, shown in Figure C-9, use the eyedropper 🖋 to select a light shade of blue, then click Apply**

   The light blue text color on the home page is not quite as easy to read as the black text.

7. **Click 🔲 next to Text color, then click the Default Color icon 🚫 at the top of the color picker**

   The Page Properties dialog box reappears with the text color setting restored to the default color. See Figure C-9. The Default Color button automatically restores the default color setting.

8. **Click OK**

   The Page Properties dialog box closes and The Striped Umbrella Web page redisplays with the default black text color and new white background color.

FIGURE C-8: Page Properties dialog box

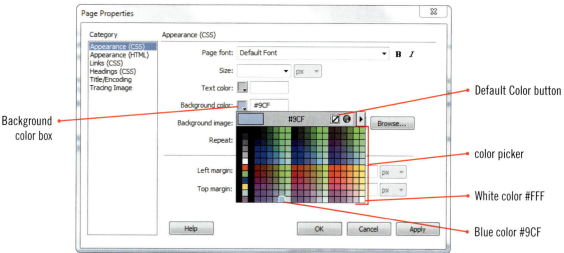

Background color box

Default Color button

color picker

White color #FFF

Blue color #9CF

FIGURE C-9: Page Properties dialog box

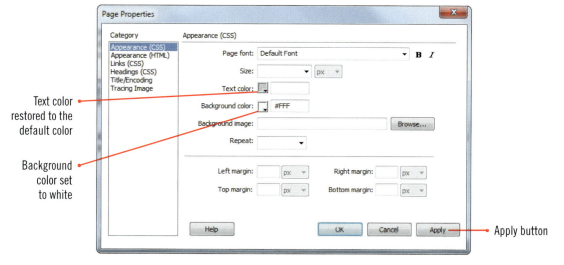

Text color restored to the default color

Background color set to white

Apply button

Using Web-safe colors

Prior to 1994, colors appeared differently on different types of computers. In 1994, Netscape developed the first **Web-safe color palette**, a set of colors that appears consistently in all browsers and on Macintosh, Windows, and UNIX platforms. The evolution of video cards has made this less relevant today, although understanding Web-safe colors may still prove important given the limitations of other online devices, such as cell phones and PDAs. If you want your Web pages to be viewed across a wide variety of computer platforms, choose Web-safe colors for all your page elements. Dreamweaver has two Web-safe color palettes: Color Cubes and Continuous Tone. Each palette contains the 216 Web-safe colors. Color Cubes is the default color palette; however, you can choose another one by clicking Modify on the Application bar (Win) or Menu bar (Mac), clicking Page Properties, clicking the Appearance (CSS) or (HTML) category, clicking the Color picker next to the Background or Text color boxes, clicking the color palette list arrow,

then clicking the desired color palette. Figure C-10 shows the list of color palette choices. See the Adobe Help files for more information about Web-safe colors.

FIGURE C-10: Color palettes

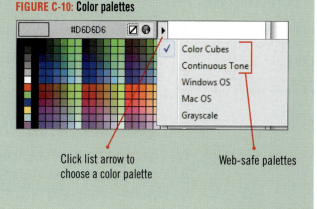

Click list arrow to choose a color palette

Web-safe palettes

Creating and Formatting Text

Text is an important part of any Web page. You can enter text directly in Dreamweaver, import it (Win only), or copy and paste text from another document. When you are entering text, each time you press [Enter] (Win) or [return] (Mac), you create a new paragraph in the HTML code. Each paragraph is surrounded by <p> tags. Once you enter or import text, you can format it in Dreamweaver by changing the font, size, and color, just as in other programs. **Headings** are six different HTML text sizes that you can apply to text: Heading 1 (the largest size) through Heading 6 (the smallest size). Using a heading format is a way of showing the importance level of selected text in relation to other text on the page. Examples of tags that show emphasis are the bold tag, <strong>, and the italic tag, <em>. While you can set some formatting characteristics with HTML tags, the preferred practice is to use CSS for most formatting. The current menu bar does not include links to all of the main pages so you decide replace it with a link to each main page and format it using an HTML heading format. You also apply the italic setting to the contact information to help users locate it more easily.

STEPS

QUICK TIP

Make sure the text is selected properly—the next keystroke will replace the selected items. If you have difficulty selecting text, try [Backspace] or [Delete].

1. **Position the insertion point to the left of A in About Us, then drag to select About Us - Spa - Cafe, as shown in Figure C-11**

   The current menu bar is selected. A small icon may appear next to the selected text. If you click this icon, you will bring up the **Code Navigator**, a small window that opens with code for the selected page element. You will learn more about the Code Navigator in Unit D.

2. **Type Home - About Us - Spa - Cafe - Activities, using spaces on either side of the hyphens**

   This text becomes the page's new menu bar. A **menu bar** is a set of text or graphic links that is used to navigate to other pages in your Web site.

3. **Position the insertion point to the left of H in Home, then drag to select Home - About Us - Spa - Cafe - Activities**

   The new menu bar appears selected.

4. **Click the HTML button on the Property inspector to open the HTML Property inspector if necessary, click the Format list arrow in the HTML Property inspector, then click Heading 4**

   The Heading 4 format is applied to the menu bar, as shown in Figure C-12. The text appears bold and a little larger in size now.

5. **Position the insertion point after the period following "...want to go home", as shown in Figure C-12, press [Enter] (Win) or [return] (Mac), then type The Striped Umbrella**

   Pressing [Enter] (Win) or [return] (Mac) creates a paragraph break with a <p> tag. Even a single character is considered a paragraph if it is preceded and followed by a paragraph break. Paragraphs can share common formatting, such as alignment settings.

QUICK TIP

Line breaks are useful when you want to apply the same formatting to text but place it on separate lines. The HTML code for a line break is <br />.

6. **Press and hold [Shift], press [Enter] (Win) or [return] (Mac) to create a line break**

   You can create separate lines within a paragraph by entering a line break after each line. A **line break** places text on separate lines without creating a new paragraph, which enables you to apply common formatting attributes to separate lines of text.

7. **Enter the following information, repeating the instructions in Step 6 to place a line break at the end of each line:**

   25 Beachside Drive
   Ft. Eugene, Florida 33775
   (555) 594-9458

QUICK TIP

The Italic button is located in both the CSS and HTML Property inspectors, but each one produces different results. The HTML Italic button formats selected text.

8. **Position the pointer to the left of The Striped Umbrella, click and drag to select all of the information you entered in Step 7, click the Italic button I in the Property inspector, then click anywhere to deselect the text**

   The contact information appears as italicized text. See Figure C-13.

FIGURE C-11: Replacing the current menu bar

Selected text

Click indicator to bring
up the Code Navigator

FIGURE C-12: Formatting the new menu bar

New menu bar
with Heading 4
format applied

Format list arrow

HTML Property
inspector

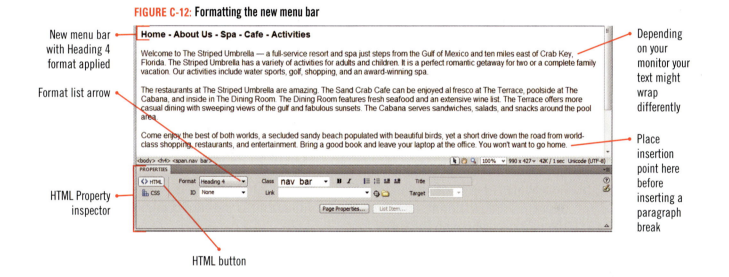

Depending
on your
monitor your
text might
wrap
differently

Place
insertion
point here
before
inserting a
paragraph
break

HTML button

FIGURE C-13: Adding and formatting the contact information

Contact
information
with italic
format applied

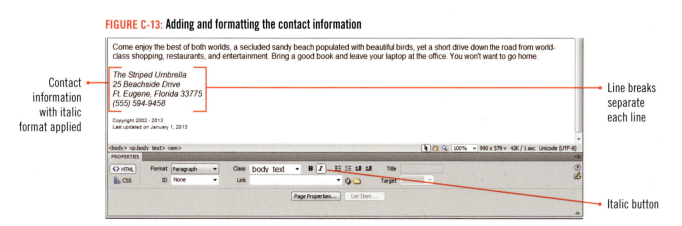

Line breaks
separate
each line

Italic button

Adding Links to Web Pages

Links, or hyperlinks, are specially formatted text or images that users click to navigate through and between Web sites. Users are more likely to return to Web sites that have a user-friendly navigation system and interesting links to other Web pages or sites. After a link has been clicked in a browser window, it is called a **visited link**, and it changes by default to a purple color in the browser window. The default color for links that have not yet been clicked is blue. When creating Web pages, it is important to avoid **broken links**, which are links that are unable to access the intended destination file. In addition to the links that you create to enable users to move from page to page, a helpful link to include is a **point of contact**, a place on a Web page that gives users a means of contacting the Web site source if they have questions or problems. A **mailto: link**, an e-mail address for users to contact the Web site's headquarters, is a common point of contact. You create links for each of the menu items to their respective Web pages in The Striped Umbrella Web site. You also create an e-mail link to the club manager at The Striped Umbrella.

STEPS

1. **Double-click Home in the menu bar**

   You use this selected text to make a link.

2. **Click the Browse for File icon ☐ next to the Link text box in the HTML Property inspector, as shown in Figure C-14, then navigate to the striped_umbrella site root folder if necessary**

   The Select File dialog box opens. The contents of the striped_umbrella site root folder are listed.

3. **Click index.html, as shown in Figure C-15, verify that Document is selected in the Relative to pop-up menu then click OK (Win) or Choose (Mac)**

   The Select File dialog box closes.

4. **Click anywhere on the home page to deselect Home**

   Home is underlined and blue, the default color for links, indicating that it is a link. When users click the Home link in a browser window, the index.html page opens.

5. **Repeat Steps 1–4 to create links for About Us, Spa, Cafe, and Activities, using about_us.html, spa.html, cafe.html, and activities.html as the corresponding files, then click anywhere on the page**

   All five links are now created for The Striped Umbrella home page. See Figure C-16.

6. **Position the insertion point immediately after the last digit in the telephone number, press and hold [Shift], then press [Enter] (Win) or [return] (Mac)**

   A line break is created.

7. **Click the Insert panel list arrow on the Insert panel, click Common if necessary, then click Email Link**

   The Email Link dialog box opens.

8. **Type Club Manager in the Text text box, press [Tab], type manager@thestripedumbrella.com in the E-Mail text box, as shown in Figure C-17, then click OK**

   The email link to the Club Manager appears under the telephone number.

9. **If the email link does not appear in italics, position the pointer to the left of Club Manager, click and drag to select the text, click the Italic button 𝐼 in the HTML Property inspector, then click anywhere to deselect the text**

   The Club Manager link appears in italics to match the rest of the contact information.

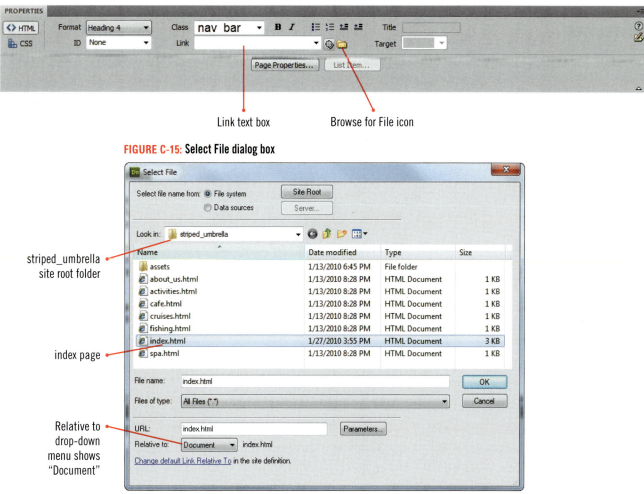

FIGURE C-14: Creating a link using the Property inspector

Link text box

Browse for File icon

FIGURE C-15: Select File dialog box

striped_umbrella site root folder

index page

Relative to drop-down menu shows "Document"

FIGURE C-16: Links added to menu bar items

The Striped Umbrella
25 Beachside Dr. • Ft. Eugene, Florida 33775

Home - **About Us** - **Spa** - **Cafe** - **Activities**

Welcome to The Striped Umbrella — a full-service resort and spa just steps from the Gulf of Mexico and ten miles east of Crab Key, Florida. The Striped Umbrella has a variety of activities for adults and children. It is a perfect romantic getaway for two or a complete family vacation. Our activities include water sports, golf, shopping, and an award-winning spa.

Links to Home, About Us, Spa, Cafe, and Activities pages

FIGURE C-17: Email Link dialog box

Email Link

Text for e-mail link that will appear on the Web page

Text: Club Manager

Email: manager@thestripedumbrella.con

OK

Cancel

Help

Link information

Using the History Panel

The **History panel** shows the steps that you have performed while editing and formatting a particular document in Dreamweaver. To **edit** a page means to insert, delete, or change content by, for example, inserting a new image, adding a link, or correcting spelling errors. Remember that formatting, in contrast, means to change just the appearance of page elements. The History panel records all of the tasks that you perform and displays them in the order in which you completed them. If you make a mistake while editing or formatting a page, you can undo your previous steps. Simply drag the slider up next to the step you want to revert to, as shown in Figure C-18. This is a more efficient way to undo steps than using the Edit, Undo command. You want to add a horizontal rule to divide the banner and menu bar from the rest of the page as well as use the History panel to undo the changes you don't like.

STEPS

1. **Click Window on the Application bar (Win) or Menu bar (Mac), then click History**
   The History panel opens, and the steps you have already performed during this session, such as Make Hyperlink and Line Break, display in the panel window.

2. **Click the Panel options button ▼≡ on the History panel title bar, click Clear History, as shown in Figure C-18, then click Yes in the Dreamweaver warning box**
   The steps that were previously listed in the History panel are cleared and the panel is empty.

QUICK TIP
A horizontal rule can also be inserted by clicking Horizontal rule in the Common category on the Insert panel.

3. **Position the insertion point to the left of the words Welcome to The Striped Umbrella in the first line of text, click Insert on the Application bar (Win) or Menu bar (Mac), point to HTML, then click Horizontal Rule**
   A horizontal rule, or line, appears on the page above the first paragraph and remains selected.

4. **If "pixels" is not displayed in the width pop-up menu, click the width list arrow in the Property inspector, click pixels, type 950 in the W text box, then press [Enter] (Win) or [return] (Mac)**
   The width of the horizontal rule changes to 950 pixels wide and the step is recorded in the History panel.

5. **Click the Align list arrow in the Property inspector, then click Left**
   The horizontal rule is left-aligned on the page. Compare your Property inspector settings to Figure C-19.

6. **Select 950 in the W text box, type 80, click the Width list arrow, click %, click the Align list arrow, then click Center**
   The horizontal rule is set to 80% of the width of the window and is center-aligned. When you set the width of a horizontal rule as a percentage of the page rather than in pixels, it resizes itself proportionately when viewed on different-sized monitors and resolutions. You prefer the way the rule looked when it was wider, a set width, and left-aligned.

7. **Drag the slider on the History panel up until it is pointing to Set Alignment: left, as shown in Figure C-20, then release it**
   The bottom three steps in the History panel appear gray, indicating that these steps have been undone, and the horizontal rule returns to the left-aligned, 950-pixel width settings.

8. **Click File on the Application bar (Win) or Menu bar (Mac), then click Save**

Using the History panel

Dragging the slider up and down in the History panel is a quick way to undo or redo steps. However, the History panel offers much more. It can "memorize" certain steps and consolidate them into one command. This is a useful feature for steps that you need to perform repeatedly. However, some Dreamweaver features, such as steps performed in the Files panel, cannot be recorded in the History panel. The default number of steps that the History panel will record is 50, unless you specify otherwise in the General Preferences dialog box. Setting this number higher requires additional memory, and may affect the speed at which Dreamweaver functions.

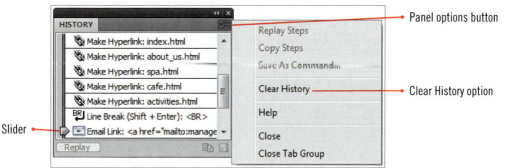
FIGURE C-18: History panel

Panel options button

Clear History option

Slider

FIGURE C-19: Property inspector settings for horizontal rule

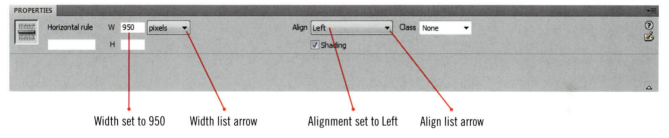

Width set to 950   Width list arrow   Alignment set to Left   Align list arrow

---

FIGURE C-20: Resetting horizontal rule properties using the History panel

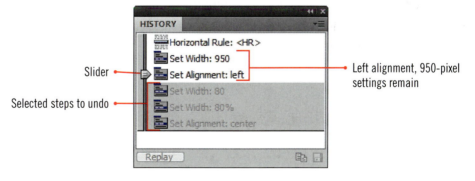

Slider

Selected steps to undo

Left alignment, 950-pixel settings remain

Checking your screen against book figures

To show as much of the Document window as possible, most figures appear with the Standard toolbar hidden. Keep in mind that Dreamweaver will "remember" the screen arrangement from the last session when it opens each time. This may mean that you would have to open, close, collapse, or expand the various panels, toolbars, and inspectors to match your screens to the figures in the book. This is not really necessary unless you need a panel that is not open to complete a step. The rulers may also be displayed in figures in Design view. To turn this feature on or off, use the View, Rulers, Show command.

Viewing HTML Code

XHTML is the newest standard for HTML code. Although the default files created in Dreamweaver are XHTML files, the file extension is .html, and the code is referred to as "HTML." It is often helpful to view the code while editing or formatting a Web page to understand how the code is working. You can use the **Reference panel** to find answers to coding questions covering topics such as HTML, JavaScript, and accessibility. The built-in electronic reference books supplied with Dreamweaver are available using the Book pop-up menu on the Reference panel. Dreamweaver also has a feature that tells you the last date that changes were made to a Web page. 🎨🖌️ Although you are satisfied with the placement of the horizontal rule on the page, you decide to use the Reference panel to research how to change its color. You also want to add a code so that the date will automatically update each time the page is saved.

STEPS

1. **Click Window on the Application bar (Win) or Menu bar (Mac), click History to close the History panel, then click the horizontal rule**
   The horizontal rule is selected.

2. **Click the Show Code view button** `Code` **on the Document toolbar**
   The highlighted HTML code represents the selected horizontal rule on the page. The Coding toolbar is docked along the left side of the document window.

3. **If necessary, click to select the Line Numbers and Word Wrap option buttons on the Coding toolbar, as shown in Figure C-21**
   The option buttons on the Coding toolbar appear white with a black border when they are selected. The Line Numbers and Word Wrap options make it easier to navigate code. **Line numbers** provide a point of reference when locating specific sections of code. **Word wrap** keeps all code within the width of the Document window so you don't have to scroll to read long lines of code. It is easier for you to read and select the lines of code as you research the <hr> tag using the Reference panel.

4. **Click Window on the Application bar (Win) or Menu bar (Mac), point to Results, click Reference, if necessary click the Book list arrow in the Reference Panel to select O'REILLY HTML Reference, click the Tag list arrow to select HR if necessary, as shown in Figure C-22**
   The HR tag appears in the Tag text box in the Reference panel menu bar; HR is the HTML code for horizontal rule tag.

5. **Read the information about horizontal rules**
   The color of rules can be changed by using CSS; this will be covered in Unit D.

6. **Click the Panel options button** ▾☰ **on the Results panel title bar, then click Close Tab Group**
   The Results tab group closes.

7. **Scroll down if necessary in the Document window, select January 1, 2013, then press [Delete]**
   The date is deleted.

8. **Scroll down the Common category on the Insert panel until the Date object button appears, click Date to open the Insert Date dialog box, click March 7, 1974, in the Date format options list, click the Update automatically on save check box if necessary to select it, as shown in Figure C-23, then click OK**
   The Insert date dialog box closes and the JavaScript code for the date is added to the page. The current date will be placed on the page each time the page is opened and saved.

9. **Click the Show Design view button** `Design` **on the Document toolbar**
   The index page appears in Design view in the Document window.

FIGURE C-21: Code view options

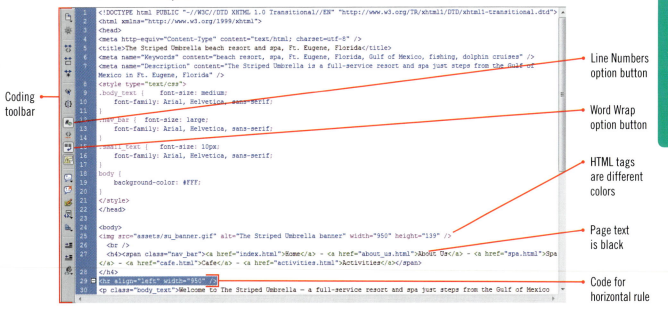

Coding toolbar

Line Numbers option button

Word Wrap option button

HTML tags are different colors

Page text is black

Code for horizontal rule

FIGURE C-22: <HR> tags information displayed in the Reference panel

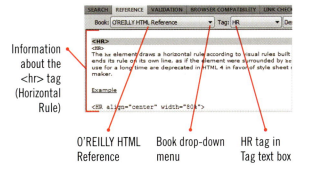

Information about the <hr> tag (Horizontal Rule)

O'REILLY HTML Reference

Book drop-down menu

HR tag in Tag text box

FIGURE C-23: Insert Date dialog box

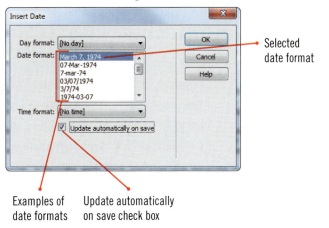

Selected date format

Examples of date formats

Update automatically on save check box

Design Matters

Using Code view to edit pages

Some designers prefer to make changes to their pages by typing directly into the code, rather than working in Design view, because they feel that this gives them more precise control. Some features, such as JavaScript functions, are often added to pages by copying and pasting code into the existing page's HTML code. **JavaScript** is code that adds interaction between the user and the Web page, such as rollovers or interactive forms. **Rollovers** are screen elements that change in appearance as the pointer rests on them. You can view the HTML code in Dreamweaver by using Code view or Code and Design view. This enables you to view the HTML code and the page content in different colors, highlight HTML code that contains errors, and **debug**, or correct, HTML errors.

Understanding XHTML vs. HTML

You can save Dreamweaver files in many different file formats, including XHTML, HTML, JavaScript, CSS, or XML, to name a few. XHTML (eXtensible HyperText Markup Language), which is based on XML (eXtensible Markup Language), is an extension of HTML 4 and has become the standard language used to create Web pages. Using XHTML rather than HTML combines the advantages of both HTML and XML content and is the next step in the evolution of the Internet. You can still use HTML (HyperText Markup Language) in Dreamweaver; however, it is no longer considered the standard language. In Dreamweaver CS5 you can easily convert existing HTML code to XHTML-compliant code by using the File, Convert command and choosing a new document type.

Testing and Modifying Web Pages

As you develop your Web pages, you should test them frequently. The best way to test a Web page is to preview it in a browser window to make sure it appears the way you expect it to. You should also check to see that the links work properly, that there are no typographical or grammatical errors, and that you have included all of the necessary information for the page. You decide to view The Striped Umbrella home page in Dreamweaver to check its appearance in a simulated window size, preview it using your default browser, make adjustments to the page, then preview the changes in the browser.

STEPS

TROUBLE

(Windows only) You cannot resize a document in the Document window if it is maximized. Click the Document window Restore Down button before attempting to resize the window. If, due to your monitor size, you cannot see the status bar, try hiding some toolbars or the Property inspector, then repeat Step 1.

1. Click the Restore down button 🖻 on your Document window if necessary, click the Window Size pop-up menu on the Status bar, then click 760 × 420 (800 × 600, Maximized), as shown in Figure C-24

   The page is resized to simulate what it would look like in a browser with an 800 × 600 screen resolution. Although the most common screen size that designers use today is 1024 × 768 or higher, many users restore down individual program windows to a size comparable to 800 × 600 or more to accommodate several windows opened simultaneously. This is strictly a matter of personal preference.

2. Maximize the Document window, click File on the Application bar (Win) or Menu bar (Mac), click Save, click the Preview/Debug in browser button 🌐 on the Document toolbar, then click Preview in [your default browser]

   The page opens in your default browser window.

3. Click the Close button ❌ in your browser window, scroll down if necessary and highlight the period after the "...go home" text, then type "!"

   An exclamation point replaces the period after "...go home".

TROUBLE

If a message appears asking if you want to allow blocked content, click the Information bar, then click Yes in the Security Warning dialog box that asks if you want to run active content.

4. Click File on the Application bar (Win) or Menu bar (Mac), click Save, click 🌐 on the Document toolbar, then click Preview in [your default browser]

   The Striped Umbrella home page displays in your browser window. See Figure C-25. You can also press the F12 key (Win) to preview a page in the default browser.

5. Click the About Us link on the menu bar to display one of the blank pages you created in Unit B, then click the Back button on the Address bar (Win) or the Navigation toolbar (Mac)

   The index page reappears in the browser window.

6. Repeat Step 5 to test the Spa, Cafe, and Activities links

   Each link opens a corresponding blank page in the browser window since you haven't placed any text or images on them yet.

TROUBLE

If you are asked to configure your default e-mail client, answer the questions in the series of dialog boxes that appear.

7. Click the Club Manager link

   The default mail program on your computer opens with a message addressed to manager@ thestripedumbrella.com.

8. Close the email message dialog box, close the browser window, close the index page, then click Exit on the File menu (Win) or Quit on the Dreamweaver menu (Mac) to close the Dreamweaver program

FIGURE C-24: Using the Window Size menu to simulate different screen resolutions

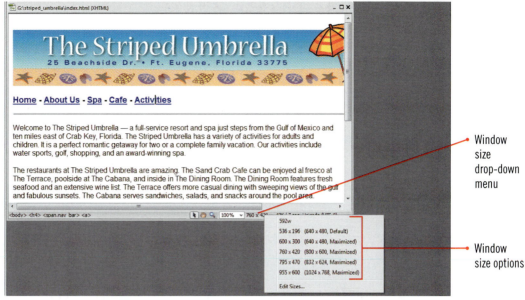

Window size drop-down menu

Window size options

FIGURE C-25: The finished page

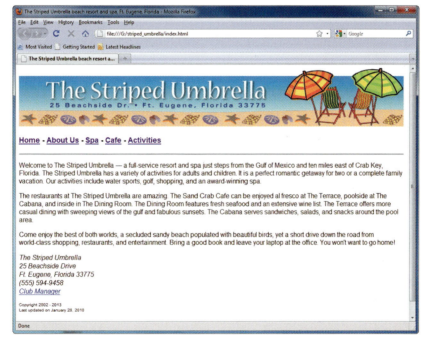

Design Matters

Using smart design principles

As you view your pages in the browser, take a critical look at the symmetry of the page. Is it balanced? Are there too many images for the amount of text, or too few? Does everything "heavy" seem to be on the top or bottom of the page, or do the page elements seem balanced, with the weight evenly distributed between the top, bottom, and sides? Use design principles to create a site-wide consistency for your pages. Horizontal symmetry means that the elements are balanced across the page. Vertical symmetry means that they are balanced down the page. Diagonal symmetry balances page elements along the invisible diagonal line of the page. Radial symmetry runs from the center of the page outward, like the petals of a flower.

These principles all deal with balance; however, too much balance is not good, either. Sometimes it adds interest to place page elements a little off center to have an asymmetrical layout. Color, white space, text, and images should all complement each other and provide a natural flow across and down the page. The rule of thirds—dividing a page into nine squares like a tic-tac-toe grid—states that interest is increased when your focus is on one of the intersections in the grid. The most important information should be at the top of the page where it is visible without scrolling—"above the fold," as they say in the newspaper business.

Practice

For current SAM information, including versions and content details, visit SAM Central (http://www.cengage.com/samcentral). If you have a SAM user profile, you may have access to hands-on instruction, practice, and assessment of the skills covered in this unit. Since various versions of SAM are supported throughout the life of this text, check with your instructor for the correct instructions and URL/Web site for accessing assignments.

Concepts Review

Label each element in the Dreamweaver window shown in Figure C-26.

FIGURE C-26

1. _____	6. _____
2. _____	7. _____
3. _____	8. _____
4. _____	9. _____
5. _____	10. _____

Match each of the following terms with the statement that best describes its function.

11. Style
12. Head section
13. Body section
14. Page Properties dialog box
15. Heading 1
16. Heading 6
17. Edit a page
18. Format a page

a. The part of a Web page that includes text, graphics, and links
b. A named group of formatting characteristics
c. Includes the default Web page settings
d. The smallest heading size
e. Make adjustments in the appearance of page elements
f. Insert, delete, or change page content
g. The largest heading size
h. The part of a Web page that includes the page title and meta tags

Select the best answer from the following list of choices.

19. The head section of a Web page can include:

  a. keywords.

  b. descriptions.

  c. Meta tags.

  d. all of the above.

20. Links that have been previously clicked are called:

  a. active links.

  b. links.

  c. visited links.

  d. broken links.

21. A Web-safe palette contains _____ colors.

  a. 256

  b. 216

  c. 125

  d. 250

22. The _____ on the History panel is used to undo or redo several steps.

  a. scroll bar

  b. pointer

  c. slider

  d. Undo/Redo tool

23. An example of a point of contact is a:

  a. heading.

  b. title.

  c. mailto: link.

  d. keywords.

24. The Dreamweaver default color palette is the:

  a. Continuous Tone.

  b. Color Cubes.

  c. Windows OS.

  d. Mac OS.

Skills Review

Important: *If you did not create the Web sites used in the preceding exercises in Unit B, you need to create a site root folder for each Web site and define the Web sites using files your instructor provides. See the "Read This Before You Begin" section for more detailed instructions.*

1. **Plan the page layout.**
   a. Using a word processor or a piece of paper, list three principles of good page design that you have learned, then list them in order of most important to least important, based on your experiences.
   b. Explain why you chose these three concepts and why you selected the order you did.

2. **Create the head content.**
   a. Start Dreamweaver.
   b. Use the Files panel to open the Blooms & Bulbs Web site.
   c. Open the index page, then view the head content.
   d. Insert the following keywords: **garden**, **plants**, **nursery**, **flowers**, **landscape**, and **greenhouse**.
   e. Insert the following description: **Blooms & Bulbs is a premier supplier of garden plants and trees for both professional and home gardeners.**
   f. Switch to Code view to view the HTML code for the head section.
   g. Switch to Design view.
   h. Save your work.

3. **Set Web page properties.**
   a. View the page properties.
   b. Change the background color to a color of your choice, then apply it to the page, leaving the dialog box open.
   c. Change the background color to white.
   d. Save your work.

4. **Create and format text.**
   a. Replace the hyphens in the current menu bar with a split vertical bar (the top of the backslash key) separated by a space on either side to separate the items.
   b. Place the insertion point at the end of the last sentence in the second paragraph, then add a paragraph break.
   c. Type the following text, inserting a line break after each line.
      Blooms & Bulbs
      Hwy 43 South
      Alvin, Texas 77511
      555-248-0806
   d. Delete the date in the "Last updated" line, then replace it with a date that will update automatically each time the page is saved, using the March 7, 1974 format.
   e. Using the HTML Property inspector, italicize the copyright statement and last updated statement.
   f. Save your work.

5. **Add links to Web pages.**
   a. Link the word *Home* on the menu bar to index.html.
   b. Link *Our Plants* to plants.html.
   c. Link *Newsletter* to newsletter.html.
   d. Link *Workshops* to workshops.html.
   e. Link *Tips* to tips.html.
   f. Using the Insert panel, create an e-mail link under the telephone number with a line break between them; type **Customer Service** in the Text text box and **mailbox@blooms.com** in the E-Mail text box.

6. **Use the History panel.**
   a. Open and clear the History panel.
   b. Using the Insert menu, insert a horizontal rule right before the first paragraph.
   c. Using the Property inspector, left-align the rule and set the width to 950 pixels.
   d. Edit the horizontal rule to center-align it with a width of 70%.

Skills Review (continued)

    e. Use the History panel to change the horizontal rule back to left-aligned with a width of 950 pixels.

    f. Close the History panel.

    g. Save your work.

7. View HTML code.

    a. Use Code view to examine the code for the horizontal rule properties, the e-mail link, and the date in the "Last updated" statement.

    b. Return to Design view.

8. Test and modify Web pages.

    a. Using the Window Size pop-up menu on the status bar, view the page at two different sizes. (*Hint*: Recall that if you select a size that is larger than your workspace, you may need to hide toolbars or the Property inspector to see your status bar.)

    b. Preview the page in your browser.

    c. Verify that all links work correctly, then close the browser.

    d. Add the text **We are happy to deliver or ship your purchases.** to the end of the first paragraph.

    e. Save your work, preview the page in your browser, compare your screen to Figure C-27, then close your browser.

    f. Close the page, then exit Dreamweaver.

FIGURE C-27

Important: *If you did not create the Web sites used in the exercises in Unit B, you need to create site root folders for each Web site and define the Web sites using files your instructor provides. See the "Read This Before You Begin" section for more detailed instructions.*

Independent Challenge 1

You have been hired to create a Web site for a river expedition company named Rapids Transit, located on the Buffalo River in Arkansas. In addition to renting canoes, kayaks, and rafts, they have several types of cabin rentals for overnight stays. River guides are available, if requested, to accompany clients on float trips. The owner's name is Mike Andrew.

a. Use the Files panel to open the Rapids Transit Web site.

b. Open the index page in the Rapids Transit Web site.

c. Create the following keywords: **river, rafting, Buffalo River, Arkansas, kayak, canoe**, and **float**.

d. Create the following description: **Rapids Transit is a river expedition company located on the Buffalo River in Arkansas.**

e. Change the page title to **Rapids Transit – Buffalo River Outfitters**.

f. Edit the menu bar below the Rapids Transit banner by changing **Our Guides** to **River Guides**.

g. Enter the telephone number **(555) 365-5228** below the address, with a line break between the lines.

h. Italicize the company copyright and last updated statements, then, after the phone number, enter a line break and create an e-mail link, using **Mike Andrew** for the text and **mailbox@rapidstransit.com** for the e-mail link.

i. Add links to the entries in the menu bar, using the files index.html, guides.html, rates.html, lodging.html, and before.html in the rapids site root folder. (Recall that these files don't have any content yet, but you can still link to them. You will add content to the pages as you work through the remaining units of the book.)

j. Delete the horizontal rule.

k. Delete the date in the last updated statement and change it to a date that will be automatically updated when the page is saved, using the March 7, 1974 data format. Reformat the date to match the rest of the line if necessary.

l. View the HTML code for the page, noting in particular the code for the head section.

m. View the page in Design view in two different window sizes, save your work, then test the links in your browser window, as shown in Figure C-28.

n. Close the browser, close the page, then exit Dreamweaver.

FIGURE C-28

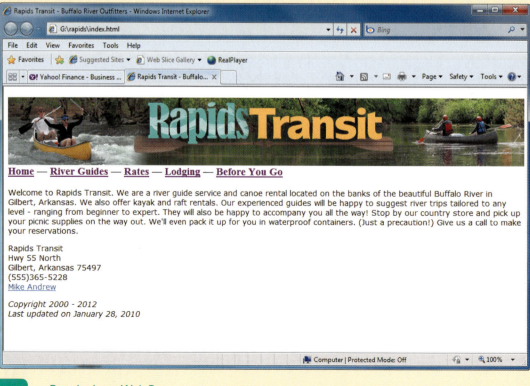

Independent Challenge 2

Your company is designing a new Web site for a travel outfitter named TripSmart. TripSmart specializes in travel products and services. In addition to selling travel products such as clothing, luggage, and accessories, they promote trips and offer travel advice. Their clients range from college students to families to vacationing professionals. The owner, Thomas Howard, has requested a dynamic Web site that conveys the excitement of traveling. Refer to Figure C-29 as you work through the following steps.

a. Open the TripSmart Web site, then open its index page.

b. Create the following keywords: **travel, traveling, tours, trips, vacations**.

c. Create the following description: **TripSmart is a comprehensive travel store. We can help you plan trips, make the arrangements, and supply you with travel gear.**

d. Change the page title to read **TripSmart: Serving all your travel needs**.

e. Change the menu bar below the banner to read **Home - Tours - Newsletter - Services - Catalog**.

f. Add links to the menu bar entries, using the files index.html, tours.html, newsletter.html, services.html, and catalog.html. (Recall that these files don't have any content yet, but you can still link to them. You will add content to the pages as you work through the remaining units of the book.)

g. Replace the date in the "Last updated" statement with a date that will update automatically when the file is saved.

h. Add the following contact information between the last paragraph and copyright statement using line breaks after each line: **TripSmart**, **1106 Beechwood**, **Fayetteville**, **AR 72604**, **555-848–0807**.

i. Immediately beneath the telephone number, place an Email link using **Contact us** as the text and **associate@tripsmart.com** for the link.

j. Insert a horizontal rule that is 950 pixels wide and left-aligned above the contact information.

k. View the HTML code for the page, noting in particular the head section code.

l. View the page in two different window sizes, save your work, then test the links in your browser window.

m. Close the page and exit Dreamweaver.

FIGURE C-29

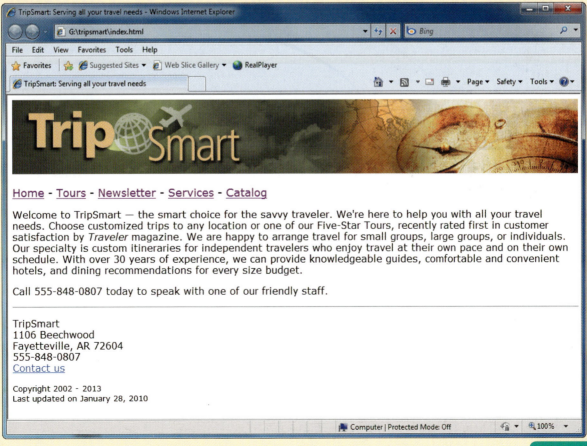

Independent Challenge 3

Angela Lou is a freelance photographer. She is searching the Internet for a particular type of paper to use in printing her digital images. She knows that Web sites use keywords and descriptions to increase traffic from search engines such as Google and Bing. She is curious as to how keywords and descriptions work with search engines. Write your answers to these questions on paper or using your word processor.

a. Connect to the Internet, then go to www.snapfish.com to see the Snapfish Web site's home page, as shown in Figure C-30.

b. View the page source by clicking View on the menu bar, then clicking Source (Internet Explorer) or Page Source (Mozilla Firefox). (*Hint*: Press the Alt key if the menu is hidden.)

c. Can you locate a description and keywords?

d. How many keywords do you find?

e. How many words are in the description?

f. In your opinion, is the number of keywords and words in the description about right, too many, or not enough?

g. Use a search engine such as Google (www.google.com), type the words **photo quality paper** in the Search text box, then press [Enter] (Win) or [Return] (Mac).

h. Choose a link in the list of results and view the source code for that page. If you see a message asking if you want to allow blocked content, click Allow. Do you see keywords and a description? Do any of them match the words you used in the search? (You may have to scroll down quite a bit to find the keywords. Try using the Find feature to quickly search the code.)

i. If you don't see the search words in keywords or descriptions, do you see them in the body of the pages?

j. Save your work, then exit all programs.

FIGURE C-30

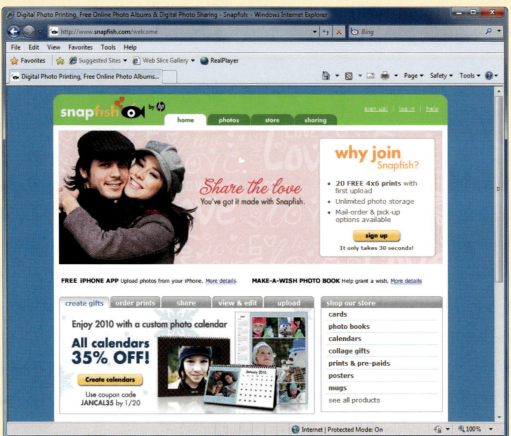

© 2009 The Snapfish by HP Web site used with permission from Snapfish by HP www.snapfish.com

Real Life Independent Challenge

This assignment will continue to build on the personal Web site that you created in Unit B. In this lesson, you will work with your home page.

a. Insert a brief description and a list of meaningful keywords for your home page in the appropriate locations.

b. Insert an effective title for your home page.

c. Format the home page attractively, creating a strong contrast between your page background and your page content.

d. Add links from the home page to your other pages.

e. Insert an e-mail link.

f. Insert a "Last updated" statement that includes a date that updates automatically when you save the file.

g. Preview the home page in your browser, verifying that each link works correctly.

h. Check the page for errors in content or format and edit as necessary.

i. Save your work, close the page, and exit the program.

Visual Workshop

Your company has been selected to design a Web site for a catering business named Carolyne's Creations. You are now ready to add content to the home page and apply formatting options to improve the page appearance, using Figure C-31 as a guide. Open your Carolyne's Creations Web site and modify the index page to duplicate Figure C-31. (*Hint*: Remember to add an appropriate description and keywords, and revise the last updated statement so it will automatically update when the page is saved.)

FIGURE C-31

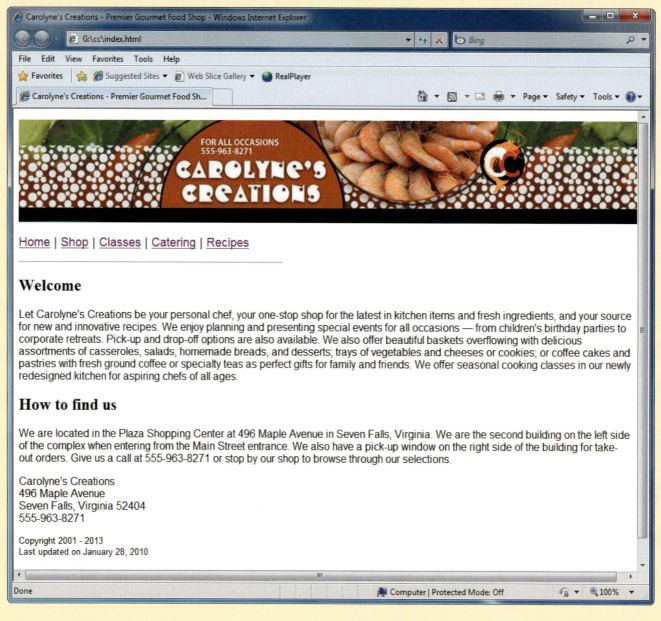

Working with Text and Cascading Style Sheets

The content of most Web pages is text-based. Because text on a computer screen can be more tiring to read than text on a printed page, you should strive to make your Web page text attractive and easy to read. Dreamweaver has many options for enhancing text, including HTML properties for paragraphs and lists, as well as Cascading Style Sheets (CSS). CSS are used to assign sets of common formatting characteristics to page elements, such as paragraph text, lists, and table data.  You decide to group content on the spa page for The Striped Umbrella Web site using lists to make the page more readable. Using lists to format text is also considered to be more accessible for users using screen readers. You want to use CSS to make these types of formatting changes consistent throughout the Web site.

OBJECTIVES

Import text

Set text properties

Create an unordered list

Understand Cascading Style Sheets

Create a style in a new Cascading Style Sheet

Apply and edit a style

Add styles to a Cascading Style Sheet

Attach a Cascading Style Sheet to a page

Check for spelling errors

Importing Text

Entering text in Dreamweaver is as easy as entering text in a word processing program. The Dreamweaver text editing features, listed in Table D-1, are similar to those in word processing programs. If you have existing text to place on a page, you can either copy and paste it, or import it from the source program, such as Microsoft Word or Excel. To ensure that text is readable, you can use alignment, indentation, headings, and lists to organize the content on the page. Your manager has given you a list of services to include on The Striped Umbrella spa page. The document, which contains a list of spa services and descriptions, was created in Microsoft Word, then saved as a Word document. You open the spa page, import the text, and use the Clean Up Word HTML command to remove any unnecessary tags.

STEPS

1. **Start Dreamweaver, click the Site list arrow (Win) ▼ or ♦ (Mac) on the Files panel, then click The Striped Umbrella, if it isn't already selected**

   The Striped Umbrella Web site opens in the Files panel.

2. **Click File on the Application bar (Win) or Menu bar (Mac), click Open, navigate to the drive and folder where you store your Data Files, double-click dwd_1.html, save it as spa.html in the striped_umbrella root folder, overwriting the existing file but not updating links, then close dwd_1.html**

   The banner displays at the top of the page since you have previously saved it in the Web site assets folder when you saved the home page. The small image under the banner, however, appears as a broken link since it has not been saved yet in the Web site. The source of this file, named sea_spa_logo.jpg, is in the unit_d Data Files assets folder. You must copy it to the assets folder in the striped_umbrella root folder by using the Property inspector to select the original image source.

3. **In Design view, click the gray broken image, click the Browse for File icon 🗀 next to the Src text box in the Property inspector, navigate to the drive and folder where you store your Data Files, double-click sea_spa_logo.jpg in the assets folder, then click anywhere on the page**

   The image is deselected, the file is copied to the assets folder in the site root folder, and the logo appears correctly on the page.

TROUBLE
If the newly copied file is not visible, click the Refresh button 🔁 on the Files panel toolbar.

4. **Click the plus sign (Win) or expander arrow (Mac) next to the assets folder in the Files panel to expand it, if necessary**

   Two images are listed in the assets folder, su_banner.gif and sea_spa_logo.jpg, as shown in Figure D-1.

5. **Click to the right of the logo to place the insertion point on the spa.html page**

6. **Click File on the Application bar (Win) or Menu bar (Mac), point to Import, click Word Document, browse to the folder where you store your Data Files, then double-click spa.doc (Win); or double-click spa.doc from where you store your Data Files, select all, copy, close spa.doc, then paste the copied text on the spa page in Dreamweaver (Mac)**

   Mac users cannot use the Import, Word command. The text from the Word file is placed beside and wraps under the logo, as shown in Figure D-2. Although you may not see evidence of unnecessary code on the page, it is always a good idea to remove any unnecessary tags that are added by Microsoft Word.

QUICK TIP
If a dialog box opens stating that Dreamweaver was unable to determine the version of Word used to generate this document, click OK, click the Clean up HTML from list arrow, then select Word 2000 and newer, if necessary.

7. **Click Commands on the Application bar (Win) or Menu bar (Mac), then click Clean Up Word HTML**

   The Clean Up Word HTML dialog box opens.

8. **Click to select each check box in the Clean Up Word HTML dialog box if necessary, click OK, then click OK again**

   The Clean Up Word HTML dialog box closes.

FIGURE D-1: The Striped Umbrella Web site with the assets folder expanded

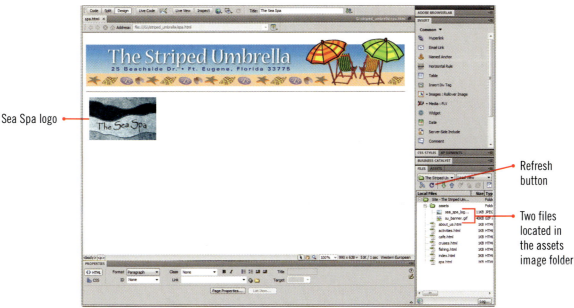

Sea Spa logo

Refresh button

Two files located in the assets image folder

FIGURE D-2: Spa page with text imported

Text is placed beside and wraps below the image

The Sea Spa Services

Massages
Facials
Body Treatments

Massages

Sports Massage
Our deepest massage for tense and sore muscles. Not recommended for first-time massage clients.

Swedish Massage
A gentle, relaxing massage. Promotes balance and wellness. Warms muscle tissue and increases circulation.

TABLE D-1: Dreamweaver text editing features

feature	menu	function	feature	menu	function
Find and Replace	Edit	Finds and replaces text on the current Web page, the entire Web site, or in selected files	Font	Format	Selects font combinations for a browser or allows you to create custom font combinations
Indent and Outdent	Format	Indents selected text to the right or left	Style	Format	Sets various styles, such as bold and italic
Paragraph Format	Format	Sets paragraph, H1 through H6, and preformatted text	CSS Styles	Format	Provides options for applying a rule, creating a new CSS rule, attaching a style sheet, converting or moving rules, and applying Design-Time Style Sheets
Align	Format	Aligns text with the left or right margin, justifies it, or centers it on the page	Color	Format	Sets text color
List	Format	Creates unordered, ordered, or definition lists	Check Spelling	Commands	Runs a spell check on the page

Setting Text Properties

You can format text on a Web page in many ways to enhance its appearance. Text formatting attributes such as paragraph formatting, heading styles, fonts, size, color, alignment, indents, and CSS styles are easy to change using either the HTML Property inspector or the CSS Property inspector. Some formatting options are available with both the HTML and CSS Property inspectors, while some are specific to each. Using standard fonts is wise because those set outside the default range may not be available on all computers. As you format your pages, it is important to read the code for each element to see how it is written. The more fluent you are with code, the easier it will be when you have to **debug** the site (correct coding errors). HTML code is built from a series of **tags** surrounded by < and > symbols. Tags instruct the browser how to display each page element. You want to format the new text on the spa page to improve its appearance. You also want to examine the code for the formatting commands to understand the HTML tags that are generated.

STEPS

QUICK TIP
To apply character formats such as bold and italic, you must select the paragraph rather than click within the text.

1. **Click the HTML button** `<> HTML` **on the Property inspector if necessary, scroll up if necessary, then click anywhere within the words** *The Sea Spa Services*

    The words *The Sea Spa Services* are classified as a paragraph; even a single word is considered a paragraph if there is a hard return or paragraph break after it. Paragraph commands are applied by clicking the insertion point within the paragraph text. The Property inspector shows the settings for the paragraph with the insertion point placed inside of it; Paragraph appears in the Format text box.

2. **Click the Format list arrow, then click Heading 2**

    The Heading 2 format is applied to the Sea Spa Services paragraph.

3. **Repeat Steps 1 and 2 to add the Heading 4 style to Massages, Facials, and Body Treatments next to the logo**

    The Heading 4 format is applied, as shown in Figure D-3.

TROUBLE
Mac users may notice that Design view and Code view do not scroll together as shown in Figure D-4.

4. **Click the Show Code and Design views button** `Split` **on the Document toolbar**

    The HTML code for the headings displays in the left window, as shown in Figure D-4. The first tag in each pair begins the code and the last tag ends the code. The HTML code for a Heading 4 tag begins with <h4> and closes with </h4>. The Heading 2 code is the same, except with a *2* instead of a *4*.

5. **Click the Show Design view button** `Design` **on the Document toolbar, then save your work**

    The spa page redisplays in Design view with its changes saved.

Importing and linking Microsoft Office documents

Adobe makes it easy to transfer data between Microsoft Office documents and Dreamweaver web pages. To import a Word or Excel document with a PC, click File on the Application bar, point to Import, then click either Word Document or Excel Document. Select the file you want to import, then click the Formatting list arrow to choose among importing Text only; Text with structure (paragraphs, lists, and tables); Text, structure, basic formatting (bold, italic); or Text, structure, full formatting (bold, italic, styles) before you click Open. The option you choose depends on the importance of the original structure and formatting. Always use the Clean Up Word HTML command after importing a Word file. On a Mac, open the file you

want to import, copy the text, then paste it to an open page in Dreamweaver in Design view.

You can also create a link to a Word or Excel document on your Web page. Simply drag the Word or Excel document from its current location to the place on the page you want the link to appear; if the document is located outside the site, you can browse for it using the Site list arrow on the Files panel, Explorer (Win), or Finder (Mac). Next, select the Create a link option button in the Insert Document dialog box, then save the file in your site root folder so it will be uploaded when you publish your site. If it is not uploaded, the link will be broken.

FIGURE D-3: Applying paragraph formats to paragraph

Text with the Heading 2 format applied

Text with the Heading 4 format applied

This line will wrap correctly when viewed in a browser window

Format list arrow

FIGURE D-4: Show Code and Design view

Show Code and Design views button

The code that is displayed in Code view reflects the position of the insertion point on the page

Code reflects insertion point position within paragraph

H2 tags

H4 tags

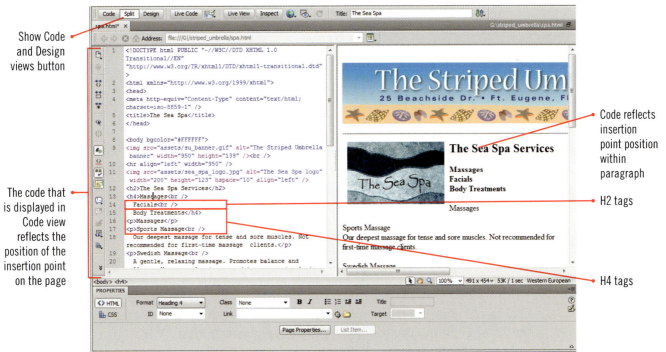

Creating an Unordered List

You can break up the monotony of large blocks of text by dividing them into smaller paragraphs or by organizing them as lists. Dreamweaver utilizes three types of lists: unordered lists, ordered lists, and definition lists. **Unordered lists**, also called bulleted lists, are lists of items that do not need to be placed in a specific order. Each item is usually preceded by a small filled circle (known as a **bullet**) or a similar icon. Numbered lists, or **ordered lists,** are lists of items that must be placed in a specific order, and each item is preceded by a number or a letter. **Definition lists** are similar to unordered lists, but do not use numbers or bullets. They are displayed with a hanging indent and are often used with terms and definitions, such as in a dictionary or glossary. You decide to organize the types of services into logical groups to make them easier to read. You want to create an unordered list for each of the spa service items.

STEPS

> **QUICK TIP**
> You can extend an unordered list to add more bullets by pressing [Enter] (Win) or [return] (Mac) once at the end of the list. To end an unordered list, press [Enter] (Win) or [return] (Mac) twice.

1. **Select the three spa service items and their descriptions under the Massages heading**
   Sports Massage, Swedish Massage, and Hot Stone Massage and their descriptions are selected.

2. **Click the Unordered List button ☷ on the HTML Property inspector**
   The spa service items redisplay as an unordered list, as shown in Figure D-5.

> **TROUBLE**
> If you accidentally include the contact information/hours paragraph as part of your list, click Edit, Undo, then repeat step 3.

3. **Repeat Steps 1 and 2 to create unordered lists of the spa service items under the Facials and Body Treatments headings**
   Each group of services redisplays as an unordered list.

4. **Click to place the insertion point within any of the items in the first unordered list, double-click the right side of the HTML Property inspector to expand it if necessary, then click the List Item button in the Property inspector**
   The List Properties dialog box opens.

> **QUICK TIP**
> Some browsers may not display the square bullets correctly. If not, they default to the circular bullets.

5. **Click the Style list arrow, click Square, as shown in Figure D-6, then click OK**
   The bullets appear as squares rather than circles in the unordered list.

6. **Repeat Steps 4 and 5 to format the other two unordered lists**

7. **Click to place the insertion point before the first item in the first unordered list, then click the Show Code view button `Code` on the Document toolbar**
   The page displays in Code view. The HTML tags surrounding the unordered list are `<ul>` and `</ul>`. Each of the items is surrounded by `<li>` and `</li>` tags, as shown in Figure D-7.

8. **Click the Show Design view button `Design` on the Document toolbar to return to Design view, then save your work**

Working with Text and Cascading Style Sheets

FIGURE D-5: Creating an unordered list

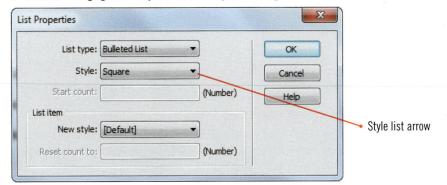

Massages

- Sports Massage
  Our deepest massage for tense and sore muscles. Not recommended for first-time massage clients.
- Swedish Massage
  A gentle, relaxing massage. Promotes balance and wellness. Warms muscle tissue and increases circulation.
- Hot Stone Massage
  Uses polished local river rocks to distribute gentle heat. Good for tight, sore muscles. Balances and invigorates the body muscles. Advance notice required.

FIGURE D-6: Changing the list style in the List Properties dialog box

List Properties

List type: Bulleted List

Style: Square ← Style list arrow

Start count: _____ (Number)

List item

New style: [Default]

Reset count to: _____ (Number)

OK   Cancel   Help

FIGURE D-7: Viewing an unordered list in Code view

Beginning unordered list tag →

Beginning list item tag →

Closing list item tag ←

Closing unordered list tag →

```
15        Body Treatments</h4>
16    <p>Massages</p>
17    <ul type="square">
18    <li>Sports Massage<br />
19        Our deepest massage for tense and sore muscles. Not recommended for first-time massage  clients.</li>
20        <li>Swedish Massage<br />
21        A gentle, relaxing massage. Promotes balance and wellness. Warms muscle tissue  and increases circulation.</li>
22        <li>Hot Stone Massage<br />
23        Uses polished local river rocks to distribute gentle heat. Good  for tight, sore muscles. Balances and invigorates
the body muscles. Advance  notice required. </li>
24    </ul>
```

Using ordered lists

Ordered lists contain numbered or lettered items that need to appear in a particular order, such as listing the steps to accomplish a task. For example, if you followed directions to drive from point A to point B, each step would have to be executed in order or you would not successfully reach your destination. For this type of sequential information, ordered lists can add more emphasis than bulleted ones. Dreamweaver uses several options for number styles, including Roman and Arabic. The HTML tags that surround ordered lists are `<ol>` and `</ol>`.

Design Matters

Coding for the semantic Web

You may have heard the term *semantic* Web. The word *semantics* refers to the study of word or sentences meanings. So the term **semantic Web** refers to the way page content, such as paragraph, text or list items, can be coded to emphasize their meaning to users. HTML tags such as the `<p>` tag, used for marking paragraphs, and the `<ul>` tag, used for marking unordered lists, provide a clear meaning of the function and significance of the paragraphs or lists. **Semantic markup**, or coding to emphasize meaning, is a way to incorporate good accessibility practice. CSS styles affect the appearance of Web page content while semantic markup enhances the meaning of the content. Both techniques work together to provide well-designed Web pages that are attractive and easy to understand.

Understanding Cascading Style Sheets

Cascading Style Sheets (CSS) consist of sets of formatting rules that create styles. You create CSS when you want to apply the same formatting attributes to Web page elements, such as text, elements, and tables. A style sheet can contain one or more different styles, such as heading or body text, saved within a descriptive name. You can apply styles to any element in a document or, if you choose, to all of the documents in a Web site. If you edit an existing style, all the page elements you have formatted with that style will automatically update. You decide to research the ways CSS can save you time and provide your site with a more consistent look.

As you plan to use CSS in a Web site, keep in mind the following:

• **Advantages of using CSS**

CSS are made up of individual **rules**, or sets of formatting attributes, such as font-family and font-size. These rules create styles that are applied to individual page elements including text, headings, and horizontal rules. CSS are great time savers and provide continuity across a Web site by applying the same style to all elements of a given type. After you apply styles, you can edit the rules definition. Once you complete the definition, every item to which you've applied that style will then be automatically updated to reflect the changes. CSS separate content from layout, which means that you can make editing changes without affecting formatting and vice versa.

• **CSS classified by location**

One way to categorize styles is by the location where they are stored. An **external style sheet** is a single, separate file with a .css file extension that can be attached to a page in a Web site. This type of style sheet determines the formatting for various page elements and can contain many individual styles. If you have an external style sheet with 10 styles, you would only need to create one file with 10 styles defined within it, rather than 10 separate style sheet files. You can then attach this style sheet file to all of the pages in the same Web site (or to pages in other Web sites) to apply all of the specific styles. **Internal style sheets** are contained in the code for an individual Web page and can be embedded or inline styles. An **embedded style** consists of code that is stored in a page's head content while an **inline style** is stored in a page's body content. While you are learning, you will create styles of each type. In a work environment, however, you will primarily use external styles.

• **CSS classified by function**

Another way to classify CSS is by their function. A **Class style** can be used to format any page element, such as a paragraph of text or an image. An **HTML style** is used to redefine an HTML tag, such as changing the color of a horizontal rule or a heading tag. An **Advanced** or **Compound style** is used to format combinations of page elements. For example, you could define an Advanced style that determines how all images are displayed inside a div tag.

• **The CSS Styles panel**

You use the CSS Styles panel to create, edit, and apply styles. The panel has two views: All (Document) Mode and Current Selection Mode. Figure D-8 shows the CSS Styles panel in All (Document) Mode, which lists all attached and embedded styles. When you select a rule in the All Rules pane, that rule's properties appear in the Properties pane at the bottom of the panel. Figure D-9 shows the CSS Styles panel in Current Selection mode, which shows the properties for the page element at the current position of the insertion point. You can edit the properties for the rule in the Properties pane. The small pane between the Summary for selection pane and the Properties pane in Current mode is called the Rules pane, which shows the location of the current selected rule in the open document.

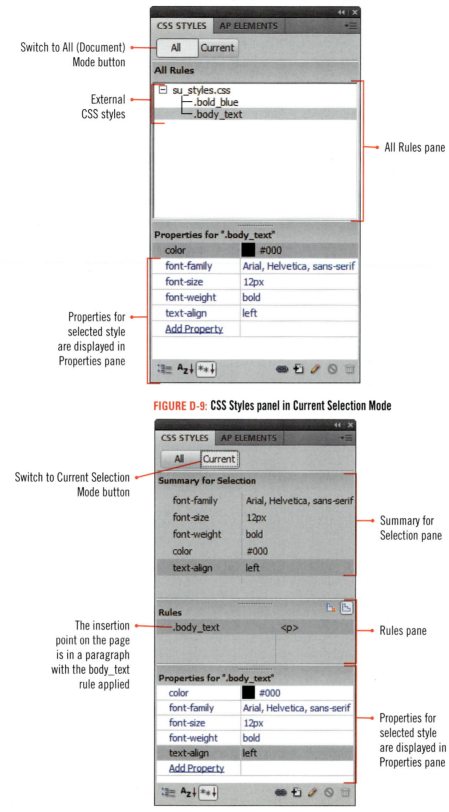

Switch to All (Document) Mode button

External CSS styles

Properties for selected style are displayed in Properties pane

All Rules pane

FIGURE D-9: CSS Styles panel in Current Selection Mode

Switch to Current Selection Mode button

The insertion point on the page is in a paragraph with the body_text rule applied

Summary for Selection pane

Rules pane

Properties for selected style are displayed in Properties pane

Using the CSS and HTML Property inspector

You apply CSS styles using either the CSS or HTML Property inspectors. You first select the element on the page, then apply a style from the Property inspector. In the HTML Property inspector, you select a style from the Class list box. In the CSS Property inspector, you select a style from the Targeted Rule list box. You change back and forth between the two Property inspectors by clicking the HTML button `<> HTML` or CSS button `CSS`.

Creating a Style in a New Cascading Style Sheet

The steps for creating the first style in a new style sheet are different from the steps for creating additional styles in an existing style sheet. Creating the first style in a new style sheet is a two-step process. When you create the first style, you have not yet created the style sheet, so you must first name the style sheet file in which you want to save the first style. Once you have named and saved the style sheet file, you can then add new styles to it. If you decide to change a style later, you only have to change the CSS rule and all the items will be updated automatically. You decide that the same formatting style should be applied to each of the spa service headings. You want to use CSS to apply the same style to each item.

STEPS

1. **Click Window on the Application bar (Win) or Menu bar (Mac), click CSS Styles if necessary, then click the Switch to All (Document) Mode button** [All] **under the CSS Styles panel tab**
    The CSS Styles panel opens in the CSS tab group. This panel is where you can add, delete, edit, and apply styles. All (Document) Mode displays all styles in the open document.

    > **QUICK TIP**
    > If you do not create a style before you begin formatting page elements, Dreamweaver will prompt you to create a new style after you make your first formatting choice.

2. **Click the New CSS Rule button** [⊡] **in the Properties pane on the CSS Styles panel, click the Selector Type list arrow in the New CSS Rule dialog box, if necessary, to select Class (can apply to any HTML element), then type bold_blue in the Selector Name text box**
    The Class option creates a new custom style that can apply to any HTML tag.

3. **Click the Rule Definition list arrow, click (New Style Sheet File), compare your screen to Figure D-10, then click OK**
    The Save Style Sheet File As dialog box opens, prompting you to name the Cascading Style Sheet file and store it in the Web site's root folder. The name of the new rule is bold_blue. The New Style Sheet File option makes the CSS style available for use in the entire Web site, not just the current document.

    > **QUICK TIP**
    > You can also create a new rule using the New CSS Rule command in the CSS Property inspector.

4. **Type su_styles in the File name text box (Win) or the Save As text box (Mac), then click Save**
    The CSS Rule Definition for bold_blue in su_styles.css dialog box opens. This dialog box allows you to choose attributes, such as font color and font size, for the CSS rule.

5. **Click the Font-family list arrow, click Arial, Helvetica, sans-serif; click the Font-size list arrow, click 14, leave the size measurement unit as px, click the Font-style list arrow, click normal; click the Font-weight list arrow, then click bold**
    The font-family, size, style, and weight settings are updated. Keeping the measurement at pixels (px) in the size measurement drop-down menu ensures that the text will be an absolute size when viewed in the browser.

    > **TROUBLE**
    > If the CSS rule does not appear, click the plus sign (Win) right-pointing triangle (Mac) next to the css file in the CSS Styles panel to expand it and see the styles listed in the file. If the styles do not appear, click [All].

6. **Click the Color box** [▣] **to open the color picker, click #006, as shown in Figure D-11, click OK, then click the Refresh button** [↻] **on the Files panel**
    The CSS rule named bold_blue appears in the CSS Styles panel, preceded by a period in the name. The **Related Files toolbar** displays under the file tab (Win) or file title bar (Mac) listing the style sheet file name su_styles.css. The Related Files toolbar, which displays the names of files related to the open document file, is used to quickly access files that are linked to the open document. The su_styles.css file appears in the file listing for the Web site, as shown in Figure D-12, with a different file extension from the HTML files. You may have to scroll down to see the su_styles.css file listed.

7. **Click the Show Code view button** [Code] **on the Document toolbar**
    The HTML code linking to the su_styles.css file appears in the Head section, as shown in Figure D-13. The bold_blue rule appears indented under the file su_styles.css in the CSS Styles panel.

8. **Click File on the Application bar (Win) or Menu bar (Mac), then click Save All**

FIGURE D-10: Adding a new CSS Rule in the New CSS Rule dialog box

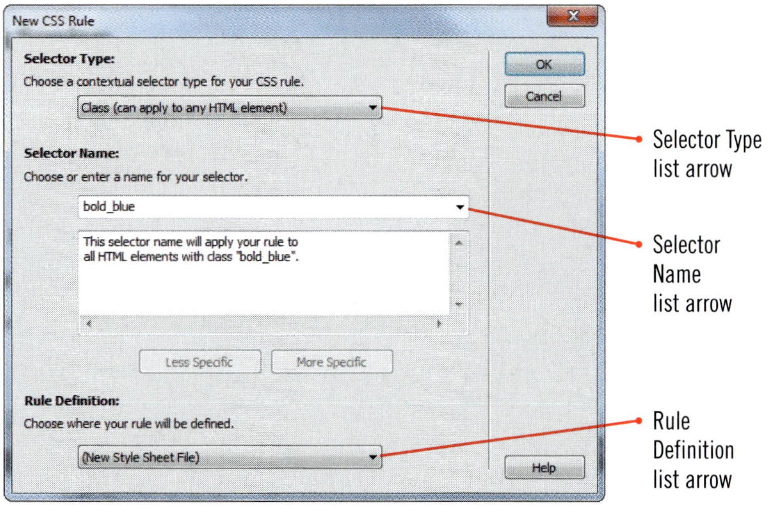

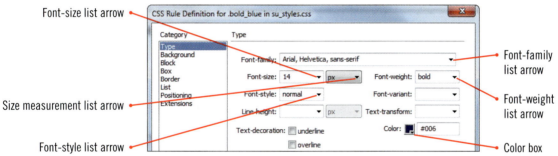

Selector Type list arrow

Selector Name list arrow

Rule Definition list arrow

FIGURE D-11: CSS Rule Definition for .bold_blue in su_styles.css dialog box

Font-size list arrow

Font-family list arrow

Size measurement list arrow

Font-weight list arrow

Font-style list arrow

Color box

FIGURE D-12: The Striped Umbrella site with the su_styles.css file listed

FIGURE D-13: Code view showing link to style sheet file

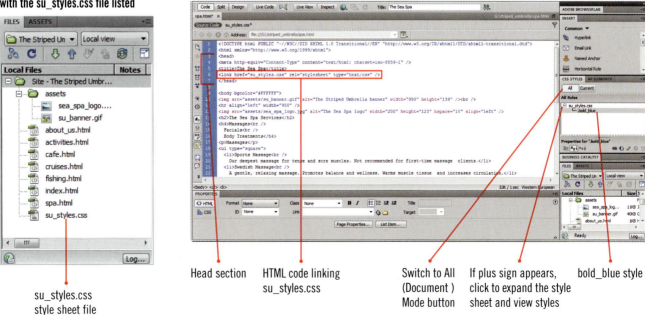

su_styles.css style sheet file

Head section

HTML code linking su_styles.css

Switch to All (Document) Mode button

If plus sign appears, click to expand the style sheet and view styles

bold_blue style

Applying and Editing a Style

After creating a style sheet, it is easy to apply its styles to page elements. If you are not satisfied with the results after applying a style, you can edit the rule to change the formatting of all elements to which that style applies. To apply a style, you select the text or page element to which you want to apply the style, remove any manual formatting, and then select the style from the Property inspector. 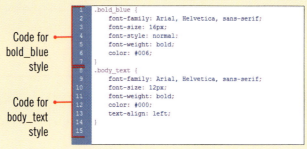 You want to apply a color style to each unordered list heading as well as increase their size to make them stand out.

STEPS

> **QUICK TIP**
>
> You can also click the Class list arrow in the HTML Property inspector to apply the bold_blue style.

1. **Click the Show Design view button** Design **on the Document toolbar, then click the CSS button** CSS **to switch to the CSS Property inspector**

   The spa page redisplays in Design view.

2. **Select the unordered list heading Massages, click the Targeted Rule list arrow on the CSS Property inspector, then click bold_blue, as shown in Figure D-15**

   The bold_blue style is applied to the Massages heading. The Font-family, Font-size, Font-weight, Color, and Font-style text boxes on the Property inspector all reflect the bold_blue settings.

> **QUICK TIP**
>
> You can press [Ctrl][Y] (Win) or [command] [Y] (Mac) to redo (repeat) an action.

3. **Repeat Step 2 to apply the bold_blue style to the Facials and Body Treatment unordered list headings**

   The bold_blue style is applied to each unordered list heading.

> **QUICK TIP**
>
> If a rule is not selected, the Edit Rule button becomes the Edit Style Sheet button and opens the css file for editing.

4. **Click the bold_blue rule in the CSS Styles panel, then click the Edit Rule button** ✎ **on the CSS Styles panel**

   The CSS Rule Definition for bold_blue in su_styles.css dialog box opens. This same dialog box that you used to create the original rule is used to edit a .css file.

5. **Click the Font-size list arrow, click 16, as shown in Figure D-16, click OK, then deselect the text**

   The unordered list headings appear on the page with a larger text size style applied, as shown in Figure D-17. The bold_blue rule includes a larger text size, in addition to a color formatting adjustment.

6. **Click File on the Application bar (Win) or Menu bar (Mac), then click Save All**

   The changes to both the spa document file and the style sheet file are saved.

Understanding CSS code

You can also use CSS styles to format page content other than text. For example, you can use CSS to format backgrounds, borders, lists, and images. A CSS style consists of two parts: the selector and the declaration. The **selector** is the name or the tag to which the style declarations have been assigned. The **declaration** consists of the property and the value. An example of a property would be font-family. An example of a value would be Arial. Figure D-14 shows the coding for two CSS styles in a style sheet.

FIGURE D-14: Code for two styles in the su_styles.css file

Code for bold_blue style

Code for body_text style

```
1   .bold_blue {
2       font-family: Arial, Helvetica, sans-serif;
3       font-size: 16px;
4       font-style: normal;
5       font-weight: bold;
6       color: #006;
7   }
8   .body_text {
9       font-family: Arial, Helvetica, sans-serif;
10      font-size: 12px;
11      font-weight: bold;
12      color: #000;
13      text-align: left;
14  }
15
```

FIGURE D-15: Applying a style to text

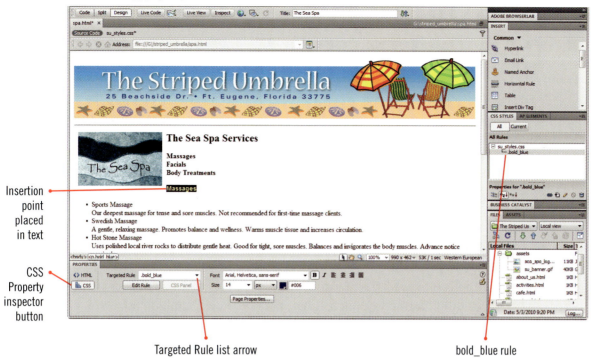

Insertion point placed in text
CSS Property inspector button
Targeted Rule list arrow
bold_blue rule
The Striped Umbrella
25 Beachside Dr. • Ft. Eugene, Florida 33775
The Sea Spa Services
Massages
Facials
Body Treatments
Massages
Sports Massage
Our deepest massage for tense and sore muscles. Not recommended for first-time massage clients.
Swedish Massage
A gentle, relaxing massage. Promotes balance and wellness. Warms muscle tissue and increases circulation.
Hot Stone Massage
Uses polished local river rocks to distribute gentle heat. Good for tight, sore muscles. Balances and invigorates the body muscles. Advance notice
Targeted Rule .bold_blue
Edit Rule
CSS Panel
Font Arial, Helvetica, sans-serif
Size 14 px #006
Page Properties...

FIGURE D-16: Editing the bold_blue rule

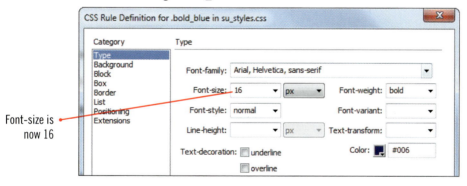

Font-size is now 16
CSS Rule Definition for .bold_blue in su_styles.css
Category
Type
Background
Block
Box
Border
List
Positioning
Extensions
Type
Font-family: Arial, Helvetica, sans-serif
Font-size: 16 px
Font-weight: bold
Font-style: normal
Font-variant:
Line-height: px
Text-transform:
Text-decoration: underline
overline
Color: #006

FIGURE D-17: Viewing text after editing the Font-size property

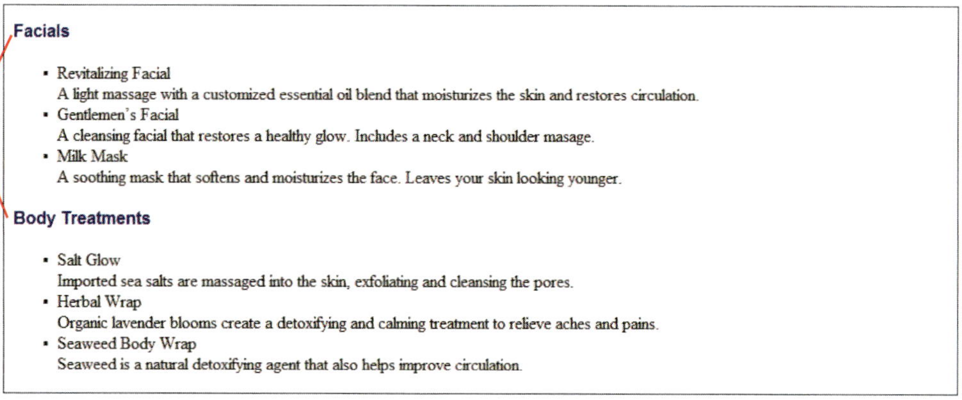

Unordered list headings with larger font-size and color formatting applied
Facials
Revitalizing Facial
A light massage with a customized essential oil blend that moisturizes the skin and restores circulation.
Gentlemen's Facial
A cleansing facial that restores a healthy glow. Includes a neck and shoulder masage.
Milk Mask
A soothing mask that softens and moisturizes the face. Leaves your skin looking younger.
Body Treatments
Salt Glow
Imported sea salts are massaged into the skin, exfoliating and cleansing the pores.
Herbal Wrap
Organic lavender blooms create a detoxifying and calming treatment to relieve aches and pains.
Seaweed Body Wrap
Seaweed is a natural detoxifying agent that also helps improve circulation.

Adding Styles to a Cascading Style Sheet

Once you have created a style sheet, it is easy to add additional styles to it. Generally, the more styles you have defined in a Style Sheet, the more time you can save. Ideally, you should create styles for all page elements. You add styles by using the New CSS Rule button in the CSS Styles panel. You should use the same style sheet for each page to ensure that all your elements have a consistent appearance. You decide to add two new styles in the su_styles.css file, one for the spa services heading and one for the spa service groups.

1. **Click the New CSS Rule button 🗒 on the CSS Styles Panel**
   The New CSS Rule dialog box opens.

2. **Click the Selector Type list arrow, click Class (can apply to any HTML element), type body_text in the Selector Name text box, click the Rule Definition list arrow, click su_styles.css, as shown in Figure D-18, then click OK**
   The CSS Rule Definition for .body_text in su_styles.css dialog box opens.

3. **Click the Font-family list arrow, click Arial, Helvetica, sans-serif, click the Font-size list arrow, click medium, click the Font-weight list arrow, then click normal**
   The font is set to a medium sized, normal weight, Arial, Helvetica, sans-serif font-family.

4. **Click the Color box ▣, then select color #000**
   The color for the body_text style is set to black.

5. **Click Block in the Category list, click the Text-align list arrow, click left, as shown in Figure D-19, then click OK**
   The body_text style is set to display left-aligned on the page. The .body_text style is added to the CSS Styles panel list.

   > **QUICK TIP**
   > If you click the insertion point within text or select text that has an applied style, that style appears in the Class list box in the HTML Property inspector, or the Targeted Rule list box in the CSS Property inspector.

6. **Select the items and descriptions in the first unordered list under the Massages heading, click the HTML button ‹› HTML, click the Class list arrow on the HTML Property inspector, click body_text, then click anywhere on the page to deselect the text**
   The body_text rule is applied to the spa service items in the first unordered list. See Figure D-20.

7. **Repeat Step 6 to apply the body_text style to the other two unordered lists and the last paragraph at the bottom of the spa page**

8. **Click File on the Application bar (Win) or Menu bar (Mac), then click Save All**
   The changes are saved to both the spa document file and the style sheet file.

Using font combinations in styles

When you are setting rule properties for text, it is wise to apply font combinations. That way, if one font is not available, the browser will apply a similar one. For instance, with the font family "Arial, Helvetica, sans-serif", the browser will first check the user's system for the Arial font, then, if it can't find the Arial font, it will look for the Helvetica font and so on. If you prefer to use a different set of fonts than the ones Dreamweaver provides, click the Font list arrow on the CSS Property inspector, click Edit Font list, then choose from the available fonts listed. You can also select font combinations in any dialog box with a Font-family option.

FIGURE D-18: Creating a new CSS rule in the su_styles.css file

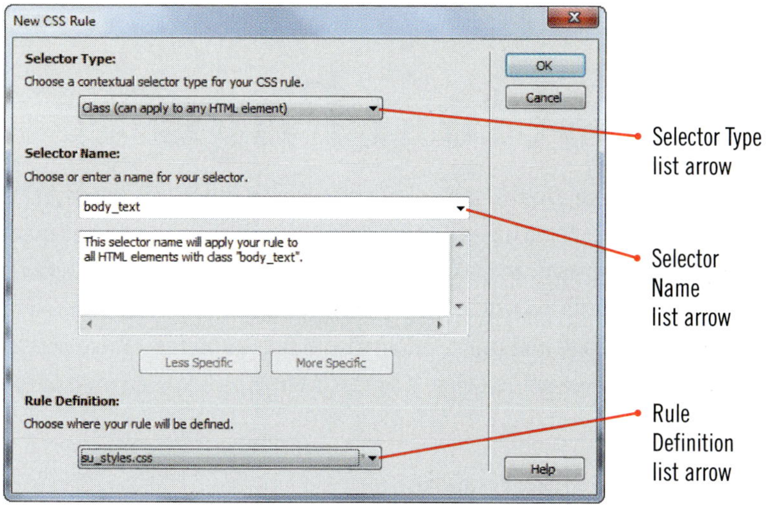

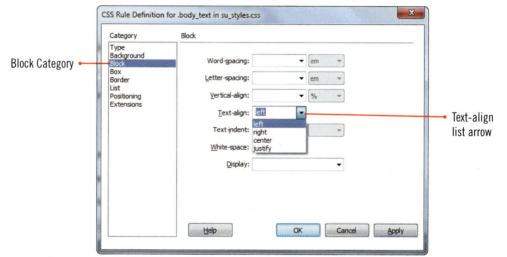

Selector Type
list arrow

Selector
Name
list arrow

Rule
Definition
list arrow

FIGURE D-19: Selecting the Text-align property for the body_text rule

Block Category

Text-align
list arrow

FIGURE D-20: body_text style applied to the first unordered list items

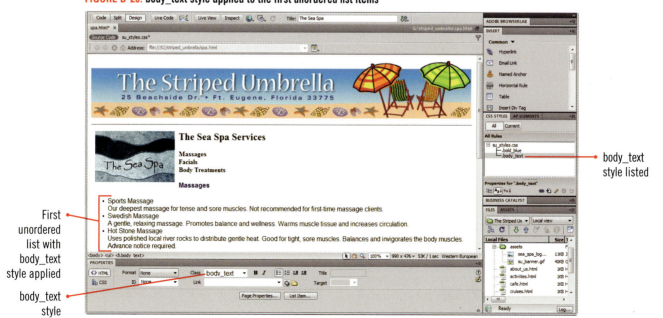

body_text
style listed

First
unordered
list with
body_text
style applied

body_text
style

Attaching a Cascading Style Sheet to a Page

After creating an external style sheet, you should attach it to the rest of the pages in your Web site to utilize the full benefit. Being able to define a rule and apply it to page elements across all the pages of your Web site means that you can make hundreds of formatting changes in a few minutes. Style sheets create a more uniform look from page to page and lead to cleaner code. You decide to attach the su_styles.css file to the home page and use it to format the paragraph text. Since you already have an internal style on the index page, you want to delete it so the external style will be used to format the paragraph text instead.

STEPS

QUICK TIP

(Win) To switch between open documents, click the tab for the document you wish to view, or press [Ctrl][Tab].

1. **Open the index.html page**

   Since an external style sheet has yet to be created for the index page, the external style sheet is not listed in the CSS Styles panel. In order to use an external style sheet with other pages in the Web site, you must first attach the style sheet file to each page.

2. **Click the Attach Style Sheet button** 🔗 **on the CSS Styles panel**

   The Attach External Style Sheet dialog box opens.

QUICK TIP

If you don't see your styles listed, click the plus sign (Win) or right-pointing triangle (Mac) next to su_styles.css in the CSS Styles panel.

3. **Click Browse next to the File/URL text box, click su_styles.css in the Select Style Sheet File dialog box if necessary, click OK (Win) or Choose (Mac); compare your screen to Figure D-21, then click OK**

   The Attach External Style Sheet dialog box closes and the su_styles.css style sheet file appears in the CSS Styles panel, indicating that the file is attached to the index page. In addition to the su_styles.css external style sheet, some internal styles are also listed in the CSS Styles panel such as the internal style called body_text, which shares the same name as the style in the external style sheet.

4. **Click the body_text style under <style> in the CSS Styles Panel in the internal style sheet, then click the Delete CSS Rule icon** 🗑

   The internal body_text style is deleted from the CSS Styles panel, and the external body_text style takes over the formatting for all text with the body_text rule applied. See Figure D-22.

5. **Compare your screen to Figure D-23, click File on the Menu bar (Win) or Application (Mac), click Save All, then close the index page**

   The changes are saved to the spa document file, the index document file, and the style sheet file.

Design Matters

Choosing fonts

There are two classifications of fonts: sans-serif and serif. **Sans-serif** fonts, such as the font you are reading now, are made up of plain characters without any strokes at the top and bottom of letters. They are used frequently for headings and subheadings in printed text. Examples of sans-serif fonts are Arial, Verdana, and Helvetica. **Serif** fonts are more ornate, with small extra strokes at the top and bottom of the characters. They are generally easier to read in printed material because the extra strokes lead your eye from one character to the next. Examples of serif fonts are Times New Roman, Garamond, and Georgia. Many designers feel that sans-serif fonts are preferable for files read electronically, while serif fonts are preferable for printed materials. When choosing fonts, limit each Web site to three font variations or less. Avoid using a tiny font size that viewers will have to enlarge or font colors that are difficult to see against the page background.

FIGURE D-21: Attaching the su_styles.css file to the index page

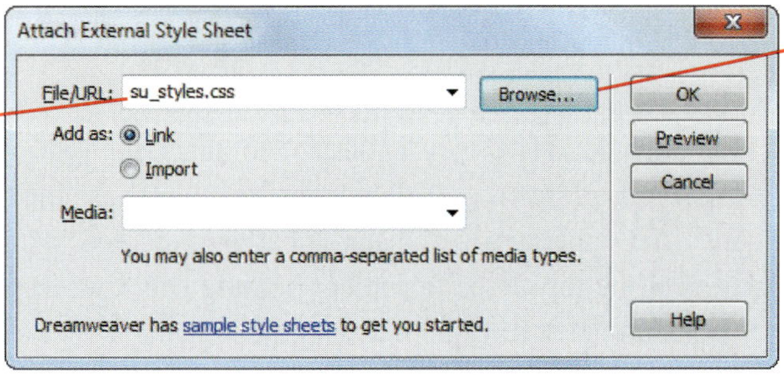

Name of external style sheet
to attach to the page

Browse button

Attach External Style Sheet

File/URL: su_styles.css   Browse...   OK

Add as: ● Link
○ Import   Preview
                    Cancel
Media:

You may also enter a comma-separated list of media types.

Dreamweaver has sample style sheets to get you started.   Help

FIGURE D-22: CSS Styles panel with internal body_text style deleted

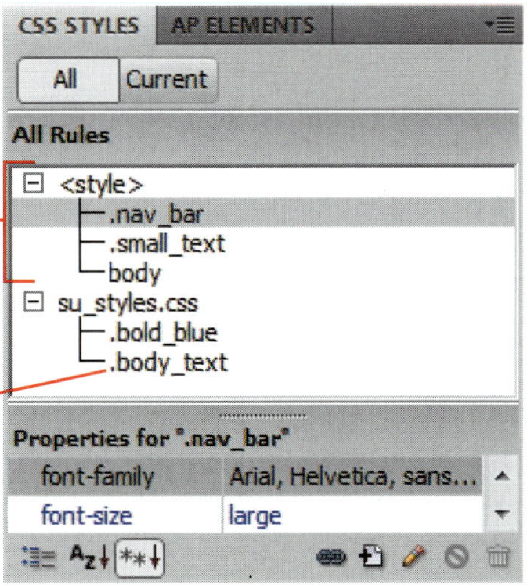

CSS STYLES   AP ELEMENTS

All   Current

All Rules

☐ <style>
    ├ .nav_bar
    ├ .small_text
    └ body
☐ su_styles.css
    ├ .bold_blue
    └ .body_text

List of internal styles
with the body_text
style removed

New body_text style added
to the external style sheet

Properties for ".nav_bar"
font-family   Arial, Helvetica, sans...
font-size   large

FIGURE D-23: The index.html page with the external style applied

The Striped Umbrella
25 Beachside Dr. • Ft. Eugene, Florida 33775

Home - About Us - Spa - Cafe - Activities

Welcome to The Striped Umbrella — a full-service resort and spa just steps from the Gulf of Mexico and ten miles east of Crab Key, Florida. The Striped Umbrella has a variety of activities for adults and children. It is a perfect romantic getaway for two or a complete family vacation. Our activities include water sports, golf, shopping, and an award-winning spa.

The restaurants at The Striped Umbrella are amazing. The Sand Crab Cafe can be enjoyed al fresco at The Terrace, poolside at The Cabana, and inside in The Dining Room. The Dining Room features fresh seafood and an extensive wine list. The Terrace offers more casual dining with sweeping views of the gulf and fabulous sunsets. The Cabana serves sandwiches, salads, and snacks around the pool area.

Come enjoy the best of both worlds, a secluded sandy beach populated with beautiful birds, yet a short drive down the road from world-class shopping, restaurants, and entertainment. Bring a good book and leave your laptop at the office. You won't want to go home!

Checking for Spelling Errors

Dreamweaver has a feature for checking spelling errors that is similar to those you have probably used in word processing programs. It is very important to check for spelling and grammatical errors before publishing a page. A page that is published with errors will cause the user to immediately judge the site as unprofessional, and the accuracy of the information presented will be in question. It is a good idea to start a spell check at the top of the document because Dreamweaver searches from the insertion point down. If your insertion point is in the middle of the document, you will receive a message asking if you want to check the rest of the document, which wastes time. If a file you create in a word processor will be imported into Dreamweaver, make sure to run a spell check in the word processing program before you import it. You want to check the spelling on the spa page and correct any errors.

STEPS

QUICK TIP
You can also press [Ctrl][Home] to move the insertion point to the top of the document. (Mac users may not have a [home] key depending on their keyboard.)

1. **Place the insertion point in front of The Sea Spa Services paragraph**

2. **Click Commands on the Application bar (Win) or Menu bar (Mac), then click Check Spelling**
   The Check Spelling dialog box opens, as shown in Figure D-24. The word *masage* is highlighted on the spa page, indicating a misspelled word.

3. **Click massage. in the Suggestions list if necessary, then click Change**
   The Check Spelling dialog box closes and a Dreamweaver dialog box opens stating that the Spell check is complete.

4. **Click OK**
   The Dreamweaver dialog box closes and the spa page redisplays with the word *massage* spelled correctly.

5. **Click File on the Application bar (Win) or Menu bar (Mac), click Save, click the Preview/Debug in browser icon, then preview the spa page in your browser window**
   The spa page opens in your browser window as shown in Figure D-25.

6. **Close your browser, close all open pages, then exit Dreamweaver**

Using Find and Replace

Another useful editing command is Find and Replace, which is located on the Edit menu. You can use this command to make individual or global text edits in either Design or Code view. It is similar to Find and Replace commands in word processing programs, except that there is an added advantage in Dreamweaver. You can use Find and Replace to easily search through code if you are trying to locate and correct coding errors. For example, if you want to find a tag that formats a font with a specific color, you can search for that color number in the code. If you are searching for internal links that are incorrectly set as absolute links, you can enter the search term *src = "file"* to help you to locate them. You will learn more about absolute links in Unit F.

FIGURE D-24: Using the Check Spelling command

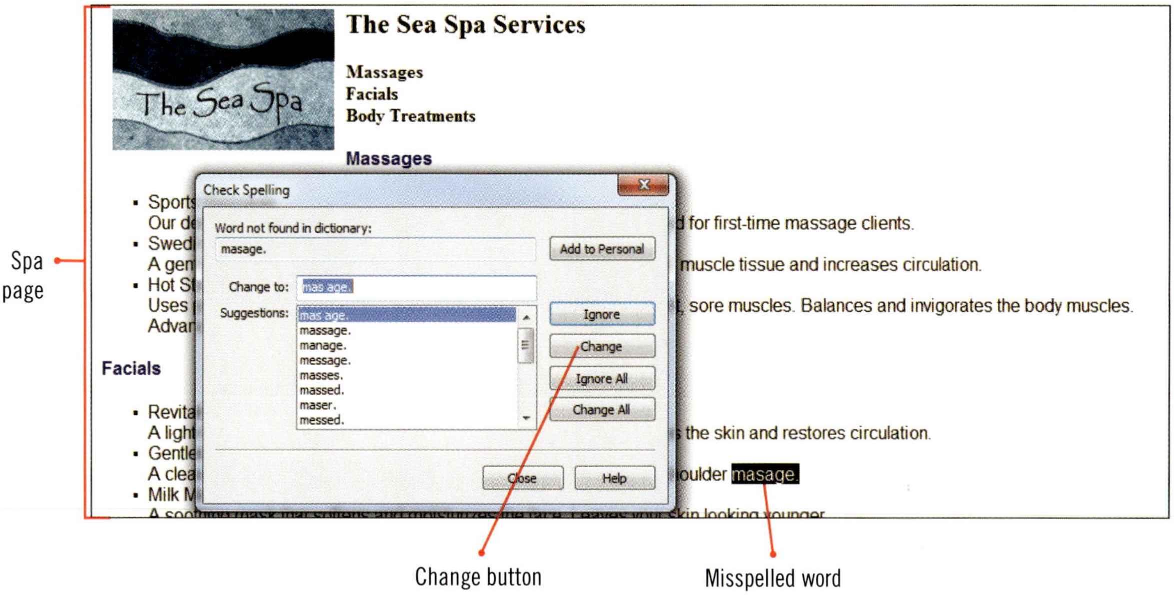

Spa page — Change button — Misspelled word

FIGURE D-25: The finished product

Practice

Concepts Review

For current SAM information, including versions and content details, visit SAM Central (http://www.cengage.com/samcentral). If you have a SAM user profile, you may have access to hands-on instruction, practice, and assessment of the skills covered in this unit. Since various versions of SAM are supported throughout the life of this text, check with your instructor for the correct instructions and URL/Web site for accessing assignments.

Label each element in the document window, as shown in Figure D-26.

FIGURE D-26

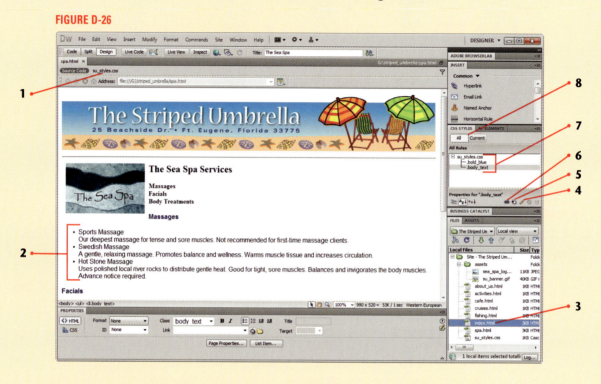

1. _____
2. _____
3. _____
4. _____
5. _____
6. _____
7. _____
8. _____

Match each of the following terms with the statement that best describes it.

9. **Sans-serif font**
10. **Property inspector**
11. **Ordered lists**
12. **Unordered lists**
13. **CSS styles**
14. **CSS Rule**
15. **External style sheet**
16. **Selector**
17. **Declaration**
18. **Serif font**

a. Numbered lists

b. Font without extra strokes at top and bottom

c. A set of formatting attributes that creates a style

d. A file attached or linked to a Web page to format page elements

e. A style property and the value

f. Bulleted lists

g. A panel used for formatting page elements

h. The name or tag to which style declarations have been assigned

i. Font with extra strokes at the top and bottom

j. Sets of formatting attributes to format page elements

Select the best answer from the following list of choices.

19. The button used to select color is:

  a.

  b.

  c.

  d.

20. External CSS files are saved with the filename extension:

  a. .css

  b. .cas

  c. .stl

  d. .csf

21. A CSS Class Style name in the Styles panel is preceded by a:

  a. pound sign.

  b. period.

  c. dash.

  d. number.

22. Styles that are part of the head content of a Web page are called:

  a. external styles.

  b. embedded styles.

  c. inline Styles.

  d. HTML styles.

23. The type of style used to redefine an HTML tag in the New CSS Rule dialog box is called:

  a. an Advanced style.

  b. a Class style.

  c. a Tag style.

  d. a Compound style.

Skills Review

Important: *If you did not create this Web site in Unit B and maintain it in Unit C, you will need to create a site root folder for this Web site and define the Web site using files your instructor will provide. See the "Read This Before You Begin" section of this book for more detailed instructions.*

1. **Import text.**
   a. Start Dreamweaver.
   b. Open the Blooms & Bulbs Web site.
   c. Open dwd_2.html from the drive and folder where you store your Unit D Data Files.
   d. Save the file as **tips.html** in the site root folder of your Blooms & Bulbs Web site, overwriting the existing file, and not updating links.
   e. Verify that the path for the banner is linked to the banner in the assets folder of the Blooms & Bulbs Web site.
   f. Select the broken image, then browse to find the butterfly.jpg file from the drive and folder where you store your Data Files to copy it to the assets folder of the Blooms & Bulbs Web site.
   g. With the insertion point to the right of the butterfly image, import (Win) or copy and paste (Mac) the Word document gardening_tips.doc from the drive and folder where you store your Unit D Data Files.
   h. Save the changes to the tips page, then close the dwd_2.html page.
   i. Use the Clean Up Word HTML command on the tips page (Win).

2. **Set text properties.**
   a. Enter a paragraph break before the Seasonal Gardening Checklist heading, then select the Seasonal Gardening Checklist heading.
   b. Format the text with the Heading 3 format.
   c. Select the Basic Gardening Tips heading and format it with a Heading 3 format.
   d. Save your work.

3. **Create an unordered list.**
   a. Select the items under the Seasonal Gardening Checklist.
   b. Format the list of items as an unordered list. (*Hint*: Be sure *not* to select the return at the end of the last line or you will accidentally create a fifth item.)
   c. Select the items under Basic Gardening Tips, then format them as an ordered list.

4. **Understand Cascading Style Sheets.**
   a. Using a word processor or piece of paper, list the types of CSS categorized by their location in a Web site.
   b. Using a word processor or piece of paper, list the types of CSS categorized by their function in a Web site.

5. **Create a Style in a new Cascading Style Sheet.**
   a. Open the CSS Styles panel, if necessary.
   b. Create a new Class style named **bold_gray** in a new style sheet file.
   c. Save the new style sheet file with the name **blooms_styles.css** in the blooms folder.
   d. Set the Font-family for the body_text style as Arial, Helvetica, sans-serif.
   e. Set the Font-size as small, the Font-weight as bold, then the Color as #333.
   f. Save all files.

6. **Apply and edit a style.**
   a. Apply the bold_gray style to the words *Fall*, *Winter*, *Spring*, and *Summer*.
   b. Edit the style to increase the text size to medium.
   c. Save all files.

Skills Review (continued)

7. Add styles to a Cascading Style Sheet.

   a. Create a new Class style named **body_text** in the blooms_styles.css file.

   b. Set the Font-family as Arial, Helvetica, sans-serif.

   c. Set the Font-size as medium, the Font-style as normal, then the Color as #000.

   d. Use the Block category to set the Text-alignment to left.

   e. Apply the body_text style to all text on the page that does not have a heading style or a CSS Style assigned.

   f. Save all files.

8. Attach a Cascading Style Sheet to a page.

   a. Open the index page in the Blooms & Bulbs Web site.

   b. Attach the blooms_styles.css file to the index page.

   c. Delete the internal body_text style so the external body_text style will format the paragraphs of text.

   d. Save all files.

9. Check for spelling errors.

   a. Close the index page, then return to the tips page.

   b. Run a spell check on the tips page.

   c. Preview the page in your Web browser window, then compare your screen to Figure D-27.

   d. Close your browser, then Exit (Win) or Quit (Mac) Dreamweaver.

FIGURE D-27

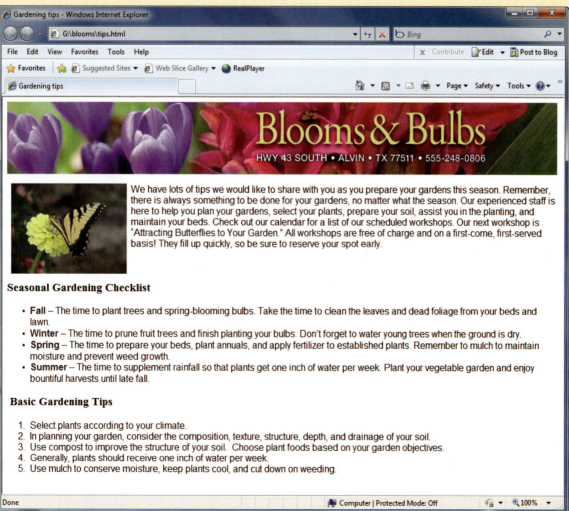

Important: *If you did not create the following Web sites in Unit B and maintain them in Unit C, you will need to create a root folder for the Web sites in the following exercises and define the Web sites using files your instructor will provide. See the "Read This Before You Begin" section in this book for more detailed instructions.*

Independent Challenge 1

You have been hired to create a Web site for a river expedition company named Rapids Transit, located on the Buffalo River in Arkansas. In addition to renting canoes, kayaks, and rafts, they have several types of cabin rentals for overnight stays. River guides are available, if requested, to accompany clients on float trips. The clients range from beginners to experienced floaters. The owner's name is Mike Andrew. Mike has asked you to add a page to the Web site that will describe the lodge, cabins, and tents that are available to their customers.

a. Start Dreamweaver.

b. Open the Rapids Transit Web site.

c. Open the file dwd_3.html from the drive and folder where you store your Unit D Data Files, then save it as **lodging.html** in the Rapids Transit Web site, replacing the existing file, but not updating links.

d. Verify that the rapids banner path is set to the assets folder in the Web site.

e. Create an unordered list from the four types of lodging and their rates.

f. Create a new Class style named **body_text,** then save it in a new style sheet file named rapids_transit.css using the following settings: Font-family, Arial, Helvetica, sans-serif; Font-size, 14; Font-style, normal.

g. Apply the body_text style to all text on the page *except* the navigation bar.

h. Create a new class style in the rapids_transit.css style sheet for the lodging choices named **paragraph_header**.

i. Format the paragraph_header style with the following settings: Font-family Arial, Helvetica, sans-serif; Font-size 14; Font-style normal; Font-weight bold; and Color #036.

j. Apply the paragraph_header style to the text The Lodge, Jenny's Cabins, and John's Camp at the beginning of the first three paragraphs.

k. Attach the rapids_transit.css file to the index page, then delete the internal body_text style and the `<style>` tag in the CSS Styles panel, allowing the external body_text style to format the paragraph of text on the page.

l. Create a new class style in the rapids_transit.css style sheet named **contact_info** using Arial, Helvetica sans-serif; italic style; size 14, color #000; then apply it to the contact information on the index page.

m. Close the file dwd_3.html, then save your work using the Save All command on the File menu.

n. Preview the index page in your browser window, click the Lodging link, compare your screen to Figure D-28, close your browser window, close all files, then exit Dreamweaver.

FIGURE D-28

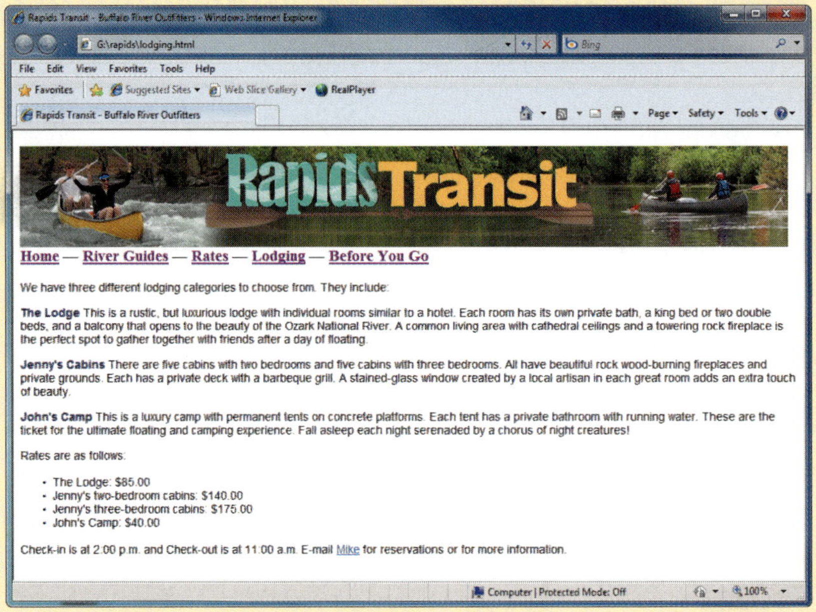

Independent Challenge 2

You are a marketing specialist for a travel outfitter named TripSmart. TripSmart specializes in travel products and services. In addition to selling luggage and accessories, they sponsor trips and offer travel advice. You company is designing a new Web site and your job is to update the newsletter page on the current Web site with some timely travel tips.

a. Start Dreamweaver, then open the TripSmart Web site.

b. Open the file dwd_4.html and save it as **newsletter.html** in the TripSmart Web site, replacing the existing file, but not updating links.

c. Verify that the banner path is set to the assets folder of the Web site, then close dwd_4.html.

d. Create an ordered list from the 10 items on the page, starting with Be organized.

e. Create a new class style called **body_text,** then save it in a new style sheet named **tripsmart_styles.css**.

f. Choose a font, size, style, color, and weight of your choice for the body_text style.

g. Apply the body_text style to all the text on the page *except* the Ten Tips for Stress-Free Travel paragraph heading.

h. Create another class style in the tripsmart_styles.css style sheet called **list_heading** with a font, size, style, color, and weight of your choice, then apply it to the Ten Tips for Stress-Free heading.

i. Create another class style in the tripsmart_styles.css style sheet named **list_term** with settings of your choice, then apply it to each ordered list item that begins each ordered list.

j. Type **Travel Tidbits** in the document title text box.

k. Attach the style sheet to the index page, then delete the internal body_text style, allowing the external body_text style to format the paragraphs of text on the page.

l. Create another class style in the tripsmart_styles.css style sheet named **contact_info** with settings of your choice, apply it to the contact information on the page, save your work, then close the page.

m. Save your work, preview the newsletter page in your browser window, then compare it to Figure D-29 as an example for a possible solution.

n. Close your browser, close the file, then exit Dreamweaver.

FIGURE D-29

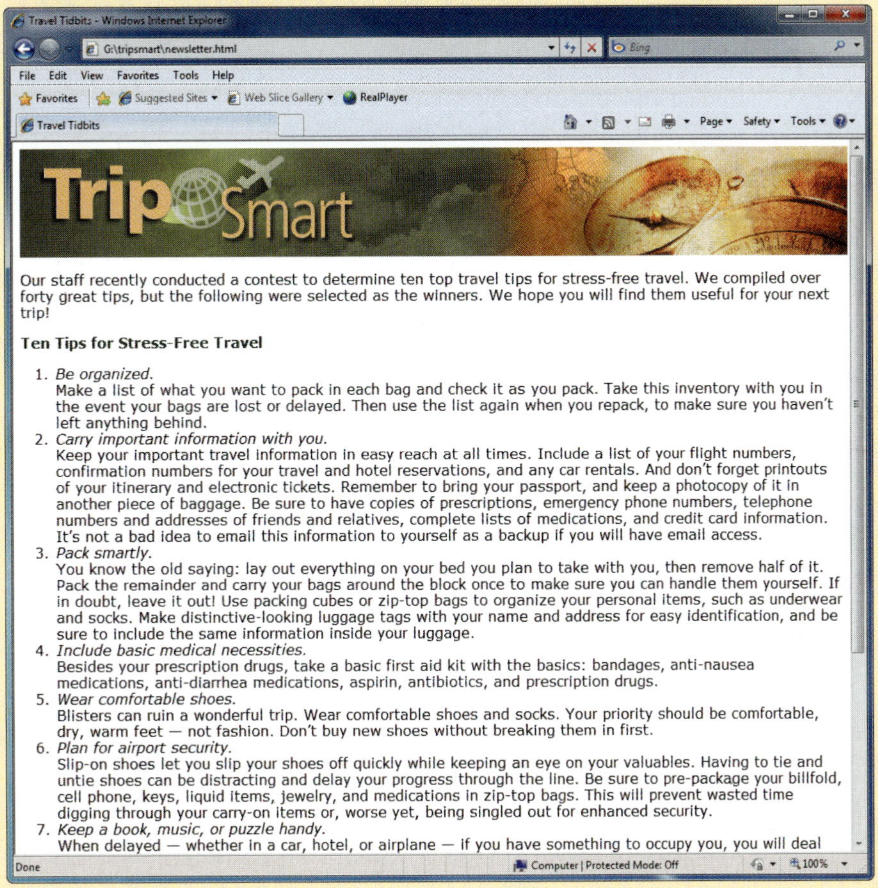

Independent Challenge 3

Dr. Chappel is a government historian who is conducting research on the separation of church and state. He is using the Library of Congress Web site to find relevant information. Write your answers to the questions below on paper or using your word processor.

a. Connect to the Internet, then go to The Library of Congress Web site at www.loc.gov, shown in Figure D-30.

b. Is the content well organized?

c. What font or fonts are used on the pages for the main text? Are the same fonts used consistently on the other pages in the Web site?

d. Are there any ordered or unordered lists on the Web site? If so, how are they used?

e. View the source to see if CSS styles are used on the pages in the Web site.

f. Use a search engine to find another Web site of interest. Compare and contrast the use of text formatting on this site to that used on the Library of Congress Web site.

FIGURE D-30

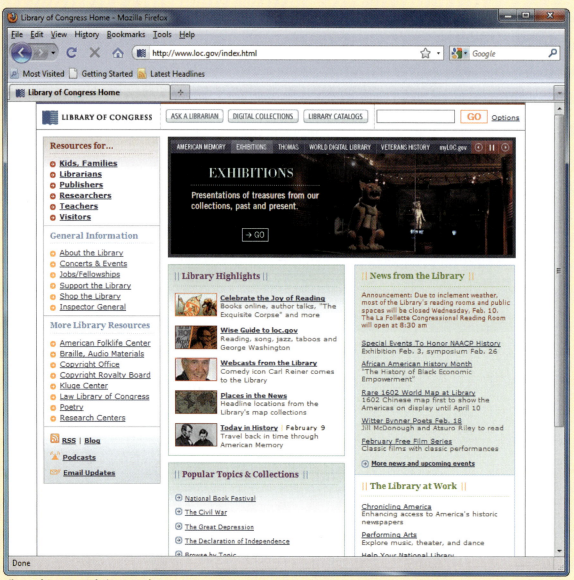

Library of Congress Web site – www.loc.gov

Real Life Independent Challenge

This assignment will continue to build on the personal Web site that you created in Unit B and modified in Unit C. You have created and developed your index page. In this lesson, you will work with one of the other pages in your Web site.

a. Consult your wireframe, then decide which page you would like to develop in this lesson.

b. Create content for this page, then format the text attractively on the page using settings for font, size, text color, style, and alignment.

c. Format some of the text on the page as either an ordered or unordered list.

d. Create a style sheet with a minimum of two styles, then apply a style to all text on the page.

e. Attach the style sheet to any of the pages you have already developed, then apply styles to all text.

f. Save the file, then preview the pages in your browser window.

After you are satisfied with your work, verify the following:

a. Each completed page has a page title.

b. All links work correctly.

c. The completed pages appear correctly using at least two screen resolutions.

d. All images are properly placed with a path to the assets folder of the Web site.

e. A style sheet is used to format text.

Visual Workshop

Your company has been selected to design a Web site for a catering business named Carolyne's Creations. Open the Carolyne's Creations Web site, open the file dwd_5.html, then save it as **recipes.html** in the Carolyne's Creations Web site, replacing the original file. Close dwd_5.html, then format the page using styles so it looks similar to Figure D-31. (The text may wrap slightly different if you are using a browser other than Internet Explorer and a monitor with a different screen resolution.) Save the file pie.jpg from the drive and folder where you store your Unit D Data Files to your Web site assets folder (*Hint*: Use the following styles and settings to match the figure, and save them in a CSS file named cc_styles.css.)

.headings	.body_text
Font-family: Arial, Helvetica, sans-serif	Font-family: Arial, Helvetica, sans-serif
Font-size: medium	Font-size: medium
Font-weight: bold	Font-weight: normal
Color: #600	Color: #000

If you have not maintained this Web site from the previous unit, then contact your instructor for assistance.

FIGURE D-31

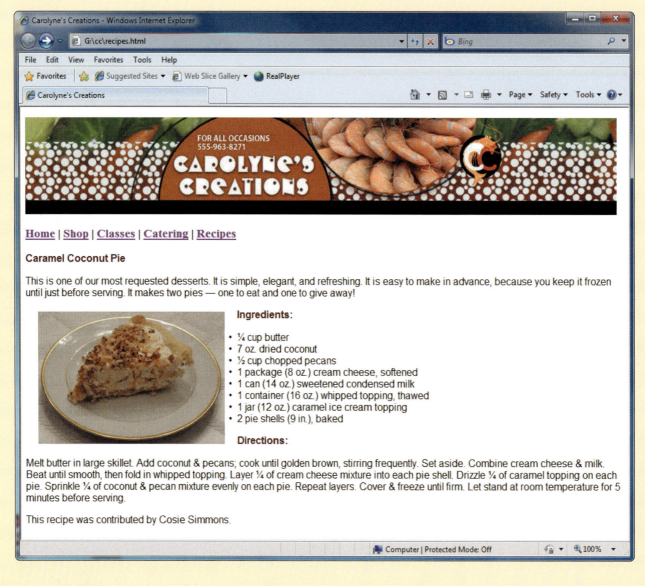

Using and Managing Images

Web pages with images are more interesting than pages with just text. You can position images on your Web pages, then resize them, add borders, and customize the amount of space around them. You can also use images as a Web page, table, or CSS layout block background. In this unit you learn how to incorporate images into a Web site and how to manage them effectively using the Assets panel. A photographer recently did a photo shoot of The Striped Umbrella property for some new brochures. You decide to incorporate several of the images on the about_us page so that the beauty of the resort comes across.

OBJECTIVES

Insert an image

Align an image

Enhance an image

Use alternate text and set Accessibility preferences

View the Assets panel

Insert a background image

Delete image files from a Web site

Create and find images for a Web site

Examine copyright rules

Inserting an Image

Images you import into a Web site are automatically added to the Assets panel. The **Assets panel**, located with the other panels on the right side of your workspace, lists the assets of the Web site, such as images and colors. As you add images to a Web page, the page **download time** (the time it takes to transfer the file to a user's computer) increases. Pages that download slowly discourage users from staying on the site. To add an image to a page, you can either use the Insert, Image command on the Application bar (Win) or Menu bar (Mac), use the Images button in the Common category on the Insert panel, or drag an image from the Assets panel onto the page. You want to place several photos of the resort on the about_us Web page and check the file size of each in the Assets panel.

STEPS

TROUBLE

Your download time shown may vary according to the Connection Speed preferences set for your Status bar. To change your settings, click Edit (Win) or Dreamweaver (Mac) on the Application bar (Win) or Menu bar (Mac), click Preferences, then click Status Bar.

1. **Start Dreamweaver, open The Striped Umbrella Web site, open dwe_1.html from the drive and folder where you store your Unit E Data Files, save it as about_us.html in the striped_umbrella root folder, overwriting the existing file and not updating the links, then close dwe_1.html**

   The about_us page displays in Design view in your workspace. The Status bar displays the download time for the current Web page, as shown Figure E-1.

2. **Click the Attach Style Sheet button** 🔗 **in the CSS Styles panel, attach the su_styles.css style sheet, then apply the body_text style to all of the paragraph text on the page, including the menu bar**

   The style sheet for the Web site is attached to the about_us page, and the body_text style is applied to the menu bar, heading, and two paragraphs.

3. **Click to the left of the word *When* in the first paragraph to place the insertion point, select the Common category on the Insert panel if necessary, scroll down and click the Images list arrow on the Insert panel, then click Image**

   The Select Image Source dialog box opens. This is the same dialog box you have been using to copy images from the Data Files folder to your site assets folder when you save new pages with images.

QUICK TIP

The Image Tag Accessibility Attributes dialog box contains Dreamweaver accessibility features, which you will learn about later in the unit.

4. **Navigate to the drive and folder where you store your Unit E data files, double-click club_house.jpg from the assets folder, type Club House as the Alternate text in the Image Tag Accessibility Attributes dialog box if prompted, then click OK**

5. **Click the Refresh Button** ↻ **on the Files panel toolbar if necessary**

   The club house image appears at the beginning of the first paragraph, as shown in Figure E-2. As indicated in the Files panel list, the club house image is located in the Web site assets folder. This is the location that will be used to load the image in the browser when the page is viewed.

QUICK TIP

You need to select club_house.jpg to see the thumbnail.

6. **Save the file, click the Assets panel tab, click the Images button** 🖼️ **on the Assets panel if necessary, then click** ↻ **at the bottom of the Assets panel, if necessary**

   The three images you added to The Striped Umbrella Web site—club_house.jpg, sea_spa_logo.jpg, and su_banner.gif—are listed in the Assets panel. When the Images button is selected, the Assets panel displays the images in the current Web site which, as shown in Figure E-3, is split into two windows. The lower window lists all of the images in the Web site, while the top window displays a thumbnail of the image currently selected in the list. The Dimensions column lists the height and width of each image.

TROUBLE

If the file names don't appear in the Files or Assets panels, click the Refresh button ↻, or click ↻ while you hold down the [Ctrl] key.

7. **Repeat Steps 3 and 4 to insert the boardwalk.png image at the beginning of the second paragraph, if prompted use Boardwalk to the Beach as alternate text, then save your work**

   The boardwalk image appears on the page at the beginning of the second paragraph and boardwalk.png is added to the list of images in the Assets panel. The Assets panel lists the four images shown in Figure E-4.

FIGURE E-1: Status bar displaying page download time

> convenient place to pick up any items that you may have forgotten to bring along, in addition to an extensive inventory of bathing suits, sandals, and other beachwear.

`<body>`   100%   975 x 582   43K / 1 sec   Western European

PROPERTIES

Your screen size might differ

Page download time (yours might differ, depending on connection speed)

FIGURE E-2: About_us page with image inserted

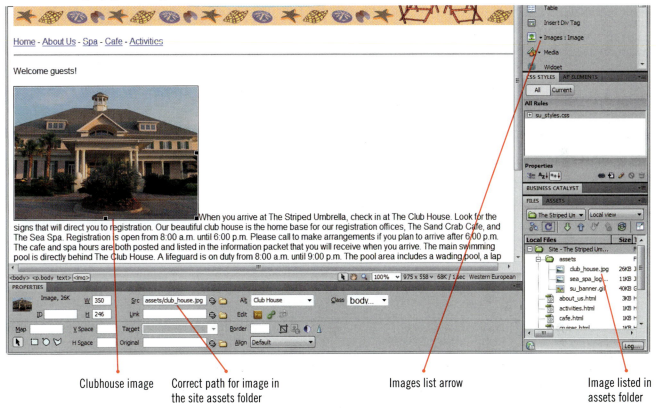

Clubhouse image

Correct path for image in the site assets folder

Images list arrow

Image listed in assets folder

FIGURE E-3: Assets panel listing for The Striped Umbrella Web site

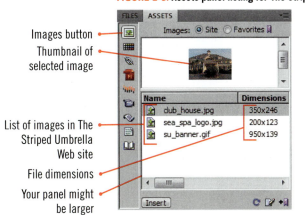

Images button

Thumbnail of selected image

List of images in The Striped Umbrella Web site

File dimensions

Your panel might be larger

FIGURE E-4: Assets panel with images listed

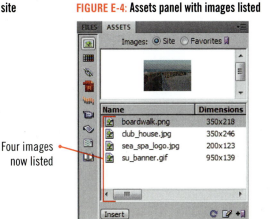

Four images now listed

Aligning an Image

Like text, images can be positioned on the page in relation to other page elements. Positioning an image is called **aligning** the image. You align an image by selecting it and then using one of the alignment options displayed in the Property inspector. See Table E-1 for a description of each alignment option. When you first place an image on a page, it has the **Default** alignment which aligns the bottom of the image with the text **baseline**—the bottom of the line of text, not including descending portions of characters such as y or g. You should experiment with the options to find the best alignment for your image. After experimenting with several alignment options, you decide to stagger the alignment of the images on the page to make it appear more balanced.

STEPS

QUICK TIP
You can double-click the right side of the Property inspector to return it to its original size.

1. **Scroll to the top of the page, click the club house image to select it, double-click the empty space in the right side of the Property inspector to expand it if necessary, then click the Align list arrow in the Property inspector**

   The expanded Property inspector displays additional settings, including those for image maps, horizontal and vertical spacing, border size, and alignment settings. The 10 alignment options appear in the Align drop down list, as shown in Figure E-6.

2. **Click Left**

   The club house image is aligned to the left side of the paragraph. The text is repositioned to align with the top and right sides of the photo.

QUICK TIP
Your text may wrap differently.

3. **Scroll down the page if necessary, click the boardwalk image to select it, click the Align list arrow in the Property inspector, then click Right**

   The boardwalk image is aligned to the right of the paragraph. The text is repositioned to align with the top and left sides of the image. The two images are aligned in staggered positions on the page, as shown in Figure E-7.

4. **Save your work, click the Preview/Debug in browser button on the Document toolbar, then click Preview in [your browser name]**

   The about_us Web page looks much better with the images staggered to the left and right sides of the page.

5. **Close the browser window**

   The about_us page reappears in Design view.

Design Matters

Using dynamic images

To make a page even more interesting, you can place images on the page that change frequently, such as a group of several images that are set to automatically cycle on and off the page, called **dynamic images**. You can use dynamic images to display multiple items with a similar layout. For example, a Web site for a retail store might display images of current sale items in one window on a Web page, one item at a time. To insert dynamic images, you must first create a Spry Data Set to store the images using the [+] button in the Bindings panel. You then insert the images on the page using the Data sources option, rather than the File system option, in the Select Image Source dialog box, as shown in Figure E-5.

FIGURE E-5: Using the Data sources option

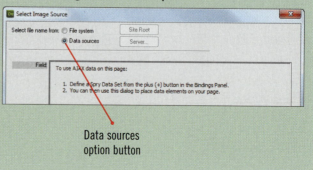

Data sources
option button

FIGURE E-6: Alignment options for images

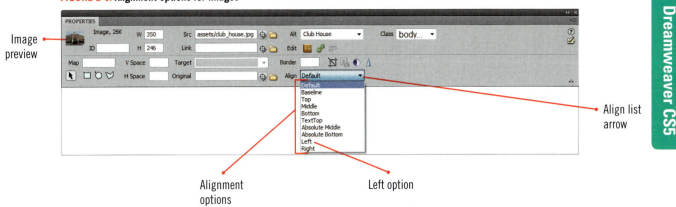

Image preview

Align list arrow

Alignment options

Left option

FIGURE E-7: Aligned images on the about_us page

Left-aligned image

Right-aligned image

TABLE E-1: Aligning elements to text

alignment option	description
Default	The default setting in which the element is aligned with the text baseline. The default can vary by browser.
Baseline	The element is aligned with the baseline of the text.
Top	The element is aligned with the top of the tallest item, whether that item is text or another object.
Middle	The element is aligned with the text baseline or another object at the vertical middle of the image.
Bottom	The bottom of the item is aligned with the bottom of the text.
TextTop	The element is aligned with the top of the tallest character in a line of text.
Absolute Middle	The element is aligned with the absolute middle of the current line.
Absolute Bottom	The element is aligned with the bottom of a text line or another object. This applies to letters that fall below the baseline, such as the letter y.
Left	The element is placed on the left margin with text wrapping to the right.
Right	The element is placed on the right margin with text wrapping to the left.

Enhancing an Image

After you select, place, and align an image on a Web page, you can enhance its appearance. You can improve an image's appearance in Dreamweaver using borders, cropping, resizing, adjusting its brightness and contrast, and adjusting the horizontal and vertical space around an image. **Borders** are like frames that surround an image to make it stand out on the page. **Cropping** an image removes part of the image, both visually (on the page) and physically (the file size). A cropped image is smaller and takes less time to download. **Horizontal** and **vertical space** refers to blank space above, below, or on the sides of an image that separates the image from other elements on the page. You decide to enhance the images on the about_us page by adding borders around the images, and adjusting the horizontal and vertical space around each image.

STEPS

1. **Click the club house image to select it**

2. **Type 1 in the Border text box in the Property inspector, press [Tab], then click anywhere on the page to deselect the image**
   The surrounding text wraps very close to the side of the image, as shown in Figure E-8. There is not much space between the text and the image. A black border with a thickness of 1 pixel will appear around the image when previewed in your browser.

3. **Repeat Steps 1 and 2 for the boardwalk image**
   The border is applied to the boardwalk image as well. A black border will appear around the image when it is previewed in your browser.

4. **Click the club house image to select it, type 10 in the V Space text box in the Property inspector, press [Tab], type 10 in the H Space text box, press [Tab], then deselect the image**
   V Space refers to vertical space above and below the image. H Space refers to horizontal space on the sides of the image. You like the way the text is more evenly wrapped around the image, so you decide to apply the same option to the boardwalk image.

5. **Repeat Step 4 to apply the same vertical and horizontal settings to the boardwalk image**
   The two images are surrounded by the new horizontal and vertical space settings. The text does not wrap as tightly around the images.

6. **Click the boardwalk image to select it, note the W and H settings in the Property inspector, click the Crop button in the Property inspector, then click OK to close the Dreamweaver warning message that says you are about to permanently alter the image**

7. **Position the pointer over the bottom-center resizing handle, as shown in Figure E-9, slowly move the handle up toward the center of the image to remove part of the boardwalk, then double-click the image to crop it**
   The boardwalk image appears smaller, and the values in the W and H text boxes in the Property inspector change to reflect the new file dimensions.

8. **Click Edit on the Application bar (Win) or Menu bar (Mac), click Undo Crop (Win) or Undo (Mac) to restore the image to the original size, then save the file**
   The boardwalk image returns its original size.

Resizing an image using the Property inspector

To save space on a Web page, you can crop an image. If you prefer to keep the entire image, you can just resize it on the page. Simply select the image, then drag a selection handle toward the center of the image. Since dragging a selection handle can distort an image, press and hold [Shift] then drag a corner selection handle to retain the image's original proportions (You can also enlarge an image using these methods.) After you drag an image handle to resize it, the image dimensions in the Property inspector appear in bold and a black Refresh icon appears to the right of the dimensions. If you click the Refresh icon, the image reverts to its original size. Do not use this method to significantly resize an image. Instead, resize it using an image editor and save a copy of it with the new settings.

FIGURE E-8: Adding a border to an image

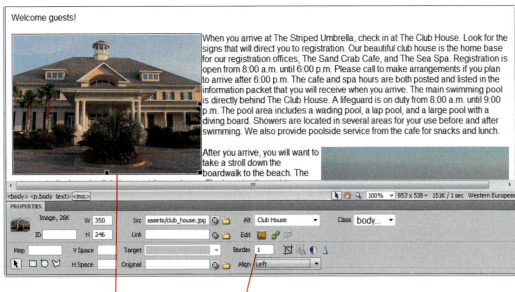

Image will have a border when displayed in the browser

New border size

FIGURE E-9: Cropping an image

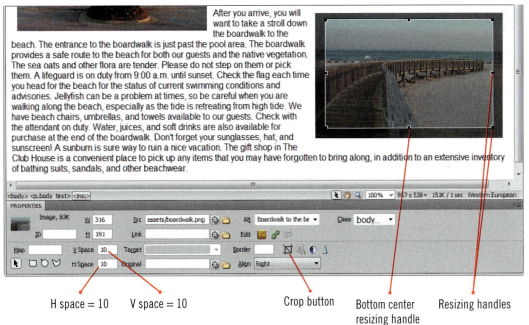

H space = 10   V space = 10   Crop button   Bottom center resizing handle   Resizing handles

Design Matters

Resizing graphics using an external editor

Each image on a Web page takes a certain amount of time to download, depending on the size of the file and the speed of the user's Internet connection. Larger files (in terms of kilobytes, not width and height) take longer to download than smaller files. Many designers feel that an ideal page should download in less than five or six seconds; to ensure that your page downloads quickly, your images should have the smallest file size possible while maintaining the necessary level of image quality. If you need to significantly resize an image, use an external image editor instead of resizing it in Dreamweaver; resizing in Dreamweaver affects how an image appears onscreen, but does not alter the image file itself. Cropping an image in Dreamweaver, however, *will* modify the image file and decrease its overall size. As a general rule, it is better to crop your images using an external editor when you are making a significant change. Always save a copy of the original file first before you crop it, then use the copy of the file to make your edits. This will always keep the original file intact in case you need it later. Think of your original images as your negatives; they must be protected for future needs.

Using Alternate Text and Setting Accessibility Preferences

One of the easiest ways to make your Web page viewer-friendly and more accessible to individuals with disabilities is through the use of alternate text. **Alternate text** is descriptive text that can be set to appear in place of an image while the image is downloading. Some browsers can be set to display only text and to download images manually. In such instances, alternate text is used in place of images. Alternate text can be read by a **screen reader**, a device used by individuals with visual impairments to convert written text on a computer monitor to spoken words. Using a screen reader and alternate text, these users can have an image described to them in detail. You should also use alternate text when inserting form objects, text displayed as images, buttons, frames, and media files to enable screen reader usage. When loading a new installation of Dreamweaver, all the accessibility preferences are turned on by default. To make the alternate text more descriptive for screen readers, you want to edit the alternate text that describes each of the images on the about_us page. You also verify that the Images option in the Accessibility preferences is set so you will not forget to enter alternate text for each image.

STEPS

1. **Click the club house image to select it, select the text in the Alt text box in the Property inspector, type The Striped Umbrella Club House, press [Tab], then save the file**
   The alternate text is entered for the image, as shown in Figure E-10.

2. **Repeat step 1 to edit the alternate text for the boardwalk image to read Boardwalk to our private beach**
   The alternate text is entered for the image, as shown in Figure E-11.

> **QUICK TIP**
> Once you set the Accessibility preferences, they will be in effect for all of your Web sites. You will not have to set each Web site separately.

3. **Click Edit on the Application bar (Win) or Dreamweaver on the Menu bar (Mac), click Preferences, click Accessibility in the Category list, click the four Accessibility check boxes to select them if necessary, as shown in Figure E-12, then click OK**
   With these options selected, Dreamweaver will prompt you to enter alternate text for new objects you add to the Web site, including images.

> **QUICK TIP**
> If your Save option is not active, you do not need to save your file. However, you can use the Save All command in the File menu to make sure any changes you have made to an open page are saved.

4. **Save your work**

FIGURE E-10: Editing the alternate text for the club house image

Alternate text

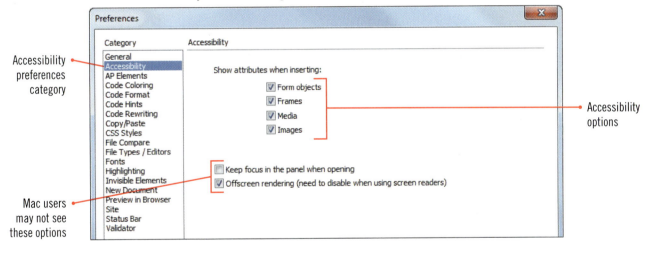

FIGURE E-11: Editing the alternate text for the boardwalk image

FIGURE E-12: Accessibility Preferences dialog box

Accessibility
preferences
category

Accessibility
options

Mac users
may not see
these options

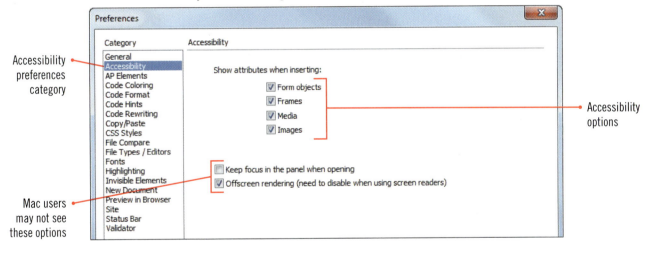

Design Matters

Providing for accessibility with alternate text

The use of alternate text is the first checkpoint listed in the Web content Accessibility Guidelines (WCAG), Version 2.0, from the World Wide Web Consortium (W3C). It states that a Web site should "provide text alternatives for any non-text content so that it can be changed into other forms people need, such as large print, Braille, speech, symbols, or simpler language." To view the complete set of accessibility guidelines, go to the Web Accessibility Initiative page

(www.w3.org/WAI). A general rule is that if you need to enter more than 50 characters of alternate text, you should create a separate file with the information you want to convey. Enter the location of the file in the Long Description text box that appears under the Alternate Text text box in the Image Tag Accessibility Attributes dialog box that opens when you insert a new image.

Viewing the Assets Panel

As you have learned, the **Assets panel** displays all of the assets in a Web site. It is important to understand how the Assets panel organizes your assets so you can quickly identify and locate the various assets in your site. There are nine categories of assets, each represented by a button on the Assets panel: Images, Colors, URLs, SWF, Shockwave, Movies, Scripts, Templates, and Library. There are two options for viewing the assets in each category. You can click the Site option button to view all the assets in a Web site, or the Favorites option button to view those assets that you have designated as **favorites**—assets that you expect to use repeatedly while you work on the site. For more information about this topic see the *Using favorites in the Assets panel* Clues to Use box in this lesson. You can also use the Assets panel to insert images on your page by either dragging an asset to the page, or by selecting the image and clicking the Insert button. So far, your Web site includes several images and colors. You explore the Assets panel to understand how Dreamweaver organizes the image files and keeps track of the colors used in the site.

STEPS

QUICK TIP

Make sure that the page you have open is in the current Web site. If you open a page outside the current Web site, the Assets panel will not display the assets associated with the open page.

1. **Click the Assets tab in the Files Tab group, if necessary**

   The first time you use the Assets panel, it displays the Images category; after that, it displays the category that was selected during the last Dreamweaver session.

QUICK TIP

You can click the column headings in the Assets panel to sort the files by Name, Dimensions, Size, Type, and Full Path.

2. **Click the Images button on the Assets panel, if necessary**

   Each time you click a category button, the contents in the Assets panel window change. Figure E-13 displays the Images category, and lists the four images in the Web site. Remember to click the Refresh button if you don't see all of your assets listed.

TROUBLE

If you see another color listed, click the Refresh button to remove it.

3. **Click the Colors button to display the Colors category**

   Three colors are listed in the Web site, as shown in Figure E-14. They are black, blue, and white. The black and blue colors are used for formatting text and are located in the external style sheet. The white color formats the page background color and is in an embedded style sheet. The Type column shows that each color is listed as Websafe. You learned about Websafe colors in Unit C.

Using the terms *graphics* and *images*

In discussing Web pages, people often use the terms *graphics* and *images*. This text uses the term *graphics* to refer to most non-text items on a Web page, including photographs, logos, menu bars, Flash animations, graphs, background images, and illustrations. Any of these can be called a "graphic" or a "**graphic file**." *Images* is a narrower term, referring to pictures or photographs. Image files are referred to by their file type, or file format, such as **JPEG** (Joint

Photographic Experts Group), **GIF** (Graphics Interchange Format), or **PNG** (Portable Network Graphics). See Table E-2 for descriptions for each of these formats. This text refers to the pictures that you see on the pages as "images." But don't worry too much about which term to use; many people use one term or the other according to habit, region, or type of business, or use them interchangeably.

FIGURE E-13: Assets panel showing Images category

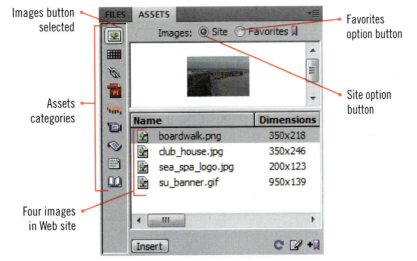

Images button selected

Assets categories

Four images in Web site

Favorites option button

Site option button

FIGURE E-14: Assets panel showing Colors category

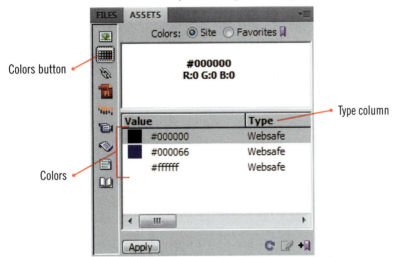

Colors button

Colors

Type column

Using Favorites in the Assets panel

For assets such as images that you plan to use repeatedly, you can place them in the Favorites list in the Assets panel to make them readily available. There are a few ways to add favorites to the Favorites list in the Assets panel. You can right-click (Win) or [ctrl]-click (Mac) an image in Design view, then click Add to Image Favorites. When you subsequently click the Favorites option button in the Assets panel, the image will display in the list. You can also right-click (Win) or [ctrl]-click (Mac) the name of an image in the Site list (when the Site option is selected in the Assets panel), then click

Add to Favorites. In addition, you can create a folder for storing assets by category by clicking the Favorites option in the Assets panel, clicking the Files panel options list arrow on the Files panel group, then clicking New Favorites Folder. You can give the folder a descriptive name, then drag assets from the Favorites list to move them to this folder. You can create nicknames for assets in the Favorites list by right-clicking (Win) or [ctrl]-clicking (Mac) the asset in the Favorites list, then clicking Edit Nickname.

Inserting a Background Image

Although you may consider them too plain, standard white backgrounds are usually the best choice for Web pages. Some pages, however, look best when they utilize background images. **Background images** are image files used in place of background colors to provide a depth and visual interest that a one-dimensional background color can't provide. Background images can create a dramatic effect; however, they may also be too distracting on an already full Web page. You should use either a background color or a background image, but not both on the same page, unless you need a background color to appear while the background image finishes downloading. If you choose to use a background image, select one that is small in file size so the page will download quickly. A **tiled image** is a small image that repeats itself across and down a Web page, appearing as individual squares or rectangles. A **seamless image** is a type of tiled image that is either blurred at the edges so that it appears to be all one image, or made from a pattern that, when tiled, appears to be one image, such as a vertical stripe.  You are pleased with the current white background color of the about_us page, but want to experiment with background images as well.

STEPS

1. **Click Modify on the Application bar (Win) or Menu bar (Mac), then click Page Properties**

   The Page Properties dialog box opens where you can add a background image from a Web page by adding a link to the background image filename.

2. **Click Browse next to the Background image text box, navigate to the drive and folder where you store your Unit E Data Files if necessary, double-click the assets folder, double-click umbrella_back.gif, then click OK**

   The file is copied to the assets folder in The Striped Umbrella Web site. A tiled background image with an umbrella repeating across the page replaces the white background on the about_us page. Since the umbrellas form distinctive squares, as shown in Figure E-15, it is easy to tell where one stops and the next starts. Although the theme of this background image fits perfectly, the text is hard to read against this busy background.

3. **Click Modify on the Application bar (Win) or Menu bar (Mac), click Page Properties, click Browse next to the Background image text box, navigate to the drive and folder where you store your Unit E Data Files if necessary, double-click stripes_back.gif from the assets folder, then click OK**

   The file is copied to the assets folder in The Striped Umbrella Web site. The umbrella background images are replaced with seamless ones containing multi-colored vertical stripes. Although the image is still technically a square, since the stripes run vertically and are parallel across the page, it is hard to tell where one image stops and the next begins. See Figure E-16.

4. **Click Modify on the Application bar (Win) or Menu bar (Mac), then click Page Properties**

   You remove a background image from a Web page by removing the background image filename in the Page Properties dialog box.

5. **Highlight the information in the Background image text box, press [Delete], click OK to close the Page Properties dialog box, then save your work**

   The about_us page background returns to white.

FIGURE E-15: about_us page with a tiled background

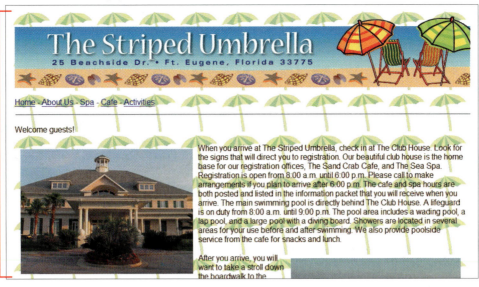

Tiled
background
with individual
square images
of umbrellas

FIGURE E-16: about_us page with a seamless background

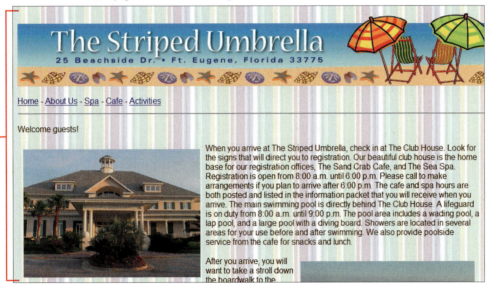

Seamless
background
with individual
square images
of vertical
stripes

Integrating Photoshop and Fireworks with Dreamweaver CS5

Dreamweaver has many functions integrated with Photoshop CS5. For example, you can copy and paste images directly from Photoshop into Dreamweaver. Dreamweaver will prompt you to optimize the image by choosing a file format and settings for using the image in a Web browser. Then it will paste the image on the page. If you want to edit the image later, select the image, then click the Edit button in the Property inspector to open the image in Photoshop. (The appearance of the Edit button will change according to the default image editor you have specified.) When you edit an image in Photoshop, you can export an updated Smart Object instantly. **Smart Objects** are layers with image source information that allow an image to be modified nondestructively without losing the original data. Photoshop users can set Photoshop as the default image editor in Dreamweaver for specific image file formats. Click Edit on the Application bar, click Preferences (Win), or click Dreamweaver, click Preferences (Mac), click File Types/Editors, click the Extensions plus sign button, select a file format from the list, click the Editors plus sign button, use the Select External Editor dialog box to browse to Photoshop (if you don't see it listed already), then click Make Primary. Search the Adobe Web site (www.adobe.com) for a tutorial on Photoshop and Dreamweaver integration. Fireworks is another commonly used default image editor. Use the same steps to select it rather than Photoshop.

Deleting Image Files from a Web Site

As you work on a Web site, it is very common to accumulate files that are never used on any page in the site. One way to avoid accumulating unnecessary files is to look at an image first, before you copy it to the default images folder. If the file has already been copied to the default images folder, however, you should delete it (or at least move it to another location) to ensure that the Assets panel only lists the assets actually used in the Web site. This practice is considered good Web site management. To delete a file from the Assets panel, you can access the Locate in Site command, which is useful if you have a large number of images to search. If you just have a single file to delete, you can use the Delete command in the Files panel. Since you decided not to use the two background images on the about_us page, you want to delete them from the assets folder.

STEPS

> **QUICK TIP**
> C will not appear on the Assets panel when the Favorites option is selected.

1. **Display the Assets panel if necessary, click the Images button** **on the Assets panel, verify that the Site option is selected, then click the Refresh button** C **on the Assets panel**

   The two background files remain in the Images list on the Assets panel. Even though you have deleted them from the page, you have not yet deleted them from the Web site assets folder.

> **TROUBLE**
> If the file is not listed, click C.

2. **Right-click (Win) or [ctrl]-click (Mac) stripes_back.gif in the Assets panel, then click Locate in Site, as shown in Figure E-17**

   The Files panel opens with the stripes_back.gif file selected.

> **TROUBLE**
> If your stripes_back.gif file is not selected, select it.

3. **Press [Delete] to delete the file, then click Yes in the confirmation dialog box**

   The stripes-back.gif file is no longer listed in the Assets panel because it has been deleted from the Web site.

4. **Select the file umbrella_back.gif in the Files panel, then press [Delete]**

   Because you deleted the file from the Web site assets folder, it no longer appears in the Files panel.

5. **Save your work, then preview your file in your browser**

   Your about_us page is presently completed and should resemble Figure E-18.

6. **Close the page, then Exit (Win) or Quit (Mac) Dreamweaver**

Inserting files with Adobe Bridge

You can manage project files, including video and Camera Raw files, with a file management tool called Adobe Bridge that is included with Dreamweaver. Bridge provides an easy way to view files outside the Web site before bringing them into the Web site. It is an integrated application, working with other Adobe programs, such as Photoshop and Illustrator. You can also use Bridge to add meta tags and search text in your files. To open Bridge, click the Browse in Bridge command on the File menu or click the Browse in Bridge button on the Standard toolbar.

FIGURE E-17: Using the Assets panel to locate a file in a site

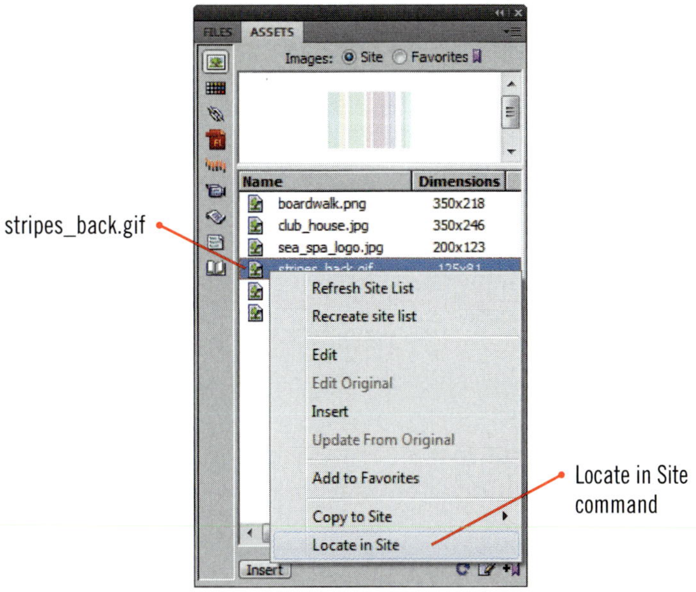

stripes_back.gif

Locate in Site command

FIGURE E-18: The finished page

Design Matters

Image file management

It is a good idea to have an additional storage location for your image files in addition to the Web site's assets folder. Keep all original image files outside the Web site and save them once with their original settings. As you edit them, save them using a different name.

This way, you will always be able to find the original file before it is resized or edited. You may also have files you don't want to use now but may need later. Store them outside your Web site to keep them from cluttering up the assets folder.

Creating and Finding Images for a Web Site

There are several resources for locating high-quality images for a Web site. You can create images from scratch using an image editing or drawing program, such as Fireworks, Illustrator, or Photoshop, or use original photographs for colorful, rich images. You can also purchase images as clip art collections. **Clip art collections** are groups of image files collected on CDs and sold with an **index**, or directory, of the files. The Internet, of course, is a great source for finding images. Stock photos are collections of photos on Web sites that are available to use by either paying a single fee per photo or a subscription fee for downloading multiple images. Table E-2 describes three image types that can be used on Web pages. Now that you understand how to incorporate images into The Striped Umbrella Web site, you explore the advantages and disadvantages of the different ways to accumulate images.

DETAILS

- ### Original images

  Programs such as Fireworks and Photoshop give you the ability to create and modify original artwork. These image editing programs have numerous features for manipulating images. For example, you can adjust the color, brightness, or size of an image. You can also set a transparent background for an image. **Transparent backgrounds** contain transparent pixels, rather than pixels with color, resulting in images that blend easily on a Web page background. Only certain file types can be used to create transparent images, such as gifs and pngs. Figure E-19 shows an example of an image with a colored background, while Figure E-20 has a similar image with a transparent background placed on top of another image. Illustrator is a drawing program that is used to create original vector graphics, which can then be converted to a usable format for Web publication, such as jpg, gif, or png files.

- ### Original photography

  High-quality photographs can greatly enhance a Web site. Fortunately, digital cameras and scanners have made this venture much easier than in the past. Once you scan a photograph or shoot it with a digital camera, you can further enhance it using an image editing software program, such as Photoshop or Fireworks. Photographs taken with digital cameras often have large file sizes, so be sure to create resized copies using an image editing program such as Photoshop before placing them on Web pages. If you don't have Photoshop or another image editor, many digital cameras come with their own basic software that you can use to resize and enhance images.

- ### Clip art collections

  Clip art collections are available from computer software retailers, office supply stores, and over the Internet. Not all clip art is **royalty-free**, however—that is, free for the purchaser to copy and publish without restrictions—so be sure to read the terms of the copyright statement in the user's manual. The company which distributed the clip art collection may charge a fee when its images are used for certain purposes, such as in advertisements.

- ### The Internet

  There are many Web sites from which you are able to copy images, but look carefully for copyright statements regarding the legal use of images. Stock photos sites, such as iStockphoto, are excellent resources used by many professional designers. To use these sites, you first sign up to become a member, then you either purchase images as you need them, or purchase a subscription, which allows you to pay a set price for the number of files you expect to download each year. There are many collections of images online that are free, but some sites require that you credit them on your Web site with either a simple statement or a link to their Web site. Images that are labeled as public domain are free to use without restrictions. Figure E-21 is an example of a source for public domain images. If you are uncertain about whether you may use an image you find on a Web site, it's best to either contact the site's owner or find another image to use. *If you copy and paste images you find while accessing other Web sites and use them for your own purposes, you may be violating copyright laws.*

FIGURE E-19: Image with colored background

FIGURE E-20: Image with transparent background

Images with transparent backgrounds can be placed on top of other images

FIGURE E-21: Example of a Web site with public domain images

TABLE E-2: Common graphic file formats for Web page images

format (file extension)	stands for	details
.jpg, .jpeg	Joint Photographic Experts Group	Pixel-based; a Web standard. Can set image quality in pixels per inch (ppi), which affects file size. Supports millions of colors. Use for full-color images, such as photographs or those with life-like artwork.
.png	Portable Network Graphics	Can be compressed for storage and quicker download, without loss of picture quality. Supports variable levels of transparency and control of image brightness on different computers. Used for small graphics, such as bullets and banners, as well as for complex photographic images.
.gif	Graphics Interchange Format	Limited to 256 colors. Low color quality and limited detail are not suitable for printing. Small file size means faster transmission. Suitable for images with only a few colors, such as cartoons, simple illustrations, icons, buttons, and horizontal rules. This format is used for transparent images.

Examine Copyright Rules

The Internet has made it possible to locate compelling and media-rich content to use on Web sites. But just because you find content does not mean that you can use it however you want or under any circumstance. Learning about copyright law can help you decide whether and how to use content created and published by someone other than yourself. Before you decide whether to use media you find on a Web site, you must decide whether you can comply with its licensing agreement. A **licensing agreement** is the permission given by a copyright holder that conveys the right to use the copyright holder's work under certain conditions. Web sites have rules that govern how a user may use its content, known as **terms of use**. Figures E-22 and E-23 are good examples of clear terms of use for the Library of Congress Web site. You decide to do some research on copyright law in relation to downloaded content from the Internet. There are several concepts to understand.

DETAILS

- **Intellectual property**

  Intellectual property is a product resulting from human creativity. It can include inventions, movies, songs, designs, clothing, and so on. The purpose of copyright law is to promote progress in society—not expressly to protect the rights of copyright owners. However, you should always assume that the majority of work you might want to download and use in a project is protected by either copyright or trademark law.

- **Copyright**

  A **copyright** protects the particular and tangible expression of an idea, not the idea itself. If you wrote a story about aliens crashing in Roswell, New Mexico, no one could copy or use your specific story without permission. However, anyone could write a story using a similar plot or characters—the actual idea is not copyright-protected. Generally, copyright protection in the United States lasts for the life of the author plus 70 years (most countries have similar regulations). A copyright attaches to a work as soon as it is created; you do not have to register it with the U.S. Copyright Office.

- **Trademark**

  A **trademark** protects an image, word, slogan, symbol, or design used to identify goods or services. For example, the Nike swoosh and the Google logo are images protected by trademark. Trademark protection lasts for 10 years, with 10-year renewal terms; it can last indefinitely provided the trademark is in active use.

- **Fair use**

  The law builds in limitations to copyright protection. One limitation to copyright is fair use. **Fair use** allows limited use of copyright-protected work. For example, you could excerpt short passages of a film or song for a class project. Determining if fair use applies to a work depends on the purpose of its use, the nature of the copyrighted work, how much you want to copy, and the effect on the market or value of the work. There is no clear formula on what constitutes fair use. It is always decided by the courts on a case-by-case basis. Except in cases of fair use, you must obtain permission from the copyright holder to use the work.

- **Derivative work**

  A **derivative work** is a work based on another pre-existing work, such as a movie adaptation of a book or a new musical arrangement of an existing song. Derivative works are included in the six rights of a copyright owner: reproduction (including downloading), creation of derivative works, distribution to the public, public performance, public display, and public performance by digital audio transmission of sound recordings. By default, only a copyright holder can create a derivative work of his or her original work.

- **Public domain**

  Work that is not protected by copyright is said to be in the public domain. Anyone can use it however they wish for any purpose, free of charge. In general, photos and other media on federal government Web sites are in the public domain. Web sites will often state if their images or other content are in the public domain. However, even if the Web site name includes the phrase "public domain," it does not necessarily mean that all content on that site is in the public domain. It is better to err on the side of caution than to risk violating copyright laws.

FIGURE E-22: Example of a Web site with a terms of use policy

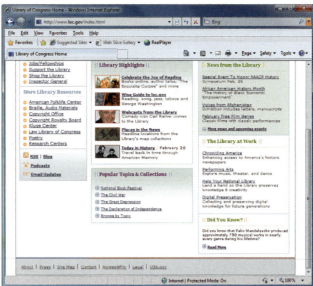

FIGURE E-23: Library of Congress terms of use policy

Using proper methods to cite content

The familiar © symbol (or the word *Copyright*) is no longer required to indicate copyrighted materials, nor does it automatically register your work, but it does serve a useful purpose. When you post or publish the copyright term or symbol, you are stating clearly to those who may not know anything about copyright law that this work is claimed by you and is not in the public domain. If someone violates your copyright, your case is made even stronger if your notice is clearly visible. That way, violators can never claim ignorance of the law as an excuse for infringing. Common notification styles include using the word *Copyright* with the year, as in "Copyright 2013, Course Technology," or by using the copyright symbol ©, as in "© 2013 Course Technology."

You must provide proper citation for materials you incorporate into your own work. The following source was used for this lesson content and is referenced as follows:

• Waxer, Barbara M., and Baum, Marsha L. 2006. *Internet Surf and Turf – The Essential Guide to Copyright, Fair Use, and Finding Media*. Boston: Thomson Course Technology.

In addition to words that you quote verbatim, copyrights apply to ideas that you summarize or paraphrase. One prominent set of guidelines for how to cite material found in print or on the Web (including text, images, sound, video, blogs, email and text messages, and so forth) is produced by the American Psychological Association (APA). To view these guidelines in detail, go to the APA Web site at www.apastyle.org. Other widely used guidelines are available from the Modern Language Association (www.mla.org) and the Chicago Manual of Style (www.chicagomanualofstyle.org).

Practice

Concepts Review

For current SAM information, including versions and content details, visit SAM Central (http://www.cengage.com/samcentral). If you have a SAM user profile, you may have access to hands-on instruction, practice, and assessment of the skills covered in this unit. Since various versions of SAM are supported throughout the life of this text, check with your instructor for the correct instructions and URL/Web site for accessing assignments.

Label each element shown in Figure E-24.

FIGURE E-24

1. _____
2. _____
3. _____
4. _____
5. _____
6. _____
7. _____
8. _____

Match each of the following terms with the statement that best describes it.

 9. **Assets panel**
10. **JPEG**
11. **Aligning an image**
12. **Background image**
13. **Favorites list**
14. **Refresh button**
15. **Tiled image**
16. **Seamless image**
17. **Alternate text**
18. **Border**

a. Positioning an image on a page
b. Updates the current list of assets in the Assets panel
c. Includes only those assets designated as Favorites
d. Small image that repeats across and down a Web page
e. Used in place of a background color
f. Used by screen readers to describe an image
g. A frame placed around an image
h. An image file format
i. Small background image that is tiled, but appears to be one image
j. Lists all the assets of the Web site, including favorites

Select the best answer from the list of choices.

19. **The following category is not found on the Assets panel:**
    a. URLs
    b. Colors
    c. Tables
    d. Movies

20. **When you no longer need files in a Web site, you should:**
    a. leave them in the Assets panel.
    b. drag them off the Web page to the Recycle bin.
    c. place them in the Site list.
    d. delete them from the Web site.

21. **Background images:**
    a. are never appropriate.
    b. are always appropriate.
    c. cannot be tiled.
    d. can be seamless.

22. **Tiled background images generally:**
    a. can be seamless.
    b. appear as many small squares on a Web page.
    c. appear as many rows across a Web page.
    d. all of the above.

Skills Review

Important: *If you did not create this Web site in Unit B and maintain it during the preceding units, you will need to create a root folder for this Web site and define the Web site using files your instructor will provide. See the "Read This Before You Begin" section in this book for more detailed instructions.*

1. **Insert an image.**
   a. Start Dreamweaver.
   b. Open the Blooms & Bulbs Web site.
   c. Open dwe_2.html from the drive and folder where you store your Unit E Data Files, then save it as **plants.html** in the Blooms & Bulbs Web site, overwriting the existing plants.html file but not updating the links.
   d. Close dwe_2.html.
   e. Insert the rose_bud.jpg file from the assets folder in the drive and folder where you store your Unit E Data Files, in front of the words *Who can resist....* (Enter alternate text, if prompted.)
   f. Insert the rose_bloom.jpg file in front of the words *For ease of growing....* (Enter alternate text, if prompted.)
   g. Insert the two_roses.jpg file in front of the words *The Candy Cane....* (Enter alternate text, if prompted.)
   h. Attach the blooms_styles.css file to the plants page.
   i. Apply the body_text style to all of the paragraph text on the page.
   j. Apply the HTML heading 3 format to the text *Featured Spring Plant: Roses!*
   k. Save your work.

2. **Align an image.**
   a. Select rose_bud.jpg, then use the Property inspector to left-align the image.
   b. Right-align the rose_bloom.jpg image and left-align the two_roses.jpg image.
   c. Save your work.

3. **Enhance an image.**
   a. Select rose_bud.jpg and apply a 1 pixel border to it.
   b. Add a 1 pixel border to the rose_bloom.jpg image and the two_roses.jpg image.
   c. Add vertical spacing of 10 pixels and horizontal spacing of 20 pixels around each image.
   d. Save your work.

4. **Use alternate text.**
   a. If you did not add alternate text in Step 1 above, select the rose_bud.jpg image, then use the Property inspector to enter **Rose bud on bird bath** as alternate text.
   b. If necessary, add the alternate text **Rose bloom** for the rose_bloom.jpg image, and **Candy Cane Floribunda** for the two_roses.jpg image.
   c. If necessary, edit the Web site preferences to set the Accessibility prompt for images.
   d. Save your work.

Skills Review (continued)

5. View the Assets panel.

a. Display the Assets panel, if necessary.

b. View the Images list to verify that there are five images in the list. Refresh the Images list, if necessary.

c. View the Colors list to verify that there are three Web-safe colors.

6. Insert a background image.

a. Use Page Properties to insert the daisies.jpg file as a background image and refresh the Assets panel. (This file is in the assets folder in the drive and folder where you store your Unit E Data Files.)

b. Save the page, then view it in your browser.

c. Close the browser window.

d. Remove the daisies.jpg image from the background, then save the file.

7. Delete image files from a Web site.

a. Delete the daisies.jpg file from the Files panel.

b. Refresh the Files panel and verify that the daisies.jpg file has been removed from the Web site. (You may have to refresh the Site list first.)

c. Preview the page in the browser, compare your users with Figure E-25, and close the browser. (Your text may wrap differently.)

d. Close the page, Exit (Win) or Quit (Mac) Dreamweaver.

FIGURE E-25

Blooms & Bulbs
HWY 43 SOUTH • ALVIN • TX 77511 • 555-248-0806

Featured Spring Plant: Roses!

Who can resist the romance of roses? Poets have waxed poetically over them throughout the years. Many persons consider the beauty and fragrance of roses to be unmatched in nature. The varieties are endless, ranging from floribunda to hybrid teas to shrub roses to climbing roses. Each variety has its own personality and preference in the garden setting. Pictured on the left is a Summer Breeze Hybrid Tea bud. This variety is fast growing and produces spectacular blooms that are beautiful as cut flowers in arrangements. The enchanting fragrance will fill your home with summer sweetness. They require full sun. Hybrid teas need regular spraying and pruning, but will reward you with classic blooms that will be a focal point in your landscaping and provide you with beautiful arrangements in your home. They are well worth the effort!

For ease of growing, Knock Out® roses are some of our all-time favorites. Even beginners will not fail with these garden delights. They are shrub roses and prefer full sun, but can take partial shade. They are disease resistant and drought tolerant. You do not have to be concerned with either black spot or dead-heading with roses such as the Knock out®, making them an extremely low-maintenance plant. They are also repeat bloomers, blooming into late fall. The shrub can grow quite large, but can be pruned to any size. The one you see on the right is Southern Belle. Check out all our varieties as you will not fail to have great color with these plants.

The Candy Cane Floribunda shown on the left is a beautiful rose with cream, pink, and red stripes and swirls. They have a heavy scent that will remind you of the roses you received on your most special occasions. These blooms are approximately four inches in diameter. They bloom continuously from early summer to early fall. The plants grow up to four feet tall and three feet wide. They are shipped bare root in February.

Important: *If you did not create the following Web sites in Unit B and maintain them during the preceding units, you will need to create a root folder for the Web sites in the following exercises and define the Web sites using files your instructor will provide. See the "Read This Before You Begin" section for more detailed instructions.*

Independent Challenge 1

You have been hired to create a Web site for a river expedition company named Rapids Transit, located on the Buffalo River in Arkansas. In addition to renting canoes, kayaks, and rafts, they have lodging for overnight stays. River guides are available, if requested, to accompany clients on float trips. The clients range from experienced floaters to beginners. The owner's name is Mike Andrew. Mike has asked you to develop the page that introduces the Rapids Transit guides available for float trips. Refer to Figure E-26 as you work on this page.

a. Start Dreamweaver and open the Rapids Transit Web site.

b. Open dwe_3.html from the drive and folder where you store your Unit E Data Files and save it in the Rapids Transit Web site as **guides.html**, overwriting the existing file but not updating links.

c. Close dwe_3.html.

d. Check the path for the Rapids Transit banner and reset the path to the assets folder for the Web site, if necessary.

e. Verify that the Rapids Transit banner has alternate text. If it doesn't, add it.

f. Insert the image buster_tricks.jpg at an appropriate place on the page. (This file is in the assets folder in the drive and folder where you store your Unit E Data Files.)

g. Create alternate text for the buster_tricks.jpg image, add a border to the image, then left-align it.

h. Crop the image as shown in Figure E-26 and add some horizontal and vertical space around the image.

i. Format the text on the page appropriately by attaching the rapids_transit.css style sheet and applying the body_text style to the paragraph text.

j. Save your work, preview the page in the browser, then compare your workspace to Figure E-26. (Your image location, border size, and vertical and horizontal space settings may differ.)

k. Close the browser and Exit (Win) or Quit (Mac) Dreamweaver.

FIGURE E-26

Home — River Guides — Rates — Lodging — Before You Go

We have four of the best river guides you will ever find — Buster, Tucker, Max, and Scarlett. Buster has been with us for fourteen years and was born and raised here on the river. Tucker joined us two years ago "from off" (somewhere up north), but we've managed to make a country boy out of him! Max and Scarlett are actually distant cousins and joined us after they graduated from college last year. They're never happier than when they're out on the water floating and fishing. Each of our guides will show you a great time on the river.

Our guides will pack your supplies, shuttle you to the put-in point, maneuver the raging rapids for you, and then make sure someone is waiting at the take-out point to shuttle you back to the store. They haven't lost a customer yet! Give us a call and we'll set up a date with any of these good people. Here's a photo of Buster showing off his stuff. The river is always faster and higher in the spring. If you want to take it a little slower, come visit us in the summer or fall. Leave your good camera at home, though, no matter what the time of the year. You may get wet! Life jackets are provided and we require that you wear them while on the water. Safety is always our prime concern.

Independent Challenge 2

Your company is designing a new Web site for TripSmart, a travel outfitter. TripSmart specializes in travel products and services. In addition to selling travel products, such as luggage and accessories, they sponsor trips and offer travel advice. Their clients range from college students to families and vacationing professionals. You are now ready to work on the destinations page. Refer to Figure E-27 as you work through the following steps.

a. Start Dreamweaver and open the TripSmart Web site.

b. Open dwe_4.html from the drive and folder where you store your Unit E Data Files and save it in the TripSmart Web site as **tours.html**, overwriting the existing tours file but not updating links.

c. Close dwe_4.html.

d. Check the path for the TripSmart banner and reset the path to the assets folder for the Web site, if necessary.

e. Attach the tripsmart_styles.css file to the page, then apply the HTML heading 2 format to the Destination: Spain heading and the body_text style to the rest of the text on the page. (*Hint*: You probably formatted your styles differently from the example, so your text may look different than Figure E-27.)

f. Change the Web site preferences to prompt you to add alternate text as you add new images to the Web site, if necessary.

g. Insert the images bull_fighter.jpg and stallion.jpg at the appropriate places on the page, adding alternate text for each image. (These files are in the assets folder in the drive and folder where you store your Unit E Data Files.)

h. Add a border to each image, then choose an alignment setting for each one.

i. Add the page title **Destination: Spain**, then add appropriate horizontal and vertical spacing around both images.

j. Save your work, preview the page in the browser, then compare your page to Figure E-27 for one possible design solution.

k. Close the browser and Exit (Win) or Quit (Mac) Dreamweaver.

FIGURE E-27

Destination: Spain

Our next trip to Spain has now been scheduled with a departure date of May 5 and a return date of May 23. This deluxe tour begins in Madrid and ends in the beautiful city of Barcelona. Come join us and enjoy some of Spain's greatest treasures. In addition to ancient cathedrals and magnificent vistas, we will see such sights as the remote town of Ronda, the location of the oldest bullring in Spain. Ronda is perched on a 300-foot gorge of El Tajo. Private coach transportation will be arranged for you to visit Ronda as you are en route from Granada to Seville.

We will also visit Jerez de la Frontera, the home of the Royal Andalusian School of Equestrian Art where you will experience a stunning performance by the "dancing stallions." These magnificent stallions seem to defy gravity as they perform to Spanish classical music. After the performance we will visit a bodega for a tour and sherry tasting, then enjoy dinner in one of Jerez's finest restaurants. Other itinerary stops include Toledo and Cordoba.

To provide the finest in personal attention, this tour will be limited to no more than sixteen persons. The price schedule is as follows: Land Tour and Supplemental Group Air, $5,500.00; International Air, $1,350.00; and Single Supplement, $1,000.00. Entrance fees, hotel taxes, and services are included in the Land Tour price. A deposit of $500.00 is required at the time the booking is made. Trip insurance and luggage insurance are optional and are also offered for an extra charge. A passport and visa will be required for entry into Spain. Call us at 555-848-0807 for further information and the complete itinerary from 8:00 a.m. to 6:00 p.m. (Central Standard Time).

d Independent Challenge 3

Donna Wasson raises and shows horses professionally. She is learning how to use Dreamweaver to be able to create a Web site to showcase her horses. She would like to look at some other Web sites about horses to get a feel for the types of images she may want to use in her site. Use a word processor or paper to answer the questions below.

a. Connect to the Internet and go to USHorse.biz (www.ushorse.biz), as shown in Figure E-28.

b. How are background colors used? Would you have selected different ones? Why, or why not?

c. Evaluate the images used in the Web site. Do they add interest to the pages, or are they distracting? Was alternate text used for any or all of the images?

d. How long did the home page take to download on your computer? In your opinion, was it too slow?

e. Are there too few images, too many, or just enough to add interest?

f. Go to Google (www.google.com) or Yahoo! (www.yahoo.com) to find another horse Web site.

g. Compare the site you found to the USHorse.biz site by answering questions b through e above.

FIGURE E-28

USHorse.biz Web site used with permission from www.USHorse.biz

Real Life Independent Challenge

This assignment will continue to build on the personal Web site that you created in Unit B. You have created and developed your index page. You have also added a page with either an ordered or an unordered list, and a CSS Style Sheet with a minimum of two styles. In this lesson, you work with one of the other pages of your Web site.

a. Consult your storyboard and decide which page you would like to develop in this lesson.

b. Create content for this page and format the text attractively on the page using styles for all formatting.

c. Set the Accessibility option to prompt you for alternate text for new images added to the Web site, if necessary.

d. Add at least two images with appropriate alternate text. Resize the images in an image-editing program if they are too large to place on the Web page.

e. Align and enhance the images to place them attractively on the page.

f. Document the source for the images and print some proof that they are in the public domain. Use your own photographs or drawings if you have difficulty obtaining public domain images.

g. Document the estimated download time for the page and the setting you used to estimate download time.

h. Save the file and preview the page in a browser.

After you are satisfied with your work, verify the following:

a. Each completed page has a page title.

b. All links work correctly.

c. The completed pages show well using a screen resolution of 1024 × 768.

d. All images are properly set showing a path to the assets folder of the Web site.

e. All images have alternate text and are legal to use.

Visual Workshop

Your company has been selected to design a Web site for Carolyne's Creations, a small catering business. Open your Carolyne's Creations Web site. Chef Carolyne has asked you to create a page that displays featured items in the kitchen shop. Open dwe_5.html from the drive and folder where your Unit E Data Files are stored. Save the file as **shop.html** in the Carolyne's Creations Web site, then add the paella_pan.jpg image from the drive and folder where you store your Unit E Data Files to create the page shown in Figure E-29. (*Hint*: You will need to attach the cc_styles.css style sheet to the page.) Apply the HTML heading 3 format to the menu bar, the body_text style to the paragraphs, and the headings style to the heading "January Special: Paella Pans". Add horizontal space and a border to the paella_pan image.

FIGURE E-29

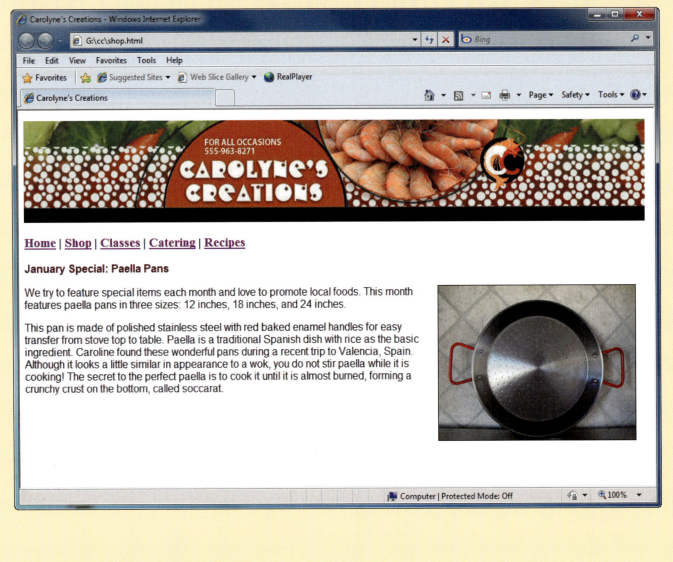

Creating Links and Menu Bars

As you learned in Unit C, links are the real strength of a Web site, because they give users the freedom to open various Web pages as they choose. You created a menu bar using a group of text links that helps users to navigate between pages of a Web site. In this unit, you will learn how to create a Spry menu bar and another type of link called an image map. A **Spry menu bar** is one of the preset widgets in Dreamweaver that creates a dynamic, user-friendly menu bar. A **widget** is a piece of code that allows users to interact with the program interface. An **image map** is an image with clickable areas defined on it that, when clicked, serve as links to take the user to another location. You begin working on the link structure for The Striped Umbrella Web site. You add links to area attractions on the activities page, create a menu bar that will be used on all pages in the Web site, create an image map, and run some site management reports.

OBJECTIVES

Understand links and paths

Create an external link

Create an internal link

Insert a named anchor

Create internal links to named anchors

Create a Spry menu bar

Add menu bar items

Format a menu bar

Copy a menu bar to other pages

Create an image map

Manage Web site links

Understanding Links and Paths

You can use two types of links on Web pages. **Internal links** are links to Web pages within the same Web site, and **external links** are links that connect to pages in other Web sites or to e-mail addresses. Internal and external links both have two important parts that work together. The first part of a link is what the user actually sees and clicks, such as a word, an image, or a button. The second part of a link is the **path**, which is the name and physical location of the Web page file that opens when the link is clicked. A link is classified as internal or external based on the information in its path. External paths reference links with a complete Web address, while internal paths reference links with a partial address, based on the relation of the destination page to the page with the link. A link that returns an error message, or a **broken link**, occurs when files are renamed or deleted from a Web site, the filename is misspelled, or the Web site is experiencing technical problems. You spend some time studying the various types of paths used for internal and external links.

DETAILS

- ### Absolute paths

  Absolute paths are used with external links. They reference links on Web pages outside the current Web site, and include **"http"** (hypertext transfer protocol) and the **URL** (Uniform Resource Locator), or address, of the Web page. When necessary, the Web page filename and the folder hierarchy are also part of an absolute path. Figure F-1 shows an example of an absolute path.

- ### Relative paths

  Relative paths are used with internal links. They reference Web pages and graphic files within one Web site and include the filename and the folder hierarchy where the file resides. Figure F-2 shows an example of a relative path. Relative paths are further classified as root-relative (relative to the root folder) and document-relative (relative to the current document).

- ### Root-relative paths

  Root-relative paths are referenced from a Web site's root folder. As shown in Figure F-3, a root-relative path begins with a forward slash, which represents the Web site's root folder. This method is used when several Web sites are published to one server, or when a Web site is so large that it uses more than one server.

- ### Document-relative paths

  Document-relative paths reference the path in relation to the Web page that appears, and do not begin with a slash. A document-relative path includes only a filename if the referenced file resides in the same folder as the current Web page. For example, index.html and spa.html both reside in the site root folder for The Striped Umbrella. So you would simply type spa.html to link to the spa page from the index page. However, when an image is referenced in the assets folder, since the assets folder is a subfolder of the site root folder, you must include the word assets/ (with the slash) in front of the filename, for example, assets/the_spa.jpg. See Figure F-4 for an example of a document-relative path.

  In the exercises in this book, you will use document-relative paths because it is assumed that you will not use more than one server to publish your Web sites. For this reason, it is very important to make sure that the Relative to text box in the Select File dialog box is set to Document, rather than Site Root, when creating links. This option can also be set in the Site Setup dialog box.

FIGURE F-1: An example of an absolute path

Hypertext transfer protocol

http://www.northark.edu/schedules.html

Web site URL   Filename

FIGURE F-2: An example of a relative path

images/banner.jpg

Folder name   Filename

FIGURE F-3: An example of a root-relative path

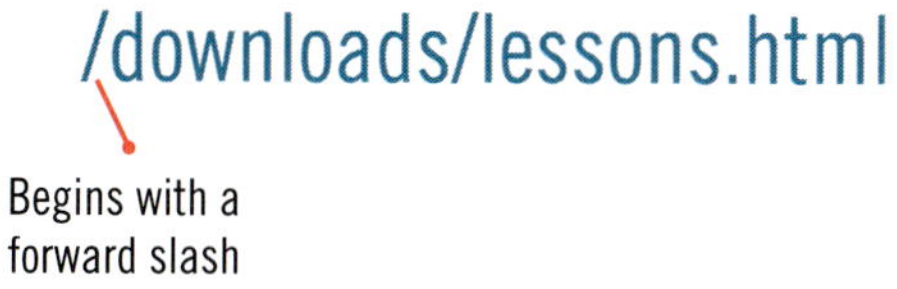

/downloads/lessons.html

Begins with a
forward slash

FIGURE F-4: An example of a document-relative path

downloads/lessons.html

Begins with either a folder
name or a filename

Creating an effective navigation structure

When you create a Web site, it's important to consider how your users will navigate from page to page within the site. A menu bar is a critical tool for moving around a site, so it's important that all text, buttons, or icons you use on a menu bar have a consistent look across all pages. If you use a complex menu bar, such as one that incorporates JavaScript or Flash, it's a good idea to include plain text links in another location on the page for accessibility. Otherwise, users might become confused or lost within the site.

A navigation structure can include more links than those included in a menu bar, however. For instance, it can contain other sets of links that relate to the content of specific pages. They can be placed at the bottom or sides of a page in a different format. No matter how you decide to design your navigation structure, make sure that every page includes a link back to the home page.

Creating an External Link

As you have learned, external links use absolute paths, which must include the complete name and path of the Web address to link to the destination Web page successfully. Because the World Wide Web is a constantly changing environment, you should check external links frequently. Web sites may be up one day and down the next. If a Web site changes server locations or shuts down because of technical difficulties, the links to it may become broken. An external link can also become broken when an Internet connection is not working properly. Broken links, like misspelled words on a Web page, indicate that the Web site is not being maintained diligently. Guests staying at The Striped Umbrella often ask for information about family activities in the surrounding area. Links to interesting attractions are helpful not only to currently registered guests, but to attract potential ones as well. You decide to create external links on the activities page that link to two Web sites for area attractions.

STEPS

1. Open The Striped Umbrella Web site, open dwf_1.html from the drive and folder where you store your Unit F Data Files, then save it as activities.html in the striped_umbrella site root folder, overwriting the existing file but not updating links

   The new activities page opens in Design view. The activities page describes two popular area attractions of interest to resort guests. There are two broken image placeholders that represent images that must be copied to the Web site.

2. Close dwf_1.html

   > **TROUBLE**
   > If you don't see the image in the data files folder, remember to browse to the Unit F Data Files assets folder to locate the heron_waiting_small.jpg image.

3. Select the leftmost broken image, click the Browse for File icon 📁 next to the Src text box in the Property inspector, select heron_waiting_small.jpg from the assets folder in the location where you store your Unit F Data Files, click OK to save the image in your assets folder, then click to the right of the placeholder

   The heron _waiting_small image is copied to the Web site and now appears on the page.

4. Select the rightmost broken image, then repeat Step 3 to place the second image, two_dolphins.jpg on the page

5. Attach the su_styles.css file, then apply the body_text style to the paragraphs of text on the page (not to the menu bar)

6. Scroll to the bottom of the page if necessary, then select the Blue Angels text in the second to the last paragraph on the page

   You use the Blue Angels text to create an external link to the Blue Angels Web site.

7. Click the Link text box in the HTML Property inspector, type http://www.blueangels.navy.mil, compare your screen to Figure F-5, then press [Tab]

   The Blue Angels text is now a link to the Blue Angels Web site.

   > **TROUBLE**
   > If your link does not work correctly, check for typing errors in the link path. If the link is typed correctly, the site may be down and you should remove the link until you can verify that it is working correctly.

8. Click File on the Application bar (Win) or Menu bar (Mac), click Save, click the Preview/Debug in browser button 🌐, click Preview in [your browser], click Blue Angels on the Web page, verify that the link works, then close your browser window

9. Scroll to the bottom of the page if necessary, select the USS Alabama text in the last paragraph on the page, then repeat Steps 7 and 8 to create the link for the USS Alabama text, using the URL http://www.ussalabama.com

We have many activities for you to choose from, here at the resort and in the surrounding area.

Some of our visitors enjoy local fishing trips. We have a small fleet of boats that will take you out for either a half or a full day. Or you can surf cast, right from the beach. But beware of Ralph, our resident blue heron. He knows what you fishermen have in your coolers and if you aren't careful, he'll take your catch off your hands and make a quick getaway!

And don't forget our dolphin cruises. We have a unique approach — two boats speed along, side by side, about 50 yards apart. The dolphins love it because it generates a huge wake. You'll see them jumping right between the boats! You can arrange for tickets for fishing excursions or dolphin cruises at The Club House desk.

Check out these links for kid-friendly attractions in the area:

The famous Blue Angels, the nation's oldest flying aerobatic team, are stationed at the

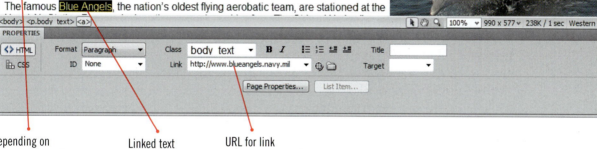

Depending on your window and screen settings, your text may wrap differently

Linked text

URL for link

Design Matters

Ensuring error-free URLs

It is easy to make mistakes when you type long and complex URLs. One way to minimize errors is to copy and paste the URL of the Web page that you would like to include as an external link in your Web site. To do this, open the Web page then copy the link information in the Address text box (Internet Explorer) or the Location bar (Mozilla Firefox). Next, select the link text on your Web page, then paste the link information in the Link text box in the HTML Property inspector.

Creating an Internal Link

As you know, a Web site usually contains individual pages for each category or major topic covered in the site. Within those pages, internal links are used to provide a way to move quickly from page to page. The home page should provide intuitive navigation to individual pages for each category or major topic covered in a Web site. A good rule of thumb is to design your Web site so that users are never more than three or four clicks away from the page they are seeking. Refer to your wireframe frequently as you create pages to help manage your site's navigation structure. 🔹 You want to create an easy way for users to access the fishing and cruises pages from the activities page, so you create internal links on the activities page that will link to each of them.

STEPS

1. **Using Figure F-6 as a reference, select fishing excursions in the third paragraph**

   You use the fishing excursions text to create an internal link to the fishing page.

QUICK TIP

You can also select the file to which you want to link in the Files panel and drag it to the Link text box or use the Point to File icon 🌐 in the Property inspector to create an internal link.

2. **Click the Browse for File icon 📁 next to the Link text box in the HTML Property inspector, make sure the Relative to text box is set to Document, then double-click fishing.html in The Striped Umbrella root folder in the Select File dialog box**

   Since you designated the fishing.html page as the target for the fishing excursions link, fishing.html is listed in the Link text box in the HTML Property inspector, as shown in Figure F-6.

3. **Select dolphin cruises in the same sentence**

   You use the dolphin cruises text to create an internal link to the cruises page.

4. **Click 📁 in the Property inspector, double-click cruises.html in the Select File dialog box, then save your work**

   The dolphin cruises text is now an internal link to the cruises page in The Striped Umbrella Web site. There are now nine links on the activities page: seven internal links (five on the menu bar and two in the paragraph text linking to the fishing and cruises pages), and two external links (the Blue Angels and USS Alabama Web sites), as shown in Figure F-7.

5. **Close the activities page**

Design Matters

Linking to the home page

Every page in your Web site should include a link to the home page so a viewer who has become "lost" in your site can quickly go back to the starting point without relying on the Back button. Don't make users rely on the Back button on the browser toolbar to find their way back to the home page. It's possible that the user's current page might have opened as a result of a search and clicking the Back button will take the user out of the Web site, which is not a good thing!

FIGURE F-6: Creating an internal link on the activities page

Selected text used for the link

Selected text links to the fishing page

Browse for File icon

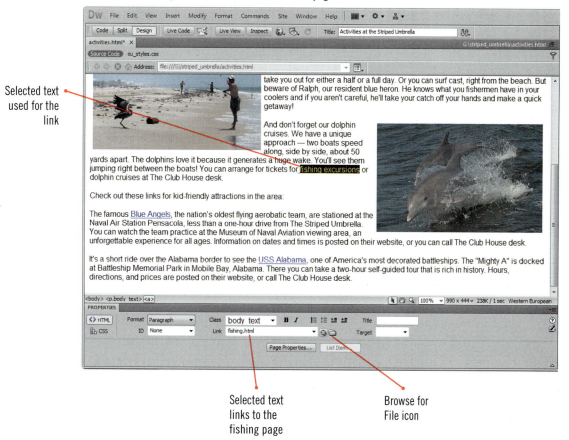

FIGURE F-7: Viewing the internal and external links on the activities page

Internal links

External links

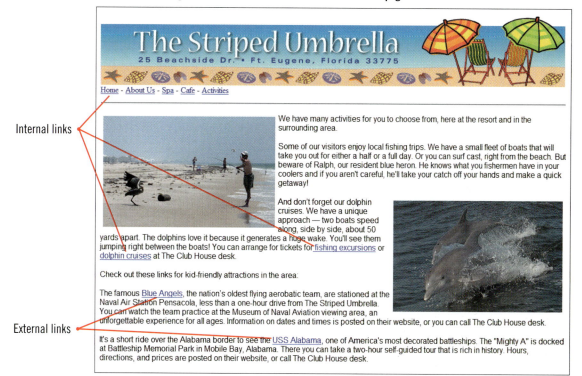

Inserting a Named Anchor

Some Web pages have so much content that users must scroll repeatedly to get to information at the top and bottom of the page. To make it easier for users to navigate to specific areas of a page without scrolling, you can use a combination of internal links and named anchors. A **named anchor** is a specific location on a Web page that is represented by an icon and an assigned descriptive name. You then create internal links on the page that the user clicks to browse to the named anchor location. For example, you can insert a named anchor called "top" at the top of a Web page, then create a link at the bottom of the page that, when clicked, will display the anchor location (the top of the Web page) when viewed in the browser. You can also insert named anchors at strategic places on a Web page, such as before paragraph headings. The name chosen for a named anchor should be short and reflect its page location. Also, you should use only lowercase characters; do not use spaces or special characters, or begin an anchor name with a number. The logical order for creating and linking to named anchors is to create a named anchor before you create its link to avoid possible errors. The Spa Services categories on the spa page contain lists of the names and descriptions of the services offered for each category. To allow users to quickly find the services they are interested in without scrolling up and down the page, you insert four named anchors on the spa page: one for the top of the page and the other three for the Massages, Facials, and Body Treatments lists of services.

STEPS

1. **Open the spa.html page, click View on the Application bar (Win) or Menu bar (Mac), point to Visual Aids, then click Invisible Elements to select it, if necessary**
   The Invisible Elements menu item must be selected in order for named anchor locations to be visible on the page in Design view.

2. **Click The Striped Umbrella banner, then press the left arrow key on your keyboard**
   The location for the first named anchor is positioned at the top of the page directly before the banner.

3. **Click the Common category on the Insert panel, if necessary**
   The command for inserting a named anchor object is located in the Common category on the Insert panel.

> **TROUBLE**
> If you don't see the Named Anchor icon on the page, make sure that Invisible Elements is selected in the Visual Aids menu.

4. **Click Named Anchor on the Insert panel, type top in the Anchor name text box in the Named Anchor dialog box, as shown in Figure F-8, then click OK**
   The Named Anchor icon appears before The Striped Umbrella banner. It may be above it or to the left of it depending on the size of your document window in the workspace.

5. **Click to place the insertion point to the left of the Massages heading, click Named Anchor on the Insert panel, type massages in the Anchor name text box, then click OK**
   The second named anchor appears before the Massages heading.

6. **Repeat Step 5 to insert named anchors to the left of the Facials and Body Treatments headings, using the following names: facials and body_treatments**
   Named anchors appear blue when selected and yellow when not selected, as shown in Figure F-9. The name of the selected anchor appears in the Property inspector.

7. **Save your work**

FIGURE F-8: Named Anchor dialog box

Anchor name text box

Named Anchor command

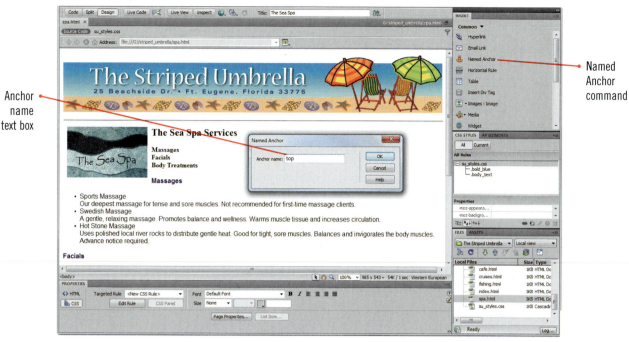

FIGURE F-9: Named anchor icons

Named anchors

Selected named anchor

Name of selected named anchor

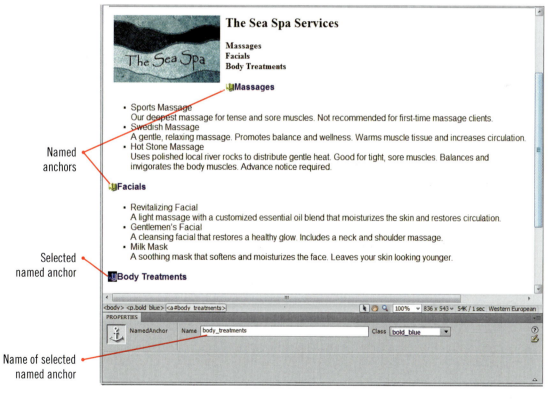

Creating Internal Links to Named Anchors

Named anchors act as targets for internal links. A **target** is the location on a Web page that displays in the browser when a link is clicked. You use the Point to File icon in the Property inspector to connect an internal link to a named anchor. Now that the named anchors are in place, you are ready to set up links for users to quickly access the information on the Web page. You want to create internal links for the four named anchors and link them to each named anchor on the spa page. You also decide to create a text link at the bottom of the page to make it easy for users to return to the top of the page.

STEPS

1. **Using Figure F-10 as a guide, select the Massages heading to the right of The Sea Spa logo, then click and drag the Point to File icon ⊙ in the HTML Property inspector on top of the massages named anchor in front of the Massages heading, as shown in Figure F-10**

   The named anchor massages is the target for the massages link. When viewing the spa_page in the browser, the list of massages will display at the top of the window when massages is clicked. The name of a named anchor is always preceded by a pound (#) sign in the Link text box in the HTML Property inspector, as shown in Figure F-10.

2. **Repeat Step 1 to create internal links for the Facials and Body Treatments headings by first selecting each heading next to the logo, then clicking and dragging ⊙ to the facials and body_treatments named anchors**

   The Massages and Body Treatments headings are now links to the Massages and Body Treatments unordered lists of services.

3. **Click at the end of the last line on the page, press [Enter] (Win) or [return] (Mac), then type Top of page**

   The Top of page text will be used to link to the named anchor at the top of the page. If the text you want to use for a link to a named anchor and the named anchor itself are far apart on the page, you can scroll up or down the page as much as you need to and still use ⊙ to create the link. As long as the text is still selected, it is not necessary to be able to see it when you point to the named anchor.

4. **Repeat Step 1 again to link the Top of page text to the named anchor in front of the banner**

   The Top of page text is now a link to the Top named anchor to the left of the banner at the top of the page.

   > **QUICK TIP**
   > To enable or disable the Code Navigator, click View on the Application bar (Win) or Menu bar (Mac), click Code Navigator, then click the Disable check box.

5. **Click anywhere in the Top of page text, wait for a few seconds until the Click indicator to bring up the Code Navigator icon ✳ appears, then click ✳**

   The Code Navigator, as shown in Figure F-11, indicates that the Top of Page text has the body_text rule applied to it. When you placed the insertion point at the end of the paragraph and entered a paragraph break, the formatting was retained.

6. **Save your work, preview the spa page in your browser, test each link, then close your browser**

   The page can only scroll as far as there is text on the page, so you may not see much change depending on your window size.

FIGURE F-10: Using the Point to File icon

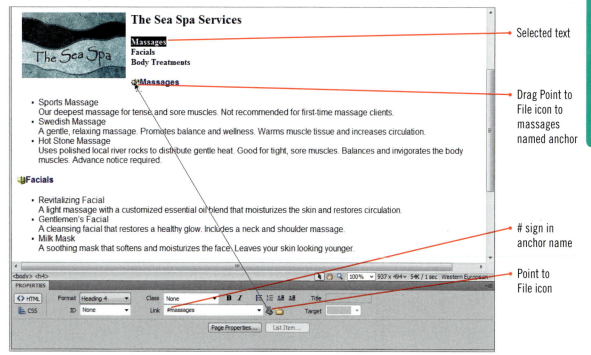

Selected text

Drag Point to File icon to massages named anchor

\# sign in anchor name

Point to File icon

FIGURE F-11: Code Navigator displaying rule name

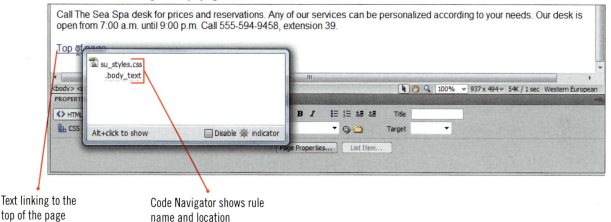

Text linking to the top of the page

Code Navigator shows rule name and location

Using the Code Navigator

When you click on a page element either in Code view or in Design view, wait a second or two; the Click indicator to bring up the Code Navigator icon ☀ will appear (you can also [Alt]-click (Win) or [Ctrl]-click (Mac) to display it instantly). Clicking ☀ will open a pop-up window called the Code Navigator. As you recall from Unit C, the **Code Navigator** lists the CSS rule name linked to the page element, along with the name of the style sheet that contains the rule. Pointing to the rule name will display the properties and values of the rule, as shown in Figure F-12. This is a quick way to view the rule definition. If you click the rule name, the code for the rule will open in Code and Design views, where you can then edit it.

FIGURE F-12: Code Navigator displaying rule properties

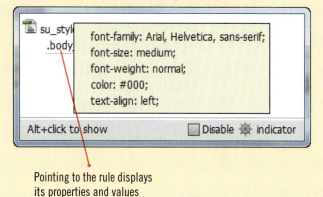

Pointing to the rule displays its properties and values

Creating a Spry Menu Bar

Recall from Unit C that a **menu bar** is a set of text or image links that can be used to navigate between pages of a Web site. To make your site more visually appealing, you can use special effects to create a more professional look for your menu bars. One way to do this is to insert a Spry menu bar. A **Spry menu bar** is a type of menu bar that uses unordered lists, CSS, and Javascript to create an interactive menu bar with pull-down submenus. **Spry**, or **Spry framework**, is open source code developed by Adobe Systems to help designers quickly incorporate dynamic content on their Web pages. Each link in a Spry menu bar is called an **item**. When you add a Spry menu bar, by default it first appears with placeholder text and generic settings for the menu bar properties, such as the width and background color for each item in the menu. The current menu bar for The Striped Umbrella site is a set of five text links. While they work perfectly well, you would like a more professionally designed look. You begin by creating a Spry menu bar that will contain five items: home, about us, cafe, spa, and activities.

STEPS

1. **Select the banner on the spa page, press the right arrow key, then press [Shift] [Enter] (Win) or [Shift] [return] (Mac)**
    The insertion point is positioned between the banner and the horizontal rule.

> **QUICK TIP**
> The Spry Menu Bar button is also in the Layout category on the Insert panel.

2. **Click the Insert panel list arrow on the Insert panel, click the Spry category, scroll down, if necessary, to click Spry Menu Bar, then click to select the Horizontal layout option button in the Spry Menu Bar dialog box, as shown in Figure F-13**
    The Horizontal layout option specifies that the menu bar will be placed horizontally on the page.

3. **Click OK**
    The Spry menu bar, which will be referred to from now on simply as the menu bar, displays selected under the banner. The menu bar contains four items by default and each item contains placeholder text, such as Item 1. Right above the upper left corner of the menu bar is the Spry menu bar label containing the default label name: MenuBar1. The Property inspector shows the menu bar properties. It lists the default items and submenu items, along with text boxes for linking each item and submenu item to the appropriate pages.

4. **Select MenuBar1 in the Menu Bar text box in the Property inspector, then type MenuBar**
    Item 1 is selected in the Item column (first column on the left) in the Property inspector.

5. **Select Item 1 in the Text text box in the right side of the Property inspector, type Home, select Item 1.1 in the first submenu column (second column) in the Property inspector, as shown in Figure F-14, then click the Remove menu Item button ⊟ above the first submenu column**
    Item 1 is renamed Home and the default submenu item Item 1.1 is deleted.

> **QUICK TIP**
> You can add sub-menu items by clicking the Add menu item button ➕.

6. **Click ⊟ two more times**
    The remainder of the default submenu items—Item 1.2 and Item 1.3—for the Home item are deleted as well.

7. **Click the Browse for File icon ▭ next to the Link text box in the Property inspector, double-click index.html in the site root folder, then compare your Property inspector to Figure F-15**
    The Home item is linked to the home page.

8. **Click to place the insertion point to the right of the menu bar, enter a line break, compare your screen to Figure F-16, save your file, then click OK to close the Copy Dependent Files dialog box**
    The menu bar displays with the first item named Home linked to the home page. The supporting files that are needed to format the Spry menu bar and make it function properly are added to the site root folder. A new SpryAssets folder is added that contains a JavaScript file, a CSS file, and some images that are used in the Spry menu bar.

FIGURE F-13: Spry Menu Bar dialog box

Horizontal
layout option
button

FIGURE F-14: Property inspector with Menu Bar properties

Menu Bar
text box

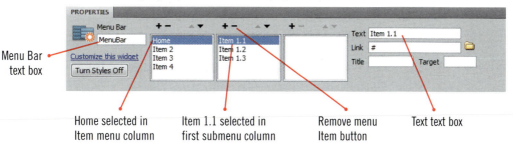

Home selected in
Item menu column

Item 1.1 selected in
first submenu column

Remove menu
Item button

Text text box

FIGURE F-15: Home item for the menu bar

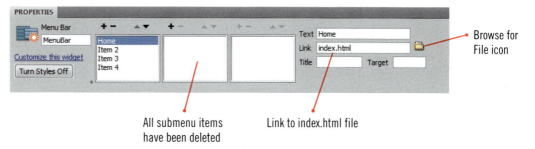

Browse for
File icon

All submenu items
have been deleted

Link to index.html file

FIGURE F-16: The Spry menu bar on the spa page

Spry Menu
Bar label

Item 1 is
renamed
"Home"

Inserting a Fireworks menu bar

Another option for adding a menu bar to your page is to create a menu bar in Adobe Fireworks, open Dreamweaver, then import the menu bar onto the Web page. Once you've created the Fireworks menu bar, you export the Fireworks file to a Dreamweaver site root folder. This file contains the HTML code that defines the menu bar properties. Next, open the appropriate Web page in Dreamweaver where you want to insert the menu bar, then use the Insert, Image Objects, Fireworks HTML command to add the HTML code to the page. You can also use Dreamweaver to import rollover images and buttons created in Fireworks.

Adding Menu Bar Items

After you create a menu bar, you can modify it by adding new menu items or submenu items or deleting those that you do not need. Submenus are also called **child menus**. Submenu items can also have submenus under them. The Property inspector is used to add, delete, rename, and link Spry menu items to pages in your Web site. You are ready to add the rest of the menu and submenu items to the menu bar so users will have access to each of the main pages from the menu bar. You want to rename the rest of the default menu items, add one additional menu item, then add two submenu items under the activities item for the cruises and fishing pages.

1. Click the Spry Menu Bar: MenuBar tab if necessary, then click Item 2 in the Item menu column (first column) in the Property inspector, select Item 2 in the Text text box, then type About Us

   Item 2 is renamed About Us.

2. Click the Browse button ☐ next to the Link text box, click about_us.html in the site root folder, then click OK

   The About Us menu item is linked to the about_us page.

3. Repeat Steps 1 and 2 to rename Item 3 Sand Crab Cafe and link it to the cafe.html page in the site root folder

4. Delete each submenu item under the Sand Crab Cafe menu item, then click OK to close the warning box confirming the removal of each of the submenus

   The submenu items under the Sand Crab Cafe menu item are deleted.

5. Repeat Steps 1 and 2 to rename Item 4 The Sea Spa and link it to the spa.html page in the site root folder

   The Sea Spa menu item is linked to the spa page and remains selected in the Property inspector.

6. Click the Add menu item button ✚ above the Item menu column (first column), select Untitled Item, in the Text text box type Activities, then link it to the activities.html page

   The new menu item, Activities, is linked to the activities page and remains selected in the Property inspector.

7. Click ✚ above the first submenu column (second column), select Untitled Item, type Cruises in the Text text box, then link it to the cruises.html page

   A new submenu item, Cruises, is added under the Activities menu item that will link to the cruises page.

8. Repeat Step 7 to add another submenu item named Fishing, link it to the fishing.html page, save your work, then compare your screen to Figure F-17

   A second submenu item is added under the Activities menu item that will link to the fishing page.

9. Click the Switch Design View to Live View button [Live View] on the Document toolbar, view the menu bar, then compare your screen to Figure F-18

   Live View shows you what the page will look like when opened in a browser. Not only is it a faster way to view your page than previewing it in a browser but it shows the interactive elements functioning. For more information about Live View read the Clues to Use box *Viewing your Page in Live View*.

10. Click [Live View] again

    The spa page redisplays in your workspace in Design view without the interactive elements being functional.

FIGURE F-17: Adding menu items and submenu items to the menu bar

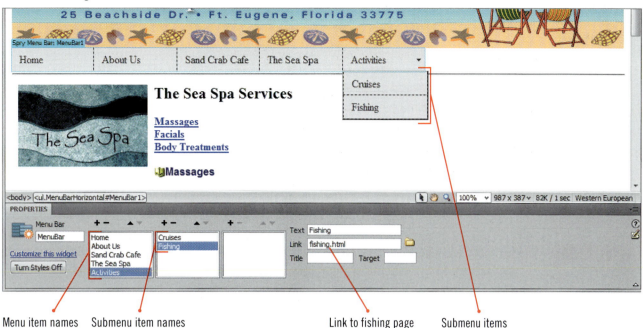

Menu item names — Submenu item names — Link to fishing page — Submenu items

FIGURE F-18: Viewing the spa page in Live View

Switch Design View to Live View button

Menu bar as it will appear in a browser

Viewing your page in Live View

When you view your Web pages in Dreamweaver, the page elements appear similar to the way they will look when viewed in a Web browser. Live View gives you a more accurate picture of what the page will actually look like in a browser, with interactive elements active and functioning. You use the Switch Design View to Live View button on the Document toolbar to enable Live View. Next to this button is the Shows the Live View source in code view button, which displays the code. The code remains as read-only until you click the Shows the Live View source in code view button again. When the

Switch Design View to Live View button is active, the Shows the Live View source in code view button can be toggled on or off. If Live View is not active, selecting the Shows the Live View source in code view button will turn it on. When you first click the Live View button, you may see a message that you need to install the Flash plug-in from the Adobe Web site, www.adobe.com. Once you download the plug-in, your pages can then be viewed using Live View.

Formatting a Menu Bar

Once you create a Spry menu bar, you'll need to modify the default settings to adjust the appearance of the menu bar and its items. For example, you can adjust their height or width or specify the background color of each menu item. You can add special effects for menu bar items by changing the characteristics for each item's state. A **state** is the condition of the menu item relative to the mouse pointer. You can create a rollover effect by using different background and text colors for each state to represent how the menu item appears when users move their mouse over or away from it. The settings for the menu bar and menu items reside in CSS rules. To change them, you edit the default rules that were automatically created when the Spry menu bar was inserted on the page. You format the Spry menu bar by editing the rules that control the appearance of the Spry menu bar items.

STEPS

TROUBLE
If you don't see the rule listed, click the Switch to All (Document) Mode button All in the CSS Styles panel.

1. **Click the plus sign (Win) or right pointing arrow (Mac) next to SpryMenuBarHorizonal. css in the CSS Styles panel if necessary, select the rule ul.MenuBarHorizontal, then click the Edit Rule button 🖉 on the CSS styles panel**

   The CSS Rule Definition for ul.MenuBarHorizontal in SpryMenuBarHorizontal.css dialog box opens. This is where you define the global settings for all menu and submenu items.

2. **Click Type in the Category list, click the Font-family list arrow, click Arial, Helvetica, sans-serif, click the Font-size list arrow, click 14, click the Font-size unit of measure list arrow, click px, compare your screen to Figure F-19, then click OK**

   The text size of the menu items becomes larger to reflect the new settings, which causes the text on some buttons to wrap to two lines. You want the menu bar to revert back to one line.

3. **Select the ul.MenuBarHorizontal li rule in the CSS Styles panel, click 🖉, click Box in the Category list, click the Width text box, type 190, click the Width unit of measure list arrow, click px, click in the Height text box, type 25, then compare your screen to Figure F-20**

   The width of each menu item increases to 190 pixels wide and the height is set to 25 pixels.

4. **Click Block in the Category list, click the Text-align text box arrow, select center, then click OK**

   The block settings include properties to change the spacing and alignment of the text in the menu bar. The Text-align setting adjusts the alignment of each text item on its "button." In this case, the menu items are set to appear centered within their button in the menu bar.

TROUBLE
If you don't see the u.MenuBarHorizontal a rule listed in the CSS Styles panel, click the Switch to (All) Document Mode button All .

5. **Click ul.MenuBarHorizontal a in the CSS Styles panel, click 🖉, click Type in the Category list, type #FFF in the Color text box replacing the current color, click Background in the Category list, type #09C in the Background-color text box, then click OK**

   The menu items redisplay with white text on a blue background. This is how they appear in the menu bar when the mouse is *not* positioned over them.

QUICK TIP
To locate this rule, which is the longest rule, place your mouse over each rule name to see the extended names.

6. **Click ul.MenuBarHorizontal a.MenuBarItemHover, ul.MenuBarHorizontal a.MenuBarItemSubmenuHover, ul.MenuBarHorizontal a.MenuBarSubmenuVisible in the CSS Styles panel, then click 🖉**

7. **Click Type in the Category list, type #630 in the Color text box, click Background in the Category list, type #FC9 in the Background-color text box, then click OK**

   The property values for the menu items and submenu items change to a sand background with brown text. This is how they appear when the mouse is positioned over them.

8. **Click File on the Application bar (Win) or Menu bar (Mac), click Save All, preview your page in the browser, compare your screen to Figure F-21, test each link to ensure that each works correctly, then close the browser**

   The button background colors are blue with white text when the pointer is not placed over them and sand with brown text when the pointer is positioned over them.

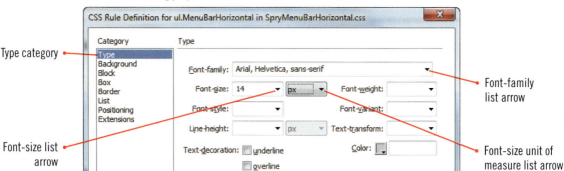

FIGURE F-19: Adding properties for the .ulMenuBarHorizontal rule

Type category

Font-family list arrow

Font-size list arrow

Font-size unit of measure list arrow

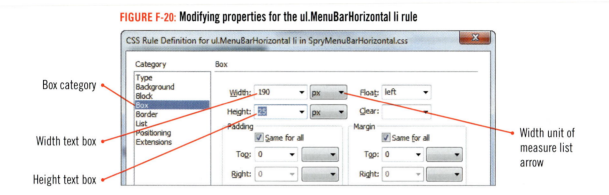

FIGURE F-20: Modifying properties for the ul.MenuBarHorizontal li rule

Box category

Width text box

Height text box

Width unit of measure list arrow

FIGURE F-21: Spa page viewed in the browser with the updated menu bar

Menu items and submenu items are blue with white text when the pointer is placed over them

Menu items and submenu items are sand colored with brown text when the pointer is placed over them

Copying a Menu Bar to Other Pages

When you create a menu bar for one page in a Web site, you should copy it to all of the other pages in the site. This practice provides continuity in the navigation structure and makes it easy for users to navigate comfortably through pages in your site.  The new Spry menu bar is an improvement over the menu bar with plain text links. You decide to replace all existing menu bars on the pages in the Web site with this menu bar to improve each page's design and promote consistency. You copy the menu bar to the about_us, index, and activities pages in The Striped Umbrella Web site.

STEPS

1. **Click the Spry Menu Bar:MenuBar tab above the top left corner of the menu bar, as shown in Figure F-22, click Edit on the Application bar (Win) or Menu bar (Mac), then click Copy**

   The menu bar is ready to be pasted on other pages in the Web site.

   QUICK TIP
   When you work on multiple open pages, use the filename tabs at the top of the Document toolbar or press [Ctrl] [Tab] to move quickly between pages.

2. **Double-click activities.html on the Files panel**

   The activities page opens.

3. **Select the original menu bar on the page, click Edit on the Application bar (Win) or Menu bar (Mac), click Paste, click to the right of the menu bar, enter a line break, compare your screen to Figure F-23, then save the page**

   The new menu bar appears on the page in place of the previous one and the new styles are added to the page.

   TROUBLE
   If you have trouble with the alignment and spacing between the banner and the menu bar, click beside the banner, change to Code view, place your insertion point after the ending < /ul> tag for the menu bar, then either type a </br> tag or return to Design view and enter a line break.

4. **Open the index page, delete the current menu bar including the heading tags, click the banner to select it, press the right arrow key, insert a line break, paste the Spry menu bar on the page, then insert a line break after the menu bar**

   The menu bar is pasted on the index page and the spacing after the menu bar is adjusted to match the other two pages.

5. **Open the about_us page, replace the current menu bar with the new menu bar, then add two line breaks after the new menu bar**

   The menu bar is pasted on the about_us page and the spacing after the menu bar is adjusted to match the home, spa, and activities pages.

   QUICK TIP
   View the pages at a high resolution to ensure that the menu bars do not break into two lines.

6. **Click File on the Application bar (Win) or Menu bar (Mac), click Save All, then preview each page in the browser**

   The menu bar appears consistently on the home, about_us, spa, and activities pages of The Striped Umbrella Web site. Although the cafe, fishing, and activities pages are not designed yet, you see that the links all work correctly.

7. **Hold the pointer over the Activities link, as shown in Figure F-24, close the browser, then close all open pages except the activities page**

   When the pointer is placed over the Activities link, the submenu drops down with the two submenu links visible and active.

FIGURE F-22: The spa page with the Spry menu bar

Spry Menu
Bar:
MenuBar tab →

FIGURE F-23: Pasting the Spry menu bar on the activities page

Spry Menu
Bar:
MenuBar tab →

FIGURE F-24: Viewing the activities submenu items in the browser

Submenu
items for
Cruises
and Fishing
pages

Creating an Image Map

Another way to create navigation links for Web pages is to create an image map. An **image map** is an image that has one or more hotspots placed on top of it. A **hotspot** is an active area on an image that, when clicked, links to a different location on the page or to another Web page. For example, a map of the world could have a hotspot placed on each individual country so that users could click a country to link to more information. Hotspots are not visible in the browser window, but when users place their pointer over the hotspot, the pointer changes to a pointing finger, indicating the presence of a link. To create a hotspot, select the image on which you want to place the hotspot, draw the hotspot with one of the shape hotspot tools in the Property inspector, then add the link information, alternate text, and target information in the text boxes in the Property inspector. You should always assign a unique name for each image map to make them more accessible to users utilizing screen readers. You want to create an image map on the activities page to provide another way for users to link to the index page.

STEPS

1. **Click The Striped Umbrella banner on the activities page to select it, then double-click a blank area on the right side of the Property inspector to expand it, if necessary**

   The Property inspector displays the drawing tools for creating hotspots on an image in the lower-left corner.

> **TROUBLE**
> If you don't see the blue rectangle, click View, point to Visual Aids, then click Image Maps to select it.

2. **Click the Rectangle Hotspot Tool button ☐ on the Property inspector, drag to create a rectangle that encompasses The Striped Umbrella name on the banner, release the mouse button, click OK to close the Dreamweaver dialog box, then compare your screen to Figure F-25**

   A shaded blue rectangle appears within the area that you outlined. This blue rectangle is the hotspot. The dialog box reminds you to add to the alternate text for the hotspot.

3. **Drag the Point to File icon ⊙ next to the Link text box in the Property inspector to index.html in the Files panel**

   The hotspot is linked to the index.html file. If the hotspot is clicked, the index file opens.

> **TROUBLE**
> If you don't see the Map text box in the Property inspector, click the image map object on the banner to select it.

4. **Select Map in the Map text box in the Property inspector, then type home**

   The image map is named home. Each image map should have a unique name, especially if a page contains more than one image map.

5. **Click the Target list arrow in the Property inspector, then click _self**

   The _self target directs the browser to display the home page in the same browser window as the activities page, rather than opening a separate window. When the hotspot is clicked, the home page opens in the same browser window. See the Clues to Use box *Setting targets for links* to learn more about how the _self property, along with other property options, are used to set targets for links.

6. **Type Link to home page in the Alt text box in the Property inspector, as shown in Figure F-26**

   The descriptive information placed in the Alt text box provides a brief clue to the user about what further information awaits if the hotspot is clicked. The alternate text is also read by screen readers to tell users what will happen if they click the image map.

7. **Save your work, preview the page in your browser window, then test the link on the image map**

   The hotspot is not visible in the browser, but if you place the mouse over the hotspot, you will see the pointer change to 🖑 to indicate a link is present.

8. **Close your browser**

FIGURE F-25: Drawing a Rectangle hotspot on The Striped Umbrella banner

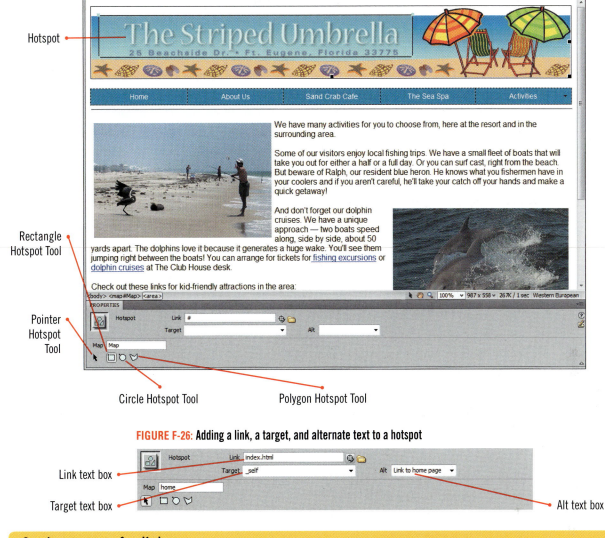

Hotspot

Rectangle
Hotspot Tool

Pointer
Hotspot
Tool

Circle Hotspot Tool   Polygon Hotspot Tool

FIGURE F-26: Adding a link, a target, and alternate text to a hotspot

Link text box

Target text box

Alt text box

Setting targets for links

You can set targets to determine how a new window will display in a browser when links on pages or in frames are clicked. A **frame** is a fixed region in a browser that can display a Web page and act independently from other pages displayed in other frames within the browser. When you set a target for a link or frame, you have four options for how the new window will open after the link is clicked. These targets are set by clicking the Target list arrow in the HTML Property inspector and selecting the target you want. The _blank target displays the destination page in a separate browser window and leaves the original window open. The _parent target displays the destination page in the parent window or frameset, replacing the original window or frameset. The _self target displays the destination page in the same window or frame. The _top target displays the destination page in the whole browser window.

Design Matters

Creating and modifying hotspots

In addition to the Rectangle hotspot tool, 🔲 there are two other helpful shape tools: a Circle hotspot tool 🔘 and a Polygon hotspot tool 🔽. These tools can be used to create any shape hotspot that you need. For instance, the Polygon hotspot tool could be used to draw an outline around each state on a map of the United States. Hotspots can be easily changed and rearranged on an image using the Pointer hotspot tool 🔺. First, select the hotspot you would like to edit, then drag one of the hotspot selector handles to change the size or shape of a hotspot. You can also move the hotspot by dragging it to a new position on the image. It is a good idea to limit the number of complex or irregularly shaped hotspots in an image because the code can become too lengthy for the page to download in a reasonable amount of time. You should also make the hotspot boundaries a little larger than they need to be to cover the area you want to set as a link. This allows a little leeway for users when they place their mouse over the hotspot by creating a larger target area for them.

Managing Web Site Links

As your Web site grows, so will the number of links on it. Checking links to make sure they work is a crucial and ongoing task that you should perform regularly. The Check Links Sitewide feature is a helpful tool for managing your links. It checks your entire Web site for the total number of links, categorizing them as OK, external, or broken, and then displays the information in the Link Checker panel. The Link Checker panel also provides a list of all the files used in a Web site, including those that are **orphaned files**, files that are not linked to any pages in the Web site. If you find broken internal links (links to files within the Web site), you should carefully check the code entered in the Link text box for errors. You can either use the Browse for File icon in the Link Checker panel to correct the link, or type the correction in the Link text box in the Property inspector. You check broken external links (links to files outside the Web site) by testing the links in your browser. Due to the volatility of the Web, it is important to check external links routinely as Web sites are often under construction or undergoing address changes. You have created three new external links in The Striped Umbrella Web site: two to external Web sites and one e-mail link. You want to make sure you entered them correctly, so you run some reports to check the site for any broken links or orphaned files.

STEPS

1. **Click Site on the Application bar (Win) or Menu bar (Mac), then click Check Links Sitewide**

   The Link Checker panel in the Results Tab group opens. By default, the Link Checker panel initially displays any broken internal links found in the Web site. The Striped Umbrella Web site has no broken links, as shown in Figure F-27.

2. **Click the Show list arrow in the Link Checker panel, click External Links, then compare your screen with Figure F-28**

   Two files are listed: the activities page and the index page. The activities page has two external links listed: one to the Blue Angels Web site and one to the U.S.S. Alabama Web site. The index page has an e-mail link listed.

3. **Click the Show list arrow, then click Orphaned Files**

   There are no orphaned files displayed in the Link Checker panel for the Web site, as shown in Figure F-29.

4. **Close the Results Tab Group, click the Assets tab on the Files Tab Group, then click the URLs button on the Assets panel**

   The list of external links in the Striped Umbrella Web site displays in the Assets panel. See Figure F-30.

5. **Close the activities page, then Exit (Win) or Quit (Mac) Dreamweaver**

FIGURE F-27: Link Checker with Broken Links results displayed

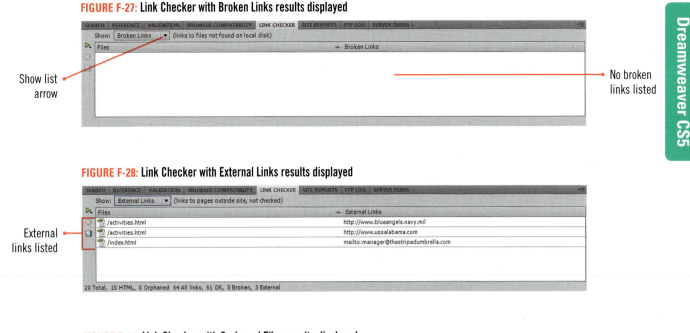

Show list arrow

No broken links listed

FIGURE F-28: Link Checker with External Links results displayed

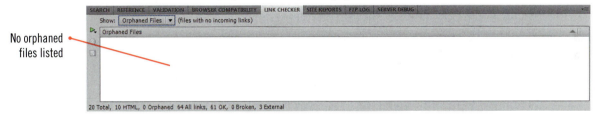

External links listed

FIGURE F-29: Link Checker with Orphaned Files results displayed

No orphaned files listed

FIGURE F-30: Assets panel with Web site external links displayed

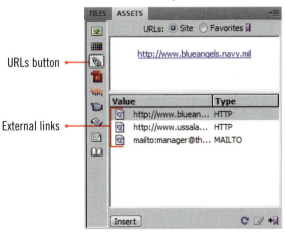

URLs button

External links

Design Matters

Designing for easy navigation

As you work on the navigation structure for a Web site, you should try to limit the number of internal links on each page. You should also provide visual clues on each page to let users know where they are, much like a "You are here" marker on a store directory at the mall, or a bread crumbs trail. A **bread crumbs trail** is a list of links that provides a path from the initial page you opened in a Web site to the page that you are currently viewing. Many Web sites provide a list of all the site's pages, called a **site map**. A site map is similar to a table of contents; it lets viewers see how the information is divided between the pages and helps them to locate the information they need quickly.

Practice

Concepts Review

For current SAM information, including versions and content details, visit SAM Central (http://www.cengage.com/samcentral). If you have a SAM user profile, you may have access to hands-on instruction, practice, and assessment of the skills covered in this unit. Since various versions of SAM are supported throughout the life of this text, check with your instructor for the correct instructions and URL/Web site for accessing assignments.

Label each element in the Dreamweaver window shown in Figure F-31.

FIGURE F-31

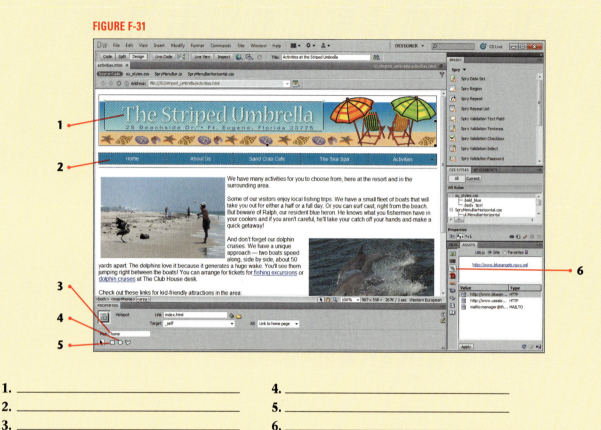

1. _____
2. _____
3. _____
4. _____
5. _____
6. _____

Match each of the following terms with the statement that best describes its function.

7. Internal links
8. External links
9. Broken links
10. Named anchor
11. Menu bar
12. Target
13. Image map
14. Hotspot
15. Orphaned file

a. Links that do not work correctly
b. A set of text or image links used to navigate between pages of a Web site
c. An image with hotspots on it
d. Links to pages within the Web site
e. Active area on an image that serves as a link
f. A location on a Web page that browsers will display when a link is clicked
g. A specific location on a Web page, represented by a special icon, that will fully display in the browser window when a user clicks the link tagged to it
h. A file that is not linked to any pages on a Web site
i. Links to pages outside the Web site

Select the best answer from the following list of choices.

16. **Which type of path begins with a forward slash?**
    a. Document-relative
    b. Root-relative
    c. Absolute
    d. Image-relative

17. **Which icon in the Property inspector do you use to connect an internal link to a named anchor?**
    a. Point to File
    b. Point to Anchor
    c. Anchor to File
    d. Point to Named Anchor

18. **The four target options for how a window will display in a browser when a link is clicked are:**
    a. _blank, _parent, _self, _top.
    b. _blank, _child, _self, _top.
    c. _blank, _parent, _child, _top.
    d. _blank, _parent, _self, _new.

19. **To see all links in a Web site, you click which icon on the Assets panel?**
    a. Links
    b. Paths
    c. URLs
    d. Anchors

20. **Which dialog box shows you a list of orphaned files?**
    a. Orphaned Files
    b. Link Checker
    c. Check Links Sitewide
    d. Assets

Skills Review

Important: *If you did not create this Web site in Unit B and maintain it during the preceding units, you will need to create a site root folder for this Web site and define the Web site using files your instructor will provide. See the "Read This Before You Begin" section for more detailed instructions.*

1. **Understand links and paths.**
   a. Write an example of an absolute path for a link.
   b. Write an example of a relative path for a link.
   c. Write a sentence explaining the difference between a document-relative path and a root-relative path.

2. **Create an external link.**
   a. Start Dreamweaver, then open the Blooms & Bulbs Web site.
   b. Open dwf_2.html from the drive and folder where you store your Unit F Data Files, save it as **newsletter.html** in the blooms site root folder, replacing the existing file and not updating links, then close dwf_2.html.
   c. Click the first broken image placeholder, grass.jpg, then browse to the drive and folder where you store your Unit F Data Files to copy it to your assets folder.
   d. Repeat Step c to replace the next two broken images for the trees.jpg and plants.jpg files, then save them to your assets folder.
   e. Scroll to the bottom of the page, then link the National Gardening Association text to http://www.garden.org.
   f. Link the Organic Gardening text to http://www.organicgardening.com.
   g. Link the Southern Living text to http://www.southernliving.com/southern.
   h. Save the file, then and preview it in your browser window.
   i. Test the links to make sure they all work correctly, then close the browser.

3. **Create an internal link.**
   a. Select the text "gardening tips" in the last sentence in the Gardening Issues paragraph.
   b. Use the Point to File icon to link the text to the tips.html page.
   c. Change the page title to **Gardening Matters**.
   d. Save the file, test the link in your browser, then close the browser.
   e. Open the plants page, then add a new paragraph to the bottom of the page: **In addition to these marvelous roses, we have many annuals, perennials, and water plants that have just arrived.**
   f. Apply the body_text rule to the paragraph if necessary.

Skills Review (continued)

    g. Use the Files panel to create three new blank files in the site root folder named: annuals.html, perennials.html, and water_plants.html.

    h. Link the "annuals" text to the annuals.html file, link the "perennials" text to the perennials.html file, then link the "water plants" text to the water_plants.html file.

    i. Save your work, test the links in your browser, then close the browser. (*Hint*: These pages do not have content yet, but are serving as placeholders.)

4. Insert a named anchor.

    a. Switch to the newsletter page, then show the invisible elements if necessary.

    b. Insert a named anchor in front of the Grass subheading, then name it **grass**.

    c. Insert a named anchor in front of the Trees subheading, then name it **trees**.

    d. Insert a named anchor in front of the Plants subheading, then name it **plants**.

    e. Save the file.

5. Create an internal link to a named anchor.

    a. Using the Point to File icon in the Property inspector, create a link from the word grass in the Gardening Issues paragraph to the grass named anchor.

    b. Create a link from the word trees in the Gardening Issues paragraph to the trees named anchor.

    c. Create a link from the word plants in the Gardening Issues paragraph to the plants named anchor.

    d. Save the file, then test the links in your browser window.

6. Create a Spry menu bar.

    a. Enter a line break after the banner on the newsletter page.

    b. Use the Spry category on the Insert panel to insert a Spry menu bar with a horizontal layout under the banner.

    c. Replace MenuBar1 in the Menu Bar text box in the Property inspector with the name **MenuBar**.

    d. Replace the name Item 1 in the Text text box with **Home**, then remove all submenu items from the Home item.

    e. Link the Home item to the index.html file.

    f. Insert two line breaks after the menu bar, then save the file, copying the dependent files.

7. Add menu bar items.

    a. Rename the Item 2 menu item with the name **Newsletter**, then link it to the newsletter page.

    b. Rename the Item 3 menu item with the name **Plants**, then link it to the plants page.

    c. Rename the Item 4 menu item with the name **Tips**, then link it to the tips page.

    d. With the Tips menu item selected, add a new menu item with the name **Workshops**, then link it to the workshops page.

    e. With the Plants menu item selected, rename submenu Item 3.1 **Annuals**, then link it to the annuals.html page.

    f. With the Plants menu item selected, rename submenu Item 3.2 **Perennials**, then link it to the perennials.html page.

    g. With the Plants menu item selected, rename submenu Item 3.3 **Water Plants**, then link it to the water_plants.html page.

    h. With the Annuals submenu item selected, delete its two submenu items.

8. Format a menu bar.

    a. Expand the SpryMenuBarHorizonal.css in the CSS Styles panel, then edit the rule ul.MenuBarHorizontal with the following settings: Font-family: Arial, Helvetica, sans-serif; Font-size: 14 px.

    b. Edit the rule ul.MenuBarHorizontal li rule with the following settings: Box Width: 190 px; Box Height: 25 px; Block Text-align: center.

    c. Edit the following rule: ul.MenuBarHorizontal a with the following settings: Type Color: #030; Background-color: #99F.

    d. Edit the following rule: ul.MenuBarHorizontal a.MenuBarItemHover, ul.MenuBarHorizontal a.MenuBarItemSubmenuHover, ul.MenuBarHorizontal a.MenuBarSubmenuVisible with the following settings: Type Color: #FFC; Background-color: #030.

    e. Save your work, then test the menu bar on the page in the browser to make sure everything works correctly.

9. **Copy a menu bar to other pages.**

   a. Select and copy the menu bar, then open the index page.

   b. Select the banner, press the right arrow key, click the Format list arrow in the HTML Property inspector, then click None if necessary.

   c. Paste the menu bar at the insertion point, then delete the existing menu bar created with text links.

   d. Remove any extra space between the new menu bar and the horizontal rule by switching to Code view and removing any <p> tags that you see.

   e. Return to Design view; when you are satisfied with the page, save your work, then close the index page. (*Hint*: To be sure that both pages have the same amount of space between the menu bar and the horizontal rule, you can copy the code between the menu bar and the horizontal rule from one page and paste it to the other page.)

   f. Open the plants page, paste the menu bar under the banner, then add a horizontal rule. (*Hint*: Copy the code after the menu bar, including the code for the horizontal rule, from the index or newsletter pages, then paste it into the code for the plants page. Place your insertion point right after the code for the banner before you paste.)

   g. Save the plants page.

   h. Repeat Step f to add a menu bar and horizontal rule on the tips page, then save the tips page.

   i. Preview all pages in the browser window, checking the spacing for each page to ensure a uniform look, then close the browser. (*Hint*: The workshops, annuals, perennials, and water_plants pages are serving as placeholder pages and do not have content yet.)

10. **Create an image map.**

    a. On the newsletter page, create a rectangle hotspot over the words *Blooms & Bulbs* on the Blooms & Bulbs banner.

    b. Name the image map **home**, then link it to the index page.

    c. Set the target as _top.

    d. Enter the alternate text **Link to home page**.

    e. Save all pages, then preview the newsletter page in the browser, testing all links. Refer to Figure F-32 to check your work.

11. **Manage Web site links.**

    a. Recreate the Site Cache, then use the Check Links Sitewide command to view broken links, external links, and orphaned files.

    b. Refresh the Site list in the Files panel if you see broken links or orphaned files. If any exist, locate them, analyze them, then correct any errors you find.

    c. View the external links in the Assets panel. Exit (Win) or Quit (Mac) Dreamweaver.

FIGURE F-32

Gardening Matters

Welcome, fellow gardeners. My name is Cosie Simmons, the owner of Blooms & Bulbs. My passion has always been my gardens. Ever since I was a small child, I was drawn to my back yard where all varieties of beautiful plants flourished. A lush carpet of thick grass bordered with graceful beds is truly a haven for all living creatures. With proper planning and care, your gardens will draw a variety of birds and butterflies and become a great pleasure to you.

Gardening Issues

There are several areas to concentrate on when formulating your landscaping plans. One is your grass. Another is the number and variety of trees you plant. The third is the combination of plants you select. All of these decisions should be considered in relation to the climate in your area. Be sure and check out our gardening tips before you begin work.

Grass

Lawn experts classify grass into two categories: cool-climate and warm-climate. The northern half of the United States would be considered cool-climate. Examples of cool-climate grass are Kentucky bluegrass and ryegrass. Bermuda grass is a warm-climate grass. Before planting grass, whether by seeding, sodding, sprigging, or plugging, the ground must be properly prepared. The soil should be tested for any nutritional deficiencies and cultivated. Come by or call to make arrangements to have your soil tested. When selecting a lawn, avoid letting personal preferences and the cost of establishment be the overriding factors. Ask yourself these questions: What type of lawn are you expecting? What level of maintenance are you willing to provide? What are the site limitations?

Trees

Before you plant trees, you should evaluate your purpose. Are you interested in shade, privacy, or color? Do you want to attract wildlife? Attract birds? Create a shady play area? Your purpose will determine what variety of tree you should plant. Of course, you also need to consider your climate and available space. Shape is especially important in selecting trees for ornamental and shade purposes. Abundant shade comes from tall trees with long spreading or weeping branches. Ornamental trees will not provide abundant shade. We carry many varieties of trees and are happy to help you make your selections to fit your purpose.

Plants

There are so many types of plants available that it can become overwhelming. Do you want border plants, shrubs, ground covers, annuals, perennials, vegetables, fruits, vines, or bulbs? In reality, a combination of several of these works well. Design aspects such as balance, flow, definition of space and focalization should be considered. Annuals provide brilliant bursts of color in the garden. By selecting flowers carefully to fit the conditions of the site, it is possible to have a beautiful display without an unnecessary amount of work. Annuals are also great as fresh and dry cut flowers. Perennials can greatly improve the quality of your landscape. Perennials have come and gone in popularity, but today are as popular as ever. Water plants are also quite popular now. We will be happy to help you sort out your preferences and select a harmonious combination of plants for you.

Further Research

These are some of my favorite gardening links. Take the time to browse through some of the information they offer, then give me a call at (555) 248-0806 or e-mail me at cosie@blooms&bulbs.com.

National Gardening Association
Organic Gardening
Southern Living

Important: *If you did not create the following Web sites in Unit B and maintain them during the preceding units, you must create a site root folder for the Web sites in the following exercises and define the Web sites using files your instructor will provide. See the "Read This Before You Begin" section for more detailed instructions.*

Independent Challenge 1

You have been hired to create a Web site for a river expedition company named Rapids Transit, located on the Buffalo River in Gilbert, Arkansas. In addition to renting canoes, kayaks, and rafts, they have lodging available for overnight stays. River guides are available to accompany clients on float trips. The owner's name is Mike Andrew. Mike has asked you to create a new Web page that lists helpful links for his customers. Refer to Figure F-33 as you work on this page.

   a. Start Dreamweaver, then open the Rapids Transit Web site.
   b. Open dwf_3.html in the drive and folder where you store your Unit F Data Files, then save it as **before.html**, replacing the existing file and without updating the links. You need to save the young_paddler.gif file (the photo) in the assets folder of the Rapids Transit Web site, then correct the path for the banner if necessary.
   c. Close the file dwf_3.html.
   d. Create the following links:
   Buffalo National River   http://www.nps.gov/buff/
   Arkansas, the Natural State   http://www.arkansas.com/
   Buffalo River Floater's Guide   http://www.ozarkmtns.com/buffalo/index.asp
   e. Attach the rapids_transit css style sheet, then apply a style to all text on the page.

Independent Challenge 1 (continued)

f. Design a Spry menu bar for the page. The menu bar should include the following items: Home, Our Guides, Rates, Lodging, and Before You Go. Link the menu items to the appropriate files in your Rapids Transit site. Delete all submenus.

g. Copy the completed menu bar to the guides, index, and lodging pages. Preview each page in the browser window to make sure the menu bar doesn't "jump," or shift position, when you move from page to page. (*Hint*: If you are having problems with spacing issues, look for stray `<p>`, `</br>`, or heading tags on your pages and remove them if necessary.)

h. Save your work, then test all links in your browser window.

i. Run reports for locate any broken links or orphaned files, then correct any that exist.

j. Exit your browser, then close all files and exit Dreamweaver.

FIGURE F-33

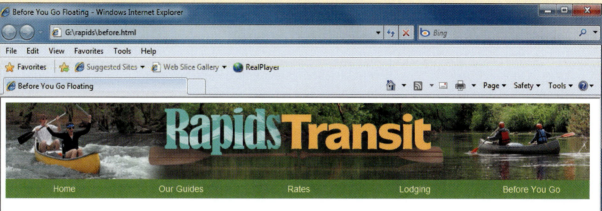

Independent Challenge 2

Your company is designing a new Web site for TripSmart, a travel outfitter. TripSmart specializes in travel products and services. In addition to selling travel products, such as luggage and accessories, they sponsor trips and offer travel advice. Their clients range from college students to families to vacationing professionals. You are now ready to work on the services page. This page will include several helpful links for clients to use in planning trips.

a. Start Dreamweaver, then open the TripSmart site.

b. Open the file dwf_4.html from the drive and folder where you store your Unit F Data Files, save it as **services.html** in the tripsmart root folder, replacing the existing file but not updating the links, then close dwf_4.html.

c. Apply the list_heading style from the attached style sheet to the four paragraph headings, then apply the body_text style to the rest of the text on the page. (*Hint*: the Helpful Links in Travel Planning is the fourth paragraph heading, but is not shown in the figure.)

d. Create the following links using the text in the unordered list at the bottom of the page:

CNN Travel Channel — http://www.cnn.com/TRAVEL
US Department of State — http://travel.state.gov
Yahoo! Currency Converter — http://finance.yahoo.com/currency-converter
The Weather Channel — http://www.weather.com

e. Create named anchors called **reservations**, **outfitters**, **tours**, and **links** in front of the respective headings on the page, then link each named anchor to "Reservations", "Travel Outfitters", "Escorted Tours", and "Helpful Links in Travel Planning" (respectively) in the first paragraph.

Independent Challenge 2 (continued)

f. Create a Spry menu bar that links to the home, tours, newsletter, services, and catalog pages, replacing any existing menu bars. Delete all submenus.

g. Copy the menu bar to the other completed pages in the Web site: index, newsletter, and tours pages, replacing any existing menu bars. (*Hint*: If you are having problems with spacing issues, look for stray <p>, < /br>, or heading tags on your pages and remove them if necessary.)

h. Save any unsaved changes, preview the services page in the browser window, as shown in Figure F-34, then test all links.

i. Use the Link Checker to check for broken links and orphaned files.

j. Exit your browser, then close all files and exit Dreamweaver.

FIGURE F-34

TripSmart has several divisions of customer service to assist you in planning and making reservations for your trip, shopping for your trip wardrobe and providing expert guide services. Give us a call and we will be happy to connect you with one of the following departments: Reservations, Travel Outfitters, or Escorted Tours. If you are not quite ready to talk with one of our departments and would prefer doing some of your own research first, may we suggest beginning with our Helpful Links in Travel Planning.

Reservations
Our Reservations Department is staffed with five Certified Travel Agents, each of whom is eager to assist you in making your travel plans. They have specialty areas in Africa, the Caribbean, South America, Western Europe, Eastern Europe, Asia, Antarctica, and Hawaii and the South Pacific. They also specialize in Senior Travel, Family Travel, Student Travel, and Special Needs Travel. Call us at *(555) 848-0807* extension 75 or e-mail us at *Reservations* to begin making your travel plans now. We will be happy to send you brochures and listings of Internet addresses to help you get started. We are open from 8:00 a.m. until 6:00 p.m. CST.

Travel Outfitters
Our travel outfitters are seasoned travelers that have accumulated a vast amount of knowledge in appropriate travel clothing and accessories for specific destinations. Climate and seasons, of course, are important factors in planning your wardrobe for a trip. Area customs should also be taken in consideration so as not to offend the local residents with inappropriate dress. When traveling abroad, we always hope that our customers will represent our country well as good ambassadors. If they can be comfortable and stylish at the same time, we have succeeded! Our clothing is all affordable and packs well on long trips. Most can be washed easily in a hotel sink and hung to drip-dry overnight. Browse through our on-line catalog, then give us a call at *(555) 433-7844* extension 85. We will also be happy to mail you a catalog of our extensive collection of travel clothing and accessories.

Escorted Tours
Our Escorted Tours department is always hard at work planning the next exciting destination to offer our TripSmart customers. We have seven professional tour guides that accompany our guests from the United States point of departure to their point of return.

Our current feature package tour is to Spain. Our local escort is Don Eugene. Don has traveled Spain extensively and enjoys sharing his love for this exciting country with others. He will be assisted after arrival in Spain with the services of archeologist JoAnne Rife, anthropologist Christina Elizabeth, and naturalist Iris Albert. Call us at *(555) 848-0807* extension 95 for information on the Spain trip or to learn about other destinations being currently scheduled.

Helpful Links in Travel Planning
The following links may be helpful in your travel research. Happy surfing!

- CNN Travel Channel - News affecting travel plans to various destinations
- US Department of State - Travel warnings, passport information, and more
- Yahoo! Currency Converter - Calculate the exchange rate between two currencies
- The Weather Channel - Weather, flight delays, and driving conditions

Independent Challenge 3

Dr. Joan Sullivent's patients often ask her questions about the current treatment protocol for Parkinson's disease, a debilitating neurological disease. She would like to post some helpful links in her clinic Web site to provide information for her patients. She begins her research at the National Institutes of Health Web site.

a. Connect to the Internet, then go to the National Institutes of Health Web site at www.nih.gov.

b. What do you like or dislike about the menu links?

c. Note the placement and appearance of the menu bar. Does it use text, images, or a combination of the two to form the links?

d. Using your favorite search engine, locate at least five helpful links that Dr. Sullivent should consider for her site, including the National Institutes of Health site pictured in Figure F-35.

FIGURE F-35

National Institutes of Health (NIH) Web site - www.nih.gov

Real Life Independent Challenge

This assignment will continue to build on the personal Web site that you created in Unit B. In Unit C you created and developed your index page. In Unit D you added a page with either an ordered or an unordered list, and a CSS style sheet with a minimum of two styles. In Unit E you added a page that included at least two images. In this lesson, you work with one of the other pages in your Web site.

    a. Consult your wireframe and decide which page you would like to develop in this lesson.

    b. Create content for this page and format the text attractively on the page using styles.

    c. Add at least three external links to this page.

    d. Think about a creative use for an image map, then add it to the page.

    e. Add at least one named anchor and link to it.

    f. Design a menu bar linking to the main pages of your Web site, then copy it to all of the main pages.

    g. Save the file, then preview the page in the browser window.

After you are satisfied with your work, verify the following:

    a. Each completed page has a page title.

    b. All links work correctly.

    c. The completed pages display correctly using a screen resolution of 1024 × 768.

    d. All images are properly set showing a path to the Web site assets folder.

    e. All images have alternate text and are legal for you to use.

    f. The Link Checker shows no broken links or orphaned files. If there are orphaned files, note your plan to link them.

Visual Workshop

You are continuing your work on the Carolyne's Creations Web site that you started in Unit B and developed in subsequent units. Chef Carolyne has asked you to create pages describing her cooking classes offered every month. Use the following files for the tasks noted: dwf_5.html to replace the classes.html page; dwf_6.html to create a new children.html page; and dwf_7.html to create a new adults.html page. (Remember not to update the links when prompted.) Copy all new images, including the new banner, cc_banner_with_text.jpg, to the assets folder in the Web site. Last, create an image map at the bottom of the banner on the classes page with hotspots for each link and copy it to all pages in the Web site, replacing all existing menu bars. Create an e-mail link on the classes page using the text "Sign me up!" and carolyne@carolynescreations.com for the link. Create links in the last sentence to the adults' and children's pages, as shown in Figure F-36. Refer to Figures F-36, F-37, and F-38 as you complete this project. Check that each completed page uses styles from the cc_styles.css file, and attach and apply these styles if you find pages without styles. (*Hint*: Remember to remove any formatting around the banners to prevent any pages from appearing to "jump.") Check for broken links and orphaned files. You will see that the former banner, cc_banner.jpg, is now an orphaned file.

FIGURE F-36

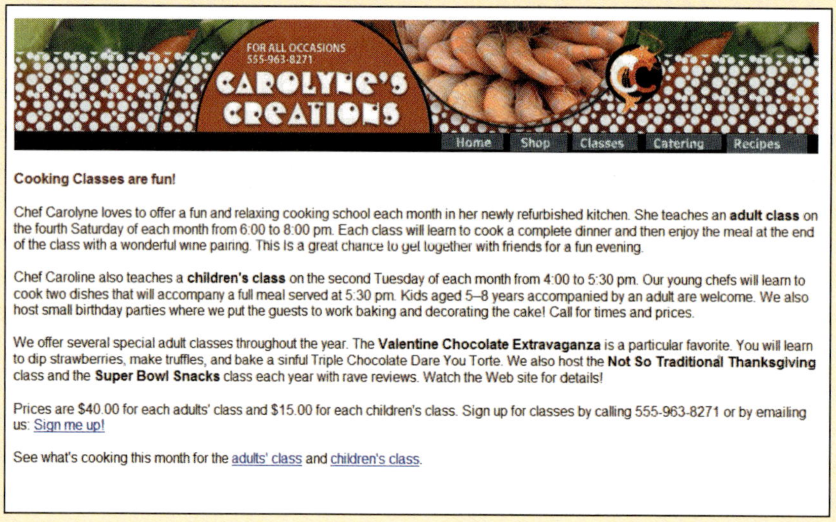

FIGURE F-37

FIGURE F-38

Using CSS for Page Layout

You have learned how to position elements on a Web page using alignment and paragraph settings. These settings let you create simple Web pages, but they limit your design choices. The best way to position page elements is to use Cascading Style Sheets (CSS). You have already learned to use CSS to format individual page elements. Now you will learn to use CSS to place your content on pages using divs. This method is the preferred method of page layout. With CSS layouts, you use blocks of content formatted with CSS rules to place information on Web pages. Once you've completed this book, you will have the skills and understanding to efficiently design sites built entirely with CSS.  In this unit, you use a predesigned CSS layout with divs to redesign the index page for The Striped Umbrella Web site.

OBJECTIVES

Understand CSS layouts

Create a page using CSS layouts

Add content to divs

Edit content in divs

Edit CSS layout properties

Insert an AP div

Position and size an AP div

Add content to an AP div

Use the AP Elements panel

Understanding CSS Layouts

Web pages built with Cascading Style Sheets use div tags to place and format page content. **Div tags** are HTML code segments that set the appearance and position of blocks of Web page content. Think of div tags as building blocks. To build a Web page with a layout based on CSS, you begin by placing div tags on the page. The div tags set up the framework to position the page content, similar to the way table cells can be used to position content. **Divs** are the page elements created with div tags that are used to position and style content. They can also be referred to as layout blocks, elements, or containers. Next, you add content and format the divs to position them on the page. For beginning designers, the predesigned CSS layouts that are available with Dreamweaver CS5 make creating pages based on CSS easy. You simply choose a predesigned CSS layout, and Dreamweaver places the div tags in the page code for you. You spend some time researching how style sheets are used for page layout.

DETAILS

Before using CSS layouts for page layout, you review the following concepts:

- **Using CSS vs. tables for page layout**

  An alternative to using CSS layouts is to use tables for page layout. Most designers today, however, use tables to place data on a page, rather than as a page layout tool. You will learn about using tables to position objects in Unit H. Tables allow you to place content in rows and columns, across and down a page. You alter the position of elements inside the table cells by modifying cell dimensions or by merging and splitting cells. Like tables, divs let you organize and control element placement by creating containers to organize content on a page. Unlike tables, however, divs let you place the content anywhere on the page, giving you more layout flexibility. They also generate pages that are more compliant with current accessibility standards.

- **Using Dreamweaver CSS page layouts**

  Dreamweaver offers 16 predesigned layouts in the New Document dialog box, as shown in Figure G-1. These layouts are a great way to learn how to create page layouts based on CSS. As you select each option, a preview of the layout appears on the right side of the New Document dialog box with a description below it. Once you select a layout, you can modify it to fit your needs. One of the great advantages of using the predesigned CSS page layouts is that each of these layouts has been tested using different browsers.

- **Using div tags for other purposes**

  Div tags are used in many ways other than in CSS layouts. For example, when you center an image on a page or inside a table cell, Dreamweaver automatically inserts a div tag in the HTML code, such as `<div align="center">`. Div tags are also used to designate different colors for page elements or for text that uses a CSS style. Divs used for page layout are identified by an ID, or name. When the div tag is selected, the ID displays in both the HTML code for the div tag in the Property inspector, and in the CSS Styles panel. In Code view, the code for a div tag named header would be `<div id="header">`.

- **Using AP divs**

  One type of div is an AP div. AP stands for absolutely positioned, so an **AP div** has a specified position that doesn't change even when viewed in different-sized windows. An AP div creates a container called an **AP element**. You create an AP div by drawing the container with the Draw AP Div button, as shown in Figure G-2. You can stack AP divs on top of each other to create interesting effects such as animations. You can also use them to show or hide content on the page by using them with JavaScript behaviors. **JavaScript behaviors** are action scripts that allow you to add dynamic content to your Web pages. **Dynamic content** is content that changes either in response to certain conditions or through interaction with the user. For example, the user might enter a zip code to display a local weather forecast. The code in the JavaScript behavior would direct the AP element with the correct forecast to appear after the user enters the corresponding zip code in a text box.

FIGURE G-1: New Document dialog box

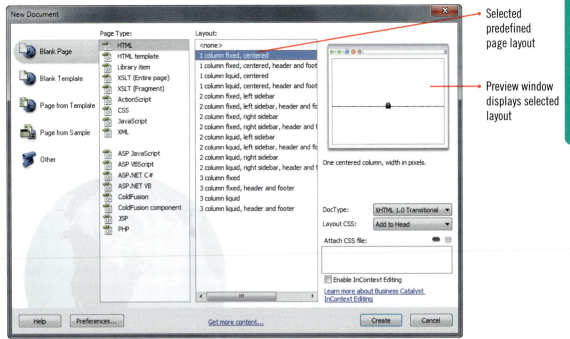

Selected predefined page layout

Preview window displays selected layout

FIGURE G-2: Inserting an AP div tag using the Draw AP Div button

Draw AP Div button

AP div icon

AP div border

AP div properties

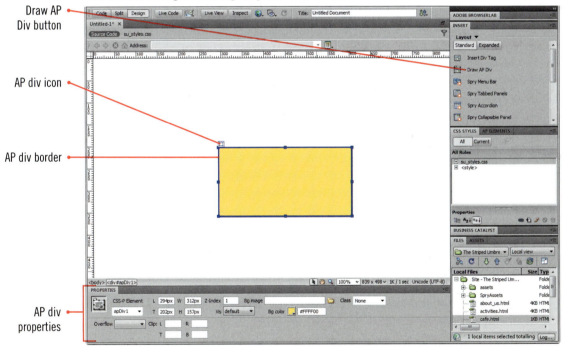

Using Dreamweaver sample pages

You can use either the Welcome Screen or the New Document dialog box, shown in Figure G-1, to create several different types of pages. The predesigned CSS page layouts make it easy for you to design accessible Web pages using CSS without being an expert in HTML code. In the Page from Sample category, CSS Style Sheet and Frameset are options that create pages you can use as starting points to develop framesets and style sheets. **Framesets** are documents that contain the instructions that tell a browser how to lay out a set of frames, which show multiple documents on a single page. It is worth the time to explore each category to understand what is available to you as a designer. Once you have selected a sample page, you can customize it to fit your needs and the site design. You can also find a variety of sample pages, or templates, on the Internet. Some sites offer templates free of charge, while others make templates available for purchase.

Creating a Page Using CSS Layouts

With the predesigned CSS layouts available in Dreamweaver, it is easy to create a page using CSS. After you choose a layout for a new page, the page opens with placeholder text displayed in the divs until you replace it with your own content. Some divs not only have placeholder text, but also instructional text on how to use or modify the default settings, such as replacing a placeholder image with your image. Each div has preset styles applied. Some of the font properties may be applied from the attributes in the CSS styles, and some may be retained from HTML headings that have been applied to the placeholder text. The properties and values of these styles are displayed in the CSS Styles panel, where you can modify them to fit your needs. Dreamweaver's predesigned CSS layouts include one-, two-, and three-column layouts. Some layouts contain features such as sidebars, headers, and footers, and some are designed with a fixed width, while others are designed to stretch across a browser window. You decide to redesign the existing index page of The Striped Umbrella Web site by creating a new page based on a predesigned CSS layout.

STEPS

1. **Open The Striped Umbrella Web site**

2. **Click File on the Application bar (Win) or Menu bar (Mac), click New, verify that Blank Page is highlighted in the left section, click HTML in the Page Type column if necessary, then click 1 column, fixed, centered, header and footer in the Layout column, as shown in Figure G-3**

   The layout description confirms that this is a fixed layout, measured in pixels. The preview of this page layout is displayed in the preview window. A **fixed layout** has columns expressed in pixels and will not change width when viewed in different window sizes. A **liquid layout** has columns expressed as percents based on the browser window width, so it will change width according to the dimensions of the browser window.

3. **If the su_styles.css file is shown in the Attach CSS file text box in the New Document dialog box, skip to Step 6. If not, click the Attach Style Sheet button 🔲 in the lower-right corner of the dialog box, then click Browse in the Attach External Style Sheet dialog box**

   The Select Style Sheet File dialog box opens.

4. **Click the su_styles.css file in the Select Style Sheet File dialog box, click OK (Win) or Choose (Mac), then click OK to close the Dreamweaver confirmation box about the document-relative path**

   The links will not be document-relative until the page is saved in the Web site.

5. **Verify that the Add as: Link option button is selected in the Attach External Style Sheet dialog box, then click OK**

   The su_styles.css file is attached to the new page, as shown in Figure G-4.

QUICK TIP
It is always better to put most, if not all, styles in an external style sheet. You can convert internal styles to external styles to keep all styles together (the number of steps it would take to list this task is space prohibitive).

6. **Click Create in the New Document dialog box, open the CSS Styles panel if necessary, then expand the <style> and su_styles.css style sheets**

   A new page opens based on the predesigned CSS layout with blocks of placeholder content as shown in Figure G-5. It contains one column of centered text, as well as a header and footer. Heading formats have been applied to the placeholder headings. There are two style sheets in the CSS Styles panel: the su_styles.css file you imported and the embedded style sheet file that is part of the predesigned page layout.

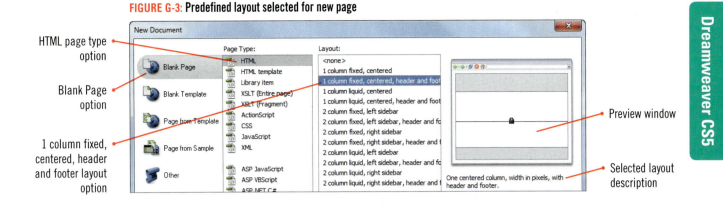

FIGURE G-3: Predefined layout selected for new page

HTML page type option

Blank Page option

1 column fixed, centered, header and footer layout option

Preview window

Selected layout description

FIGURE G-4: The su_styles.css file attached to the new page

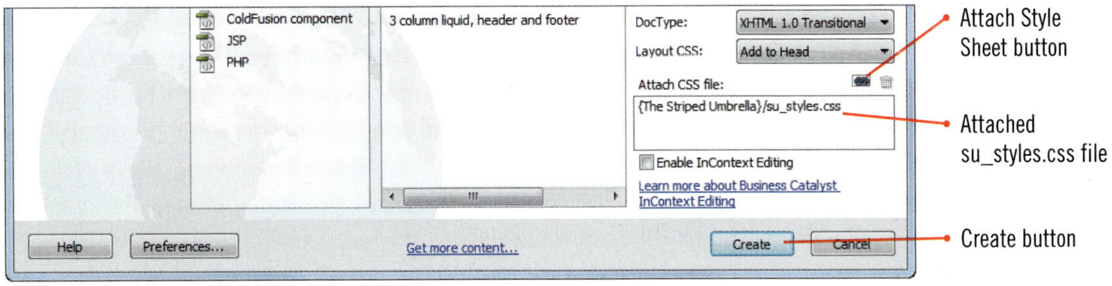

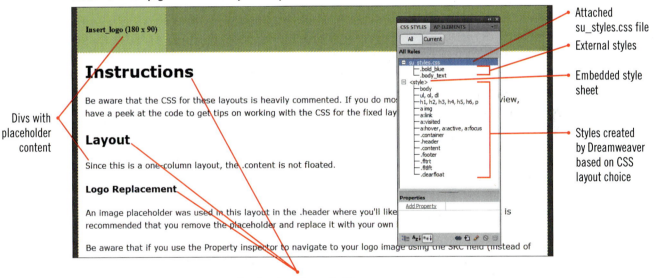

Attach Style Sheet button

Attached su_styles.css file

Create button

FIGURE G-5: New page based on CSS layout with placeholder content

Divs with placeholder content

Attached su_styles.css file

External styles

Embedded style sheet

Styles created by Dreamweaver based on CSS layout choice

Heading formats applied to placeholder headings

Design Matters

Recognizing and addressing printing issues

There are many factors that affect how a page will print compared to how it displays in a browser window. While a page background color will display in a browser window, it will not print unless the print option to print background colors is selected by the user. Although the width of the page in the browser window may fit on the screen, it could actually be too wide to print on a standard printer in portrait orientation. Also, table borders, horizontal rules, and CSS divs may not print exactly how they look in a browser. Printing your pages to see how they actually appear will allow you to address most of these issues. You can also go to a site, such as the World Wide Web Consortium (W3C) at w3.org, to find the best solution for any problems you identify.

Adding Content to Divs

A page built with all content placed inside divs makes it easy to apply formatting to all page elements. The div style properties and values set background and text colors, container widths, font settings, and alignment settings that are used to format all the images, links, tables, and text. Div styles also determine the content's position on the page. If you have developed your page content already, you can easily copy and paste it into the divs, replacing the placeholder content. You are ready to copy the content from the existing index page of The Striped Umbrella Web site and place it on the new page, replacing the placeholder content.

STEPS

1. **Open The Striped Umbrella index page, then select the three paragraphs and all contact information**

QUICK TIP
Press [Ctrl][Tab] to switch between two open pages.

2. **Copy the selected text, then switch to the new, unsaved page**

3. **Select the placeholder text between the Header and Footer, as shown in Figure G-6, paste the copied text in its place, click the Format list arrow, click Paragraph if necessary, then delete any extra space at the end of the contact information if necessary**

   The paragraphs and contact information from the index page appear in the center div on the new, unsaved page, replacing the placeholder text. This div is named content. Changing the format to paragraph removed the H1 tag that was left in the content div.

4. **Display the index page, then select and copy the two lines with the copyright and last updated information**

5. **Display the new, unsaved page, then paste the copyright and last updated information in the footer div, replacing the placeholder text, as shown in Figure G-7**

   The copyright and last updated information are placed on the new, unsaved page in the footer div.

6. **Display the index page, copy the banner, then paste it into the header div of the new, unsaved page, replacing the logo placeholder**

QUICK TIP
If you struggle with the placement of the banner and menu bar, use Code view to copy the code from the index page then paste it into the code in the new, unsaved page.

7. **Copy the menu bar from the index page into the header div of the new, unsaved page right under the banner, then enter a paragraph break after the menu bar**

   The banner displays as a broken image and the menu bar is formatted incorrectly, as shown in Figure G-8. Once you save the page in the Web site root folder, the paths and formatting will be corrected.

8. **Switch to the index page, then close it**

9. **Save the new, untitled page as index.html in The Striped Umbrella root folder, overwriting the original index page**

   The page is saved in the Web site; the menu bar displays in the correct format and the banner no longer appears as broken link, as shown in Figure G-9.

Design Matters

Understanding selector types

When you have a mixture of style classifications - embedded styles, external styles, and styles-redefining HTML tags, there is an order of precedence that is followed. Styles are ranked in order of precedence as they are applied to page elements, thus the name **cascading style sheets**. The first order of precedence is to find declarations that match the media type being used, such as a computer monitor. The second order of precedence is by importance and origin. The third order of preference is by specificity of the selector. **Pseudo class styles**, styles that determine the appearance of a page element when certain conditions are met, are considered as normal class styles. Sometimes styles with common formatting properties are grouped together to help reduce the size of style sheets. These styles are called **group selectors**.

FIGURE G-6: Selected placeholder text in new, unsaved page

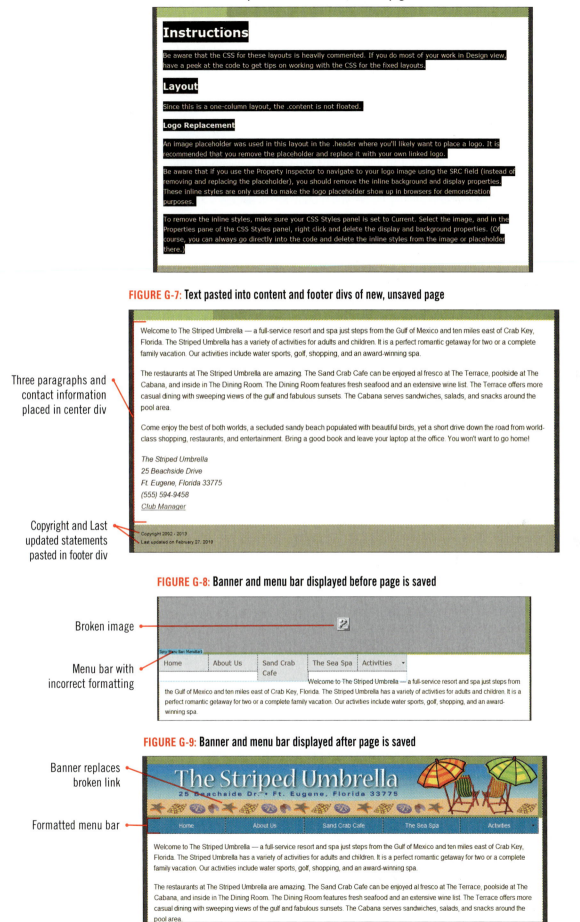

Instructions

Be aware that the CSS for these layouts is heavily commented. If you do most of your work in Design view, have a peek at the code to get tips on working with the CSS for the fixed layouts.

Layout

Since this is a one-column layout, the .content is not floated.

Logo Replacement

An image placeholder was used in this layout in the .header where you'll likely want to place a logo. It is recommended that you remove the placeholder and replace it with your own linked logo.

Be aware that if you use the Property inspector to navigate to your logo image using the SRC field (instead of removing and replacing the placeholder), you should remove the inline background and display properties. These inline styles are only used to make the logo placeholder show up in browsers for demonstration purposes.

To remove the inline styles, make sure your CSS Styles panel is set to Current. Select the image, and in the Properties pane of the CSS Styles panel, right click and delete the display and background properties. (Of course, you can always go directly into the code and delete the inline styles from the image or placeholder there.)

FIGURE G-7: Text pasted into content and footer divs of new, unsaved page

Three paragraphs and contact information placed in center div

Welcome to The Striped Umbrella — a full-service resort and spa just steps from the Gulf of Mexico and ten miles east of Crab Key, Florida. The Striped Umbrella has a variety of activities for adults and children. It is a perfect romantic getaway for two or a complete family vacation. Our activities include water sports, golf, shopping, and an award-winning spa.

The restaurants at The Striped Umbrella are amazing. The Sand Crab Cafe can be enjoyed al fresco at The Terrace, poolside at The Cabana, and inside in The Dining Room. The Dining Room features fresh seafood and an extensive wine list. The Terrace offers more casual dining with sweeping views of the gulf and fabulous sunsets. The Cabana serves sandwiches, salads, and snacks around the pool area.

Come enjoy the best of both worlds, a secluded sandy beach populated with beautiful birds, yet a short drive down the road from world-class shopping, restaurants, and entertainment. Bring a good book and leave your laptop at the office. You won't want to go home!

The Striped Umbrella
25 Beachside Drive
Ft. Eugene, Florida 33775
(555) 594-9458
Club Manager

Copyright and Last updated statements pasted in footer div

Copyright 2002 - 2013
Last updated on February 27, 2010

FIGURE G-8: Banner and menu bar displayed before page is saved

Broken image

Menu bar with incorrect formatting

Spry Menu Bar: MenuBar1

| Home | About Us | Sand Crab Cafe | The Sea Spa | Activities ▾ |

Welcome to The Striped Umbrella — a full-service resort and spa just steps from the Gulf of Mexico and ten miles east of Crab Key, Florida. The Striped Umbrella has a variety of activities for adults and children. It is a perfect romantic getaway for two or a complete family vacation. Our activities include water sports, golf, shopping, and an award-winning spa.

FIGURE G-9: Banner and menu bar displayed after page is saved

Banner replaces broken link

The Striped Umbrella
25 Beachside Dr. • Ft. Eugene, Florida 33775

Formatted menu bar

| Home | About Us | Sand Crab Cafe | The Sea Spa | Activities ▾ |

Welcome to The Striped Umbrella — a full-service resort and spa just steps from the Gulf of Mexico and ten miles east of Crab Key, Florida. The Striped Umbrella has a variety of activities for adults and children. It is a perfect romantic getaway for two or a complete family vacation. Our activities include water sports, golf, shopping, and an award-winning spa.

The restaurants at The Striped Umbrella are amazing. The Sand Crab Cafe can be enjoyed al fresco at The Terrace, poolside at The Cabana, and inside in The Dining Room. The Dining Room features fresh seafood and an extensive wine list. The Terrace offers more casual dining with sweeping views of the gulf and fabulous sunsets. The Cabana serves sandwiches, salads, and snacks around the pool area.

Editing Content in Divs

After you replace placeholder content in divs with your Web site's content, you will probably want to adjust some of the formatting. Styles that you have previously applied might conflict with the div styles, so you may want to remove redundant style properties, such as font and alignment settings. It is generally better to use an external style sheet to format text, to provide consistency across the site. External style sheets use global styles. **Global styles** are styles used to apply common properties for certain page elements, such as text, links, or backgrounds. When you have styles that are defined in both an external style sheet and in styles defined by div tags, you should evaluate which styles makes the most sense to use, based on the content each is intended to format. The styles for the div tags determine the placement and appearance of the divs, so analyze them carefully before you modify them.  You continue to work on the new index page. You decide to change the menu bar alignment and remove the formatting that the new div styles have automatically applied.

STEPS

1. **Click the HTML button <> HTML to switch to the HTML Property inspector if necessary, then select the text in the second paragraph**

   The body_text style from the su_styles.css file appears in the Class text box in the HTML Property inspector to indicate the current style of the selected text.

2. **Click the Class list arrow, then click None**

   The content style (from the embedded style sheet) appears in the Class text box to indicate the new style of the selected text, as shown in Figure G-10. By removing the body_text style, the font properties from the content style are now formatting the text.

3. **Click anywhere on the page to deselect the text**

   The text in the second paragraph looks different from the text in the other two paragraphs, since it is now formatted with a different style.

   > **QUICK TIP**
   > You can also triple-click a paragraph to select it.

4. **Select the text in the second paragraph, click the Class list arrow, click body_text, then click anywhere on the page to deselect the text**

5. **Click the `<div.content>` tag in the Tag selector, then move the pointer to the middle of the div until the tooltip shown in Figure G-11 appears**

   The properties of the div appear in a tooltip, indicating that the Class for the div is content and the Tag is div.

6. **Save your work**

   The text remains selected on the page.

TABLE G-1: Div tag properties

property	function
ID	Displays the name used to identify the div in the code
Class	Displays the class style currently applied to the div
Float	Sets the float, or position, of the div in relation to adjacent elements as left, right, none, or inherit
Position	Sets the position of the div as absolute, fixed, relative, static, or inherit
Top	Sets the div position in relation to the top of the page or parent element
Right	Sets the right position of the div as either auto or inherit
Bottom	Sets the bottom position of the div as either auto or inherit
Left	Sets the div position in relation to the left side of the page or parent element
Width	Sets the width of the div, in pixels by default
Height	Sets the height of the div, in pixels by default
Overflow	Controls how the div will appear in the browser if the content is larger than the div

Using CSS for Page Layout

FIGURE G-10: Reformatting with content style

content style is now formatting the paragraph

FIGURE G-11: Viewing the div properties

<div.content> tag in the Tag selector

content style is applied to all content in content div

Properties of div displayed in tooltip

Using Visual Aids as design tools

There are several options for viewing your divs in Design view. You can choose to show or hide outlines, temporarily assign different background colors to each individual div, or view the **CSS Layout Box Model** (padding and margins included) of a selected layout. To change these options, use the View, Visual Aids menu, and then select or deselect the CSS Layout Backgrounds, CSS Layout Box Model, or CSS Layout Outlines menu choice. You can also use the Visual Aids button 🖾 on the Document toolbar.

Editing CSS Layout Properties

It is unlikely that you will find a predesigned CSS page layout that is exactly what you have in mind for your Web site. However, once you have created a page with a predesigned CSS layout, it is easy to modify the properties for individual rules to better fit your needs. If you have attached a style sheet to a page using CSS for page layout, you will see two sets of rules in the CSS Styles panel: those from the attached external style sheet and those from the style sheet created with the page that contains the properties for the CSS layout blocks. Ideally, every page element should be formatted using style sheets rather than by applying individual formatting properties with the Property inspector. You apply the rules in attached external style sheets to format individual page elements with global styles, such as text or horizontal rules. The styles generated by the CSS page layout control the formatting of the divs, including the div width and background color, but they can also include formatting for the page elements within the divs. You continue working on the new index page by changing the div formatting and the page properties.

1. **Click .header in the CSS Styles panel to select it**

   This style contains the formatting for the header div. The current formatting includes an olive green background, color #ADB96E. Rather than using the Edit Rule button in the CSS Styles panel to edit rules, you can change, add, or delete property values in the Properties pane of the CSS Styles panel.

   > **QUICK TIP**
   > You can enter either #FFFFFF or #FFF (the shorthand version).

2. **Click to select the background color #ADB96E in the CSS Styles panel properties pane, type #FFF as shown in Figure G-12, then press [Enter] (Win) or [return] (Mac)**

   The background color of the header is now white, which matches the background color in the content div.

   > **TROUBLE**
   > You may need to resize panels to be able to see the page background behind the divs.

3. **Repeat Steps 1 and 2 to change the footer rule to white**

   All of the divs contain a white background. Although the page background is still gray, you can change this feature by editing the body tag if you prefer a different color.

4. **Select the body tag in the CSS Styles panel, click to select the existing background color, type #FFF, then press [Enter] (Win) or [return] (Mac)**

   The body tag is used to format the page body—the area outside the divs. The body tag for the page is set to display a white background.

   > **QUICK TIP**
   > You can also open the CSS Rule definition dialog box by double-clicking a rule name on the CSS Styles panel.

5. **Click .container in the CSS Styles panel, click the Edit rule button ✎, then click the Border category**

   A border around the page sets it off from the extra space around it when it is viewed in a browser.

6. **Click the Top list arrow in the Style column, click solid, click the Width list arrow in the first text box in the Width column, click thin, click in the First color text box in the Color column, type #003, verify that the Same for all check box is selected in each of the three columns, compare your screen to Figure G-13, then click OK**

   The border properties are set to include a thin solid line with a dark gray color.

7. **Type The Striped Umbrella Beach Resort and Spa, Ft. Eugene, Florida in the Title text box on the Document toolbar**

8. **Save your work, then preview the page in the browser**

   The banner and menu bar are not centered on the page; adding padding to the header rule will fix this.

   > **QUICK TIP**
   > The padding property places extra space inside a div between the borders and contents.

9. **Close the browser, click .header in the CSS Styles panel, click ✎, click the Box category, click the Same for all check box in the Padding section to select it if necessary, type 5 in the Top Padding text box, then click OK**

10. **Save your work, preview the page in the browser, compare your screen to Figure G-14, then close the browser**

FIGURE G-12: Editing the properties of the header rule

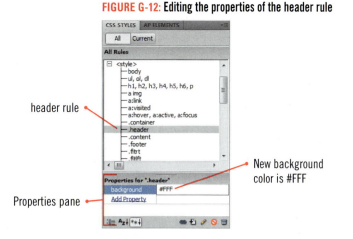

header rule

New background color is #FFF

Properties pane

FIGURE G-13: Editing the properties for the container rule

Same for all check boxes

Color text box

Style text box

Width text box

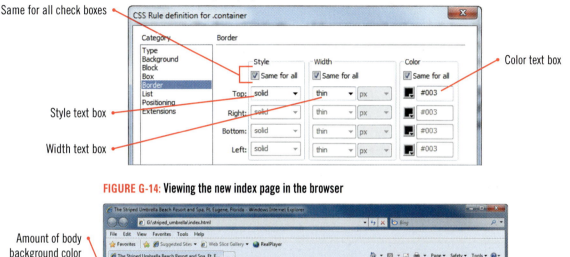

FIGURE G-14: Viewing the new index page in the browser

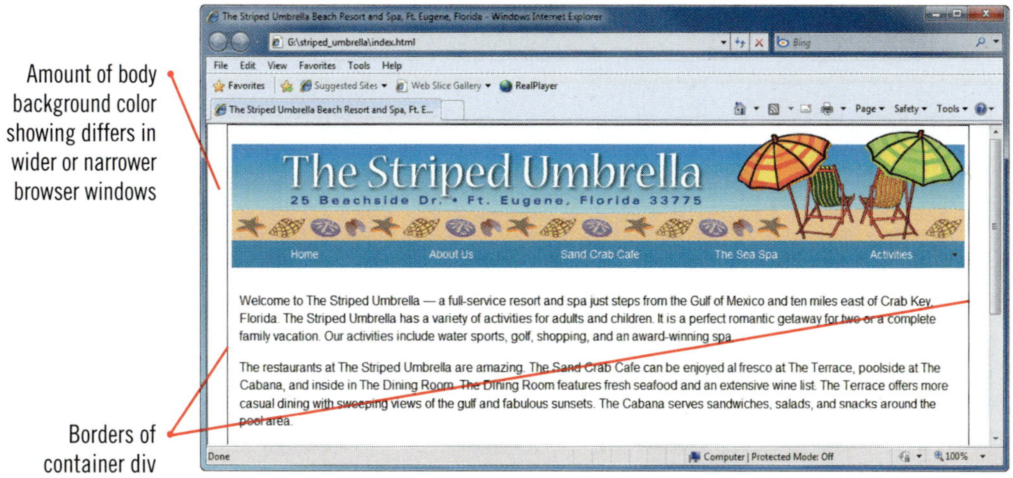

Amount of body background color showing differs in wider or narrower browser windows

Borders of container div

Inserting an AP Div

An **AP (absolutely positioned) div** is a div you use to place content on a Web page in a fixed position. AP divs are also referred to as AP elements. You can specify a selected AP div's exact position using either the Left or Top settings on the Property inspector or by editing the rule in the CSS Styles panel. (By contrast, **relative positioning** places divs relative to other page content.) You can stack AP divs on top of each other as if they were transparency sheets and specify that only certain divs be visible at certain times or in specified conditions. To insert an AP div, you click the Draw AP Div button in the Layout category on the Insert panel, then drag a rectangular shape anywhere on a page. AP divs are useful for placing time-sensitive information on a page that might be used for only a set period of time. Since it won't affect the page layout when it is added or removed, it is a useful design tool for showing temporary content, such as advertising space. **Guides** are lines you can drag onto your pages to help you place objects more precisely. Guides are not visible in the browser. Once you place a guide on the page, you can reposition it by dragging it to a different location. You have been asked to place a temporary advertisement for a children's sand castle contest on the index page. An AP div would be a good way to display the ad. You begin by inserting an AP div at the bottom of the page.

STEPS

> **TROUBLE**
> If you cannot see the 500 pixel mark on your vertical ruler, close the Property inspector to place the guide, then open it back up again once the guide is placed.

1. **Click View on the Application bar (Win) or Menu bar (Mac), point to Rulers, click Show if necessary, place the mouse pointer anywhere on the horizontal ruler, then drag a horizontal guide to the 500 pixel mark on the vertical ruler**

   When you hold your pointer over the guide, a yellow tooltip noting the exact location of the guide appears beside it.

2. **Click the Insert panel list arrow, click Layout if necessary, then click Draw AP Div**

   The pointer changes to a plus sign when placed over the page, indicating that it is ready to draw an AP div.

> **QUICK TIP**
> You can also insert an AP div using the Insert, Layout Objects, AP Div command.

3. **Using Figure G-15 as a guide, drag a rectangle in the middle of the home page, under the guide, that is approximately 300 pixels wide and 130 pixels tall**

   As you drag you can see the height and width values change in the Property inspector. A new AP div appears on the page, but it is not selected. An AP div icon ⊡ appears in the upper-left corner of the div.

> **QUICK TIP**
> You can also select an AP div by clicking one of its borders.

4. **Click the AP Div icon ⊡ above the AP div to select it**

   Sizing handles appear around the AP div, indicating that it is selected. The Property inspector options change to show properties for an AP div.

5. **With the AP div selected, select apDiv1 in the CSS-P Element ID text box in the Property inspector, type contest, then press [Enter] (Win) or [return] (Mac)**

   Giving an AP div a unique name helps you to identify the div quickly as you view the code.

6. **Select <div#contest> in the Tag selector if necessary, click the Overflow list arrow in the Property inspector, then click auto**

   The Overflow property controls how the content in an AP div will appear in a browser if there is insufficient space to fit the content in the AP div. The Auto setting enables the overflow content to display, and will add scroll bars, if necessary, at the side or bottom of the AP div when it is viewed in the browser window.

7. **Click the Vis list arrow, then click visible**

   The Vis property specifies whether the AP div is visible or not when the page loads in the browser.

8. **Compare your screen to Figure G-16, then save your work**

Using CSS for Page Layout

FIGURE G-15: New AP div added to the home page

Drag guide from horizontal ruler

Horizontal guide

500-pixel mark on vertical ruler

AP div icon

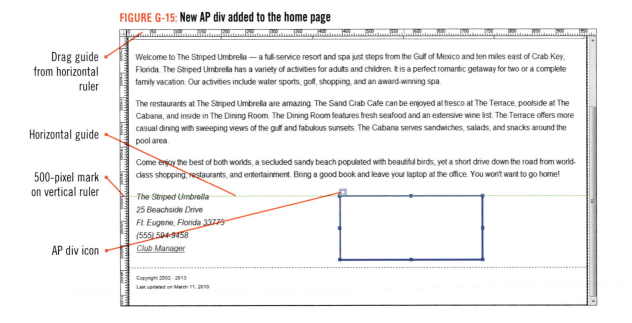

FIGURE G-16: Property inspector showing properties of selected AP div

AP div icon

Selected AP div

CSS-P Element ID text box

Overflow property

Vis property

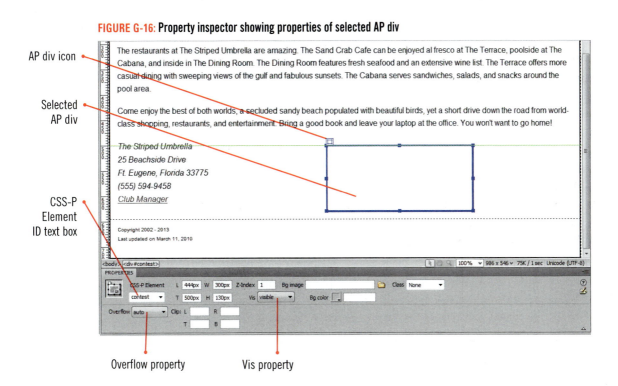

Creating special effects with AP divs

Advanced designers use AP divs to create special effects on Web pages. They might create a rollover effect so that when the user places the mouse pointer over an AP div, another AP div appears. Or they might make an AP div appear to move along a path, or change size, visibility, or position using a JavaScript feature called a **timeline**. Another effect allows users to drag AP divs across the page; this feature might be used to create a puzzle where users can move puzzle pieces into the correct position. Some interactive games allow you to drag and drop objects to target areas, such as dragging chess pieces on a virtual chessboard. In Dreamweaver, a designer would use the Behaviors panel to assign behaviors to AP divs. A **behavior** is a preset piece of JavaScript code that can be attached to divs. A behavior tells the div to respond in a specific way when an **action** occurs, such as when the mouse pointer is positioned over the div, or when a user clicks the mouse over a div. The action triggers an **event** that causes a behavior to start, such as the AP div changing size or disappearing.

Positioning and Sizing an AP Div

To use AP divs, you must understand absolute positioning. An AP div is positioned absolutely by specifying the distance between the top-left corner of the AP div and the top-left corner of the page or parent container. The default reference point is the top-left corner of the page. You control the placement of AP divs by setting attributes in the Property inspector. The **Left property (L)** specifies the distance between the left edge of an AP div and the left edge of the page or parent container, such as another div. The **Top property (T)** specifies the distance between the top edge of the AP div and the top edge of the page or div that contains it. The **Width (W)** and **Height (H) properties** specify the dimensions of the AP div in either pixels or as a percentage of the page. If your pages are based on a CSS layout that is centered on the page, you must change the default reference point from the top-left corner of the page to the top-left corner of the parent container, such as a CSS layout block. First, move the code for the AP div after the opening tag for the CSS layout block serving as the parent container. Second, edit the code for the parent container by changing the Positioning property value to relative. The AP div will then align itself in a fixed position relative to the parent container despite browser window size. The top and left properties of the AP div use the top-left corner of the parent div, rather than the top-left corner of the browser window to determine where to place the AP div. The parent div must then be set to align relatively. With the AP div in position on the index page, you edit the properties that will determine the size and position of the content on the page.

1. **Switch to Code view, select the code `<div id="contest"></div>` if necessary, then press [Ctrl][X] (Win) or [command][X] (Mac) to cut it**

   The code is removed from the page and placed on the Clipboard.

2. **Locate the code `<div class="container">`, enter a line break at the end of this code, press [Ctrl][V] (Win) or [command][V] (Mac) to paste `<div id="contest"></div>`, then compare your screen to Figure G-17**

   The placement of the AP div code is repositioned inside the opening and closing tags for the div named *container*.

   > **QUICK TIP**
   > If the CSS layout was based on a left align- ment rather than a center alignment, these steps would not be necessary.

3. **Switch back to Design view, select container rule in the CSS Styles panel, click the Edit Rule button, click Positioning in the Category list, click the Position list arrow, click relative, then click OK**

   The position property for the container rule is set to relative. The combination of changing the container rule position to relative and moving the AP div code after the container opening tag works together to ensure that the AP div remains in a constant position in the browser window, regardless of the width of the window.

4. **Click the AP div border to select the AP div if necessary, select the current text in the L text box in the Property inspector, type 420px, then press [Enter] (Win) or [return] (Mac)**

   The left side of the AP div automatically aligns with the 420px location on the horizontal ruler.

5. **Select the current text in the T text box, type 467px, then press [Enter] (Win) or [return] (Mac)**

   The top of the AP div aligns with the 470 location on the vertical ruler. In the browser window, the AP div will not appear as close to the last line of text.

   > **QUICK TIP**
   > You can press [Enter] or [Tab] to enter options in the Property inspector, but [Tab] will also move the insertion point to the next text box.

6. **Select the current text in the W text box, type 200px, press [Tab], type 175px in the H text box, press [Tab], save your work, then compare your screen to Figure G-18**

   The AP div automatically adjusts to the updated width and height specifications and the upper-left corner remains in its original position.

FIGURE G-17: AP div code repositioned after container div code

Opening tag for CSS container div

div tag for contest AP div

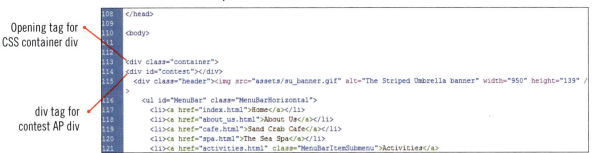

```
108  </head>
109
110  <body>
111
112
113  <div class="container">
114  <div id="contest"></div>
115    <div class="header"><img src="assets/su_banner.gif" alt="The Striped Umbrella banner" width="950" height="139" /
     >
116      <ul id="MenuBar" class="MenuBarHorizontal">
117        <li><a href="index.html">Home</a></li>
118        <li><a href="about_us.html">About Us</a></li>
119        <li><a href="cafe.html">Sand Crab Cafe</a></li>
120        <li><a href="spa.html">The Sea Spa</a></li>
121        <li><a href="activities.html" class="MenuBarItemSubmenu">Activities</a>
```

FIGURE G-18: Resized AP div

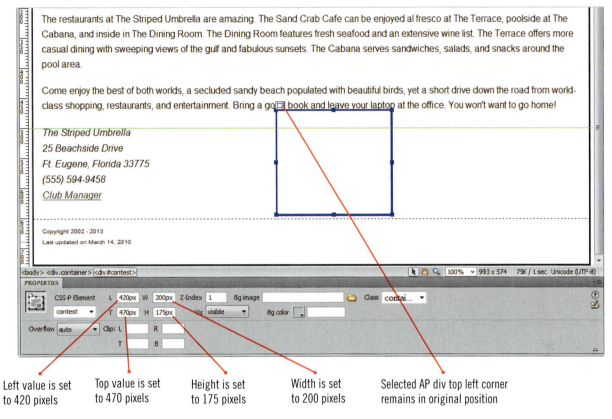

Left value is set to 420 pixels

Top value is set to 470 pixels

Height is set to 175 pixels

Width is set to 200 pixels

Selected AP div top left corner remains in original position

Understanding the z-index property

The **z-index property** in the Property inspector is used to specify the vertical stacking order of multiple AP divs on a page. If you think of the page as being AP div 0, then any number higher than that will appear on top of the page. For instance, if you have three AP divs with z-index values of 1, 2, and 3, then 1 will appear underneath 2 and 3, while 3 will always appear on top of 1 and 2. AP divs are assigned default z-index values as they are created beginning with the number 1, but you can easily change the stacking order by reassigning the z-index values in either the CSS Styles panel or in the AP Elements panel.

Design Matters

Placing the most important information first

People on the Internet are notoriously hurried and will often read only information that is located on the first screen that they see on a Web page, rather than scroll though the entire length of the page. Therefore, it is a good idea to put the most important information at the top of the page. In other words, the most important information should be on the part of the page that is visible before you have to scroll to see the rest. You can use guides to emulate a newspaper **fold line**, which represents the place where a newspaper is folded. The most important stories are usually printed "above the fold." You create guides by clicking and dragging from the horizontal or vertical ruler, down or across the page.

Adding Content to an AP Div

Because an AP div is like a separate document within a Web page, it can contain the same types of elements that a page contains, such as background colors, images, links, tables, and text. If you add more content than will fit in the present size, the AP div will enlarge to display the content on your page in Dreamweaver. However, when you preview the page in a browser, the amount displayed will depend on how you set your Overflow settings. As with formatting text on Web pages, you should use CSS to format text on an AP div.  You are ready to add text to advertise the date of the sand castle contest. You want to use a picture of children on the beach as a background image to add interest to the AP div.

STEPS

1. Select the AP div if necessary, then click the Browse for File icon 🗀 next to the Bg image text box in the Property inspector

   The Select Image Source dialog box opens.

QUICK TIP
If you don't see the contestants_bak.jpg in the assets folder, hold down [Ctrl] while you click the Refresh button or repeat Steps 1 and 2.

2. Navigate to the drive and folder where you store your Unit G Data Files, double-click contestants_bak.jpg from the assets folder, then compare your screen to Figure G-19

   The image fills the background of the AP div.

3. Refresh the Files panel to verify that contestants_bak.jpg was copied to the assets folder of the Web site

TROUBLE
If you are having trouble setting the insertion point, click or double-click directly in the middle of the AP div.

4. Click inside the AP div

   The insertion pointer displays as a blinking line in the upper-left corner of the div.

5. Type Sand Castle Contest July 4, press [Shift][Enter] (Win) or [Shift][return] (Mac), then type Bring your friends!

   This AP div will be placed on the index page three weeks before July 4 and then removed after the contest is over. Since it is independent from the rest of the page content, you will not need to make any page modifications other than changing the visibility property of the AP div to invisible.

TROUBLE
If you don't see the contest rule listed in the CSS Styles panel, click the plus sign next to <style> to expand it.

6. Select the contest rule in the CSS Styles panel, then click the Edit Rule button ✏️

   The contest rule was created when the AP div name "contest" was assigned to replace the default AP div name.

7. Click the Type category, as shown in Figure G-20, change the Font-family to Arial, Helvetica, sans-serif, the Font-size to small, the Font-weight to bold, the Color to #006, then click Apply

QUICK TIP
When you type text on an AP div, you should always format the text using styles in the CSS Styles panel, rather than using manual formatting.

8. Click the Block category, change the Text-align setting to center, then click OK

   The text changes to reflect the properties you have added to the contest style. It is blue and centered in the AP div.

9. Save your work, then click View on the Application bar (Win) or Menu bar (Mac), point to Rulers, then click Show to deselect it

   Hiding the rulers saves space in the document window until you need to access them.

10. Preview the page in your browser, compare your screen with Figure G-21, close your browser, make any line adjustments if necessary, save the page, then Exit (Win) or Quit (Mac) Dreamweaver

FIGURE G-19: AP div with a background image

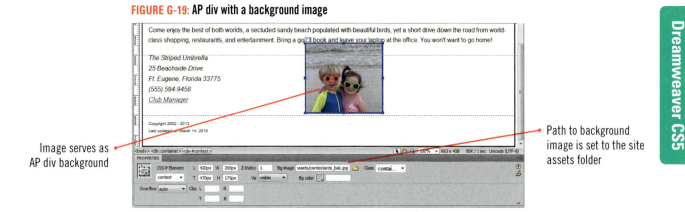

Image serves as
AP div background

Path to background
image is set to the site
assets folder

FIGURE G-20: Editing the contest style

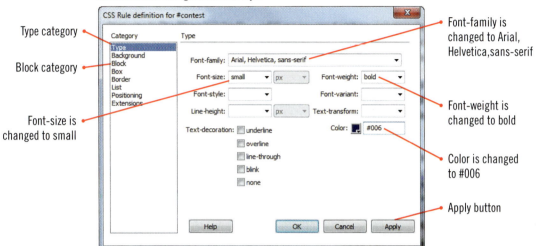

Type category

Block category

Font-size is
changed to small

Font-family is
changed to Arial,
Helvetica, sans-serif

Font-weight is
changed to bold

Color is changed
to #006

Apply button

FIGURE G-21: Index page with the formatted AP div

Understanding the Overflow property

Sometimes there is more content than will fit in the dimensions of an AP div. To account for this possibility, you can set the Overflow property to direct the browser to display the extra content or to hide it, by assigning one of four possible values. The visible value means that the AP div will stretch to display any extra content. The hidden value means that extra content will not be displayed. The scroll value means that the browser will display scroll bars in the AP div whether they are needed or not. The auto value means that extra content will be displayed, and scroll bars will be added if needed.

Using the AP Elements Panel

The easiest way to manage AP divs is with the AP Elements panel, which is in the CSS tab group next to the CSS Styles panel. The **AP Elements panel**, opened through the Window menu, is used to control the properties of all AP divs on a Web page. The AP Elements panel provides a quick way to scan the number of AP divs on a page, their names, their z-indexes, and to control their visibility settings. You study the uses of the AP Elements panel to better understand how to manage your AP divs. As you add more AP divs to the Web site pages, the need for good organization practices becomes even more important.

DETAILS

• Change AP div order and names

The AP Elements panel lists all AP divs on the open page in order of their z-index. The first AP div you create appears by default at the bottom of the stack, with the most recent at the top. You can reorder them by changing the z-index settings. Assigning an AP div a logical name that represents its content helps you quickly identify each page div. To rename an AP div, double-click its default name in the Property inspector, then enter a new name.

• Select AP divs

When you select the AP div name from the list in the AP Elements panel, the AP div will be selected on the page. This feature is helpful when you are trying to select an AP div from the bottom of a stack.

QUICK TIP

If you want to show or hide all AP divs on a page, click the header eye icon at the top of the column to toggle between all visible or all hidden.

• Control visibility

The first column in the AP Elements panel contains icons that show the visibility setting for each AP div, with eye icons representing the visibility settings. An open eye icon 👁 means that the AP div is visible on the page. A closed eye icon 👁 means the AP div is not visible on the page. If neither icon appears in the column, the AP div will inherit the visibility status of its parent object; see Figure G-22. If an AP div is not part of a group, the parent object is the Web page or CSS container. Clicking the column next to a div will toggle between the icons, thus changing the visibility settings for that div.

QUICK TIP

You can also change the z-index by entering a new value in the Z-Index text box in the Property inspector.

• Control the visible stacking order and overlaps

You can change the stacking order of an AP div by dragging the AP div name up or down in the AP Elements panel. As you drag past other names in the list, a placement line appears to let you know where the AP div would move if you released the mouse button. After you drag an element in the list, its z-index changes automatically to reflect its new position in the stacking order. See Figures G-23 and G-24.

• Change the nesting status of nested AP divs

Besides stacking, another option for placing AP divs is nesting. **Nested AP divs** are AP divs whose HTML code resides inside other AP divs. In the AP Elements panel, nested AP divs are indented under the parent AP div. See Figure G-25. Nesting AP divs ties them together for such purposes as visibility. Nested AP divs move with their parent AP divs. If you want to nest AP divs, be sure that the Prevent overlaps check box is deselected in the AP Elements panel, as shown in Figure G-25. You must also select the Nest when created within an AP div check box in the Dreamweaver Preferences dialog box, as shown in Figure G-26. To nest existing AP divs, simply [Ctrl]-drag (Win) or [option]-drag (Mac) the AP div you want to nest on top of the AP div that will be the parent in the AP Elements panel.

Understanding AP div code

As you examine the HTML code for AP divs, you will see that the code is actually split between the head section and the body section of the code. The head section contains the code that sets the position, size, overflow, and formatting. Comments are also included that provide explanation for each style. The body section contains the code for the div ID and div content. This is similar to the way CSS styles are written: the code for the CSS style, properties, and values resides in the head section for internal style sheets. For external style sheets, the code linking the style sheet to the page resides in the head section. The code where each CSS style is applied to a page element resides in the body section.

FIGURE G-22: The AP Elements panel visibility settings

Eye header icon
Open eye icon
Closed eye icon
No eye icon displayed
CSS STYLES
AP ELEMENTS
Prevent overlaps
ID
Z
contest
2
signup
outline
1

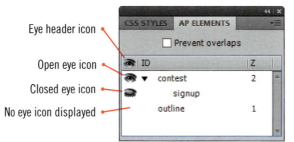

FIGURE G-23: The Outline AP div with a z-index of 2

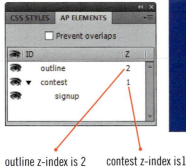

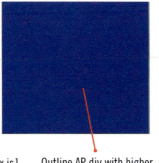

CSS STYLES
AP ELEMENTS
Prevent overlaps
ID
Z
outline
2
contest
1
signup
outline z-index is 2
contest z-index is1
Outline AP div with higher z-index positioned in front of the contest AP div

FIGURE G-24: The Outline AP div with a z-index of 1

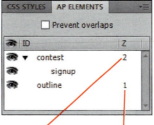

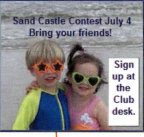

CSS STYLES
AP ELEMENTS
Prevent overlaps
ID
Z
contest
2
signup
outline
1
Sand Castle Contest July 4
Bring your friends!
Sign up at the Club desk.
contest z-index is 2
outline z-index is 1
Outline AP div with lower z-index positioned in back of the contest AP div

FIGURE G-25: Viewing a nested AP div in the AP Elements panel

Prevent overlaps check box remains unselected
signup AP div is indented under the contest AP div
CSS STYLES
AP ELEMENTS
Prevent overlaps
ID
Z
contest
2
signup
3
outline
1
Sand Castle Contest July 4
Bring your friends!
Sign up at the Club desk.

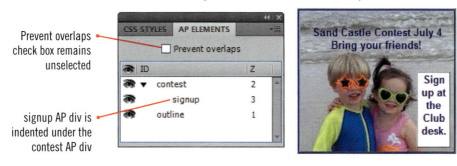

FIGURE G-26: Viewing AP Elements preferences

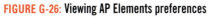

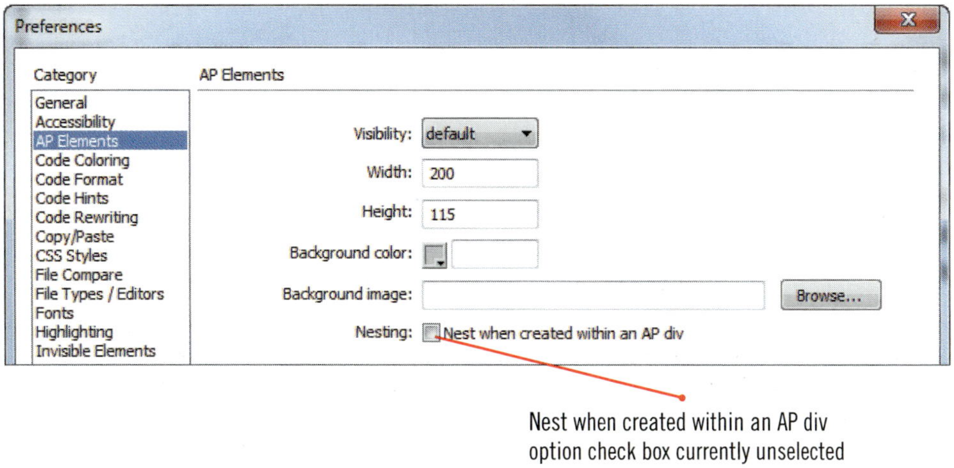

Preferences
Category
General
Accessibility
AP Elements
Code Coloring
Code Format
Code Hints
Code Rewriting
Copy/Paste
CSS Styles
File Compare
File Types / Editors
Fonts
Highlighting
Invisible Elements
AP Elements
Visibility: default
Width: 200
Height: 115
Background color:
Background image:
Browse...
Nesting: Nest when created within an AP div
Nest when created within an AP div option check box currently unselected

Practice

For current SAM information, including versions and content details, visit SAM Central (http://www.cengage.com/samcentral). If you have a SAM user profile, you may have access to hands-on instruction, practice, and assessment of the skills covered in this unit. Since various versions of SAM are supported throughout the life of this text, check with your instructor for the correct instructions and URL/Web site for accessing assignments.

Concepts Review

Label each element shown in Figure G-27.

FIGURE G-27

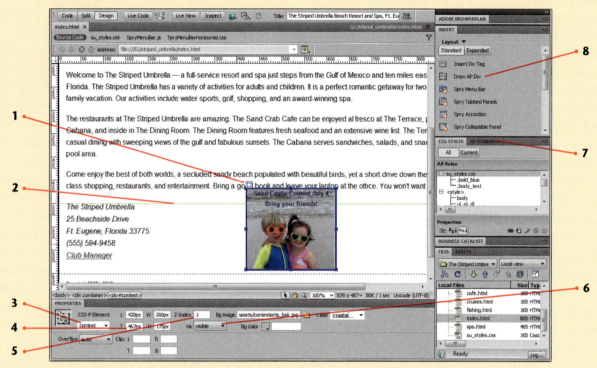

1. _____
2. _____
3. _____
4. _____

5. _____
6. _____
7. _____
8. _____

Match each of the following terms with the statement that best describes its function.

9. AP Elements panel
10. z-index property
11. div tags
12. AP div
13. Fixed layout
14. CSS page layouts
15. JavaScript behaviors
16. CSS Layout box model
17. Nested AP divs
18. Dynamic content

a. A div with a specified, fixed position on a page
b. Pages built using div tags and CSS
c. A view that displays padding and margins for AP divs
d. The location used to control the properties of AP divs
e. Page content that changes either in response to certain conditions or through interaction with the user
f. A layout with the width of content blocks based on pixels
g. An AP div whose code is inside another AP div's (parent) code
h. The property that determines the stacking order of multiple AP divs
i. Action scripts that allow you to create dynamic page content
j. HTML tags that determine the appearance and position of containers of content

Skills Review

(If you did not create this Web site in Unit B and maintain it during the preceding units, you will need to create a site root folder for this Web site and define the Web site using files your instructor will provide. See the "Read This Before You Begin" section for more detailed instructions.)

1. **Create a page using CSS layouts.**
   a. Start Dreamweaver, then open the Blooms & Bulbs Web site.
   b. Open the index page.
   c. Create a new blank HTML page with the 1 column fixed, centered, header and footer layout, then attach the blooms_styles.css file to the page if necessary.
   d. Add the page title **Blooms & Bulbs – Your complete garden center** in the Title text box.

2. **Add content to CSS layout blocks.**
   a. Switch to the index page, then copy the two paragraphs and contact information (but not the copyright or last updated information).
   b. Paste the text in the content container of the new, unsaved page, replacing the placeholder text.
   c. Switch back to the index page, then copy the copyright and last updated information.
   d. Paste the text in the footer container of the new, unsaved page, replacing the placeholder text.
   e. Switch back to the index page, then select and copy both the banner and the menu bar.
   f. Paste the banner and menu bar in the header section of the new, unsaved page, replacing the placeholder logo, then delete any extra paragraph returns if necessary. (*Hint*: The banner will be broken and the menu bar will not be formatted until you save the file.)
   g. Close the index page.
   h. Save the new, untitled page as **index.html**, overwriting the original index page.

3. **Edit content in CSS layout blocks.**
   a. Select the contact information.
   b. Verify that the body_text style was applied.

4. **Edit CSS layout properties.**
   a. Select the header rule in the CSS Styles panel to change the background color to **#FFF**, then add a five pixel-width padding to each side of the header.
   b. Select the footer rule then change the background color to **#996**.
   c. Save your work.

5. **Insert an AP div.**
   a. Use the Draw AP Div button to draw a rectangle, about two inches tall by one inch wide, on the bottom half of your page using a guide for placement.
   b. Select and rename this AP div **organic**.
   c. Set the Vis property to visible.
   d. Set the Overflow property to visible.

6. Position and size an AP div.

a. Switch to Code view, cut the code for the AP div, then paste it under the opening tag for the container rule.

b. Return to Design view, then edit the container rule to set the Position property to **relative**.

c. Select the organic AP div, then set the Left property to **445px**.

d. Set the Top property to **325px**.

e. Set the Width property to **175px**.

f. Set the Height property to **219px**.

g. Set the Z-index property to **1** if necessary.

h. Save your work.

7. Add content to an AP div.

a. Select the organic AP div if necessary, then insert the background image peaches_small.jpg from the assets folder in the drive and folder where you store your Unit G Data Files.

b. Place the insertion point in the organic AP div, then type **Organic Gardening**.

c. Insert a line break, then type **Class begins soon!**.

d. Use the Text-align property to center the text for the organic rule.

e. Save your work.

f. Preview the page in your browser, compare your screen with Figure G-28, then close the browser.

g. Make any line spacing adjustments if necessary, save the page, then exit Dreamweaver.

Skills Review (continued)

FIGURE G-28

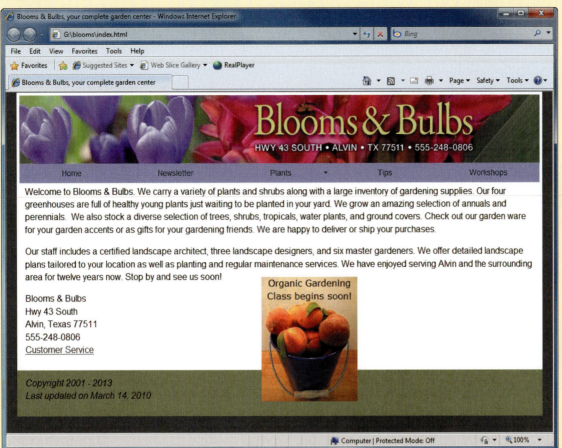

Important: If you did not create the Web sites used in the following exercises in Unit B, you need to create a site root folder for each Web site and define the Web sites using files your instructor provides. See the "Read This Before You Begin" section for more detailed instructions.

Independent Challenge 1

You continue your work on the Rapids Transit Web site. After studying Cascading Style Sheets, you decide to experiment with predesigned CSS layouts. You begin by redesigning the index page based on a CSS layout and add an AP div that can be used to show the floating conditions each day.

a. Open the Rapids Transit Web site, then open the index page.

b. Create a new HTML page based on the 1 column fixed, centered, header and footer layout, and attach the rapids_transit.css file to the page if necessary.

c. Add the page title **Rapids Transit – Buffalo River Outfitters**.

d. Copy the banner and menu bar from the index page to the new, untitled page, replacing the logo placeholder and the header placeholder text.

e. Copy the paragraph and contact information from the index page, then paste it in the content block, replacing the placeholder text.

f. Copy the copyright and last updated statement from the index page, then use it to replace the placeholder text in the footer block of the new, untitled page.

g. Close the index page, then save the new, untitled page as **index.html**, replacing the original index page.

h. Change the background color of the header block to white and add five-pixel padding to each side of the header.

i. Add an AP div about one inch tall and two inches wide, then name it **river_level**.

j. Set the following properties for the river_level AP div: the left position to **500px**, the top position to **325px**, the width to **245px**, and the height to **80px**.

k. Set the background color of the AP div to **#FFCC33**, then add an inset border that is a dark tan. (*Hint*: The inset border option is in the Border category.)

l. In the AP div, add the text **Current River Conditions: good floating today with a few Class II spots**, using line breaks after the words *Conditions*: and *today*.

m. Edit the river_level type rule properties to change the Font-family to Verdana, Geneva, sans-serif; the Font-size to medium; and the Text-align to center.

n. Switch to Code view, cut the code for the AP div, then paste it under the opening tag for the container rule.

o. Edit the container rule to set the Position property to **relative**.

p. Make any spacing adjustments necessary, save your work, then preview the page in the browser.

q. Compare your screen to Figure G-29, then close the browser. (*Hint:* Your page will probably look different from the figure depending on the formatting choices you have made.)

r. Close the page, then exit Dreamweaver.

Independent Challenge 1 (continued)

FIGURE G-29

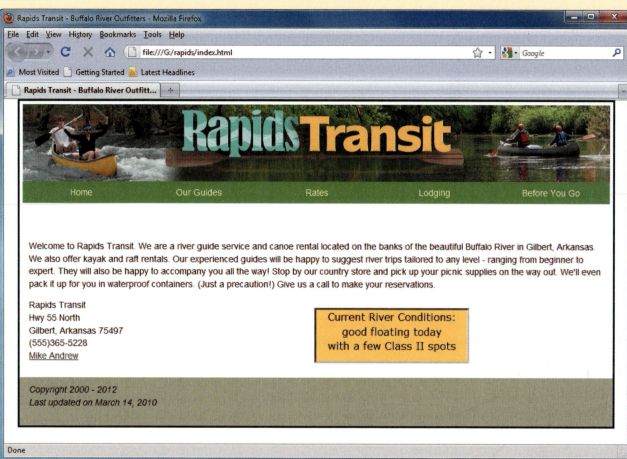

Independent Challenge 2

You continue your work on the TripSmart Web site. The owner, Thomas Howard, wants you to create a section on the index page that promotes a new tour to San Francisco.

a. Open the TripSmart Web site, then open the index page.

b. Create a new HTML page based on the 1 column fixed, centered, header and footer CSS page layout, then attach the tripsmart_styles.css file if necessary.

c. Copy the banner and menu bar, the page body and content information, and the copyright and last updated information from the index page, then paste it into the new, unsaved page, replacing all header, content, and footer placeholder content.

d. Close the index page.

e. Save the new page as the index page, overwriting the original index page.

f. Check the formatting for each text block to make sure each is formatted with a style from one of the style sheets, then apply a style to any unformatted text.

g. Edit the header rule to add five-pixel padding on each side, then change the background color to white.

h. Add a border of your choice to the container rule.

i. Change the background color of the page to white.

j. Draw an AP div that is approximately two inches tall and four inches wide in the middle of the page, then name it **tour**.

k. Set the background image of the AP div to sea_lions.jpg from the drive and folder where you store your Unit G data files.

l. Adjust the dimensions of the AP div by dragging the handles to show as much of the image as you want.

m. Draw another AP div named san_francisco that is approximately one-half inches tall by two inches wide with a background color of your choice.

n. Type the text **San Francisco this fall! Call today!** in the san_francisco AP div, then refer to Figure G-30 to adjust the placement of the two AP divs on the page.

o. Edit the san_francisco rule in the CSS Styles panel to include a border and text alignment of your choice.

p. Edit the container rule to change the Position value to relative.

q. Change to Code view, then move the code for the san_francisco div and the tour div below the opening tag for the container rule.

r. Add the page title **TripSmart: Serving all your travel needs**.

s. Save your work, preview the page in your browser, compare your screen to Figure G-30, close your browser, make any spacing adjustments necessary for the AP div size or position, then close the index page.

t. Exit Dreamweaver.

Independent Challenge 2 (continued)

FIGURE G-30

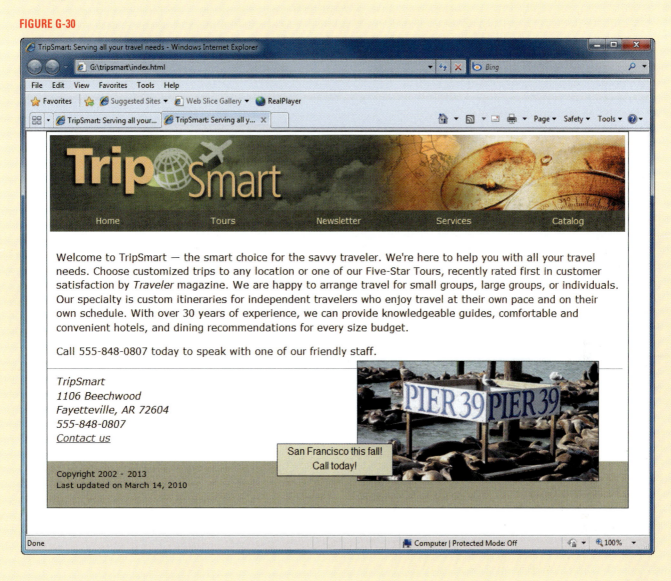

Independent Challenge 3

Hernandez Santoro has recently been asked to redesign a Web site for a new restaurant. He has decided to use CSS for page layout. Because he has never developed a Web site based on CSS before, he decides to look at some other restaurant Web sites for ideas and inspiration. He asked you to analyze the way the James at the Mill Restaurant Web site was built.

a. Connect to the Internet, then go to www.jamesatthemill.com, as shown in Figure G-31.

b. View the source code for the index page and locate the HTML tags that control the CSS on the page.

c. How is CSS used on this site?

d. List at least five div IDs that you find on the index page.

e. Use the Reference panel in Dreamweaver to look up two sets of code used in this site for page layout that you don't understand.

FIGURE G-31

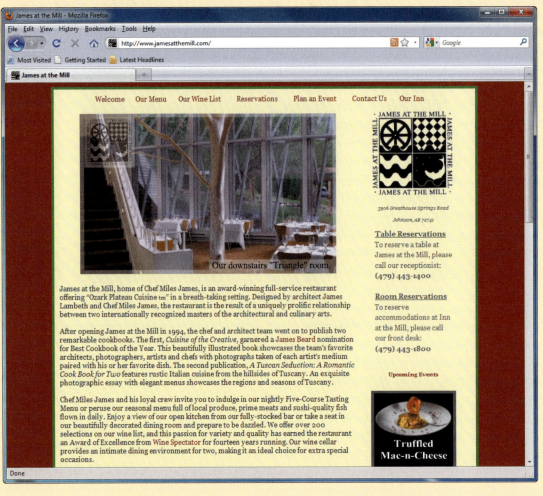

Real Life Independent Challenge

For this assignment, you will continue to work on the Web site that you have been developing since Unit A. You are building this Web site from unit to unit, so you must do each Real Life Independent Challenge to complete your Web site. There are no Data Files supplied. You will continue building your Web site by designing and completing a page that uses CSS for page layout.

a. Consult your wireframes to decide which page to create and develop for this unit. Draw a sketch of the page to show how you will use CSS to lay out the content.

b. Create the new page for the site using one of the predesigned CSS layouts. Add or edit the divs and AP divs on your page, making sure to name each one.

c. Add text, images, and background colors to each div.

d. Copy the menu bar from an existing page to the new page.

e. Update the menu bar, if necessary, to include a link to the new page.

f. Consider using the new page as an example to redesign the existing pages with CSS.

g. Save your work, preview each page in your browser, then make any necessary modifications to achieve a clean, consistent, attractive design for each page.

h. Close your browser, close all open pages, then exit Dreamweaver.

Visual Workshop

Use Figure G-32 as a guide to continue your work on the Carolyne's Creations Web site. Replace the index page with a new page based on the 1 column fixed, centered, header and footer CSS page layout. Remember to attach the Web site style sheet to the page. Draw an AP div on the page and insert the cream_cheese_eggs.jpg image from the Unit G Data Files assets folder. Draw another AP div on the page that overlaps the first one for the catering text. Change the properties of the divs so the AP divs will retain their positions on the page regardless of the width of the browser window. (*Hint*: Remember to add the page title. The footer background color used in the figure is #C63.)

FIGURE G-32

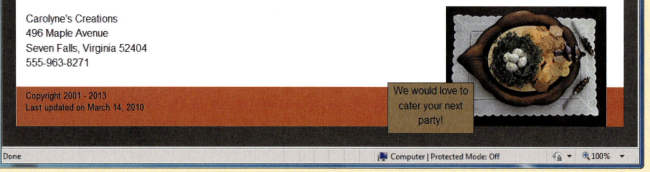

Positioning Page Content with HTML Tables

You have learned how to place elements on a page, align them, and enhance them through various formatting options, including divs and CSS. Another way to position page elements is by using tables. **Tables** are placeholders made up of small boxes called **cells**, where you can insert text and images. Cells are arranged horizontally in rows and vertically in columns. The main advantage of using tables is that you can specify the placement of each object on a Web page. Tables are most often used to place lists of data, such as item names, prices, and sizes. Most designers use a combination of divs, CSS, and tables to place page content, choosing the tool that is the best suited to improve the page appearance, accessibility, and funtionality. In this unit, you learn how to create and format tables, work with table rows and columns, and format the contents of table cells. You begin by replacing the current cafe placeholder page with one that is based on a CSS layout. You add a table to position the cafe dining room names and hours so the guests know their dining options at various times during the day.

OBJECTIVES

Understand table modes

Insert a table

Resize tables, rows, and columns

Merge and split cells

Insert and align images in table cells

Add text

Format and modify cell content

Format cells

Understanding Table Modes

There are two ways to insert a table in Dreamweaver. You can use the Table button in either the Common or Layout category on the Insert panel or use the Application bar (Win) or Menu bar (Mac) to access the Insert and Table commands. When you insert, edit, or format a table, you have a choice of two ways to view the table: Standard mode and Expanded Tables mode. **Standard mode** displays the table with no extra space added between the table cells. **Expanded Tables mode** is similar to Standard mode but has expanded table borders and temporary space between the cells to make it easier to work with individual cells. You choose the mode that you want by clicking the Standard mode button or the Expanded Tables mode button in the Layout category on the Insert panel. It is common to switch between modes as you work with tables in Dreamweaver. Expanded Tables mode is used most often when you are doing precise work with small cells that are difficult to select or move between. You can also use the Import Tabular Data command on the Insert, Table Objects menu to place an existing table with its data on a Web page. You review the two modes for inserting and viewing tables using the Standard and Expanded Tables modes.

DETAILS

- ### Inserting a table in Standard mode

  Standard mode is the mode you have used for page layout up to this point. To insert a table in Standard mode, you click the Standard mode button in the Common or Layout category on the Insert panel, then click the Table button. You then enter values for the number of rows and columns, the table width, border size, cell padding, and cell spacing in the Table dialog box. The **width** refers to the distance across the table, which is expressed either in pixels or as a percentage of page width. This difference is significant. When expressed as a percentage, the table width adjusts to the width of the page in the browser window. When expressed in pixels, the table width does not change, regardless of the size of the browser window. The **border** is the outline or frame around the table and the individual cells. It is expressed in pixels. **Cell padding** is the distance between the cell content and the **cell walls**, the lines inside the cell borders. **Cell spacing** is the distance between cells. Figure H-1 shows an example of a table viewed in Standard mode.

- ### Viewing a table in Expanded Tables mode

  Expanded Tables mode lets you view a table with expanded table borders and temporary cell padding and cell spacing. Since table rows and columns appear magnified when viewed on the page, this mode makes it easier to see how many rows and columns you actually have in your table. It is often difficult, especially after splitting empty cells, to place the insertion point precisely in a table cell, because empty cells can be such small targets. The Expanded Tables mode lets you see each cell clearly. After you select a table item or place the insertion point, it's best to return to Standard mode to maintain the WYSIWYG environment. **WYSIWYG** is the acronym for "What You See Is What You Get." This means that your Web page should look the same in the browser as it does in the Web editor. You can toggle between the Expanded Tables mode and Standard mode by pressing [Alt] [F6]. Figure H-2 shows an example of a table in Expanded Tables mode.

Using HTML table tags

When formatting a table, you should understand the basic HTML tags used to define it. The tags that define a table are `<table>` and `</table>`. The tags that define table rows are `<tr>` and `</tr>`. The tags that define table data cells are `<td>` and `</td>`. Dreamweaver places the ` ` code into each empty table cell at the time it is created. The ` ` code inserts a nonbreaking space; this is a space that appears in a fixed location to keep a line break from separating text into two lines or, in the case of table cells, to keep an empty cell from collapsing. Some browsers collapse an empty cell, which can ruin the look of a table. The nonbreaking space appears in the cell by default until it is replaced with content.

Positioning Page Content with HTML Tables

FIGURE H-1: Table viewed in Standard mode

Selected table with no additional space added between cells

Tag selector

Property inspector expanded to access cell properties

Layout category

Standard mode button

Table button

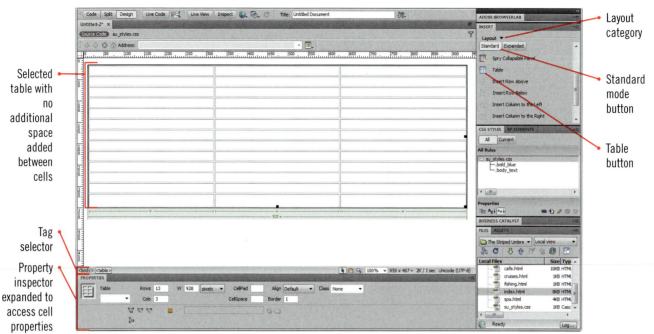

FIGURE H-2: Table viewed in Expanded Tables mode

Increased space between table cells

Expanded Tables mode button

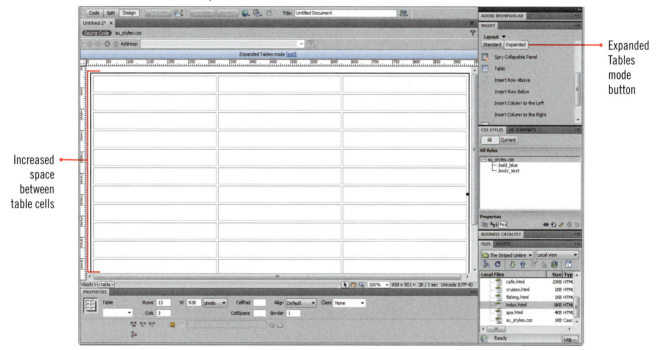

Using visual aids

Dreamweaver lets you hide or display page features, such as table borders, image maps, and frame borders that are known as **visual aids**; they appear in Design view but not in the browser. You can control the visual aids display using the View menu or the Visual Aids button  on the Document toolbar. You can show or hide all visual aids or selectively show or hide individual items. Table borders and similar features are helpful as you edit and format a page, but hiding them lets you quickly view how the page will appear in the browser without having to open it in the browser window.

Inserting a Table

Before you begin creating a table, it is important to decide what information you want to convey and how you want to achieve the desired look. Writing or sketching an overall plan before you begin saves a lot of development time. If you plan to insert images into a table, you should first determine where you want them to appear. You should also consider whether you want the table borders and the cell walls to appear in the browser. If you make a table "invisible" by setting the border value to zero, the user will not be aware that you used a table to arrange the text or images on the page. After consulting with the restaurant manager, you sketch your idea for organizing the dining room information into a table on the cafe page, as shown in Figure H-3. You begin the process by creating a table with three columns and five rows.

STEPS

1. **Start Dreamweaver, open The Striped Umbrella Web site, open the file dwh_1.html from the drive and folder where you store your Unit H Data Files, save it as cafe.html in the striped_umbrella site root folder, overwriting the existing file without updating links, then close the dwh_1.html file**

   The two broken image placeholders that display on the cafe page represent images that need to be copied to the Web site assets folder.

2. **Click the first broken image placeholder, click the Browse for File icon □ next to the Src text box in the Property inspector, then double-click cafe_logo.gif from the assets folder in the location where you store your Unit H Data Files**

   The broken image is replaced with the logo for the Sand Crab Cafe and the file cafe_logo.gif is placed in the Web site assets folder.

3. **Repeat Step 2 to correct the second broken image and copy cafe_photo.jpg to the Web site assets folder**

   The broken image is replaced with the image of the Sand Crab Cafe and the file cafe_photo.gif is saved in the Web site assets folder.

> **QUICK TIP**
>
> The Table command is also located in the Common category of the Insert panel.

4. **With the insertion point to the right of the cafe photo, enter a paragraph break, then click Table in the Layout category of the Insert panel**

   The Table dialog box opens.

> **QUICK TIP**
>
> There is a difference between leaving the Cell padding and Cell spacing text boxes blank and typing a zero in them. Typing a zero as their values will remove any space between table cells.

5. **Type 5 in the Rows text box, 3 in the Columns text box, 600 in the Table width text box, click the Table width list arrow, click pixels, type 0 in the Border thickness text box (leave the Cell padding and Cell spacing options blank), click Top in the Header section if necessary, type This table lists the cafe hours for each dining room. (including the period) in the Summary text box, compare your screen to Figure H-4, then click OK**

   A table with five rows and three columns displays on the page. Because the table is selected, the table settings that you entered in the Table dialog box are listed in the Property inspector. Table settings can be modified by changing their values in the Property inspector.

6. **Click the `<table>` in the tag selector, click the Align list arrow in the Property inspector, as shown in Figure H-5, click Left if necessary, then save your work**

   The table appears left-aligned in the div, but the table summary information you entered in the Summary text box is not visible. The summary does not appear when the page is displayed in the browser window, but is read by screen readers.

Selecting a table

There are several ways to select a table in Dreamweaver. You can click the insertion point in the table, click Modify on the Application bar (Win) or Menu bar (Mac), point to Table, then click Select Table. You can also select a table by moving the pointer slowly to the top or bottom edge of the table, then clicking the table border when the pointer changes to ⊞. Finally, if the insertion point is inside the table, you can click `<table>` on the tag selector.

FIGURE H-3: Sketch for the table on the cafe page

FIGURE H-4: Table dialog box

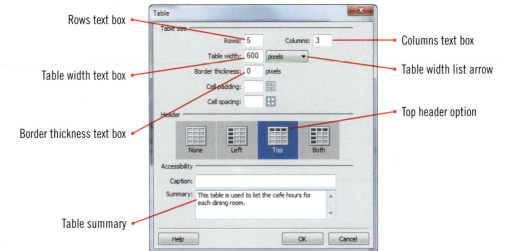

Rows text box

Columns text box

Table width text box

Table width list arrow

Border thickness text box

Top header option

Table summary

FIGURE H-5: Table inserted and aligned on the cafe page

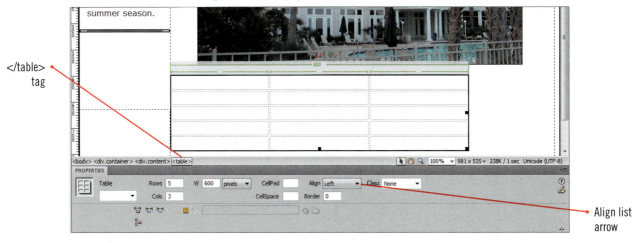

</table>
tag

Align list
arrow

Design Matters

Setting table and cell widths for page layout

If you use a table to position all text and images on a Web page, you should consider setting the width of the table in pixels. The table will remain one size, regardless of the size of the browser window. If you set the width using a percentage, the table will resize itself if the browser window's size is changed. Most designers use a resolution setting of 800 × 600 or 1024 × 768. By choosing a table width of slightly under 800, the page will closely match the browser window's size. Users with higher resolutions will see the page with extra space outside the page borders. You can also set each cell width as either a percent of the table or as pixels, depending on the table design. If you anticipate that users will print the page, consider making the table narrower than usual so it will fit on a printed page.

Resizing Tables, Rows, and Columns

After creating a table, you can resize it, along with its individual rows and columns, by adjusting the borders. Table H-1 lists the options for resizing tables, rows, and columns. When you resize a column or a row or change a cell width or height, the corresponding rows, columns, or cells are automatically resized as a result. You resize cells using either pixels or a percent of the table, depending on your design needs. Cells resized as a percent maintain that percent in relation to the width or height of the entire table if the table is resized. It is a good idea to set the cell widths before you enter the table content; otherwise, the widths tend to shift as you enter the data. Now that your table is created, you want to ensure that the contents of the three columns will be distributed according to your plan and will not shift as you place the content. You set the width of each cell and also experiment with resizing a row's height.

QUICK TIP
Type the % sign next to a number you want expressed as a percent. Otherwise, it will be expressed in pixels.

1. **Click inside the first cell in the bottom row, type 30% in the W text box in the Property inspector, then press [Tab]**
   The cell width setting appears above the first column, as shown in Figure H-6, indicating that the cell width is set to 30% of the table width. Changing the width of a cell changes the width of its entire column. As you add content to the table, this column will remain 30% of the width of the table.

QUICK TIP
If your widths do not add up to 100%, the table may not appear as you intend.

2. **Repeat Step 1 for the next two cells in the bottom row, using 30% for the middle cell and 40% for the last cell**
   The combined widths of the three cells add up to 100%.

QUICK TIP
The height of a row also automatically increases to accommodate the height of its contents.

3. **Place the pointer over the bottom border of the first row until the pointer changes to a resizing pointer ⤓, click and drag downward as shown in Figure H-7, to increase the height of the row slightly, then release the mouse button**
   The color of the row border becomes darker as you select and drag it. Although the height of the top row would make the heading stand out, you hold off on placing the content in that row until you see whether the default height works just as well.

4. **Click Window on the Application bar (Win) or Menu bar (Mac), click History to open the History panel if necessary, then drag the slider in the History panel up until the Set Height command is dimmed**
   The Set Height command is undone and the row returns to the original height.

5. **Close the History panel, then save the file**

FIGURE H-6: Changing the width of an individual cell

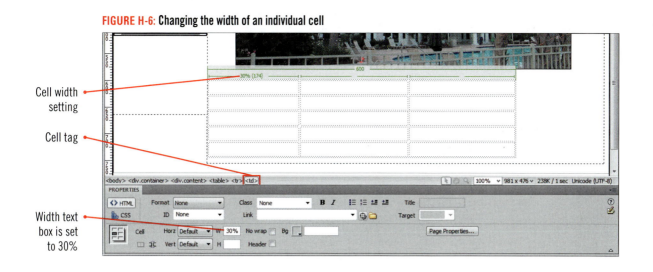

Cell width setting

Cell tag

Width text box is set to 30%

FIGURE H-7: Changing the height of a single row

Resized row

Resizing pointer

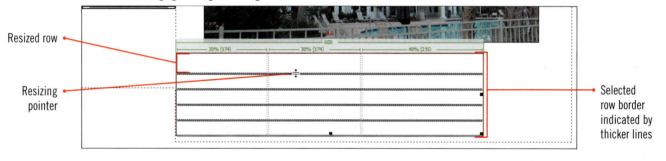

Selected row border indicated by thicker lines

TABLE H-1: Resizing tables, rows, and columns

task	action
To resize a table	Drag the right-corner selection handle
To resize the width of all columns simultaneously	Drag the middle-right selection handle
To resize the height of all rows simultaneously	Drag the middle-bottom selection handle
To change column widths and row heights individually	Drag the interior cell borders up, down, or to the left or right, or either place the insertion point in a cell or select a cell, then assign values in the W and H text boxes in the Property inspector

Resetting table widths and heights

Once you've experimented with resizing columns and rows in a table, you may decide to return to the default column widths and row heights. To accomplish this task, select the table, click Modify on the Application bar (Win) or Menu bar (Mac), point to Table, then click Clear Cell Heights or Clear Cell Widths. You can also use these commands to eliminate any extraneous space in a cell. Using the Clear Cell Heights command aligns a cell border with the bottom of an inserted image.

Merging and Splitting Cells

In addition to resizing table columns and rows, you may need to adjust the table cells by splitting or merging them. **Splitting** a cell divides it into multiple rows or columns, while **merging** cells combines multiple adjacent cells into one cell. The ability to split and merge cells gives you more design flexibility for inserting images or text into your table. Merged cells are good placeholders for wide images or headings. For example, you could merge a row of cells to allot space for a heading. You can split merged cells and merge split cells. However, you can only merge cells that, when combined together, form the shape of a rectangle. When cells are merged, the HTML tag used to describe these cells changes from a width size tag to a column span or row span tag. 🎨 You merge the top row of cells to make room for a heading across the table. You then split one cell to make room for a new image and its descriptive text in the first column. Finally, you merge four cells to create a larger area that will be used to describe room service availability.

STEPS

1. **Click to place the insertion point in the first cell in the top row, then drag the pointer to the right to select all three cells in the top row**

    A black border surrounds the cells, indicating that they are selected.

2. **Click the Merges selected cells using spans button ▣ in the Property inspector**

    The three cells are merged into one cell, as shown in Figure H-8. The heading will display nicely in this area.

3. **Place the insertion point in the first cell in the fifth row, then click the Splits cell into rows or columns button ⌗ in the Property inspector**

    The Split Cell dialog box opens. This is where you select the Rows or Columns option, then specify the number of rows or columns you want as a result of the split.

    > **QUICK TIP**
    > To create a new row identical to the one above it at the end of a table, place the insertion point in the last cell, then press [Tab].

4. **Click the Split cell into: Rows option button to select it if necessary, type 2 in the Number of rows text box if necessary, then click OK**

    The dialog box closes, and the bottom-left cell is split into two rows. These rows will eventually contain the photograph of the featured dessert and its description.

5. **Click the Show Code view button ⬚ Code ⬚ on the Document toolbar**

    The code for the split and merged cells displays, as shown in Figure H-9. Table row and table column tags denote the column span and the nonbreaking spaces ( ) inserted in the empty cells. The tag `<td colspan="3">` refers to the three top cells that have been merged into one cell.

6. **Click the Show Design view button ⬚ Design ⬚ on the Document toolbar, select and merge the first cells in rows 2, 3, 4, and 5 in the left column, compare your screen to Figure H-10, then save your work**

    With the table framework completed, the table is now ready for content.

Using nested tables

Inserting another table inside a cell within another table creates what is called a **nested table**. Nested tables can be used effectively when you want parts of your table data to contain both visible and invisible borders. For example, you can nest a table with red borders inside a table with invisible borders. The process of creating a nested table is similar to the one used to add a new row or column to a table. Simply click to place the insertion point inside the cell where you want the nested table to appear, click Insert on the Application

bar (Win) or Menu bar (Mac), then click Table, or click the Table button on the Insert panel. A nested table is separate from the original table so you can format it however you wish. The more nested tables you add, however, the more complicated the coding becomes, making it challenging to select and edit each table. You may be able to achieve the same results by adding rows and columns or splitting cells instead of inserting a nested table.

FIGURE H-8: Merging selected cells into one cell

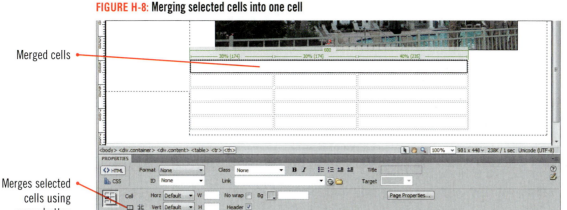

Merged cells

Merges selected
cells using
spans button

FIGURE H-9: Viewing the code for the table

Opening
<table> tag

Code for
merged
cells

Code for
row with
split cell

Closing
<table> tag

FIGURE H-10: Viewing the table after splitting and merging cells

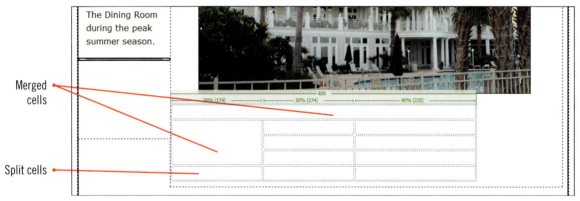

The Dining Room
during the peak
summer season.

Merged
cells

Split cells

Adding and deleting rows and columns

As you add new content to your table, you may find that you have too many or not enough rows or columns. You can add or delete one row or column at a time or add several at once, using commands on the Modify menu. When you add a new column or row, you must first select an existing column or row to which the new column or row will be adjacent. The Insert Rows or Columns dialog box lets you choose how many rows or columns you want to insert and specify where you want them placed, relative to the selected row or column. To add a new row to the end of a table, simply press [Tab].

Positioning Page Content with HTML Tables

Inserting and Aligning Images in Table Cells

You can type, import, or paste text into table cells. You insert images into cells just as you would insert them on a page. You can use the Insert panel or you can drag images onto the page from the Assets panel. As you add content to cells, the cells expand in height to make room for the content. You have a great photograph of a specialty chocolate cake that is featured in two of the dining areas. You insert the new image into the four merged cells in the first column of the table to add visual interest to the cafe page.

STEPS

1. **Click to place the insertion point in the first cell in the second row of the table (below the merged cells in the top row), change to the Common category on the Insert panel, click the Images button list arrow, click Image, navigate to the drive and folder where you store your Unit H Data Files, then double-click chocolate_cake.jpg from the assets folder**

   The Image Tag Accessibility Attributes dialog box opens. This is where you add the alternate text for screen readers.

2. **Type Chocolate Grand Marnier Cake in the alternate text box, click OK, then refresh the Files panel**

   The image of the chocolate cake displays in the merged cells and is saved in the Web site assets folder.

3. **Save your work, click the Preview/Debug in browser button ⊙ on the Document toolbar, then click Preview in [your browser name]**

   The cafe page displays in the browser window with the image positioned in the cell. The page would look better if the image was centered within the cell.

4. **Close your browser, click inside the cell in the second row with the chocolate cake image, click the Horz list arrow in the HTML Property inspector, then click Center**

   The image is horizontally centered in its cell. Compare your screen to Figure H-11.

5. **Save your work, preview the page in your browser, then compare your screen to Figure H-12**

   The table or cell borders do not appear in the browser, because the table borders are set to zero.

6. **Click each link to navigate between the pages in the Web site, then close the browser**

   Notice that the index page and the cafe page maintain a constant position in the browser. The other pages seem to "jump" or change positions slightly when you click on one of those links. The index and cafe page are both based on a CSS page layout. The others are not based on a CSS page layout. Ideally, once you have decided on a CSS page layout for one page, you would redesign all pages to use the same layout.

Using Live View to check pages

Live View is another option for previewing your pages. It is a quick way to see how your page will look without previewing the page in a browser window. Live View renders the page as though it were being viewed in a browser window with any active objects (such as a Spry menu bar) functioning. To use Live View, open a page in Design view, then click the Switch Design View to Live View button Live View . Remember, a page cannot be edited in Live View. You must exit Live View to be able to make changes to the page content.

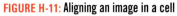

FIGURE H-11: Aligning an image in a cell

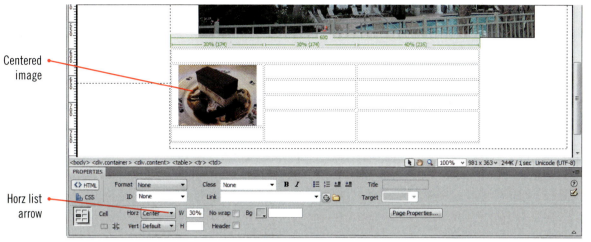

Centered image

Horz list arrow

`<body> <div.container> <div.content> <table> <tr> <td>`

FIGURE H-12: Viewing the table in a browser window

The edges of the table are not visible with the border set to zero

---

Vertically aligning cell contents

In addition to aligning cell contents horizontally, you can also align them vertically by the top, middle, bottom, or baseline of the cell. To vertically align an image, select the image, click the cell tag icon `<td>` on the tag selector or place the insertion point in the cell, click the Vert list arrow in the HTML Property inspector, then choose an alignment type. See Figure H-13.

FIGURE H-13: Vertically aligning cell contents

Vertical alignment option

Adding Text

You can enter text in table cells by typing it in the cell, copying it from another source and pasting it into the cell, or importing it into the cell from another program. You can then format the text for readability and appearance. If you import text from another program, you should use the Clean Up HTML or Clean Up Word HTML command to remove unnecessary code. You add a heading to the table and a caption for the chocolate cake image. You also add the hours of operation for the three dining areas in the second column. Finally, you include a short description of room service options as well.

STEPS

TROUBLE

If you can't see the last lines you typed, click the `<div.container>` tag on the Tag selector to refresh the container size on the screen, or resize the Dreamweaver application window.

QUICK TIP

You can press [Tab] to move your insertion point to the next cell in a row, and press [Shift] [Tab] to move your insertion point to the previous cell.

1. **Click in the first cell in the last row (below the chocolate cake image), type Chocolate, press [Shift] [Enter] (Win) or [shift] [return] (Mac), type Grand Marnier, press [Shift] [Enter] (Win) or [shift] [return] (Mac), then type Cake**

   The text appears in the first cell in the last row below the chocolate cake image.

2. **Click in the top row of the table, then type Sand Crab Cafe Hours**

   The header text appears centered and boldfaced in the table. Note that a header row in a table appears boldfaced and centered by default. Recall that the top row header was selected when the table was created. The summary does not appear when the page is displayed in the browser, but is read by screen readers.

3. **Enter the names for each dining area and its hours, as shown in Figure H-14**

   The dining room areas and respective hours are listed in the table with the font properties from the body tag applied to them through the rules of inheritance. This means that if formatting is not specified for a child tag inside a parent tag, the parent tag properties and values will format the child tag content.

4. **Merge the second and third cells in the last row, then type the room service information from Figure H-14 with a line break after _12:00 a.m._**

   The room service hours are displayed at the bottom of the table.

5. **Compare your screen to Figure H-14, then click the `<table>` tag on the Tag selector**

   The Room service information wraps to a second line, which looks a bit awkward. The width of the table could be extended to the right where there is more room.

6. **Select 600 in the W text box in the Property inspector, then type 700, press [Tab], then compare your screen to Figure H-15**

   The table is resized to 700 pixels wide, allowing room for the lengthy sentence to remain on one line.

7. **Save your work**

FIGURE H-14: Table with text added

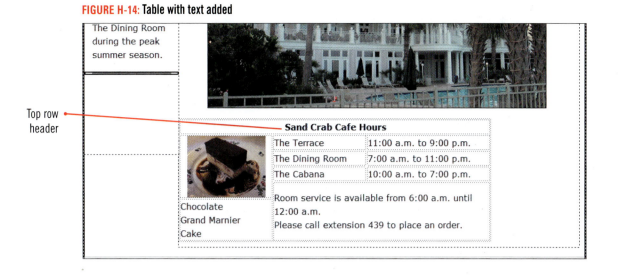

Top row header

FIGURE H-15: Table with increased width

Table width has increased

Importing and exporting tabular data

You can import and export tabular data into and out of Dreamweaver. **Tabular data** is data that is arranged in columns and rows and separated by a **delimiter**, such as a comma, tab, colon, semicolon, or similar character, that tells Dreamweaver where to break the data into table cells. **Importing** means to bring data created in another software program into Dreamweaver, and **exporting** means to save data that was created in Dreamweaver in a different file format so that other programs can read it. Files containing tabular data that are imported into Dreamweaver must first be saved as delimited text files. Programs such as Microsoft Word and Excel offer many file formats for saving files, including saving as delimited text. To import a delimited file, click File on the Application bar (Win) or Menu bar (Mac), point to Import, then click Tabular Data. The Import Tabular Data dialog box opens, offering you choices for the resulting table that will appear on the Web page. To export a table that you created in Dreamweaver, click File on the Application bar (Win) or Menu bar (Mac), point to Export, then click Table. The Export Table dialog box opens, letting you choose the type of delimiter and line breaks you want for the delimited file when you save it.

Formatting and Modifying Cell Content

In addition to changing the height and width of cells, you can apply a background color or insert a background image to fill an entire table or individual cells. You can also change border colors and border widths of cells or tables. You format cell content by changing the font, size, or color of the text, or by applying styles. You can also resize images placed in cells. If you have a simple table that can share the same formatting between all of the table elements, you can add all formatting rules to the table by adding properties and values to the `<table>` tag. Now that you have your text in place, you are ready to format it using CSS. You create a new style to use for the image caption.

STEPS

1. **Expand the CSS panel group if necessary**
   Formatting the text in the table cells will make the cafe page look more professional.

2. **Apply the body_text style to each of the cafe dining areas, hours, and room service information**
   The text changes to reflect the settings in the body_text style. You want the name of the featured dessert, Chocolate Grand Marnier Cake, to stand out on the page but there isn't an existing style that suits your needs.

3. **Click the New CSS Rule button, then create a new class style called featured_item in the su_styles.css style sheet file**
   Creating a new style for this specific text will give it a unique look.

4. **In the Type category, set the Font-size to 14, the Font-weight to bold, the Font-style to italic, the Color to #003, as shown in Figure H-16, then click OK**
   The cafe page redisplays. Since you did not specify a Font-family in the CSS Rule Definition dialog box, the font will remain the same, as it is inherited from the body rule.

5. **Select the Chocolate Grand Marnier Cake text under the chocolate cake image, click the CSS button in the Property inspector, then apply the featured_item rule to the text**
   All text on the page now has a style applied. Your screen should resemble Figure H-17.

6. **Click after the word *cake* in the bottom-left cell, then press [Tab]**
   A new row is added. Pressing the Tab key while the insertion point is in the last cell of the table creates a new row. Even though it appears as if the cell with the room service information is the last cell, it is not because of the merged cells.

7. **Merge the cells in the new row, click in the merged cells, click Insert on the Application bar (Win) or Menu bar (Mac), point to HTML, then click Horizontal Rule**
   A horizontal rule is displayed in the merged cells in the last row. Horizontal rules are used frequently to set off or divide sections on a page.

8. **Save your work, preview the cafe page in your browser, then close your browser**
   The page looks much better with the formatted text.

FIGURE H-16: Creating the featured_item rule

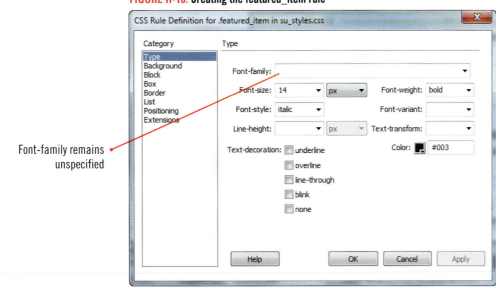

Font-family remains
unspecified

FIGURE H-17: Styles applied to text

body_text
rule applied

featured_item
rule applied

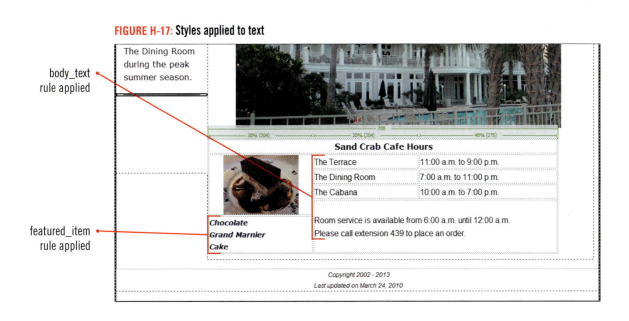

Design Matters

Setting accessibility preferences for tables

You can make tables more accessible to individuals with disabilities by adding table captions or table summaries that can be read by screen readers. A table caption will appear at the top of the table in the browser window, but a table summary will not. Using either or both of these settings adds to table accessibility. These features are especially suitable for tables that are used for presenting tabular

data. Another way to provide accessibility is by using a **table header**, which is an option used by screen readers to help viewers identify the content of a table. Table headers are automatically centered, boldfaced, and placed in the top row or left column. You create table captions, summaries, and headers using the settings found in the Table dialog box.

Formatting Cells

Formatting a cell can include setting properties that visually enhance the cell's appearance, such as setting a cell width, assigning a background color, or setting global alignment properties for the cell content. To format a cell, you need to either select the cell or place the insertion point inside the cell you want to format, then choose the appropriate cell formatting options in the Property inspector. Formatting cells is different from formatting cell contents. When you format cell contents, you must select the contents before you can format them. See the Clues to Use *Formatting cells and cell content* at the end of this lesson for more information. You decide to experiment with the placement and alignment of the current page content. You change the horizontal and vertical alignment settings for some of the table cells to improve the appearance of the cell contents on the page.

STEPS

1. **Click to place the insertion point in the cell with the chocolate cake caption**

   You position the insertion point in the cell rather than select the cell content because you are setting a global alignment for the cell contents. This is true no matter how many different types of content the cell contains.

2. **Click the Horz list arrow in the Property inspector, then click Center**

   The cell content moves to the center of the cell. Using this setting, the contents will remain aligned in the center of the cell even if the cell itself is made larger or smaller at a subsequent point.

3. **Repeat Steps 1 and 2 to horizontally center the contents of the cell with the room service information**

   Although this alignment centers the information horizontally in the cell, the room service information has been previously assigned the body_text rule, which is left-aligned. This rule is taking precedence over the cell alignment value, so it needs to be edited in order for all cell contents to be centered.

4. **Click the body_text rule in the CSS Styles panel, click the Edit Rule button , click the Block category, delete left from the Text- align text box, click OK, then compare your screen to Figure H-18**

   With the left text-align value removed from the body_text rule, the cell contents (the room service information) are now centered in the table cell. If the Text-align text box is left blank, the default alignment is left-aligned. Removing the left-alignment property value will not affect any of the cell contents already assigned to this style.

5. **Click the Switch Design View to Live View button Live View, then compare your screen to Figure H-19**

   The page displays as it will appear in your browser. The table looks more organized and professional with the new alignment settings.

6. **Save all files, preview the cafe page in your browser, then close your browser**

7. **Close all open pages, then exit Dreamweaver**

Formatting cells and cell content

As you have learned, you can format cell content using the Property inspector. Formatting cells, however, is not the same task—nor is it accomplished in the same manner—as formatting the content inside of cells. You can format a cell by simply clicking to place the insertion point inside the cell that you want to format, then choosing options in the Property inspector. For example, you can click a cell, then choose a fill color for the cell by clicking the Bg Color list arrow in the Property inspector and selecting a color. (You must expand the Property inspector to see this option.) However, to format the cell content, you must select the *content*, not the cell itself. For instance, you can set a cell's alignment to center align, but also format its contents to align differently by selecting and formatting each one individually. You can, for instance, have left-aligned text and an image in a cell that has been formatted as center-aligned.

FIGURE H-18: Setting horizontal and vertical cell alignment

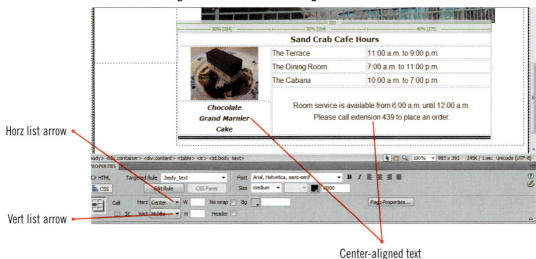

Horz list arrow

Vert list arrow

Center-aligned text

FIGURE H-19: The finished product

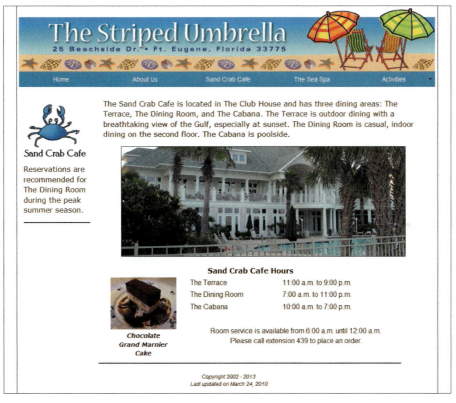

Using grids and guides for positioning page content

The View menu offers a number of options to help you position your page content more precisely. **Grids** consist of horizontal and vertical lines resembling graph paper that fill the page. You can edit the colors of the lines, the distance between them, whether they are displayed using lines or dots, and whether or not objects "snap" (automatically align) to them. **Guides** are horizontal or vertical lines that you place on the page yourself, by clicking and dragging onto the page from the vertical and horizontal rulers. Unlike grids, which fill the page, you can have as many or as few guides as you need. Both grids and guides are used to position page elements using exact measurements.

You can edit both the color of the guides and the color of the **distance**, a screen tip that shows you the distance between two guides when you hold down the control key (Win) or command key (Mac) and place the mouse pointer between the guides. You can lock the guides so you don't accidentally move them, and you can set them either to snap to page elements or have page elements snap to them. To display grids or guides, click View on the Application bar (Win) or Menu bar (Mac), point to either Grid or Guides, then select an option from the displayed menu. Grids and guides only appear in Dreamweaver—they do not display when viewed in the browser.

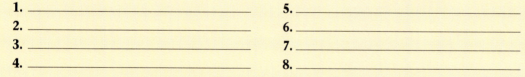
Label each element in the Dreamweaver window shown in Figure H-20.

FIGURE H-20

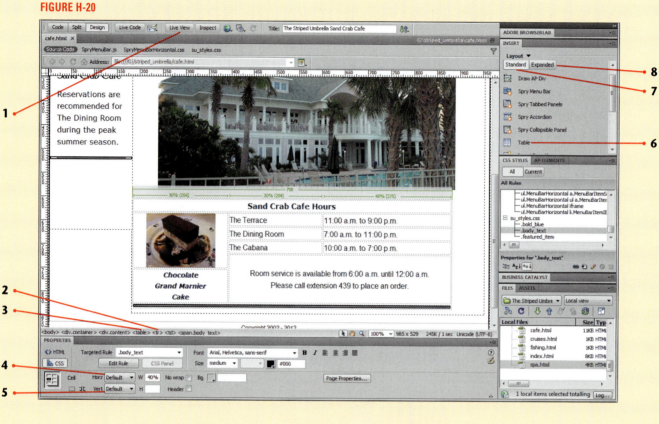

1. _____

2. _____

3. _____

4. _____

5. _____

6. _____

7. _____

8. _____

Match each of the following terms with the statement that best describes its function.

9. **Small boxes that are arranged in columns and rows**
10. **Expanded Tables mode**
11. **Cell padding**
12. **Standard mode**
13. **Border**
14. **Import**
15. **Cell spacing**
16. **Export**
17. **Tag selector**

a. The mode that displays temporary cell padding and cell spacing
b. The space between cell content and cell walls
c. Displays HTML tags for the various page components, including tables and cells
d. Cells
e. The mode that you use to create a table with a specific number of rows and columns
f. Save data that was created in Dreamweaver with a different file format
g. The space between table cells
h. The outline of a table or an individual cell
i. Bring data into Dreamweaver from another program

Select the best answer from the following list of choices.

18. **Which of the following is true about nested tables?**
    a. Only one nested table can be inserted into a table.
    b. Nested tables are inserted using the Insert Nested Table button.
    c. Nested tables can have visible or invisible borders.
    d. Nested tables cannot be formatted like regular tables.

19. **Which of the following tags is used to select a row in a table?**
    a. `<div>`
    b. `<td>`
    c. `<tr>`
    d. `<table>`

20. **Which pointer is used to select a row?**
    a.
    b.
    c.
    d.

Skills Review

Important: If you did not create this Web site in Unit B and maintain it during the preceding units, you will need to create a site root folder for this Web site and define the Web site using files your instructor will provide. See the "Read This Before You Begin" section for more detailed instructions.

1. **Understand table modes.**
   a. Open the Blooms & Bulbs Web site.
   b. Open the file dwh_2.html, then save it as **workshops.html**, overwriting the existing file without updating links.
   c. Replace the broken image placeholder with the file chives.jpg from the drive and folder where you store your Unit H Data Files.
   d. Close dwh_2.html, use the Insert panel to change to the Layout category, change to Expanded Tables mode, then click OK to close the Getting Started in Expanded Tables Mode dialog box if necessary.
   e. Return to Standard mode.

2. **Insert a table.**
   a. Select the placeholder text *sidebar* in the top left corner of the page, then delete it.
   b. Use the Insert panel to insert a table at the current insertion point location with the following settings:

      Rows = 8   Width = 175 pixels   Cell padding = 5   Header = Top
      Columns = 2   Border = 0   Cell spacing = 5

   c. Enter the text **This table is used to list the workshop schedule.** in the Summary text box.
   d. Save the file.

3. **Resize tables, rows and columns.**
   a. Select the first cell in the second row, then set the cell width to 60%.
   b. Select the second cell in the second row, then set the cell width to 40%.
   c. Save your work.

4. **Merge and split cells.**
   a. Merge the cells in the first row.
   b. Merge the cells in the last row.
   c. Save your work.

5. **Insert and align images in table cells.**
   a. Use the Insert panel to insert gardening_gloves.gif in the last row. (The gardening_gloves.gif file is located in the assets folder where you store your Unit H Data Files.)
   b. Add the alternate text **Gardening gloves** to the gardening_gloves.jpg image when prompted, then place the insertion point next to the image in the cell and set the horizontal alignment to Center.
   c. Use the tag selector to select the cell containing the gardening_gloves.jpg image, then set the vertical alignment to Top.
   d. Save your work.

6. **Add text.**
   a. Type **Scheduled Workshops** in the merged cell in the first row.
   b. Type the names and dates for the workshops listed in Figure H-21 in each row of the table.
   c. Save your work. (*Hint*: Don't worry if your table content does not look like the figure; you have yet to format the cells and cell content. If you select the `<table>` tag on the Tag selector, the cells will tighten up and make it easier to work with the table.)

7. **Format and modify cell content.**
   a. Apply the body_text style from the blooms_styles style sheet file to the names and dates for the workshops listed in Figure H-21.
   b. Edit the body_text rule by deleting the left alignment property value.
   c. Save your work.

Skills Review (continued)

8. **Format cells.**

   a. Set the horizontal alignment for the cells that contain the workshop names and dates to Center.

   b. Set the vertical alignment for the same cells to Top.

   c. Save your work, preview the page in the browser, then compare your screen to Figure H-21.

   d. Close the browser, close the page, then exit Dreamweaver.

FIGURE H-21

Important: If you did not create the following Web sites in Unit B and maintain them during the preceding units, you must create a site root folder for the Web sites in the following exercises and define the Web sites using files your instructor will provide. See the "Read This Before You Begin" section for more detailed instructions.

Independent Challenge 1

You have been hired to create a Web site for a river expedition company named Rapids Transit. The owner's name is Mike Andrew. Mike has asked you to develop the page for the Web site that lists the equipment available for rental. Refer to Figure H-22 as you work on this page.

a. Start Dreamweaver, then open the Rapids Transit Web site.

b. Open the file dwh_3.html from the drive and folder where you store your Unit H Data Files, save it as **rates.html**, overwriting the existing file without updating links, then close dwh_3.html.

c. Delete the *table* placeholder text, replace it with a table with the following settings: seven rows, four columns, 900 pixels wide, zero border, no header, then type **Table used for rental rates.** in the Summary text box. Leave the cell padding and cell spacing settings blank.

d. Center-align the table, then set each column width to 25%.

e. Merge the four cells in the first row, then import (Win) or copy and paste (Mac) the text rentals.doc from the drive and folder where you store your Unit H Data Files into the merged cells.

f. Apply the body_text style to the imported text.

g. Merge the four cells in the second row, then insert a horizontal rule in the merged cells.

h. Merge the four cells in the third row, then type **Rental Rates Per Day**.

i. Create a new class rule named **bold_gray** in the rapids_transit.css style sheet with the following settings: Font-family: Arial, Helvetica, sans-serif; Font-size: large; Font-weight: bold; Text-decoration: underline; Color: #666; and Text-align: center.

j. Apply the bold_gray rule to *Rental Rates Per Day*.

k. Enter the rental information listed in Figure H-22 in the next three rows, then apply the body_text rule to each of the cells.

l. Merge the third and fourth cells in the bottom row.

m. Insert the rt_logo.gif file from the drive and folder where you store your Unit H Data Files in the merged cells, type **Rapids Transit logo** for the alternate text, then center the image in the merged cells.

n. Enter a line break before the opening paragraph, save your work, then preview the page in your browser.

o. Close your browser, close all open pages, then exit Dreamweaver.

Independent Challenge 1 (continued)

FIGURE H-22

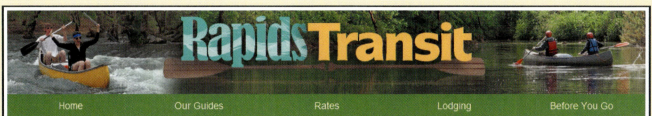

Home   Our Guides   Rates   Lodging   Before You Go

You may be wondering why we charge to rent our equipment when we are already charging a fee for the float. We do this because we have many repeat customers who have invested in their own gear. We want to be able to charge them a lower price than we charge those who don't own equipment. Therefore, the more you bring along with you, the less your float will cost! Our basic float price is $20.00 without equipment. Add the amounts on the table for the equipment you will need to the basic price, and you will have the total price of the float. We also take an action shot of you on the water that is included in the price of the float.

Rental Rates Per Day

Canoe	$9.00	Life Jacket	$3.00
Kayak	$8.00	Helmet	$2.00
Two-man raft	$7.00	Dry Packs	$1.00

Copyright 2000 - 2012
Last updated on March 24, 2010

Independent Challenge 2

Your company is designing a new Web site for TripSmart, a travel outfitter. You are now ready to work on the catalog page. The catalog page will feature three items from the latest TripSmart catalog.

   a. Start Dreamweaver, then open the TripSmart Web site.

   b. Open the file dwh_4.html, save it as **catalog.html**, overwriting the existing file, but not updating links, then close the dwh_4.html file.

   c. Insert a table in the content div with the following settings: five rows, three columns, a width of 950 pixels, a border of zero, a top header, and an appropriate table summary, then set the cell widths in the second row to 33%, 33%, and 34%.

   d. Merge the three cells in the first row, enter a line break, then type **Our products are backed with a 100% guarantee.**

   e. In the three cells in the second row, type **Protection from UV rays**; **Cool, light-weight, versatile**; and **Pockets for everything**, then set the horizontal alignment in each cell to Center. *(Note: Do not include the semi-colon punctuation.)*

   f. In the three cells in the third row, place the files hat.jpg, pants.jpg, and vest.jpg from the drive and folder where you store your Unit H Data Files, add the following alternate text to the images: **Safari Hat**, **Kenya Convertible Pants**, and **Photographer's Vest**, then set the horizontal cell alignment for each cell to Center.

   g. In the three cells in the fourth row, type **Safari Hat**, **Kenya Convertible Pants**, and **Photographer's Vest**, then center-align each cell. *(Note: do not include the comma punctuation.)*

   h. In the first cell in the fifth row, type **Item number 50501** and **$29.00** with a line break between them.

   i. Type **Item number 62495** and **$39.50** with a line break between them in the second cell in the fifth row.

   j. Type **Item number 52301** and **$54.95** with a line break between them in the third cell in the fifth row.

   k. Apply the body_text style to the three descriptions in the second row.

   l. Create a new class style in the tripsmart_styles.css style sheet named reverse_text with the following settings: Font-family: Arial, Helvetica, sans-serif; Font-size: 14; Font-style: normal; Font-weight: bold; color: #FFF.

   m. Apply the reverse_text style to the three item names under the images, then change each cell background color to #666633.

   n. Create a new class style called item_numbers with the following settings: Font-family: Arial, Helvetica, sans-serif; Font-size: 12px; Font-style: normal; Font-weight: bold; Text-align: center.

   o. Apply the item_numbers style to the three item numbers and prices.

   p. Save your work, preview the page in the browser, then compare your page to Figure H-23.

   q. Close your browser, then exit Dreamweaver.

Independent Challenge 2 (continued)

FIGURE H-23

Dell Patterson has opened a new shop called CollegeFandz, an online source for college students' clothing and collectibles. She is considering creating a Web site to promote her services and products and would like to gather some ideas before she hires a Web designer. She decides to visit Web sites to look for design ideas, and asks for your help.

a. Connect to the Internet, then go to the Neiman Marcus Web site at www.neimanmarcus.com.

b. Use the View Source command from the Page button menu (Internet Explorer) or the Page Source command on the View menu (Firefox) to view the source code and determine if the page layout is based on the use of CSS layouts, tables, or a combination of both.

c. Go to the Waterfield Designs Web site at www.sfbags.com, as shown in Figure H-24.

d. View the source code and determine if the page layout is based on the use of CSS layouts, tables, or a combination of both.

e. Using your word processing software or paper, list five design ideas that you like from either of these pages, identifying which page was the source of each idea.

f. Close your browser.

FIGURE H-24

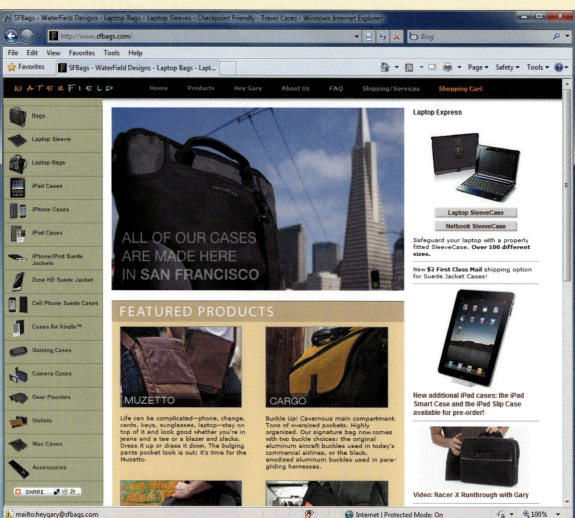

Waterfield Designs Web site used with permission from Waterfield Designs – www.sfbags.com

Real Life Independent Challenge

This assignment will continue to build on the personal Web site that you created in Unit B. In Unit C, you created and developed your index page. In Unit D, you added a page with either an ordered or an unordered list, and a style sheet with a minimum of two styles. In Unit E, you added a page that included at least two graphics. In Unit F, you added a page that included several links and an image map. In Unit G, you converted the index page to a page based on a CSS layout. In this unit, you will be working with one of the other pages in your Web site.

   a. Consult your wireframes and decide which page you would like to develop in this lesson.
   b. Sketch a layout for your page using a table for placement of some of the page elements.
   c. Experiment with splitting and merging cells and adding and deleting rows.
   d. Create content for this page and format the text attractively on the page by customizing the font, size, text color, style, and alignment.
   e. Save the file, open your browser, then preview the page.
   f. Add the data to your table.

After you are satisfied with your work, verify the following:

   a. Each completed page has a page title.
   b. All links work correctly.
   c. The completed pages view well using screen resolutions of 800 × 600 and 1024 × 768.
   d. All images are properly set showing a path to the assets folder of the Web site.
   e. All images have alternate text and are legal for you to use.
   f. The link checker shows no broken links or orphaned files. If there are orphaned files, note your plan to link them.
   g. All main pages have a consistent navigation system.

Visual Workshop

Use Figure H-25 to continue your work on the Carolyne's Creations Web site. You are now ready to begin work on a page that will showcase the catering services using a table to list menu items. Open the file dwh_5.html from the Unit H Data Files, save it as catering.html (overwriting the existing file), then begin by replacing the main content placeholder text with the table shown in Figure H-25. Use the new image from the Unit H Data Files folder called muffins.jpg. The text for the menu items can be found in the file menu items.doc. (*Hint*: Open the file in Word, then copy and paste each section to the appropriate cell in the table.) Remember to add alternate text for each new image. Make any spacing adjustments necessary to improve the page appearance. The table in Figure H-25 is 925 pixels wide.

FIGURE H-25

Collecting Data with Forms

Forms are a way to add interactivity and collect information on a Web page, by presenting users with a series of options for collecting and entering information. Dreamweaver lets you easily create forms by adding form objects to the page, such as check boxes and option buttons. The form then sends information that users enter to the host Web server to be collected and processed. Forms are useful for such things as ordering merchandise, responding to requests for customer feedback, and requesting information. The Striped Umbrella Marketing Department wants interested guests to be able to request information about the fishing and dolphin cruises online. You decide to design and add this type of form to the activities page to collect the name and address of guests who make inquiries, along with their response to an offer to send them a quarterly newsletter.

OBJECTIVES

Understand forms and form objects

Create and insert a form on a page

Add a text form field

Add a radio group

Add a check box

Insert a Submit and a Reset button

Format and test a form

Update files

Understanding Forms and Form Objects

Forms are a convenient and efficient way to obtain information from Web site users. A form can either be a page by itself, collecting several pieces of information from a user with numerous form objects, or it can take up only a small part of a page. **Form objects** are the individual form components that accept individual pieces of information. They include check boxes, radio buttons, text fields, and buttons. Many Web pages include a form with only two form objects, such as a text box and a submit button. See Figures I-1 and I-2 for examples of long and short types of forms. You can insert tables in more complex forms to help organize the objects into rows and columns. Pages can have more than one form. However, you cannot place a form inside a form. Before you begin work on the form, you review the various form objects you might use to collect information from guests.

As you create forms, you can choose from the following objects:

- **Form fields**

  A **field** is a form area into which users can insert a specific piece of data, such as their last name or address. Form fields include text fields, hidden fields, and file fields. **Text fields** can accept both numbers and letters, known as **alphanumeric** data. A text field can contain single or multiple lines of data. **Hidden fields** store information about the user and can be used by the company originating the form at a later time, such as the next time the user visits their Web site. **File fields** allow users to browse to a file on their computer and **upload** it to the form host Web server. To upload a file means to transfer a copy of the file to a server.

- **Radio buttons**

  Radio buttons are option buttons that appear as small empty circles on a form that users click to select a choice. A selected radio button has a black fill. Radio buttons in a group are mutually exclusive, meaning that the user can select only one choice at a time.

- **Check boxes**

  Check boxes are small squares on a form. To select a choice, users click to place a check mark inside the box. In contrast to a group of radio buttons, with a series of check boxes it is possible to select more than one check box.

- **Lists and menus**

  Lists and menus provide the user with a list or menu of choices to select. Lists display the choices in a scrolling format while menus display the choices in a pop-up set of choices. Lists and menus provide a fast method of entering information that may be tedious for the user to type.

- **Buttons**

  Buttons (not to be confused with radio buttons) are usually small rectangular objects containing a text label. When a user clicks a button, a task is performed, such as submitting or clearing a form. To **submit** a form means to send the information on the form to the host Web server for processing. Clearing or **resetting** the form means to erase all form entries and set the values back to the default settings.

Design Matters

Planning form layout

Before you begin creating your form, you should take the time to write down the information you want to collect and the order in which you want it to appear on the form. It's also a good idea to make a sketch of the form to make sure that all of the form objects are placed in a logical order that will make sense to the user. Position the most important information at the top of the form to make it more likely that users will complete it.

FIGURE I-1: Example of a long form

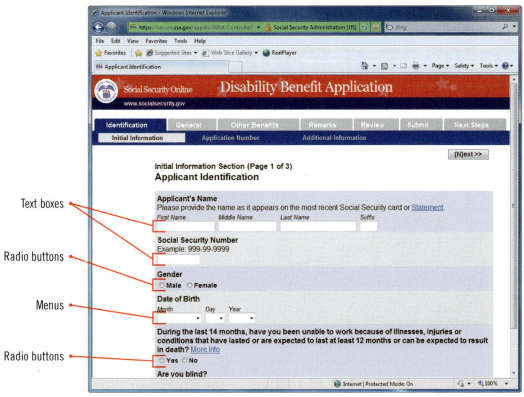

Text boxes

Radio buttons

Menus

Radio buttons

Social Security Administration Web site – www.ssa.gov

FIGURE I-2: Example of a short form

Text box

Search button is
the Submit button

Federal Bureau of Investigation Web site – www.fbi.gov

Creating and Inserting a Form on a Page

Before you can begin adding form objects to a page, you must create the form that will contain them. You create a form by using the Form command on the Insert menu, or by using the Form button on the Insert panel. When you create a form, Dreamweaver adds beginning and ending form tags to the HTML code. Once it is created, you replace the default form name with a descriptive name that the program will use when it processes the data from the form. The form on the activities page will include form objects to collect information from guests who are seeking information about fishing and dolphin cruises excursions. You create the form and then insert it at the bottom of the activities page.

STEPS

> **TROUBLE**
> If a message appears about needing to view invisible elements to see the form outline on the page, click View on the Application bar (Win) or Menu bar (Mac), point to Visual Aids, then click Invisible Elements.

1. **Start Dreamweaver, open The Striped Umbrella Web site, then open the activities.html page**

2. **Place the insertion point after the last sentence on the page, then insert a paragraph break**
   The insertion point is positioned where you want to form to reside, at the bottom of the page.

> 3. **Click the Form button in the Forms category on the Insert panel**
   The form displays as a red dotted outline (Win) or red solid outline (Mac), on the page. Although the Property inspector displays the form properties, the form objects won't display until you insert them.

> **TROUBLE**
> If form1 is not listed as the default name, select your current default name, then continue with Step 4.

4. **Select form1 in the form ID text box in the Property inspector, type feedback, press [Tab], then compare your screen to Figure I-3**
   The form ID text box now contains the name *feedback* and the Tag selector shows the form tag with the name of the form <form#feedback>. The rest of the form properties identify how the information users enter will be processed on the host server. The Action and Target fields, for example, should remain blank unless your instructor provides you with the appropriate information. (The programming involved in processing a form is beyond the scope of this book.)

5. **Click the Show Code view button** `Code`
   The form code appears, as shown in Figure I-4. The form is surrounded by beginning and ending form tags as well as the tags for the form ID, form name, form method, and form action. The form method information directs the way that the data will be sent to the server.

6. **Click the Show Design view button** `Design`
   Your page redisplays in Design view.

Design Matters

Creating user-friendly forms

When a form contains several required fields—fields that must be filled out before the form can be processed—it is a good idea to provide visual clues to alert the user. Adding asterisks in different font colors with an accompanying note is an easy way to increase the visibility of required fields. An asterisk is often placed right next to a required field with a corresponding note at either the top or the bottom of the form explaining that all fields marked with asterisks are required. This encourages users to complete these fields initially, rather than submitting the form and then receiving an error message asking them to complete required fields that were left blank.

FIGURE I-3: Form on the activities page

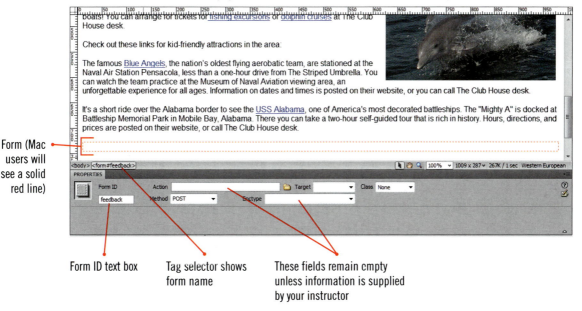

Form (Mac users will see a solid red line)

Form ID text box

Tag selector shows form name

These fields remain empty unless information is supplied by your instructor

FIGURE I-4: HTML code for the form on the activities page

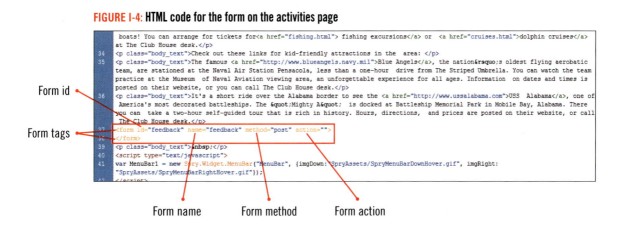

Form id

Form tags

Form name

Form method

Form action

Processing forms

An attractive, user-friendly form serves no purpose without a way to process and store the information. Sending e-mails with form information is not a time efficient or effective process. It is more practical to send form information directly to a server to read, store, and process the data. The data collection stage of form processing is called **front-end processing**, which denotes the beginning of the processing cycle. The data processing stage is accordingly called **back-end processing**, as it references the end of the processing cycle. Forms are processed according to the properties specified in the form action attribute. The **form action attribute** is the part of the form tag that specifies how the data in the form will be processed. If you do not need to save the data that a user enters on a form, it is better to use **client-side scripting**. This means that the form is processed on the user's computer. An example of this is a mortgage calculator that allows you to estimate mortgage payments. **Server-side scripting** is used if data entered on a form needs to be stored and processed on the form's host Web server. An example of this is ordering books on a bookstore Web site. Client-side scripting is written with programming languages such as JavaScript or VBScript. Server-side scripting is written with programming languages, such as Common Gateway Interface (CGI).

Adding a Text Form Field

One of the most common form fields is a text field. Dreamweaver has three types of text fields: single-line text fields, multi-line text fields, and password fields. For more information, see the Clues to Use *Understanding text fields*. Each field should have a descriptive label so users have a visual clue as to the type of information required. Form field names should not include spaces, punctuation, or uppercase letters, to ensure that they can be read properly by the program that will process the form data. You want to make sure that the form objects display in an organized manner so you place a table inside the form. You then add single-line text fields for the name and address information.

STEPS

1. **Place the insertion point inside the form if necessary, then click Table in the Common category on the Insert panel**

   The Table dialog box opens. This is where you set the table properties such as the table width, the number of rows and columns, and the accessibility tags.

2. **Set the table rows to 8, the table columns to 3, the table width to 800 pixels, the border thickness to 0, cell padding to 2, cell spacing to 1, select the Top header option if necessary, type This table is used for form layout. in the Summary text box, then click OK**

   The Table dialog box closes and the table is inserted inside the form, ready for placement of the form fields.

3. **Click the `<table>` tag on the Tag selector, click the Class text box list arrow in the Property inspector, then click body_text**

   The body_text style will be used to format all of the text in the table.

4. **Using Figure I-5 as a guide, enter the labels for your text fields into the table beginning in the first cell in the second row (press [down arrow] to move the insertion point to each position), then drag the column border to the left so that it is positioned closer to the edge of the text labels**

   The labels for the text fields are entered in the first column. The second column remains empty until you insert the next set of text fields. The top row is left blank, as the table header will be placed there.

5. **Place the insertion point in the second cell in the second row, then click the Text Field button in the Forms category on the Insert panel**

   The Input Tag Accessibility Attributes dialog box opens. This dialog box is used to enter the accessibility attributes for the form field.

6. **Type first_name in the ID text box, click the No label tag option button in the Style section to select it, click OK, type 30 in the Char width text box in the Property inspector, then type 60 in the Max chars text box**

   The text field for the First Name label is placed on the form with a black dotted outline. The Property inspector displays the text field ID first_name. The Char width and Max chars settings set the size of the text field and limit the number of characters that can be input in the field.

7. **Repeat Steps 5 and 6 to enter additional single-line text fields, using the information in Table I-1**

   All text fields are placed in the form with labels, IDs, settings for the character width that will display in the text field and the maximum characters the user can enter in each field.

8. **Drag the column border closer to the edge of the form fields, click the first_name field to select it, save your work, then compare your screen to Figure I-6 (You are only selecting this field to be able to compare your field properties with the figure.)**

   The form field properties for the first_name field are displayed in the Property inspector.

FIGURE I-5: Adding form labels for text fields

Adjusted column border

Text labels formatted with body_text style

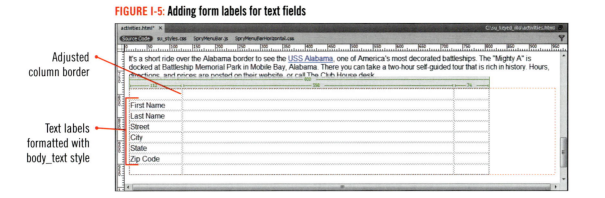

FIGURE I-6: Text form fields added to the feedback form

Text form fields

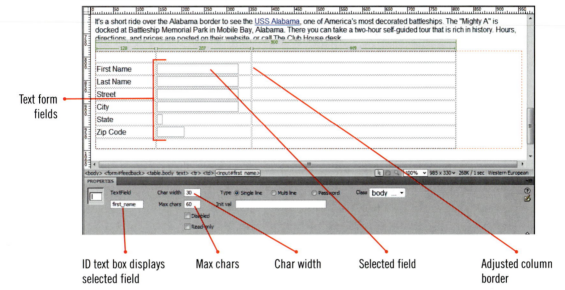

ID text box displays selected field   Max chars   Char width   Selected field   Adjusted column border

TABLE I-1: Form field attributes for the feedback form

label	ID	char width	max chars
First Name	first_name	30	60
Last Name	last_name	30	60
Street	street	30	60
City	city	30	60
State	state	2	2
Zip Code	zip_code	10	10

Understanding text fields

Single-line text fields are useful for small pieces of data, such as a name or telephone number. **Multi-line text fields**, also called **Text area fields**, are useful for entering comments that may take several sentences to complete. **Password fields** are unique fields that display asterisks or bullets in place of text on the screen, to prevent others from viewing the data as it is entered. There are three ways to create a Multi-line text field. You can click the Text Field button in the Forms category on the Insert panel, select the field, then click the Multi line option on the Property inspector. Or you can create a Text area field by clicking the Textarea button in the Forms category on the Insert panel. You can also use the Insert, Form submenu on the Application bar (Win) or Menu bar (Mac). To create a Password field, create a text field, select the field, then select the Password option in the Property inspector.

Adding a Radio Group

Radio buttons let users select options. Two or more radio buttons together are called a **radio group**. When used in a group, radio buttons are mutually exclusive; if a user tries to select two radio buttons in the same group, the first one becomes deselected when the second one is selected. Radio buttons are useful in situations where you want users to select only one choice from a group of possible choices. For example, on a shoe order form, radio buttons could represent the different shoe sizes. To order one pair of shoes, users would select only one size. It is important to include labels to help users understand how to complete each item in the form. It is also important to set an appropriate default value to form objects. A default value will prevent users from unintentionally skipping over items or mistakenly sending unintentional information when they submit the form.  You continue working on the form by adding a group of two radio buttons for users to indicate whether they would like to receive newsletters.

STEPS

1. **Select the third cells in the second, third, and fourth rows, expand the Property inspector if necessary, then click the Merges selected cells using spans button** ⬚ **in the Property inspector**

   Merging these cells provides a good-sized location to position the radio group.

2. **Place the insertion point in the newly merged cell, then type Would you like to receive our quarterly newsletters?**

   This text will appear above the radio button group so the user will understand the significance of this group.

3. **Press [Shift][Enter] (Win) or [shift][return] (Mac), then click the Radio Group button in the Forms category on the Insert panel**

   The Radio Group dialog box opens, as shown in Figure I-7. This is where you specify the name of the radio group and the label and value for each button. You can choose whether to use line breaks or a table to position the buttons.

4. **Type newsletters in the Name text box**

   The radio group is assigned the name *newsletters*.

5. **Click Radio in the first row of the Label column to select it, type Yes, then press [Tab]**

   "Yes" will display as the label for the first radio button. The default value for the first radio button is selected.

6. **Type positive**

   "Positive" is set as the value that, after users select the "Yes" option, will be sent to your script or program when the form is processed.

7. **Repeat Steps 5 and 6 for the second row of the Label and Value columns and enter the label No with a value of negative to create the second radio button**

8. **If necessary, click the Lay out using: Line breaks (
 tags) option button to select it, compare your screen to Figure I-8, then click OK**

   The radio group appears on the form.

9. **Save your work, deselect the option button if necessary, then compare your screen to Figure I-9**

TROUBLE

If you see empty space displayed at the bottom of the table, click the Table tag in the Tag selector to close it up.

Design Matters

Creating good form field labels

Because labels are so important in identifying the information that the form collects, you must use form field labels that make sense to your viewers. For example, First Name and Last Name are good form field labels because users understand clearly what information they should enter. A generic label, such as Name, isn't as specific. If creating a simple and obvious label is impossible, include a brief preceding paragraph that describes the information that should be entered

into the form field. You can add labels to a form using one of three methods: type a label in the appropriate table cell of your form; use the Label button in the Forms category on the Insert panel to link the label to the form object; or use the Input Tag Accessibility Attributes dialog box. The Input Tag Accessibility Attributes dialog box will prompt you to add a label if you have set your preferences to provide accessibility attributes for form objects.

FIGURE I-7: Radio Group dialog box properties

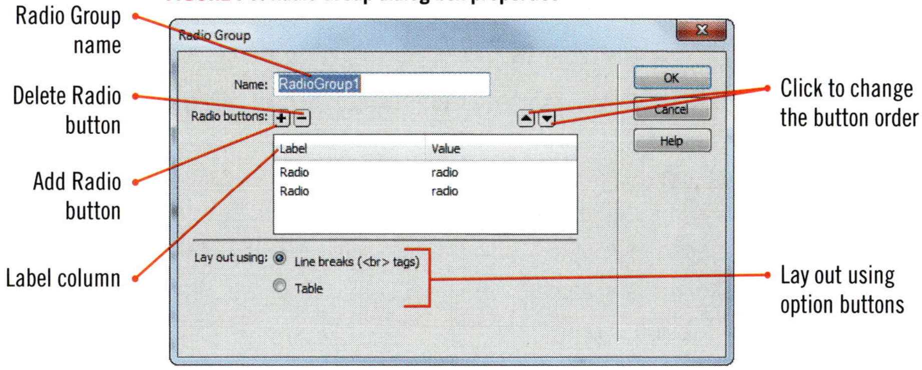

Radio Group name

Delete Radio button

Add Radio button

Label column

Click to change the button order

Lay out using option buttons

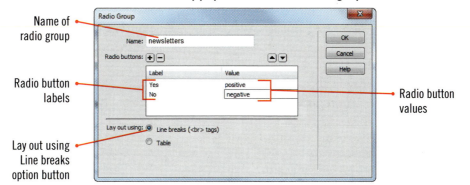

FIGURE I-8: Radio Group properties for newsletters radio group

Name of radio group

Radio button labels

Lay out using Line breaks option button

Radio button values

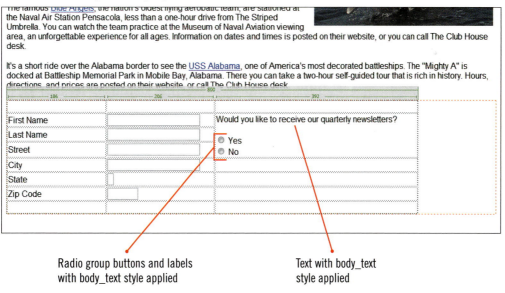

FIGURE I-9: Formatting the radio group

Radio group buttons and labels with body_text style applied

Text with body_text style applied

Design Matters

Using lists and menus

Often a form will include a field where the user is asked to select only one item, but there are so many items from which to choose that radio buttons would take too much space on the form. In those cases, lists or menus are the more appropriate choice for a form object. This form object can either take the form of a scrolling list or a shortcut menu. Lists differ from menus in that they allow form users to make multiple selections. Menus only allow one selection. Both make efficient use of space on a form.

Adding a Check Box

Check boxes are very much like radio buttons, in that a user can simply click one to select it. However, with check boxes, the user can select more than one choice when appropriate. For example, a form with hobby check box options would allow users multiple selections since many people have more than one hobby. Using check boxes rather than radio buttons gives users the opportunity to select both options. You decide to insert check boxes in the form so users can request more information about both the fishing trips and dolphin cruises.

STEPS

1. **Select the third cells in the third and fourth rows, then click the Merges selected cells using spans button ▣ in the Property inspector**
   Merging these cells provides a good location to position the check boxes.

2. **Place the insertion point in the newly merged cell, type Please select the materials you would like to receive:, then press [Shift][Enter] (Win) or [shift][return] (Mac)**
   This text will display above the check boxes. It serves as a user prompt to direct the response for the check boxes on the form.

> **QUICK TIP**
> You can also assign a tab index here, which sets the order for moving to each form object when the Tab key is pressed.

3. **Click Checkbox in the Forms category on the Insert panel**
   The Input Tag Accessibility Attributes dialog box opens. This is where you enter the ID, label, label tag style, and position. These attributes are essential for creating an accessible form.

> **QUICK TIP**
> To edit the name of a check box, click the check box to select it, then edit its properties in the Property inspector.

4. **Type fishing in the ID text box, type Fishing in the Label text box, click the Wrap with label tag option button for the style, if necessary click the After form item option button for the position as shown in Figure I-10, then click OK**
   The dialog box closes and a check box with the label *Fishing* displays in the form.

5. **Select the fishing check box on the form, then type fish in the Checked value text box in the Property inspector**
   The check box is assigned a name and a value, as shown in Figure I-11. The Initial state option button in the Property inspector is set to Unchecked; the check box will remain unselected when the form is first opened. That way you are assured that the user intended to select the check box, rather than neglecting to deselect it.

6. **Click to place the insertion point after the word *Fishing* on the form, press [spacebar] once, then repeat Steps 3 through 5 to place one more check box on the form, using Figure I-12 as a guide for the check box properties and Cruises as the label on the page**
   A check box with the label cruises appears to the right of the fishing check box on the form.

> **TROUBLE**
> If your cell widths do not match the figure, you can resize them by dragging the cell borders to match Figure I-13.

7. **Compare your screen to Figure I-13, then save your work**
   The check boxes are placed in the form.

Design Matters

Creating accessible HTML form objects

When users enter information in form fields, they use [Tab] to move the insertion point from field to field. By default, the insertion point moves through fields from left to right across the page and screen readers read from left to right. However, you can set your own tab order to override the default. For example, regardless of where the fields for First Name and Last Name are placed on the form, you can direct the insertion point to move directly from the First Name field to the Last Name field, even if there are other fields between them. To change an existing form object's tab order, right-click the form object (Win), or [Ctrl] + click the form object (Mac). Click Edit Tag `<input>`, click the Style Sheet/Accessibility category in the Tag Editor – input dialog box, then change the Tab index number. To assign the subsequent fields to move to after the user presses [Tab], type the number *2* in the Tab index box to denote the second field; type *3* to assign the third field, and so forth. You can also assign Tab Index values in the Input Tag Accessibility Attributes dialog box when you create the tag. Tab orders will only work if each tab is assigned an index number.

FIGURE I-10: Input Tag Accessibility Attributes dialog box for fishing check box

Input Tag Accessibility Attributes
ID: fishing
Label: Fishing
Attach label tag using 'for' attribute
Style: Wrap with label tag
No label tag
Position: Before form item
After form item
Access key:
Tab Index:
If you don't want to enter this information when inserting objects, change the Accessibility preferences.
OK
Cancel
Help
ID for check box
Label for check box
Wrap with label tag option button
After form item option button

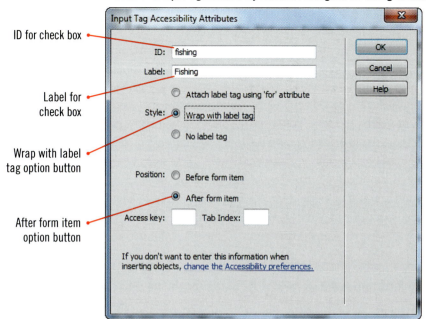

FIGURE I-11: Properties for fishing check box

PROPERTIES
Checkbox name
fishing
Checked value
fish
Initial state
Checked
Unchecked
Class
None
Checkbox name
Checked value
Unchecked Initial state option button

FIGURE I-12: Properties for cruises check box

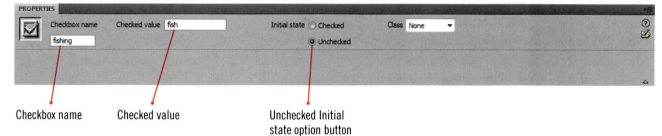

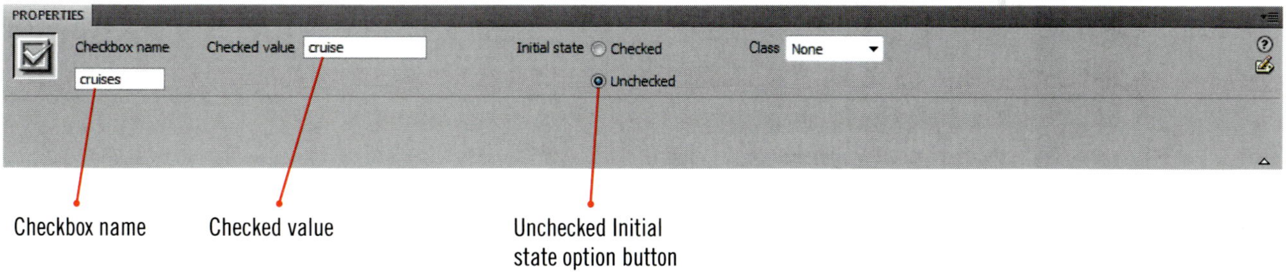

PROPERTIES
Checkbox name
cruises
Checked value
cruise
Initial state
Checked
Unchecked
Class
None
Checkbox name
Checked value
Unchecked Initial state option button

FIGURE I-13: Viewing the check boxes

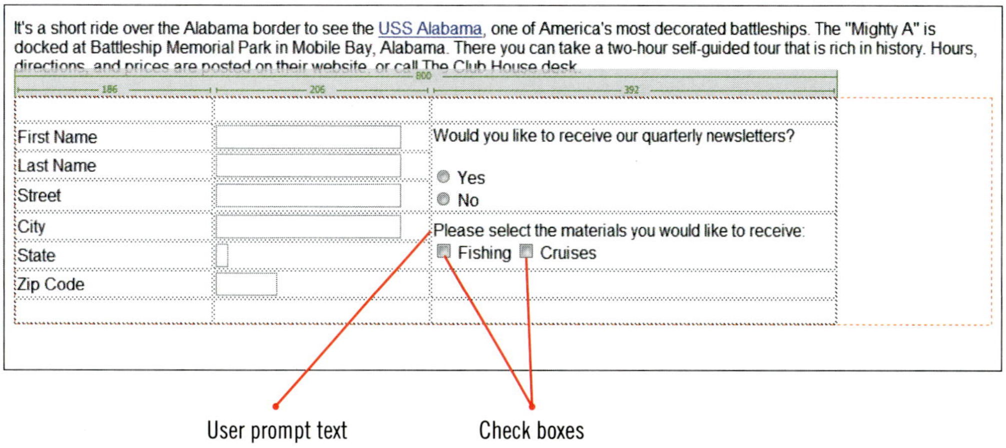

It's a short ride over the Alabama border to see the USS Alabama, one of America's most decorated battleships. The "Mighty A" is docked at Battleship Memorial Park in Mobile Bay, Alabama. There you can take a two-hour self-guided tour that is rich in history. Hours, directions, and prices are posted on their website, or call The Club House desk.
First Name
Last Name
Street
City
State
Zip Code
Would you like to receive our quarterly newsletters?
Yes
No
Please select the materials you would like to receive:
Fishing
Cruises
User prompt text
Check boxes

Inserting a Submit and a Reset Button

Buttons are small rectangular objects that have actions assigned to them. **Actions** trigger events that take place after a user clicks a button. Button properties include a name, a label, and an action. As with all selected objects, you assign button properties using the Property inspector. There are two reserved button names that have assigned meanings: Submit and Reset. These should only be used for buttons that are used to submit or reset a form; no other buttons should use these names. **Submit** means to send the form data to the processing program or script for processing. **Reset** means to clear the form fields to the original values. You want to add two buttons to the form: one that will submit the form for processing and another to clear the form in case the user needs to erase the information and start over.

STEPS

1. **Place the insertion point in the third column of the next to last row**

2. **Click Button in the Forms category on the Insert panel, click the No label tag option button in the Style section of the Input Tag Accessibility Attributes dialog box, then click OK**

   A Submit button appears on the form, without a label next to it, and the Property inspector displays its properties.

3. **If necessary, click the Submit form option button next to Action in the Property inspector, then type Submit in the Button name text box, as shown in Figure I-14**

   When a viewer clicks this Submit button, the information in the form is sent to the server for processing.

4. **Click to place the insertion point to the right of the Submit button, click Button on the Insert panel, click the No label tag option in the Input Tag Accessibility Attributes dialog box if necessary, click OK, select the newly placed Submit button, then click the Reset form option button next to Action in the Property inspector**

   The second Submit button changes to a Reset button. When a viewer clicks this Reset button, the form will clear any information he or she has typed.

5. **Verify that the Button name text box and the Value text box contain Reset, compare your screen to Figure I-15, then save your work**

Design Matters

Using the Adobe Exchange

To obtain form controls designed for creating specific types of forms, such as online tests and surveys, you can visit the Adobe Marketplace & Exchange (www.adobe.com/cfusion/exchange). This is a central storage location on the Adobe Web site for program extensions, also known as **add-ons**. You can search the site by entering keywords in a standard Search text box, similar to using the Dreamweaver Help Search text box.

FIGURE I-14: Inserting a Submit button

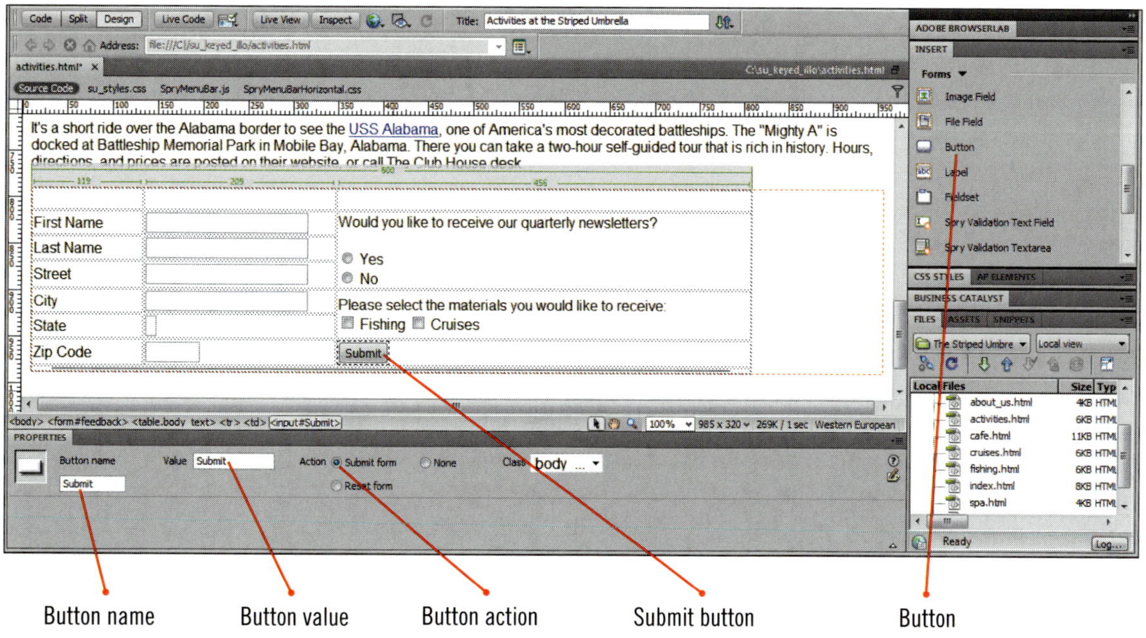

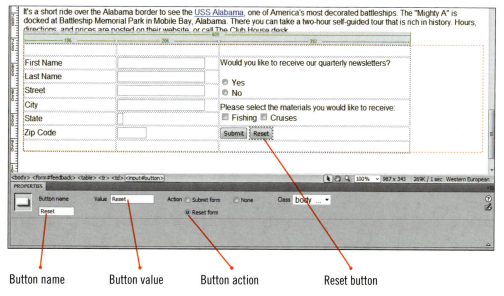

Button name   Button value   Button action   Submit button   Button

FIGURE I-15: Inserting a Reset button

Button name   Button value   Button action   Reset button

Setting the Form Properties

Once you've inserted a form, you can then assign the properties for the application that you want to process the form information and the method you want it transmitted to the processing application. The **Action property** in the Property inspector specifies the application or script that will process the form data. The **Method property** specifies the protocol used to send the form data to the Web server. The **Get**

method specifies that the data collected in the form be sent to the server as appended to the URL of the Web page in the Action property. The **Post method** specifies that the data be sent to the processing script as a binary or encrypted file, allowing you to send the data securely. This information must be obtained from your instructor in order to be able to process the form.

Formatting and Testing a Form

In addition to adding descriptive labels to each form object, there are several ways you can format a form to make it easier to use. You can add brief instructions to the top of the form that will guide the user in filling it out correctly. Simple formatting such as adding a horizontal rule above and below the form can set it off from the rest of the page content. You decide to add a short instructional sentence to serve as the form header at the top of the form, right-align some of the labels, then accentuate the form with a horizontal rule.

STEPS

1. **Merge the top three cells in the first row of the table, then type To request further information, please complete this form. in the merged cell**
   Because it is a table header, this text is automatically centered across the table and appears bold. The body_text style is applied as well.

2. **Select the labels in the first column, then set the Horizontal alignment to right**
   The labels are now closer to the text boxes, as shown in Figure I-16.

3. **Place the insertion point in the last cell in the first column of the table, select all the cells in the row, then merge them**
   The new row is merged.

4. **Place the insertion point in the newly merged cell, click Insert on the Application bar (Win) or Menu bar (Mac), point to HTML, click Horizontal Rule, then set the width to 95% and the alignment to Center in the Property inspector**
   A horizontal line displays selected at the end the form.

> **QUICK TIP**
> Recall that you can click the table tag in the tag selector to select a table.

5. **Select the table, then center the table in the form**

6. **Save your work, click the Preview/Debug in Browser icon [icon], then select Preview in [your browser name], enter some dummy data in the form, then click the Reset button**
   The Reset button works correctly, but the Submit button will not. Recall from the second lesson that you have not set the form properties to send the data to a Web server. You need additional information from your instructor to do this.

> **TROUBLE**
> If the text in column 3 wraps to two lines, drag the right table border to widen the table.

7. **Compare your finished project to Figure I-17, close your browser window, then close the page**

FIGURE I-16: Formatting text field labels

It's a short ride over the Alabama border to see the USS Alabama, one of America's most decorated battleships. The "Mighty A" is docked at Battleship Memorial Park in Mobile Bay, Alabama. There you can take a two-hour self-guided tour that is rich in history. Hours, directions, and prices are posted on their website, or call The Club House desk.

To request further information, please complete this form.

First Name

Last Name

Street

City

State

Zip Code

Would you like to receive our quarterly newsletters?

○ Yes
○ No

Please select the materials you would like to receive:

☐ Fishing ☐ Cruises

Submit   Reset

Labels are
right-aligned

FIGURE I-17: The finished project

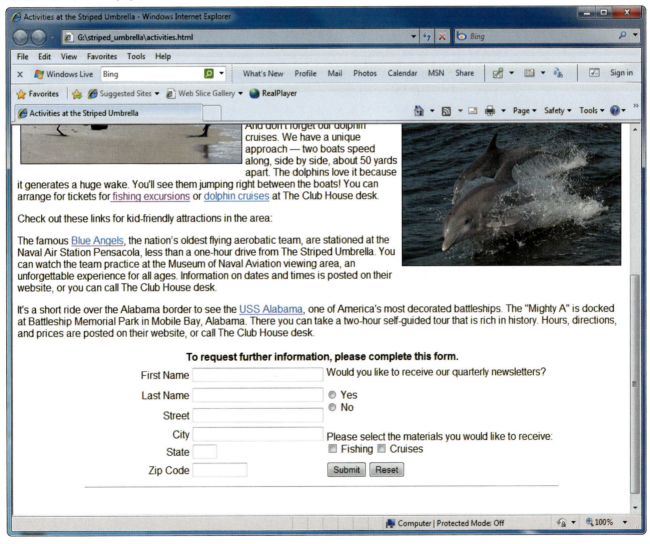

Dreamweaver CS5

Updating Files

As your Web site grows and you have additional folders and files to keep track of, it is imperative to keep your files in good order. Deleting files that are no longer needed and keeping your other files updated are important to insure quality Web sites. In Unit F, you learned to run reports to identify broken links and orphaned files. When you are using incomplete pages as placeholder pages, they will not show up as orphaned files if they contain links from other pages. Before publishing your site to a Web server, however, be sure to complete all pages; publishing incomplete pages is considered unprofessional. ▰▰▰ Now that the form for the activities page is finished, you need to finalize the fishing and cruises pages. You replace the placeholder pages with completed pages so that all of the pages are up to date.

STEPS

1. **Open the file dwi_1.html from the folder where you store your Unit I Data Files, then save it as fishing.html in the striped_umbrella root folder, overwriting the existing fishing page but not updating links**

   Although the page is saved, the image will continue to display as a broken link on the fishing page until the image is saved in the Web site.

2. **Click the broken graphic placeholder, click the Browse for File icon ▭ next to the Src text box in the Property inspector, browse to where you store your Unit I Data Files, open the assets folder, then double-click the file heron_small.jpg to copy the file to the striped_umbrella assets folder**

   The file is copied to the site assets folder.

3. **Deselect the image placeholder**

   The page displays with heron image, as shown in Figure I-18. Since the code was already in place on the page linking the su_styles.css to the file, the text is automatically updated with the body_text style. The Spry Menu bar is also formatted correctly.

4. **Close the file dwi_1.html, then close the fishing page**

5. **Open the file dwi_2.html from where you store your Unit I Data Files, then save it as cruises.html in the striped_umbrella root folder, overwriting the existing cruises page but not updating links**

   The page is saved, but the image link remains broken because the image has not been saved in the Web site.

6. **Close the dwi_2.html page, click the broken graphic placeholder, click ▭ next to the Src text box in the Property inspector, browse to where you store your Unit I Data Files, open the assets folder, then double-click the file boats.jpg to copy the file to the striped_umbrella assets folder**

   The file is copied to the site assets folder.

7. **Deselect the image placeholder**

   The image displays on the page, as shown in Figure I-19. Since the code was already in place on the page linking to the su_styles.css style sheet, the text is automatically updated with the body_text style.

QUICK TIP
Recall that you can create reports using the Reports command on the Site menu.

8. **Run reports on the Entire Current Local Site to check for Missing Alt Text and Untitled Documents**

   There are no pages with missing alternate text or missing page titles.

9. **Recreate the site cache, then run reports on broken links and orphaned files**

   There are no broken links or orphaned files.

10. **Close the page, then exit Dreamweaver**

FIGURE I-18: Fishing page updated

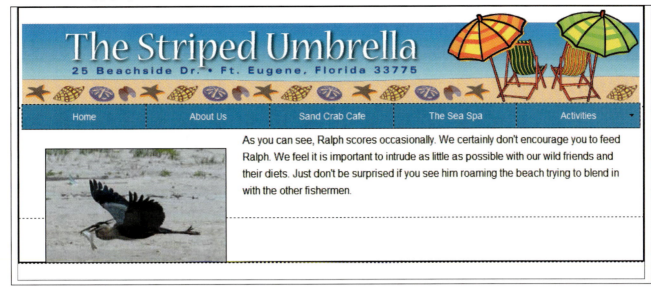

As you can see, Ralph scores occasionally. We certainly don't encourage you to feed Ralph. We feel it is important to intrude as little as possible with our wild friends and their diets. Just don't be surprised if you see him roaming the beach trying to blend in with the other fishermen.

FIGURE I-19: Cruises page updated

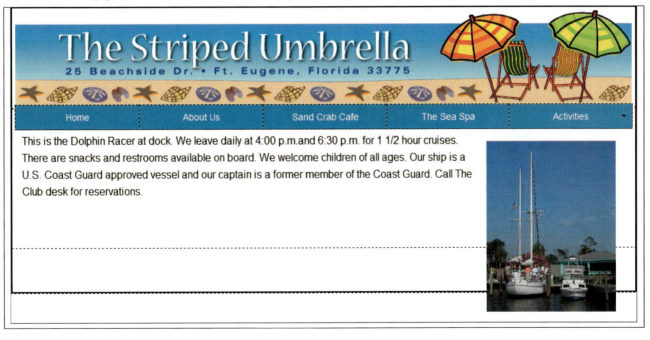

This is the Dolphin Racer at dock. We leave daily at 4:00 p.m. and 6:30 p.m. for 1 1/2 hour cruises. There are snacks and restrooms available on board. We welcome children of all ages. Our ship is a U.S. Coast Guard approved vessel and our captain is a former member of the Coast Guard. Call The Club desk for reservations.

Practice

Concepts Review

For current SAM information, including versions and content details, visit SAM Central (http://www.cengage.com/samcentral). If you have a SAM user profile, you may have access to hands-on instruction, practice, and assessment of the skills covered in this unit. Since various versions of SAM are supported throughout the life of this text, check with your instructor for the correct instructions and URL/Web site for accessing assignments.

Label each element in the Dreamweaver window shown in Figure I-20.

FIGURE I-20

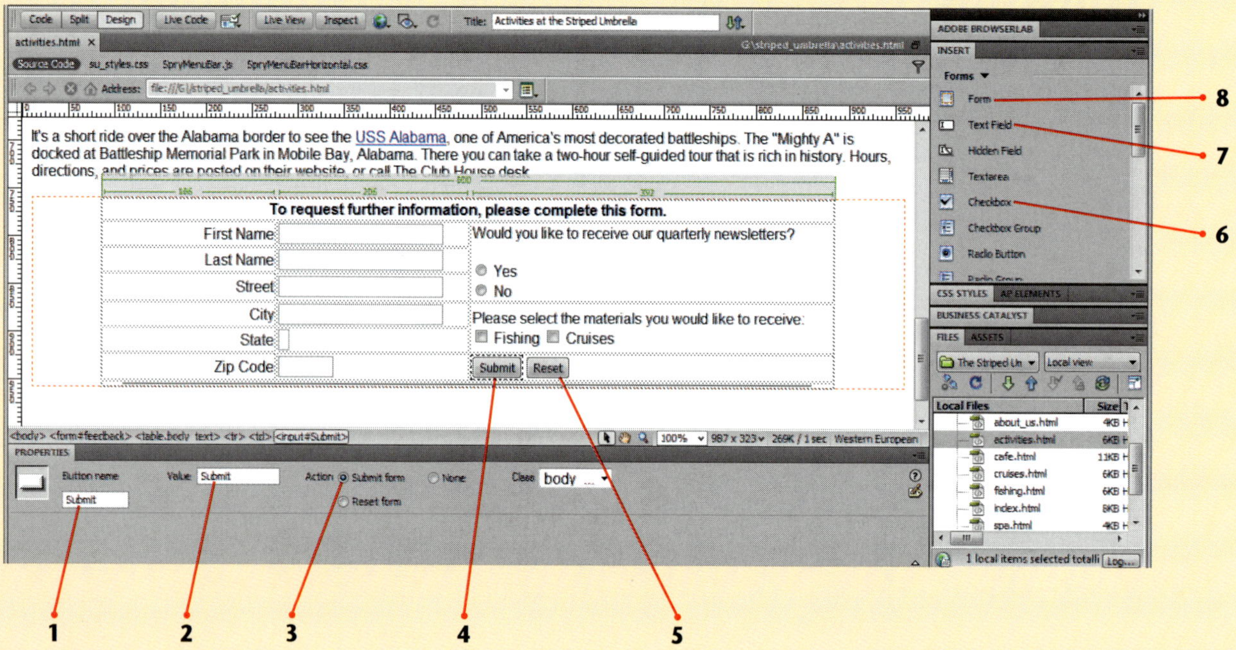

1. _____	5. _____
2. _____	6. _____
3. _____	7. _____
4. _____	8. _____

Match each of the following terms with the statement that best describes it.

9. **Check boxes**

10. **Radio buttons**

11. **Submit button**

12. **Reset button**

13. **Event**

14. **Password fields**

15. **Multi-line text fields**

a. Set(s) the form object values to the default settings

b. Are mutually exclusive; only one in each group can be selected

c. What happens after a button is clicked

d. Display(s) data as asterisks or bullets

e. Send(s) the data to be processed

f. Contain(s) space for more than one line of data

g. More than one can be selected

Select the best answer from the following list of choices.

16. **Which of the following is not classified as a form field?**
  a. text field
  b. hidden field
  c. default field
  d. file field

17. **Button properties include:**
  a. a name, a field, and an action.
  b. a name, a label, and an action.
  c. a name, a label, and a value.
  d. a name, a value, and an action.

18. **Server-side scripting means that:**
  a. the form is processed on the user's computer.
  b. the form is processed by a JavaScript program.
  c. the form is processed on the form's host server.
  d. b and c.

Skills Review

Important: If you did not create this Web site in Unit B and maintain it during the preceding units, you will need to create a site root folder for this Web site and define the Web site using files your instructor will provide. See the "Read This Before You Begin" section for more detailed instructions.

1. **Understand forms and form objects.**
  a. Refer to Figure I-21 to locate a text field, a check box, a radio button, and a Submit button.

2. **Create and Insert a form on a page.**
  a. Start Dreamweaver and open the tips.html page in the Blooms & Bulbs Web site.
  b. Place the insertion point after the last sentence on the page and add two paragraph breaks to end the ordered list.
  c. Insert a form.
  d. Name the form **tips**.
  e. View the HTML code for the form.
  f. Return to Design view.
  g. Save your work.

3. **Add a text form field.**
  a. Place the insertion point inside the form and insert a table with 9 rows and 3 columns, a width of 90%, a border of zero, the cell padding blank, cell spacing of 5, the Top header option, and a table summary **This table is used for form layout**.
  b. Center the table in the form.
  c. Using Figure I-21 as a guide, enter labels that will be used for Single line text fields in the first column, beginning in row 2.
  d. Format the table with the body_text style.
  e. Drag the column border close to the text fields.
  f. Use the information in Table I-2 to add text fields with no label tags in the column next to the labels, beginning in row 2.

TABLE I-2: Form field attributes for the tips form

label	form field ID	char width	max chars
First Name	first_name	40	40
Last Name	last_name	40	40
Street	street	40	40
City	city	40	40
State	state	2	2
Zip Code	zip_code	10	10
E-mail Address	e_mail	40	40

Skills Review (continued)

    g. Drag the column border close to the text fields.

    h. Save your work.

    i. Merge the second through fifth rows in the third column.

    j. Type **My favorite gardening tip:** in the resulting merged cell.

    k. Top-align the text.

    l. Create a line break after the text and insert a Multi-line text field (or a Textarea field) with no label tag.

    m. Name the new Textarea field **my_tips**, then set the Char width to 40 and the Num lines to 4.

    n. Click the table tag to remove any empty space displayed in the table, then save your work.

4. Add a radio group.

    a. In the third column in the last row, insert a radio group.

    b. Name the radio group **contact**.

    c. Enter the label **Please contact me with special offers** for the first radio button, then enter a value of **yes**.

    d. Enter the label **Don't contact me** for the second radio button, then enter a value of **no**.

    e. Use line breaks to lay out the radio group.

    f. Save your work.

5. Add a check box.

    a. In the cell below the text area, type **I would be interested in reading Gardening Tips:**.

    b. In the same cell, below the text, insert a check box with the label **On the Web** wrapped with the label tag after the form item, name it **on_web**, then assign it a checked value of **web**.

    c. Enter a space after the check box text, insert a check box with the label **By E-mail** wrapped with the label tag after the form item, then enter **e_mail2** as the name and **e_mail** as the checked value.

    d. Enter a space after the check box text and insert a check box with the label **By mail** wrapped with the label tag after the form item, enter **by_mail** as the name, then enter **mail** as the checked value.

    e. Save your work.

6. Insert a Submit and a Reset button.

    a. Add a new row to the table.

    b. Insert a Submit button with no label tag in the second column of the new row.

    c. Right-align the Submit button in the cell, then change the button name to **Submit**.

    d. Insert a Reset button in the third column of the new row.

    e. Verify that **Reset** is the button name, **Reset** is the value, and the action is set to **Reset form**.

    f. Save your work.

7. Format a form.

    a. Merge the cells in the top row of the table, type **Do you have a gardening tip you would like to share with us?**, then center-align the text.

    b. Right-align the labels in the first column of the form.

    c. Add a new row between the last two rows in the table, then merge all cells in the row. (*Hint*: You can place the insertion point in the last row, then use the Insert, Table Objects, Insert Row Above command.)

    d. Place a horizontal rule in the new row and format it as 90%, centered.

    e. Select the table, then set the cell spacing to 5.

    f. Save your work, preview the page in the browser, compare your screen to Figure I-21, test all fields, then test the Reset button.

    g. Close the browser.

Skills Review (continued)

8. Update files.

a. Open dwi_3.html from where you store your Data Files, then save it as **annuals.html**, replacing the original file but not updating links. Save the file coleus.jpg in the assets folder of the Web site. Close dwi_3.html.

b. Open dwi_4.html from where you store your Data Files, then save it as **perennials.html**, replacing the original file but not updating links. Save the file ruby_grass.jpg in the assets folder of the Web site. Close dwi_4.html.

c. Open dwi_5.html from where you store your Data Files, then save it as **water_plants.html**, replacing the original file but not updating links. Save the file water_lily.jpg in the assets folder of the Web site. Close dwi_5.html.

d. Save all files, run reports to check for untitled documents and missing alternate text, then, if necessary, correct any omissions that you find.

e. Check for broken links and orphaned files, then, if necessary, correct any errors that you find. (*Hint:* If you see any broken links, recreate your site cache and run the report again.)

f. Save your work, close all open files, then exit Dreamweaver.

FIGURE I-21

We have lots of tips we would like to share with you as you prepare your gardens this season. Remember, there is always something to be done for your gardens, no matter what the season. Our experienced staff is here to help you plan your gardens, select your plants, prepare your soil, assist you in the planting, and maintain your beds. Check out our calendar for a list of our scheduled workshops. Our next workshop is "Attracting Butterflies to Your Garden." All workshops are free of charge and on a first-come, first-served basis! They fill up quickly, so be sure to reserve your spot early.

Seasonal Gardening Checklist

- **Fall** – The time to plant trees and spring-blooming bulbs. Take the time to clean the leaves and dead foliage from your beds and lawn.
- **Winter** – The time to prune fruit trees and finish planting your bulbs. Don't forget to water young trees when the ground is dry.
- **Spring** – The time to prepare your beds, plant annuals, and apply fertilizer to established plants. Remember to mulch to maintain moisture and prevent weed growth.
- **Summer** – The time to supplement rainfall so that plants get one inch of water per week. Plant your vegetable garden and enjoy bountiful harvests until late fall.

Basic Gardening Tips

1. Select plants according to your climate.
2. In planning your garden, consider the composition, texture, structure, depth, and drainage of your soil.
3. Use compost to improve the structure of your soil. Choose plant foods based on your garden objectives.
4. Generally, plants should receive one inch of water per week.
5. Use mulch to conserve moisture, keep plants cool, and cut down on weeding.

Do you have a gardening tip you would like to share with us?

First Name

Last Name

Street

City

State

Zip Code

E-mail Address

My favorite gardening tip:

I would be interested in reading Gardening Tips:
☐ On the Web ☐ By E-mail ☐ By mail

◉ Please contact me with special offers
◉ Don't contact me

Submit   Reset

Important: *If you did not create these Web sites in Unit B and maintain them during the preceding units, you will need to create a site root folder for these Web sites and define the Web sites using files your instructor will provide. See the "Read This Before You Begin" section for more detailed instructions.*

Independent Challenge 1

You have been hired to create a Web site for a river expedition company named Rapids Transit, located on the Buffalo River in Northwest Arkansas. Mike Andrew, the owner of Rapids Transit, has asked you to add a form to the page that describes the three categories of lodging available. The purpose of this form will be to allow clients to request brochures for each lodging category.

    a. Open the Rapids Transit Web site.

    b. Open the page lodging.html.

    c. Place a paragraph break after the last sentence on the page and insert a form called **lodging**.

    d. Insert a table inside the form with 7 rows and 3 columns, 800 pixels wide, the border, cell spacing, and cell padding text boxes left blank, a Top header, an appropriate table summary, and center-aligned.

    e. Enter text labels in the first column beginning with the second row, using Figure I-22 as a guide.

    f. Format the table with the body_text style.

    g. Adjust the column border so it is adjacent to the text labels.

    h. Add Single line text fields with no label tags in the column next to the text labels using 40 characters for both the character width and maximum characters for all text fields except for the state and zip code; use a width of 2 for the state and 10 for the zip code. Name the fields appropriately.

    i. Adjust the column border.

    j. In the third cell in the second row type **Please check the brochures you would like to receive.**

    k. Place a check box in the third cell in the third row named **option_1** with a text label of **The Lodge** and a checked value of **lodge**.

    l. Place a check box in the third cell of the fourth row named **option_2** with a text label of **Jenny's Cabins** and a checked value of **jenny**.

    m. Place a check box in the third column of the fifth row named **option_3** with a text label of **John's Camp** and a checked value of **john**.

    n. Insert a Submit button in the third column of the last row.

    o. Insert a Reset button to the right of the Submit button in the same cell, and change the Action to **Reset form**, the button value to **Reset**, and the Button name to **Reset**.

    p. Merge the cells in the top row, then type **If you would like to receive a brochure describing our lodging choices, please complete the form below.**

    q. Insert a new row at the end of the table and merge the cells in the new row.

    r. Insert a horizontal rule with a 100% width, then copy the horizontal rule.

    s. Add a new row between the first and second rows, merge the cells if necessary, then paste the horizontal rule in the merged cells.

    t. Preview the page in the browser, compare it to Figure I-22, then test the text fields and the Reset button.

    u. Make any adjustments to improve the page, then save your work.

    v. Run reports for broken links, orphaned files, untitled documents, and missing alternate text, correcting any errors that you find.

    w. Exit Dreamweaver.

FIGURE I-22

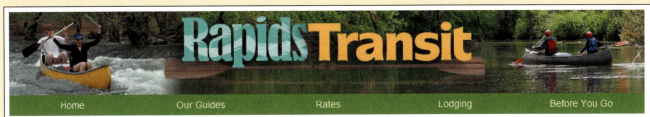

We have three different lodging categories to choose from. They include:

The Lodge This is a rustic, but luxurious lodge with individual rooms similar to a hotel. Each room has its own private bath, a king bed or two double beds, and a balcony that opens to the beauty of the Ozark National River. A common living area with cathedral ceilings and a towering rock fireplace is the perfect spot to gather together with friends after a day of floating.

Jenny's Cabins There are five cabins with two bedrooms and five cabins with three bedrooms. All have beautiful rock wood-burning fireplaces and private grounds. Each has a private deck with a barbeque grill. A stained-glass window created by a local artisan in each great room adds an extra touch of beauty.

John's Camp This is a luxury camp with permanent tents on concrete platforms. Each tent has a private bathroom with running water. These are the ticket for the ultimate floating and camping experience. Fall asleep each night serenaded by a chorus of night creatures!

Rates are as follows:

- The Lodge: $85.00
- Jenny's two-bedroom cabins: $140.00
- Jenny's three-bedroom cabins: $175.00
- John's Camp: $40.00

Check-in is at 2:00 p.m. and Check-out is at 11:00 a.m. E-mail Mike for reservations or for more information.

If you would like to receive a brochure describing our lodging choices, please complete the form below.

First Name	[_____]	Please check the brochures you would like to receive.
Last Name	[_____]	☐ The Lodge
Street	[_____]	☐ Jenny's Cabins
City	[_____]	☐ John's Camp
State	[____]	
Zip Code	[_____]	[Submit] [Reset]

Independent Challenge 2

In this exercise you will continue your work on the TripSmart Web site. The owner, Thomas Howard, wants you to create a form to collect data from users who are interested in receiving more information about one or more of the featured trips.

a. Open the TripSmart Web site, then open the tours page.

b. Insert a paragraph break after the last sentence on the page, then insert a form named **tours**.

c. Insert a table in the form that contains 11 rows, 2 columns, a table width of 800 pixels, a border thickness of 0, cell padding of 1, cell spacing of 1, a Top header, and add an appropriate table summary.

d. Center-align the table in the form, then set the cell width of the first column to 40% and the cell width for the second column to 60%.

e. Merge the cells in the top row, type **Please complete this form for additional information on these tours.**, apply the reverse_text style, then change the cell background color to #666633.

f. Beginning in the second row, type the following labels in the cells in the first column: **First Name**, **Last Name**, **Street**, **City**, **State**, **Zip Code**, **Phone**, **E-mail**, and **I am interested in:**; adjust the column border to a position of your choice; then right-align the labels and apply the body_text style to each one.

g. Insert single-line text fields in the first eight cells in the second column beginning with row 2 and assign the following names: **first_name**, **last_name**, **street**, **city**, **state**, **zip**, **phone**, and **email**; setting the Char width to **40** and the Max Chars to **100** for each of these text fields. (*Hint*: To save time create the first_name field, then use copy and paste to create the other fields, changing the name of each pasted field in the Property inspector.)

h. In the second cell of the tenth row, insert a check box wrapped with the label tag **Spain**, the name **spain**, and a checked value of **yes**.

i. Add a space after the Spain label, then repeat Step h to add another check box next to the Spain check box wrapped with the label tag **China**, the name **china**, and a checked value of **yes**.

j. Apply the body_text style to the Spain and China labels.

k. Left-align the cells with the text boxes and check boxes, then set their vertical alignment to Top.

l. Insert a Submit button and a Reset button in the second cell of the eleventh row with appropriate names and actions.

m. Insert a new merged row at the bottom of the table, then insert a horizontal rule that is 100% wide.

n. Run reports for untitled documents, missing alternate text, broken links, and orphaned files.

o. Save your work, preview the page in your browser, test the form, compare your screen to Figure I-23, close your browser, then close the destinations page.

Home   Tours   Newsletter   Services   Catalog

Destination: Spain

Our next trip to Spain has now been scheduled with a departure date of May 5 and a return date of May 23. This deluxe tour begins in Madrid and ends in the beautiful city of Barcelona. Come join us and enjoy some of Spain's greatest treasures. In addition to ancient cathedrals and magnificent vistas, we will see such sights as the remote town of Ronda, the location of the oldest bullring in Spain. Ronda is perched on a 300-foot gorge of El Tajo. Private coach transportation will be arranged for you to visit Ronda as you are en route from Granada to Seville.

We will also visit Jerez de la Frontera, the home of the Royal Andalusian School of Equestrian Art where you will experience a stunning performance by the "dancing stallions." These magnificent stallions seem to defy gravity as they perform to Spanish classical music. After the performance we will visit a bodega for a tour and sherry tasting, then enjoy dinner in one of Jerez's finest restaurants. Other itinerary stops include Toledo and Cordoba.

To provide the finest in personal attention, this tour will be limited to no more than sixteen persons. The price schedule is as follows: Land Tour and Supplemental Group Air, $5,500.00; International Air, $1,350.00; and Single Supplement, $1,000.00. Entrance fees, hotel taxes, and services are included in the Land Tour price. A deposit of $500.00 is required at the time the booking is made. Trip insurance and luggage insurance are optional and are also offered for an extra charge. A passport and visa will be required for entry into Spain. Call us at 555-848-0807 for further information and the complete itinerary from 8:00 a.m. to 6:00 p.m. (Central Standard Time).

Please complete this form for additional information on these tours.

First Name	
Last Name	
Street	
City	
State	
Zip Code	
Phone	
E-mail	

I am interested in: ☐ Spain ☐ China

[Submit] [Reset]

Independent Challenge 3

Paul Patrick and his partner Donnie Honeycutt have a construction business in Southern California. They have recently published a Web site for their business and would like to add a search form to help their customers quickly find the data they are looking for. They begin this task by researching other Web site search pages on the Internet.

- **a.** Connect to the Internet, then go to the Internal Revenue Service site at www.irs.gov.
- **b.** Click the Advanced Search link to search the IRS site, as shown in Figure I-24.
- **c.** How is the search form organized?
- **d.** What form objects were used?
- **e.** Click the Search Tips link. What information did you find to help users search the Web site?
- **f.** Find one more example of a Web site that uses a search page and explain which of the two sites you prefer and why.

FIGURE I-24

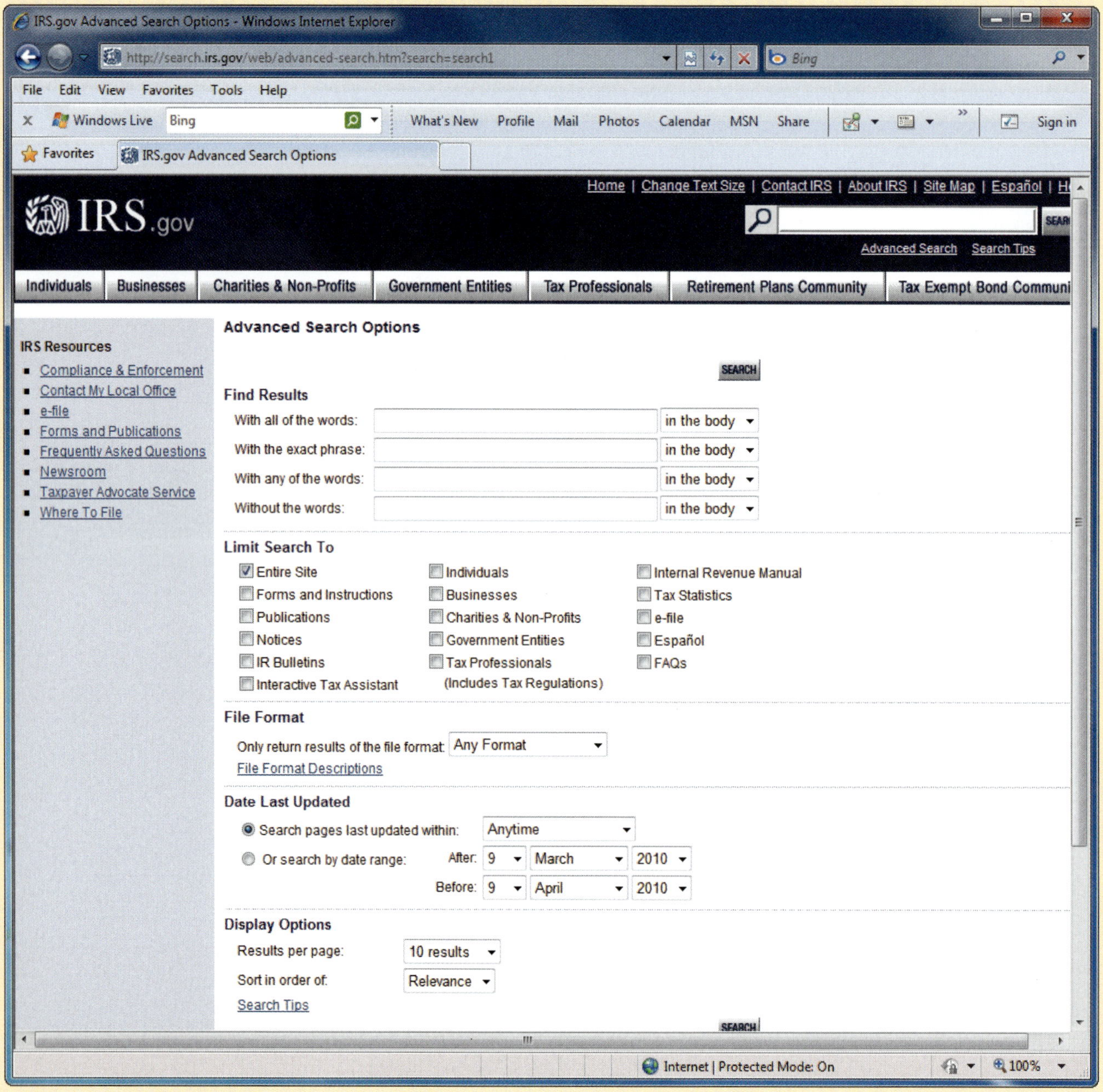

Internal Revenue Service Web site – www.irs.gov

Real Life Independent Challenge

This assignment will continue to build on the personal Web site that you created in Unit B. In Unit C, you created and developed your index page. In Unit D, you added a page with either an ordered or an unordered list, using CSS with a minimum of two styles. In Unit E, you added a page that included at least two images. In Unit F, you added a page that included several links and an image map. In Unit G, you redesigned the index page based on CSS. In Unit H, you used a table to position page elements. In this lesson, you will add a form to one of the pages in your Web site.

a. Consult your wireframes and decide which page you would like to develop in this lesson.

b. Sketch a layout for your page to place the form objects you would like to use.

c. Create the form using at least three different form objects. Include clear instructions that will help users fill out the form correctly.

d. Add text labels to each form object.

e. Add a Submit and Reset button and format them appropriately.

f. Format the form attractively to help it stand out on the page.

g. Save the file and preview the page in the browser, testing the Reset button to make sure it works correctly.

h. Make any adjustments that are necessary to improve the appearance of your form.

After you are satisfied with your work, verify the following:

a. Each completed page has a page title.

b. All links work correctly.

c. The completed pages look good using screen resolutions of 800 × 600 and 1024 × 768.

d. All images are properly linked to the assets folder of the Web site.

e. All images have alternate text and are legal to use.

f. The link checker shows no broken links or orphaned files. If there are orphaned files, note your plan to link them.

g. All main pages have a consistent navigation system.

h. The form is attractive and easy to understand and use.

Visual Workshop

Use Figure I-25 as a guide to continue your work on the Carolyne's Creations Web site. You are adding a form to the catering page that will allow customers to fax a lunch order for pick up that day. Since the customers are faxing their orders, there is no need for a Submit button. You can add a Reset button if you wish. Use form properties and settings of your choice. Run reports for missing alt text, untitled documents, broken links, and orphaned files. If cc_banner.jpg is listed as an orphaned file, delete it, as you no longer need it. (*Hint*: To match the figure, add two new rows to the existing table, merge the cells in each row, insert a horizontal rule in the first row, and insert the new form in the second row.)

FIGURE I-25

Adding Media and Interactivity

There are many ways to make a Web site more compelling for users. Most users would rather feel that they are interacting with a site, rather than passively reading information. Adding media objects, such as rollover images, behaviors, Flash video, and Flash movies, provides more interest than static text and images. You decide to add more interactivity to The Striped Umbrella Web site. You begin by exploring the various options available to you as a designer.

OBJECTIVES

Understand media objects

Add Flash objects

Add behaviors

Edit behaviors

Add rollover images

Add Flash video

Incorporate Web 2.0 technology

Understanding Media Objects

While a Web site with text and static images is adequate for presenting information, you can create a much richer user experience by adding movement and interactive elements. You can use Dreamweaver to add media objects created in other programs to the pages of your Web site. The term *media object* can have different meanings, depending on the industry it is applied to. For our purposes, **media objects** are combinations of visual and audio effects and text used to create an interactive experience with a Web site. You want to add interest to The Striped Umbrella Web site by including media objects. You begin by learning about media objects and how they can help you achieve your remaining Web site goals.

DETAILS

- ### Role of media objects

  The role of a media object is to enhance the user's experience while visiting a Web site. Thus, each media object that you add should provide a specific purpose that could not be achieved as well without it. As with the use of images, there is a fine balance between providing a rich experience for users, cluttering your Web page, and not adding enough interesting detail. Too many media objects on a page can slow the time it takes the page to load and be a problem for users with slow connection speeds. Strive to use the smallest possible file size for your media objects to keep download time at a minimum. Also, provide accessibility by using alt or title tags when you insert media objects. Figure J-1 shows an example of the NASA Web site, which uses video, rollovers, and audio files.

- ### Types of media objects

  You can use Dreamweaver to insert a variety of media effects in your Web pages, including Flash movies, Flash video, and a series of built-in JavaScript behaviors, such as sounds, rollover images, drop-down menus, Go to URLs, and menus. **Go to URLs** direct the browser to use a link to open a different window. Some of the external media file types include Adobe Fireworks menu bars, rollover images, and buttons; Flash video, sound, and animation; Flash Paper; Director and Shockwave movies and presentations; Java applets; ActiveX controls; server-side controls; and a variety of plug-ins. A **plug-in** (also called an **add-on**) is a small computer program that works with a host application, such as a Web browser, to enable it to perform certain functions. In order to play a Flash SWF file in a Web browser, you would need to install the Flash Player plug-in. In order to read Adobe PDF files, you would need to install the Adobe Reader plug-in. Plug-ins allow you to extend the capabilities of the browser to display content, letting you create complex, interactive Web sites with media effects that can be viewed within the pages themselves. Another advantage of plug-ins is that they eliminate the need to load an external document player, such as Windows Media Player.

- ### Collecting Flash objects

  A variety of downloadable Flash objects are available on the Adobe Exchange Web site, located at www.adobe.com/cfusion/exchange. At this site, you can find collections of objects, such as menus, transitions, and image galleries. You can also download a trial version of Flash to experiment with creating your own Flash objects. If you want to create Flash objects regularly, you can purchase the licensed version either as a separate program or as part of a suite of programs, such as Adobe Web Premium CS5. In addition to the Adobe site, there are many other Web sites from which you can download both free and for–purchase Flash objects.

FIGURE J-1: Web site containing media objects

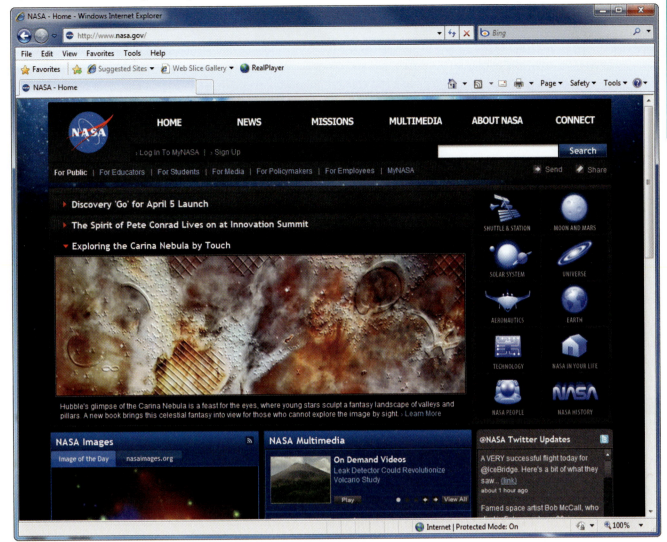

NASA Web site—www.nasa.gov

Using Adobe Flash Player to view Flash content

To view Flash movies, you need to install Adobe Flash Player. This program is included in the latest versions of Internet Explorer, Mozilla Firefox, Safari, and Opera. If you are using an older browser that does not support the version of Flash used to create your movie, you can download the latest Flash Player from the Adobe Web site, located at www.adobe.com. Almost all Internet browsers use Adobe Flash Player. When you use the Insert panel to add Flash content to a Web page, the code that links and runs the content (such as detecting the presence of Flash Player and directing the user to download it if necessary) is embedded into the page code.

Add Flash Objects

Flash is a software program that allows you to create low-bandwidth, high-quality animations and interactive elements called **Flash movies** that you can place on your Web pages. **Low-bandwidth** animations are animations that don't require a fast connection to work properly. These animations use a series of vector-based graphics to create short movies that download quickly. **Vector-based graphics** are scalable graphics that are built using mathematical formulas, rather than pixels. When you use the Insert panel to add Flash content to a Web page, the code that links and runs the content is embedded into the page code. Thus, the presence of a Flash player can be identified by the computer, which will then provide a prompt to the user to download the player if it is not detected. The original Flash file is stored as a separate file in the site root folder. Flash movies have the .swf file extension. The cafe logo displayed at the top of the cafe page is an attractive image. However, an animated logo would add movement and more interest to the page. You decide to replace the current logo image with a Flash movie.

STEPS

1. **Open the cafe page in The Striped Umbrella Web site, select the cafe logo on the left side of the page below the menu bar, then press [Delete] (Win) or [delete] (Mac)**
   The logo is deleted from the page.

2. **Click the Media button list arrow in the Common category on the Insert panel, then click SWF**
   The Select SWF dialog box opens. You use this dialog box to locate the Flash movie.

QUICK TIP
If you already have a Flash .swf file in your site root folder, you can drag and drop it from the Assets panel or Files panel instead of using the Insert panel or Insert menu.

3. **Navigate to the drive and folder where you store your Unit J Data Files, click crabdance.swf, click OK (Win) or Choose (Mac), click Yes in the Dreamweaver dialog box, then click Save**
   The movie is copied and saved in the site root folder of The Striped Umbrella Web site. An Object Tag Accessibility Attributes dialog box opens. This is where you add a title for screen readers.

4. **Type Cafe logo animation in the Title text box, click OK, select FlashID in the ID text box in the Property inspector, then type crabdance**
   A Flash movie placeholder appears on the page, as shown in Figure J-2. The title and ID provide accessibility for the Flash movie. The Loop check box in the Property inspector is currently selected, which means that the Flash movie will play continuously (loop) by default while the page is viewed.

5. **With the placeholder selected, click the Play button in the Property inspector**
   The movie plays on a continuous loop.

6. **Click Stop, click the Loop check box to deselect it, save your work, then click OK to close the Copy Dependent Files dialog box**
   Two supporting files, expressInstall.swf and swfobject_modified.js, are copied to a new Scripts folder. These files are necessary for the movie to play in the browser correctly. Deselecting the Loop check box stops the Flash movie from continuous play.

7. **Click the Switch Design View to Live View button** | Live View |, **then compare your screen to Figure J-3**
   The page is displayed in Live View, with all active content functioning. As it will do when viewed in a browser, the Flash movie plays one time and then stops.

8. **Click** | Live View |, **then save and close the cafe page**

FIGURE J-2: The Flash movie inserted on the cafe page

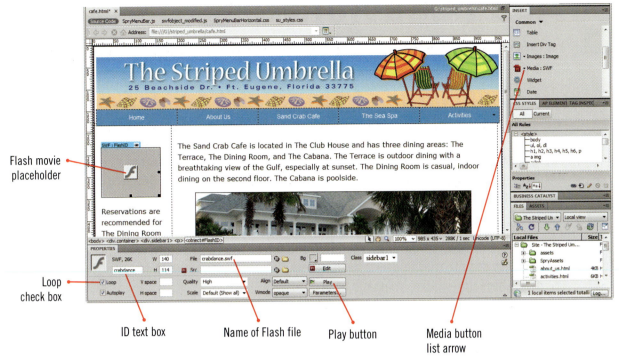

Flash movie placeholder

Loop check box

ID text box

Name of Flash file

Play button

Media button list arrow

FIGURE J-3: Viewing the Flash movie with Live View

Switch Design View to Live View button

Flash movie

Using Flash movies

Using Flash, you can create Flash movies that include multimedia elements, such as audio files (both music and voice-overs), animated objects, scripted objects, and clickable links. You can use Flash movies to add content to your existing Web site or to create an entire Web site. To add a Flash movie to a Web page, click SWF from the Media menu in the Common category on the Insert panel to open the Select SWF dialog box, and then choose the Flash movie you want to insert. As with images, always add a title tag when inserting Flash content to provide accessibility. You also need to include code that will instruct the browser to check for and load a Flash player so the user can view the Flash content on the page. To view your Flash movies, you can either use Live view or preview them in a browser window.

Add Behaviors

You can make your Web pages come alive by adding interactive elements, such as special effects, to them. These special effects are called **actions**. For example, you could attach an action to an image that would result in a descriptive drop-down message when the mouse is rolled over it. You add actions to elements by attaching behaviors to them. **Behaviors** are sets of instructions that tell the page element to respond in a specific way when an event occurs, such as when the mouse pointer is positioned over the element. When you attach a behavior to an element, Dreamweaver generates the JavaScript code for the behavior and inserts it into your page code. The Striped Umbrella staff would like guests to know ahead of time that feeding the birds and other wildlife around the property is prohibited. You decide to add an action to the activities page that will automatically open a new browser window with a related message.

STEPS

1. **Open the file dwj_1.html from the drive and folder where you store your Unit J Data Files, save it in the site root folder as wildlife_message.html without updating links, then close dwj_1.html and wildlife_message.html**

   The wildlife_message page is already linked to the su_styles.css style sheet and coded with the body_text style. (The connection became active when the file was saved to the Web site.)

2. **Open the activities page, select the heron_waiting_small image on the activities page, click Window on the Application bar (Win) or Menu bar (Mac), then click Behaviors**

   The Behaviors panel opens. With the heron_waiting_small image selected, any action that is selected will apply to the image.

   > **QUICK TIP**
   > An event can be changed by clicking it and choosing a different event.

3. **Click the Add behavior button ➕ on the Behaviors panel toolbar, as shown in Figure J-4, then click Open Browser Window**

   The Open Browser Window dialog box opens. This is where you specify the action you want to happen when an event occurs, such as a mouse click. The name of the event is onClick. Once an action is selected, the name of the event will appear by default in the left column of the Behaviors.

4. **Click Browse next to the URL to display text box to open the Select File dialog box, navigate to the site root folder if necessary, then double-click wildlife_message.html**

   You identify the location where the message resides. The message will display when the heron_waiting_small image is clicked.

5. **Type 300 in the Window width text box, type 300 in the Window height text box, type message in the Window name text box, compare your screen to Figure J-5, then click OK**

   The new dimensions will be applied to the page when it opens in a browser window.

   > **QUICK TIP**
   > The information bar at the top of the window will display specific instructions for your browser type.

6. **Save your work, preview the page in your browser, then click the heron_waiting_small image, as shown in Figure J-6**

   The wildlife_message page opens in a new browser window that is 300 pixels wide and 300 pixels high.

7. **Close both browser windows**

Using the Behaviors panel to add Actions

You can use the Behaviors panel located in the Tag panel group to insert a variety of JavaScript-based behaviors on a page. For instance, you can automate tasks, respond to visitor selections and mouse movements with drop-down menus, create games, go to a different URL, or add automatic dynamic effects to a Web page. To insert a behavior, click the Add behavior button on the Behaviors panel to open the Actions menu, then click an action from the menu. Actions are triggered by events. For instance, if you want the user to see a page element slide across the page when the element is clicked, you would attach the Slide action using the **onClick** event to trigger the action. Other examples of events are onMouseOver and onLoad. The **onMouseOver** event will trigger an action when the mouse is placed over an object. The **onLoad** event will trigger an action when the page is first loaded in the browser window.

FIGURE J-4: Behaviors panel with the Actions menu displayed

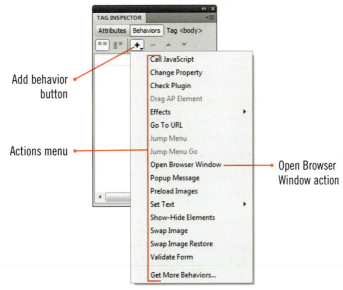

Add behavior
button

Actions menu

Open Browser
Window action

FIGURE J-5: Setting Open Browser Window options

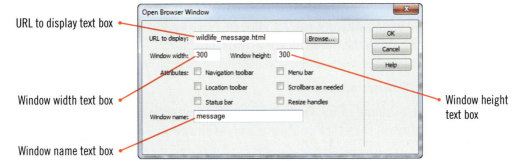

URL to display text box

Window width text box

Window name text box

Window height
text box

FIGURE J-6: Viewing the wildlife message in a browser

Wildlife message
displayed in new
browser window

Clicking the
heron_waiting_small
image triggers
the event

Using the Spry framework

Some of the behaviors that you can add to Web pages use a JavaScript library called the **Spry framework for AJAX. Asynchronous JavaScript and XML (AJAX)** is a method for developing interactive Web pages that respond quickly to user input, such as clicking a map. The JavaScript library contains **spry widgets**, which are prebuilt components for adding interactivity to pages, and **spry effects**, which are screen effects, such as fading and enlarging page elements. When you add a spry effect to a page element, Dreamweaver automatically adds a **SpryAssets folder** to the site root folder with the supporting files located inside the folder.

Adding Media and Interactivity

Edit Behaviors

Once a behavior has been added to a Web page or Web page object, it is easy to modify the action or event by using the Behaviors panel. To change an event, click the left column in the Behaviors panel to display the list of events, then choose the event you would like to use. To change the action, click the right column to display the list of actions, then choose the action you would like to use. You can edit an existing behavior by clicking the right column of the existing behavior, then clicking Edit Behavior. The current browser window that displays the wildlife message is a little too large. You want to resize the window so it will fit the message better. You would also prefer that the event for this behavior opens a new window when the mouse is simply placed over the image rather than clicked. You decide to use the Behaviors panel to make the necessary adjustments to the page.

STEPS

1. **Click the heron_waiting_small image if necessary, right-click (Win) or [control]-click (Mac) the Open Browser Window action in the right column of the Behaviors panel, then click Edit Behavior**

    The Open Browser Window dialog box opens. This is where you adjust the window properties and settings, such as establishing window dimensions, including a status bar, or adding scrollbars as needed.

2. **Change the window height to 225, click OK, save your changes, preview the page in your browser, then click the heron_waiting_small image**

    The size of the browser window with the wildlife message is smaller in size, as shown in Figure J-7.

3. **Close both browser windows**

4. **Click the left column of the Open Browser Window action in the Behaviors panel, click the events list arrow, then click onMouseOver, as shown in Figure J-8**

    The onMouseOver selection specifies that the event of placing the mouse over an image triggers an action. The Open Browser Window action remains the same.

5. **Save your work, preview the page in the browser, then move the mouse over the heron_waiting_small image**

    Simply placing the mouse over the image, rather than clicking it, triggers the Open Browser Window action.

6. **Close the browser windows, close the Behaviors panel, then close the activities page**

Using the Server Behaviors panel

In addition to the Behaviors panel, Dreamweaver also has a Server Behaviors panel, which is located in the Dynamic Content Tab group with the Databases, Bindings, and Components panels. The **Server Behaviors** panel is used to add server behaviors. Server behaviors are tools that write server-side code, such as ASP, PHP, or ColdFusion. For example, you can add code to create a login page or create a page that is password protected. You can also build search pages that will enable viewers to search a Web site for specific content. After you have created a server behavior and enabled Dreamweaver to display live data, you can add, edit, or delete the server behavior while you are in Design view, but viewing the page in Live View.

Reduced
window
size with
wildlife
message
displayed

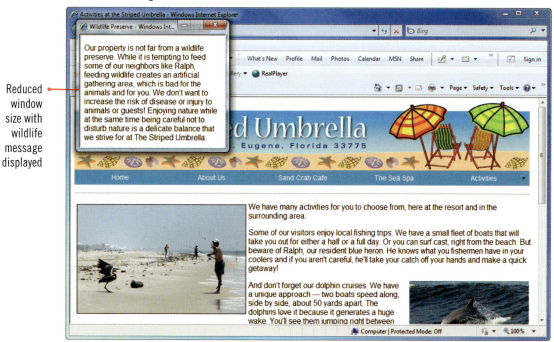

onMouseOver
event

Add Rollover Images

A **rollover image** is an image that changes its appearance when the mouse pointer is placed over it in a browser. A rollover image actually consists of two images. The first image is the one that displays when the mouse pointer is not positioned over it, and the second image is the one that displays when the mouse pointer is positioned over it. Rollover images are often used to help create a feeling of action and interest on a Web page. When a rollover image is inserted into a page, Dreamweaver automatically adds two behaviors: a Swap Image behavior and a Swap Image Restore behavior. A **Swap Image behavior** is JavaScript code that directs the browser to display a different image when the mouse is rolled over an image on the page. A **Swap Image Restore behavlor** restores the swapped image back to the original image back to the original image when the mouse is moved away from the image. You have a photograph of a dolphin that would be perfect on the activities page. To add some interactivity to the page, you decide to include the photograph as a rollover image for the current image of two dolphins.

STEPS

1. **Open the activities page of The Striped Umbrella Web site, select the image of the two dolphins, then delete it**

   The rollover image will be placed in the same position on the page as the deleted two-dolphin image.

2. **Click the Images list arrow in the Common group on the Insert panel, then click Rollover Image**

   The Insert Rollover Image dialog box opens. This is where you specify the name of the image and link to the images you will use for both the original image and the rollover image.

3. **Type dolphins in the Image name text box, click Browse next to the Original image text box, browse to the drive and folder where you store your Unit J Data Files, open the assets folder, then double-click one_dolphin.jpg**

   You specify the image name for the rollover and identify the name and location for the original image. The original image is the one that initially displays in the browser window.

   > **QUICK TIP**
   >
   > To prevent one of the images from being resized during the rollover, both images should be the same height and width.

4. **Click Browse next to the Rollover image text box, browse to the drive and folder where you store your Unit J Data Files if necessary, double-click two_dolphins.jpg, then overwrite the two_dolphins.jpg file in your Web site assets folder**

   You specify the name and location for the rollover image. The rollover image is the image that displays in the browser window when the mouse rolls over the original image. This version of the two_dolphins image is a different size from your original file.

   > **QUICK TIP**
   >
   > The Preload rollover image option ensures that the rollover image displays without a delay.

5. **Type Dolphins riding the surf in the Alternate text text box, verify that the Preload rollover image check box is selected, compare your screen to Figure J-9, then click OK**

   The single dolphin image displays on the page. The two_dolphins image will only appear in the browser window when the mouse rolls over it.

   > **TROUBLE**
   >
   > If you don't see the rollover image, temporarily direct your browser to allow blocked content.

6. **Select the image, click the Align list arrow in the Property inspector, click Right, type 10 in the H Space text box, save your work, preview the page in your browser, move your mouse pointer over the single dolphin image, then compare your screen to Figure J-10**

   The image is aligned to the right of the paragraph with additional white space added to the sides. When you point to the image, the single dolphin image is swapped with the two-dolphin image. When you move the mouse away from the image, it is swapped again.

7. **Close the browser, then click the Show Code view button** `Code`

   The code for the swap image behavior displays, as shown in Figure J-11. The code directs the browser to display the image with one dolphin "onmouseout"— when the mouse is not over the image. It directs the browser to display the image with two dolphins "onmouseover"—when the mouse is over the image.

8. **Click the Show Design view button** `Design`

Adding Media and Interactivity

FIGURE J-9: Setting rollover image properties

Image name text box

Original image text box

Rollover image text box

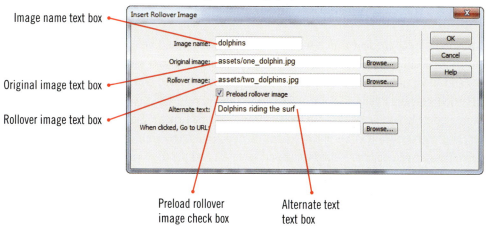

Preload rollover
image check box

Alternate text
text box

FIGURE J-10: Viewing the rollover image in a browser

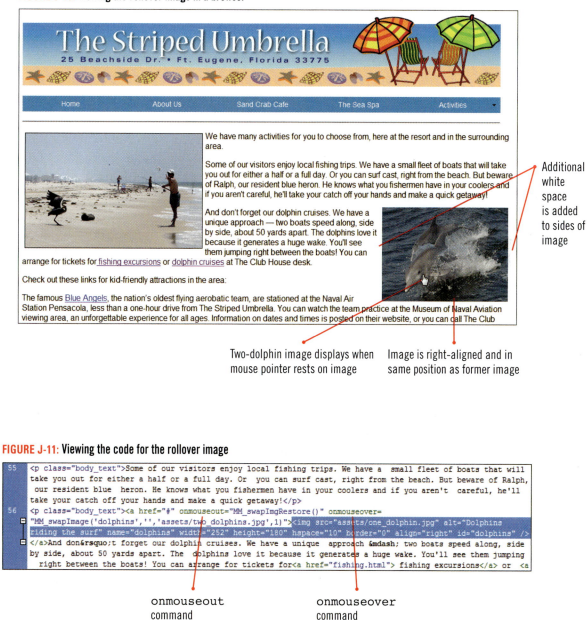

Additional
white
space
is added
to sides of
image

Two-dolphin image displays when
mouse pointer rests on image

Image is right-aligned and in
same position as former image

FIGURE J-11: Viewing the code for the rollover image

```
55  <p class="body_text">Some of our visitors enjoy local fishing trips. We have a  small fleet of boats that will
    take you out for either a half or a full day. Or  you can surf cast, right from the beach. But beware of Ralph,
     our resident blue  heron. He knows what you fishermen have in your coolers and if you aren't  careful, he'll
     take your catch off your hands and make a quick getaway!</p>
56  <p class="body_text"><a href="#" onmouseout="MM_swapImgRestore()" onmouseover=
    "MM_swapImage('dolphins','','assets/two_dolphins.jpg',1)"><img src="assets/one_dolphin.jpg" alt="Dolphins
    riding the surf" name="dolphins" width="252" height="180" hspace="10" border="0" align="right" id="dolphins" />
    </a>And don&rsquo;t forget our dolphin cruises. We have a unique  approach &mdash; two boats speed along, side
     by side, about 50 yards apart. The  dolphins love it because it generates a huge wake. You'll see them jumping
      right between the boats! You can arrange for tickets for<a href="fishing.html"> fishing excursions</a> or  <a
```

onmouseout
command

onmouseover
command

Add Flash Video

Another way to add rich media content to your Web pages is to insert video files. Of the several available video formats, one of the most popular is the Flash video format. **Flash video files** are files that include both video and audio and have an .flv file extension. There are two video types you can specify: a progressive download video or a streaming download video. See the Clues to Use box *Comparing video types* in this lesson for more detailed coverage. As with the Flash .swf file, you play the Flash video file using Flash Player. Most users already have Flash Player installed on their computers, so your movies can be easily accessed. Used sparingly, video can be an effective way to add interest and depth to your Web pages. The **skin** is the bar at the bottom of the video with the control buttons. Every guest is given a small beach umbrella anchor as a welcome gift, which then can be used to secure a beach umbrella in the sand. Since guests sometimes have trouble figuring out this procedure, you decide to add a short Flash video to the about_us page that demonstrates the process.

STEPS

1. **Using Windows Explorer (Win) or Finder (Mac), copy the file umbrella_anchor_ movie.flv from the drive and folder where you store your Unit J Data Files, paste it into The Striped Umbrella site root folder, close Windows Explorer (Win) or Finder (Mac), then return to Dreamweaver**

   The file is copied to the site root folder and ready to insert in the page.

2. **Open the about_us page, click to place the insertion point at the end of the last paragraph on the page, enter a paragraph return, click the Media list arrow on the Insert panel, then click FLV**

   The Insert FLV dialog box opens. This is where you enter the settings for the video.

3. **Click Progressive Download Video in the Video type menu if necessary, click the Browse button next to the URL text box, browse to your site root folder if necessary, then double-click umbrella_anchor_movie.flv**

   The video type and the location of the video file is specified.

4. **Click Halo Skin 1 (min width: 180) in the Skin menu, type 180 in the Width text box, type 180 in the Height text box, verify that the Constrain check box is checked, compare your screen to Figure J-12, then click OK**

   A placeholder for the movie displays on the page in Design view. The two files added to the Files panel, Halo_Skin_1.swf and FLVPlayer_Progressive.swf, are supporting files for the video file. The Halo-Skin1.swf file instructs the skin to appear and function, while the FVPlayer_Progressive.swf file prompts the movie to begin playing in the browser while it downloads.

5. **Place the insertion point to the right of the video placeholder image, press [Shift][Enter] (Win) or [Shift][return] (Mac), type Visit us at the front desk, press [Shift][Enter] (Win) or [Shift][return] (Mac), then type to pick up your complimentary Umbrella Anchor!**

   The explanatory text helps guests understand the purpose of the video.

   QUICK TIP
   The Remove Block-quote button ⬅️ removes an indent.

6. **Apply the featured_item rule to the sentence, select the video placeholder, click the left arrow to place the insertion point to the left of the placeholder, then click the Blockquote button ➡️ nine times**

   The video placeholder as well as the explanatory text shift position on the page, as shown in Figure J-13. The reformatted text is indented to the approximate center of the page where it stands out more effectively from the other information.

   QUICK TIP
   You can click the Stop button ⬛ to stop the movie before it ends.

7. **Save your work, preview the page in the browser, compare your screen to Figure J-14, click the Play button ▶, close the browser, close all open pages, then exit Dreamweaver**

FIGURE J-12: Entering the settings for the Flash video

Video type menu ●

Skin menu ●

Width text box ●

Height text box ●

Constrain check box

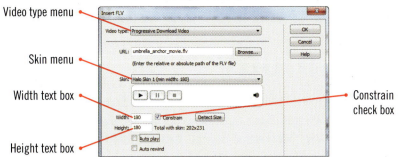

FIGURE J-13: Viewing and formatting the video placeholder

Video placeholder and text are indented on the page

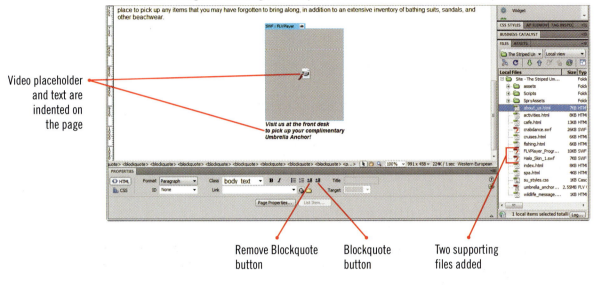

Remove Blockquote button

Blockquote button

Two supporting files added

FIGURE J-14: Viewing and playing the video in a browser

Play button

Pause button

Volume control

Stop button

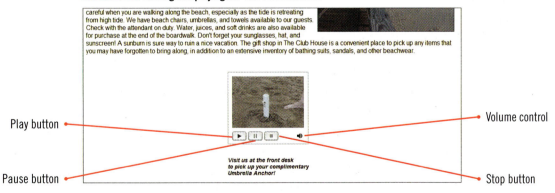

Comparing video types

Once you select a movie file to include on your Web site, you then have to decide which video type to specify. There are two types to choose from: a progressive download video or a streaming download video. A **progressive download video** will allow the video to play while it is downloading to the user's computer. A **streaming download video** is similar to a progressive download video, except that it uses buffers to gather the content as it downloads to ensure a smoother playback. A **buffer** is a temporary storage area on your hard drive that acts as a holding area for the Flash content as it is being played. Other video formats that you can link or embed in a Web page include **AVI (Audio Visual Interleave)**, the Microsoft standard for digital video, and **MPEG (Motion Picture Experts Group)** files.

Incorporate Web 2.0 Technology

The term **Web 2.0** describes the recent evolution of Web applications that facilitate and promote information sharing among Internet users. These applications not only reside on computers, but on cell phones, in cars, on portable GPS devices, and in game devices. **GPS (Global Positioning System)** devices are used to track your position through a global satellite navigation system. They are regularly used for assistance with driving directions, hiking locations, and map making. Web 2.0 applications do not simply display information; they enable users to actively direct or contribute to the Web page content. Web 2.0 technology could potentially transform The Striped Umbrella Web site from a strictly informative site to one that is interactive and fully engaging. You decide to research Web 2.0 technology and analyze which Web applications could be incorporated into the current site.

DETAILS

- ### RSS feeds and podcasts

  RSS feeds are an easy way to share information with users. **RSS (Really Simple Syndication)** feeds are regularly scheduled information downloads used by Web sites to distribute news stories, information about upcoming events, or announcements. Web users can subscribe to RSS feeds to receive regular releases of information from a site. Users can also download and play the digitally broadcasted files called **podcasts** (which stands for **Programming On Demand**) using devices such as computers or MP3 players. Many news organizations and educational institutions publish both audio and video podcasts. Video podcasts are also sometimes referred to as **vodcasts** or **vidcasts**.

- ### Social networking

  Web 2.0 also includes the ever-increasing use of social networking. **Social networking** refers to any Web-based service that facilitates social interaction among users. One example of a social networking site is **Facebook**, which allows users to set up profile pages and post information for others to view. Facebook pages often contain lots of text, images, and videos. To fully view and post to an individual's page, you must be accepted by that person as a "friend," which lets them control who has access to page content.

- ### Wikis

  The term **wiki** (named for the Hawaiian word for "quick") refers to a site where a user can use simple editing tools to contribute and edit the page content in a site. A good example is **Wikipedia**, an online encyclopedia. Wikipedia allows users to post new information and edit existing information on any topic. Although people have different opinions about the reliability of the information on Wikipedia, it is generally viewed as a rich source of information. Proponents argue that its many active and vigilant users maintain its accuracy.

- ### Blogs

  Blogs are Web sites where the Web site owner regularly posts commentaries and opinions on various topics. Content can consist of text, video, or images. Users can respond to the postings and read postings by other users as well. **Twitter** is a Web site where users post short messages, called tweets. Twitter is considered a **micro blog**, because you cannot enter more than 140 characters in each post. To use Twitter, you must first join by creating a free account. Then you can post messages about yourself, "follow" other people's tweets, and invite others to follow you. It is a quick and easy way to exchange short bits of information.

- ### Video sharing applications

  There are many video sharing applications, such as Skype, Google Video Chat, and YouTube. **Skype** and **Google Video Chat** are free applications that you use to communicate live through video conferencing, using a high-speed Internet connection and a digital video camera connected to your computer, called a **webcam**. You can also use Skype or Google Chat to make regular telephone calls over the Internet. **YouTube** is a Web site where you can view or upload or videos. To upload videos, you need to register with the site.

FIGURE J-15: Viewing Web 2.0 application links

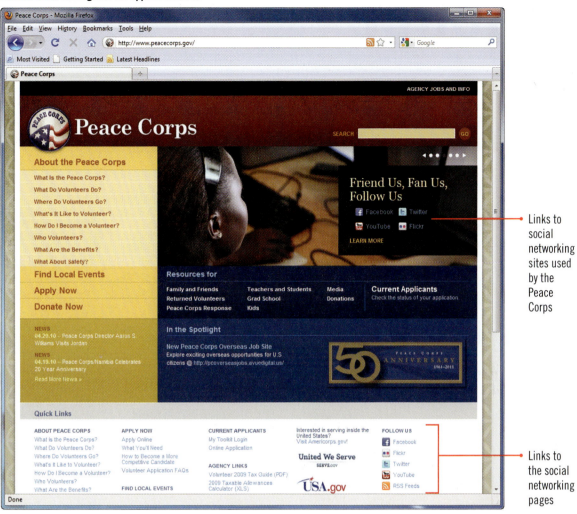

Links to social networking sites used by the Peace Corps

Links to the social networking pages

Design Matters

How to incorporate Web 2.0 components

Most Web sites today engage their users with one or more Web 2.0 component applications. The Peace Corps Web site, shown in Figure J-15, has links to Facebook, Twitter, YouTube, and RSS Feeds. When you are designing a site, one of the decisions you must make is not if but how you will incorporate technology to fully engage users. To incorporate one of these applications into your Web site, first register to set up an account on the social networking site,

then place a link on one of your site's Web pages (usually the home page) that links to the social networking site and opens your page. For example, if your Twitter account is located at www.twitter.com/your_name, add this link to your home page using the Twitter logo as a graphic link. You can download social networking sites' logos from their Web sites. You can also enter plain text links if you prefer.

Practice

Concepts Review

For current SAM information, including versions and content details, visit SAM Central (http://www.cengage.com/samcentral). If you have a SAM user profile, you may have access to hands-on instruction, practice, and assessment of the skills covered in this unit. Since various versions of SAM are supported throughout the life of this text, check with your instructor for the correct instructions and URL/Web site for accessing assignments.

Label each element in the Dreamweaver window shown in Figure J-16.

FIGURE J-16

1. _____   4. _____
2. _____   5. _____
3. _____   6. _____

Match each of the following terms with the statement that best describes it.

7. **Progressive video download**
8. **Streaming video download**
9. **Media objects**
10. **Plug-in**
11. **Vector graphic**
12. **Rollover image**
13. **Behavior**

a. Combinations of visual and audio effects and text used to create a fully engaging experience with a Web site

b. A scalable graphic that is built using mathematical formulas rather than pixels

c. A set of instructions that is attached to page elements and tells the page element to respond in a specific way when an event occurs

d. A type of download that allows a video to play before it has completely downloaded

e. An image that changes its appearance when the mouse pointer is placed over it in a browser

f. A small computer program that works with a host application to enable certain functions

g. A download that uses buffers to gather the content for a video as it downloads to ensure a smoother playback

Select the best answer from the following list of choices.

14. The file extension for a Flash video file is:
   a. .vid.
   b. .fla.
   c. .swf.
   d. .flv.

15. The panel that is used to add JavaScript functions to page elements is:
   a. the Behaviors panel.
   b. the Server Behaviors panel.
   c. the JavaScript panel.
   d. the Functions panel.

16. Which event will trigger an action when a mouse is placed over a page element?
   a. onMouseOut
   b. onMouseOver
   c. onLoad
   d. onClick

17. Web 2.0 technology includes:
   a. wikis.
   b. blogs.
   c. podcasts.
   d. all of the above

18. When you add a Spry effect to a page element, which folder is automatically created?
   a. SpryAssets folder
   b. Spry folder
   c. SpryEffects folder
   d. Effects folder

Skills Review

Important: *If you did not create this Web site in Unit B and maintain it during the preceding units, you will need to create a site root folder for this Web site and define the Web site using files your instructor will provide. See the "Read This Before You Begin" section for more detailed instructions.*

1. **Understand Media objects.**
   a. List three different types of media objects that you can add to a Web page.
   b. Write a short paragraph that explains how to make media objects accessible.
   c. Write a few sentences that explain what a plug-in does. Give two examples.

2. **Add Flash objects.**
   a. Open the Blooms & Bulbs Web site, then open the workshops page.
   b. Add a paragraph break after the last paragraph, then insert the garden_quote.swf Flash movie from the drive and folder where you store your Unit J Data Files at the insertion point.
   c. Type Garden quote in the Object Tag Accessibility Attributes dialog box, then add nine block quotes in front of the Flash object.
   d. Play the **garden_quote.swf** movie in Dreamweaver, save your work, click OK to close the Copy Dependent Files dialog box, preview the page in your browser, compare your screen to Figure J-17, then close your browser.
   e. Close the workshops page.

FIGURE J-17

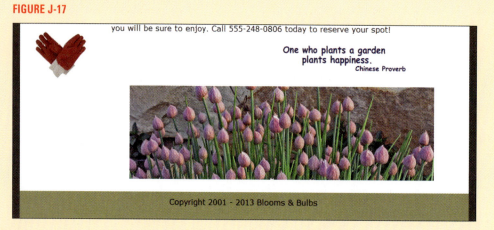

3. **Add Behaviors.**
   a. Open the water_plants page.
   b. Select the water lily image, then use the Behaviors panel to add the Appear/Fade effect so that the image will fade from 100% to 50% when clicked, select the Toggle effect check box, click OK, then save the page. (*Hint:* Dreamweaver will add a new SpryAssets folder in the site with the SpryEffects.js supporting file.)
   c. Preview the page in the browser, then close the browser. (*Hint:* Click the image to test the behavior. The image will alternate between 100% and 50% opacity each time you click the mouse.)

4. **Edit Behaviors.**
   a. Edit the behavior to use the onMouseOver action, then save your work.
   b. Preview the page in the browser. (*Hint:* Place the mouse over the image twice to test the behavior.)
   c. Close the browser, then close the water_plants page.

5. **Add Rollover images.**
   a. Open the tips page, then delete the butterfly image at the top of the page.
   b. Verify that your insertion point is still positioned at the deleted butterfly graphic location.
   c. Insert a rollover image from the drive and folder where you store your Unit J Data Files (*Hint:* Click Insert on the Application bar (Win) or Menu bar (Mac), point to Image Objects, then click Rollover Image.) Type **butterfly_rollover** as the image name, insert butterfly1.jpg from where you store your Data Files as the original image, insert butterfly2.jpg from where you store your Data Files as the rollover image, type **Butterflies** as the alternate text, then click OK.

Skills Review (continued)

    d. Left-align the rollover image, then add a horizontal space of 10 pixels around the image.

    e. Save your work, preview the page in the browser to test the rollover, close the browser, then close the tips page.

6. Add Flash video.

    a. Open the plants page, click at the end of the last sentence on the page, then insert two paragraph breaks.

    b. Insert the hanging_baskets.flv file from drive and folder where you store your Unit J Data Files folder using the following settings: Video Type: Progressive Download Video; URL: hanging_baskets.flv; Skin: Clear Skin1 (min width: 140); Width: 150; Height: 150. (*Hint:* Remember to copy the file to your site root folder first.)

    c. Insert a line break after the video placeholder, type **Join us Saturday at 9:00 a.m. for a demonstration on hanging baskets.** with a line break after the word *for*.

    d. Create a new class rule named **.video** and set the Font-family to Arial, Helvetica, sans-serif; the Font-size to small; and the Text-align to center.

    e. Select the video placeholder, press [right arrow] to place the insertion point to the right of the video placeholder, then apply the .video rule.

    f. Save your work, preview the page and play the movie in the browser, then compare your screen to Figure J-18.

    g. Close the browser, then close all open pages.

FIGURE J-18

The Candy Cane Floribunda shown on the left is a beautiful rose with cream, pink, and red stripes and swirls. They have a heavy scent that will remind you of the roses you received on your most special occasions. These blooms are approximately four inches in diameter. They bloom continuously from early summer to early fall. The plants grow up to four feet tall and three feet wide. They are shipped bare root in February.

In addition to these marvelous roses, we have many annuals, perennials, and water plants that have just arrived.

Join us Saturday at 9:00 for
a demonstration on hanging baskets.

Important: *If you did not create this Web site in Unit B and maintain it during the preceding units, you will need to create a site root folder for this Web site and define the Web site using files your instructor will provide. See the "Read This Before You Begin" section for more detailed instructions.*

Independent Challenge 1

You have been hired to create a Web site for a river expedition company named Rapids Transit, located on the Buffalo River in Northwest Arkansas. You have completed the main pages in the site, but would like to add a slideshow of some river photographs to the guides page. You have selected seven photographs to use and plan to place them on the page, replacing the existing image, as shown in Figure J-19.

a. Start Dreamweaver, then open the Rapids Transit Web site.

b. Open the guides page, then select and delete the buster_tricks image on the page.

c. Insert the file river_scenes.swf at the insertion point, adding River Scenes as the title.

d. Set the alignment of the Flash placeholder to Left.

e. Add vertical spacing of 20 pixels and horizontal spacing of 10 pixels.

f. Enter the ID **river_photos** in the ID text box.

g. Save your work, then use Live View to preview the slideshow.

h. Return to Design view, then preview the page in the browser.

i. Close the browser, close the guides page, then exit Dreamweaver.

FIGURE J-19

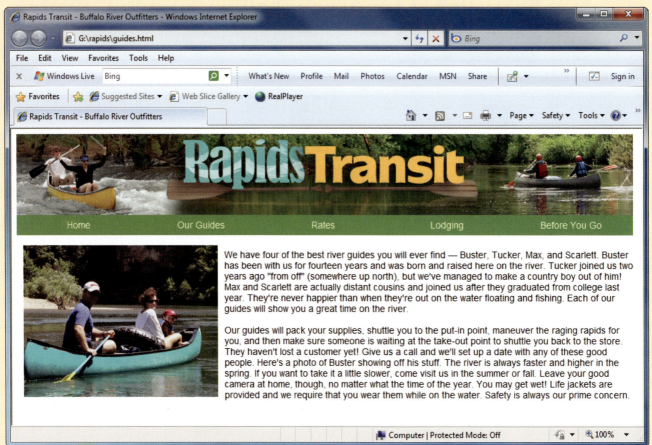

Independent Challenge 2

In this exercise, you will continue your work on the TripSmart Web site. The owner of TripSmart would like you to change the catalog page to show each of the three featured catalog items one at a time on the page. You create a Flash movie using the three featured items and place it in the page in place of the table. You then create a new page that you set to display when the Spain trip is sold out; this new page is attached as a behavior to the banner image.

a. Start Dreamweaver, open the TripSmart Web site, then open the catalog page.

b. Delete the table, then type **Our products are backed with a 100% guarantee.**

c. Add a paragraph break, insert the catalog.swf file from the drive and folder where you store your Unit J Data Files, then add the text **Catalog featured items** in the Object Tag Accessibly Attributes dialog box.

d. Add another paragraph break, then type **Call today! 555-848-0807**.

e. Create a new class rule named centered_items with settings of your choice, apply the centered_items rule to both lines of text and the Flash placeholder, then save all files. (*Hint:* Place the insertion point right before the placeholder to apply the rule.)

f. Preview the catalog page in the browser, then compare your screen to Figure J-20. (Watch for a few seconds to see the images change.)

g. Close the browser, then close the catalog page.

h. Open the file dwj_2.html from the drive and folder where you store your Unit J Data Files, then save it in the TripSmart site root folder as **spain_trip.html**, without updating links.

i. Attach the tripsmart_styles.css file to the page, then apply the body_text style to the text.

j. Close the dwj_2.html page, then save and close the spain_trip.html page.

k. Open the tours page, then attach a behavior to the banner image that, when opened, will open a new browser window that displays the spain_trip.html file. Use 300 px for the window width and 100 px for the window height. Name the window **soldout**.

l. Save your work, then preview the page in the browser to test the behavior, close the browser, then close all open pages.

FIGURE J-20

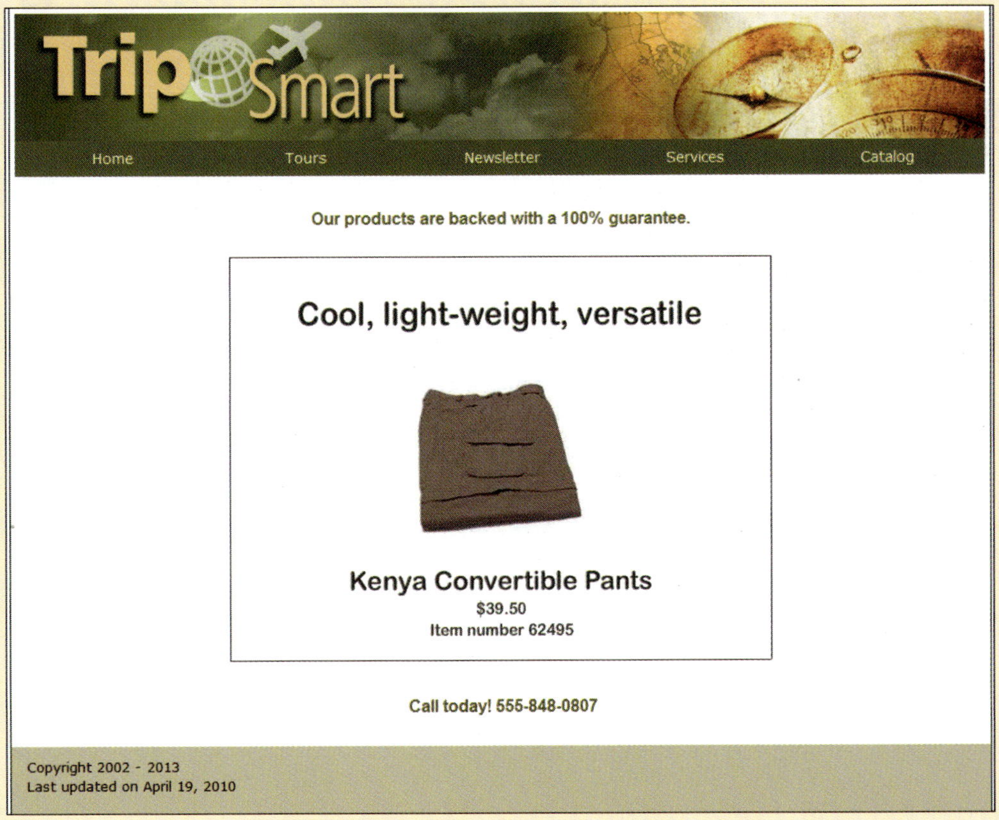

Independent Challenge 3

Angie Wolf is an amateur astronomer. She would like to design a Web site about planets. She would like to use Dreamweaver to build her Web site and incorporate Flash elements, rollovers, and video to the site.

a. Connect to the Internet then go to the United States Navy Web site at www.navy.mil, as shown in Figure J-21.

b. Search for ".swf" and ".flv" in the code for several pages to locate Flash objects.

c. Do you see any objects in the site that are made with rollover images?

d. How has adding Flash effects improved the appearance of this site?

e. Do you see any links to Web 2.0 applications that are being used? If so, list them.

f. Create a sketch of Angie's site that contains at least five pages. Indicate in your sketch what media elements you would insert in the site, including where you would add Flash objects, rollover images, and video.

FIGURE J-21

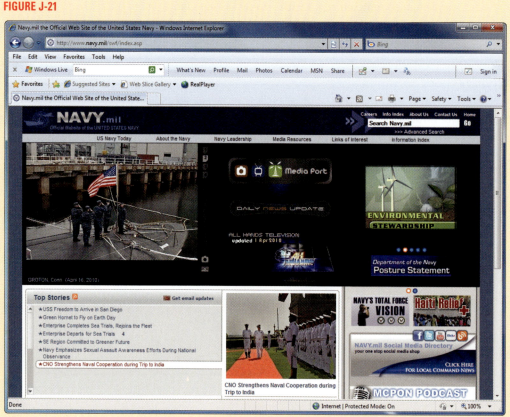

United States Navy Web site—www.navy.mil

Real Life Independent Challenge

This assignment will continue to build on the personal Web site that you created in Unit B. In Unit C, you created and developed your index page. In Unit D, you added a page with either an ordered or an unordered list, using CSS with a minimum of two styles. In Unit E, you added a page that included at least two images. In Unit F, you added a page that included several links and an image map. In Unit G, you redesigned the index page based on CSS. In Unit H, you used a table to position page elements. In Unit I, you added a form to one of the pages. In this lesson, you will continue building your site by designing and completing a page that contains rich media content or by adding media content to existing pages. After completing your site, be sure to run appropriate reports to test the site.

a. Evaluate your wireframes, then choose a page or series of pages to develop in which you will include Flash objects as well as other media content, such as rollover images, video, and behaviors.

b. Plan the content for your new page so that the layout works well with both the new and old pages in your site. Sketch a plan for your wireframes for the media content you wish to add, showing which media elements you will use and where you will place them.

c. Create or find the media you identified in your sketch, choosing appropriate formatting.

d. Add the rollover images to the page.

e. Add a video to the page.

f. Add a behavior to a page element, then specify the action you would like to use with it.

g. Run a report on your new page(s) to ensure that all links work correctly.

h. Preview the new page or pages in your browser and test all links. Evaluate your pages for content and layout.

i. Make any modifications that are necessary to improve the page.

After you are satisfied with your work, verify the following:

a. Each completed page has a page title.

b. All links work correctly and styles are used consistently for all content.

c. The completed pages are attractive using screen resolutions of 800 × 600 and 1024 × 768.

d. All images are properly linked to the assets folder of the Web site.

e. All images have alternate text and are legal to use.

f. All media content works as you intended and downloads quickly.

g. The link checker shows no broken links or orphaned files. If there are orphaned files, note your plan to link them.

h. Run reports for untitled documents and missing alternate text. Make any corrections necessary.

Visual Workshop

Use Figure J-22 as a guide to continue your work on Carolyne's Creations. You decide to add a behavior to the catering_text AP div on the index page. You would like a Grow/Shrink action to occur when the user clicks the AP div on the index page. After you have added the effect, preview the page in the browser and test the effect.

FIGURE J-22

Adding Media and Interactivity

Using Templates

When designing a new Web site, it is important to include best practices that promote consistency across the site, with each page a part of the overall design plan. The use of CSS, consistent navigation links, standard fonts, reusable assets, and library objects are some of the ways you can accomplish this design goal. Another way to promote consistency as well as save development time is to use templates. **Templates** are Web pages that contain the basic layout for related pages in a Web site. Template-based pages enable you to update your site information quickly and easily. As your organization grows, you consider the advantages of incorporating templates in your increasingly complex Web site.

OBJECTIVES

Understand templates

Create a template

Create a template based on an existing page

Create and edit editable regions

Build pages from templates

Understanding Templates

When you create a Web site, it's important to make sure that each page has a unified look so that users know they are in your site no matter what page they are viewing. Common elements, such as the menu bar and company banner, should appear in the same place on every page, and every page should have the same background color scheme. If you are the only site developer, you can easily copy elements from one page to another. As your organization grows and your Web site becomes more complex, one way to update your site and maintain a consistent appearance on every page is through the use of templates. You begin by looking at the advantages that templates offer for creating and updating Web sites. You want to learn how to use templates to streamline the work flow and create consistent page layouts.

DETAILS

- **Templates save development time, especially when different people will be creating pages for your site**

  The ideal process for using templates is for one person to create a page and save it as a template. This person is referred to as the **template author**. Other team members or content contributors can then use this template when creating additional pages for the site. A template usually consists of two types of regions: those that can be changed by others and those that cannot. **Locked regions** are areas of the page that only the template author has access to. These regions contain design elements common to every page in the site that is based on that template. The content of a locked region usually contains information that does not need to be changed on a regular basis, such as a Web site banner. **Editable regions**, in contrast, are areas in which content can be added or changed by other designers. Figure AP 1-1 shows an example of a template with an editable region.

- **Templates ensure both continuity and flexibility throughout a Web site**

  Each page that a team creates from a template is connected to the original template file, so if the template author changes the template, all pages to which the template is attached are automatically updated. **Nested templates** are templates that are based on other templates. Templates also allow for design flexibility; an **optional region** is an area in the template that other content contributors can choose to show or hide, such as time-sensitive content that you do not want displayed except on specific dates or as a result of certain conditions

- **Templates simplify the updating process**

  Web site pages based on a template, or a group of nested templates, can be quickly and easily updated. Figure AP 1-2 shows the New Document dialog box with the Blank HTML template option selected. This is the dialog box that you use to create a new template. When updates to the Web site are necessary, the template is distributed to content contributors, who, in turn, can add the appropriate content to the editable regions of each page.

FIGURE AP 1-1: Template with editable region

Editable region label

Editable region marked by blue outline

Locked region indicated by lock icon when pointer is over it

FIGURE AP 1-2: Template Type and Layout options

Blank Template options

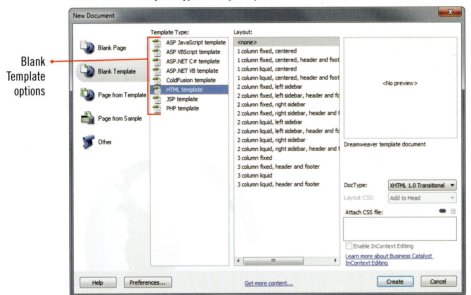

Using InContext Editing

Another way to allow users to modify Web pages is through InContext Editing (ICE). **InContext Editing** is an online service that enables users to make changes to designated editable regions on a page while viewing it in a browser. This service requires little knowledge of HTML or Dreamweaver. The commands to create editable regions are found in the InContext Editing category on the Insert panel. For more information, search either the Adobe Help files or the Adobe Web site at www.adobe.com.

Creating Templates

You can create a new template using the New Document dialog box or, if you have already created and designed a page you want for the layout and design for other pages in your site, you can save that page as a template using the Save as Template command. Templates are saved with a .dwt extension and are stored in the Templates folder in the site root folder for your Web site. If your site does not have a Templates folder, one will automatically be created for you the first time you save a template. To view a list of templates in your site, open the Templates folder in the Files panel. To preview a template before opening it, open the Assets panels, click the Templates button on the Assets panel toolbar, then click a template in the list. The template appears in the preview window, as shown in Figure AP 1-3. See Table AP 1-1 for a description of the available regions. You want to review the steps to create a new template to use for each of the activities pages.

STEPS

To create a new template:

QUICK TIP
You can also use the Template Objects command on the Insert menu to create a template or add template regions.

1. **Open Dreamweaver, select the Web site you wish to edit, click File on the Application bar (Win) or Menu bar (Mac), click New, click Blank Template, click HTML template in the Template type column, chose a layout from the Layout column, then click Create**
   In this example, as the Web page author, you select the HTML template option.

2. **Replace any existing placeholder text with your page content**
   The template placeholder text includes many helpful hints for working with the template. It's a good idea to read through the text before you delete it if it is the first time you are using the template.

QUICK TIP
If you prefer to show the Insert panel as a toolbar, drag it from its default dock position and drop it above the document window. You can then choose to display the categories as menus or as tabs by right-clicking (Win) or control-clicking (Mac) a category, then selecting Show as Tabs or Show as Menu.

3. **Select the content that you would like to use to create a template region, click the Templates list arrow in the Common category on the Insert panel, as shown in Figure AP 1-4, click one of the template region options, type a name for the region in the dialog box, click OK, then add your content to the region**
   By default, all template content is locked except for editable regions, which allows content contributors to add their own content. You will learn more about editable regions in the next lesson.

4. **Click File on the Application bar (Win) or Menu bar (Mac), click Save As, type a template name in the File name text box, then click Save**
   A Templates folder under the site root folder is created with the new template listed inside the folder, as shown in Figure AP 1-5. This Templates folder was automatically created since your site did not have an existing one.

TABLE AP 1-1

region type	definition
Editable	A region that allows users to edit the content
Optional	A region that allows users to choose to either show or hide content
Repeating	A region that contains content that is used multiple times
Editable Optional Region	A region that allows users to both edit the content and choose to show or hide the content
Repeating Table	A table that has a predefined structure and allows users to add content

FIGURE AP 1-3: Viewing a template in the Assets panel

Preview of activities_pages template

Templates button

activities_pages template

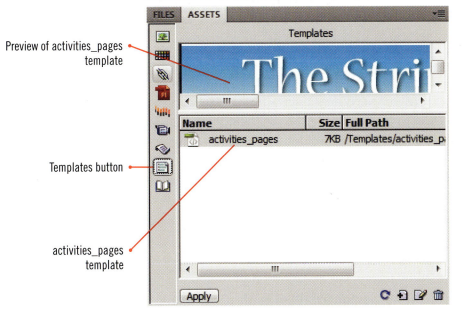

FIGURE AP 1-4: Using the Insert panel to create template regions

Templates list arrow

Make Template options

Template region options

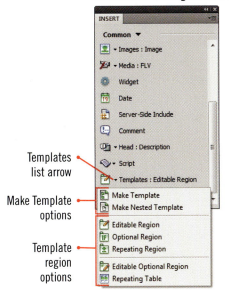

FIGURE AP 1-5: Viewing the Templates folder

Templates folder

Template file

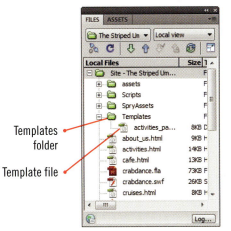

Creating Templates Based on an Existing Page

If you have already created and designed a page that you like, you can use the layout and design for other pages in your site using the Save as Template command. When you save the page as a template, all of the content on the page will be locked. In order for other users to add content to your page, you will need to create at least one editable region. This is the same procedure you follow when you create a new template that is not based on an existing page. You review the steps to create a new template based on one of the existing activities pages.

STEPS

To create a new template based on an existing page:

1. **Open an existing page**

2. **Click File on the Application bar (Win) or Menu bar (Mac), then click Save as Template**
   The Save As Template dialog box opens, as shown in Figure AP 1-6. This is where you assign a name for the template.

TROUBLE
If you don't see the Web site listed that you want to save the template in, click the Site list arrow, then select the correct Web site.

3. **Verify that the Web site name is displayed in the Site text box, type a file name for the new template in the Save as text box, click Save, then click Yes to update links**
   A Templates folder is created under the site root folder with the new template inside the folder.

FIGURE AP 1-6: Saving an existing page as a template

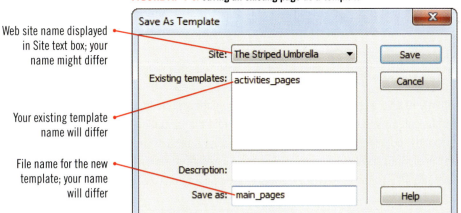

Web site name displayed in Site text box; your name might differ

Your existing template name will differ

File name for the new template; your name will differ

Finding downloadable templates

It is not necessary to create all of your templates from scratch or from existing pages. You can also use templates from outside sources, such as the Internet. A wide range of templates is available for Web page components, such as introductions and logos, as well as entire Web sites. These can include sites for businesses, charities, events, and many other venues. Go to your favorite search engine and type "Web site templates" in the Search text box. For example, www.yahootemplates.com offers many types of templates, both free and for sale.

Creating and Editing Editable Regions

By default, when you save a template, all content on the page will be locked. You must insert at least one editable region for a template to be functional. Editable regions are outlined in blue on the template page, and the names of the editable regions appear in blue shaded boxes, as shown in Figure AP 1-7. In addition to editable regions, you can also add optional regions, repeating regions, editable optional regions, and repeating tables. You want to review the steps to add an editable region to a template.

STEPS

1. **Select the existing content on the page where you want to create the editable region**

2. **Select the Common category on the Insert panel, if necessary.**

3. **Click the Templates list arrow in the Common category, then click Templates: Editable Region**

   The New Editable Region dialog box opens. This is where you specify a name for region.

4. **Type a name for the editable region in the Name text box, as shown in Figure AP 1-8, then click OK**

   The editable region appears selected on the page. A blue shaded box containing the name of the editable region displays above the top left corner of the region. To remove an editable region from a template, select the editable region in the document window, click Modify on the Application bar (Win) or Menu bar (Mac), point to Templates, then click Remove Template Markup (This does not remove the actual content from that region).

Understanding optional regions

In addition to editable regions, you can also add optional regions to a template. An **optional region** is an area in a template that users can choose to either show or hide. An optional region's visibility is controlled by the conditional statement *if*. You can specify a page element as an optional region using the New Optional Region dialog box. You can name the region and specify whether to show or hide it by default. The Editable and Optional Region dialog boxes are both accessed by clicking the Templates list arrow in the Common category of the Insert panel.

FIGURE AP 1-7: Viewing an editable region in a template

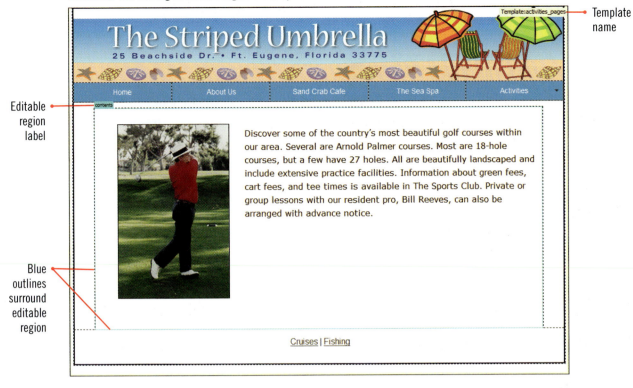

Template name

Editable region label

Blue outlines surround editable region

FIGURE AP 1-8: New Editable Region dialog box

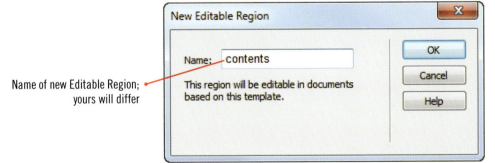

Name of new Editable Region; yours will differ

Building Pages From Templates

There are many advantages to using a template to create a page. First, it saves time since some or all of the content and format are already set. Second, it ensures that the page you create is consistent with the look and format of other pages in the site. It is important to use document-relative links for links on pages based on templates; otherwise, the links will not work. The path to a link actually goes from the template file (not from the template-based page) to the linked page. To ensure that all of your links are document-relative, select the page element to which you want to add a link, and then drag the Point to File icon from the Property inspector to the page you want to link to in the Files panel. You want to review the steps to create a page from a template.

STEPS

QUICK TIP
Another method is to right-click (Win) or [control]-click (Mac) a template in the Assets panel, and then click New from Template.

1. **Click File on the Application bar (Win) or Menu bar (Mac), then click New**
   The New Document dialog box opens. This is where you select the template you want to use to create the new page.

2. **Click Page from Template, as shown in Figure AP 1-9**

3. **Verify that the correct site name is selected in the Site column, click the name of the template in the Template for Site column, then click Create**
   A new Dreamweaver document opens, as shown in Figure AP 1-10, based on the template you selected. This is where you add content to the editable regions.

4. **Save the page**

Attaching a template to an existing page

Sometimes you might need to apply a template to a page that you have already created. For example, suppose you create a page for your department in your company's Web site, and then your manager tells you that it must be based on the template created by the marketing department. Before you attach a template to an existing page, you should delete any elements from your page that also appear in the template. For instance, if both your page and the template have a company logo, you should delete the logo on your page so that it doesn't appear twice. Once you delete the duplicate content on your page, attach the template by opening your page, selecting the template in the Assets panel, then clicking the Apply button in the Assets panel. The resulting Inconsistent Region Names dialog box enables you to specify in which regions of the template to place the document head and body content from your page. To detach a template from a page, open the page, click Modify on the Application bar (Win) or Menu bar (Mac), point to Templates, then click Detach from Template. You can also attach a template to an open page by dragging the template from the Assets panel to the Document window.

FIGURE AP 1-9: New Document dialog box

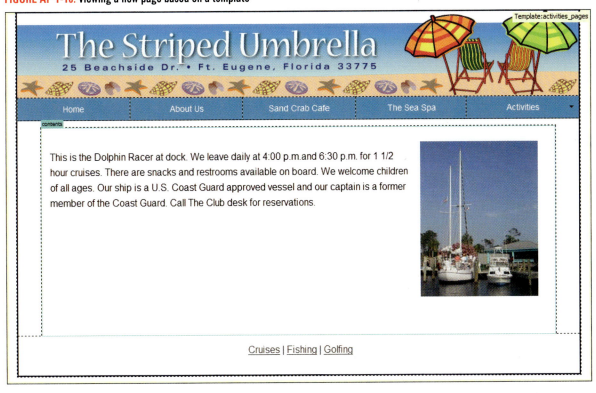

Template name; yours might differ

Page from Template

Web site name; yours might differ

Create button

FIGURE AP 1-10: Viewing a new page based on a template

Template:activities_pages

The Striped Umbrella
25 Beachside Dr. • Ft. Eugene, Florida 33775

| Home | About Us | Sand Crab Cafe | The Sea Spa | Activities |

contents

This is the Dolphin Racer at dock. We leave daily at 4:00 p.m.and 6:30 p.m. for 1 1/2 hour cruises. There are snacks and restrooms available on board. We welcome children of all ages. Our ship is a U.S. Coast Guard approved vessel and our captain is a former member of the Coast Guard. Call The Club desk for reservations.

Cruises | Fishing | Golfing

Practice

For current SAM information, including versions and content details, visit SAM Central (http://www.cengage.com/samcentral). If you have a SAM user profile, you may have access to hands-on instruction, practice, and assessment of the skills covered in this unit. Since various versions of SAM are supported throughout the life of this text, check with your instructor for the correct instructions and URL/Web site for accessing assignments.

Concepts Review

Match each of the following terms with the statement that best describes it.

1. Locked region
2. Editable region
3. Optional region
4. Nested template
5. ICE
6. Template

a. Area in a template that users can choose to either show or hide.
b. A template based on another template.
c. Area of a template that users cannot modify.
d. An online hosted service for editing pages while viewing them in a browser.
e. Area of a template where users can add or edit content.
f. Pages that can be used as a basis for creating other pages.

Select the best answer from the following list of choices.

7. **An area in a template where users can add or change content is called:**
   a. a locked region.
   b. an editable region.
   c. an optional region.
   d. a hidden region.

8. **The name of the folder that is created when a template is first saved is called:**
   a. Templates.
   b. TemplateAssets.
   c. TemplatePages.
   d. Temp.

9. **Which of the following appears when the mouse pointer is placed over a locked region in a template?**
   a. ⌖
   b. ✋
   c. ➡
   d. None of the above

10. **Which type of region must every template contain?**
    a. Repeating region
    b. Editable region
    c. Optional region
    d. Repeating table

APPENDIX
2
Dreamweaver CS5

Presenting and Publishing a Web Site

There are many items to verify and tests to run before a Web site is ready to be finalized, presented to a client for approval, and published on the Web. For instance, you need to confirm that all issues that could be affected by end-user technical factors have been resolved so that all page elements will work well under most operating environments. As recommended, testing your web site should be an ongoing process that happens throughout the development cycle. It is much easier to make incremental corrections rather than last minute corrections.  You review the many factors that contribute to successful project completion.

OBJECTIVES

Collect feedback

Conduct technical tests

Evaluate and present a Web site

Set up remote access

Publish your site

Collecting Feedback

Although you may be satisfied with the Web site that you have designed and developed, it is important to ask for and receive constructive feedback before you present it to the client and publish. Feedback is most helpful when it is solicited from a variety of sources, such as other content contributors, clients, and objective participants who are not connected to the project. Feedback should be solicited both during the project cycle and after the Web site is published. You decide to identify some of the methods you can use to collect final feedback on your Web site.

DETAILS

- ### Site usability tests

  Once you have at least a prototype of the Web site ready to evaluate, it is a good idea to conduct a **site usability test**. This process involves obtaining Web site feedback from users who are not connected to the project. Usability test participants, often selected from external marketing sources, are instructed to objectively evaluate the site based on a standard set of directions. A comprehensive usability test will include pretest questions, participant tasks, a posttest interview, and a posttest survey. The goal of this test is to obtain much-needed information as to how usable the site is to those unfamiliar with it. Typical questions include: "What are your overall impressions?", "What do you like the best and the least about the site?", and "How easy is it to navigate around the site?". It is helpful to have a test monitor observe the testers as they navigate the site to record the time it takes for them to locate information. For more detailed information about this topic, go to www.w3.org and search for "site usability test."

- ### Surveys

  Once the Web site is published, surveys are a great way to collect user feedback. A well designed survey with articulate and pertinent questions can provide you with valuable feedback regarding issues about the Web site itself or regarding the company's products or services. You can request feedback with email solicitations sent to the company's clients or request feedback from the users while they are using a Web site. Users who complete surveys are often interested in supplying helpful information to a company. However, incentives such as discounts or promotional gifts are also used to increase levels of participation. The US Navy Web site, shown in Figure AP 2-1, solicits user feedback on their Web site with a survey that the user is asked to complete and submit.

- ### Points of contact

  All Web sites should have several points of contact. A physical address, a mailing address, a telephone number, and an email address are all good points of contact. By providing your clients' users with multiple points of contact, you give them a choice as to how they would like to contact them when they have problems or questions.

- ### Web 2.0 Technology

  As you learned in Unit J, many Web sites today are incorporating some form of Web 2.0 technology to interact with their users. Blogs and other social networking sites function as valuable communication tools between companies and their target audiences. For example, posts on such applications as Twitter or Facebook provide instant information as well as allow users the opportunity to post feedback directly back to the Web site. The White House Web site, shown in Figure AP 2-2, has links to several Web 2.0 applications to encourage sharing information and gathering feedback.

FIGURE AP 2-1: The US Navy Web site with form for feedback

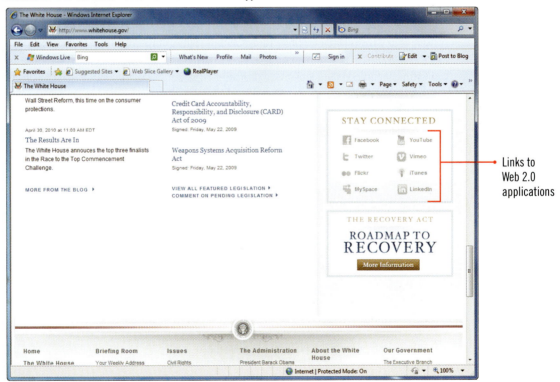

Paragraph requesting feedback from users

Form for user feedback

The US Navy Web site—www.navy.mil

FIGURE AP 2-2: The White House Web site with Web 2.0 application links

Links to Web 2.0 applications

The White House Web site—www.whitehouse.gov

Conducting Technical Tests

Dreamweaver has several helpful reports you can run to identify problems in your Web site. The more frequently you run these reports, the easier it will be to correct any errors. If you allow errors to build up, it will be more difficult to find and correct them. You should also view your pages in several different browsers so you can see what editing and formatting changes are necessary. Factors such as download speeds, screen resolutions, operating systems, and browser types that will vary by user should have been included in the development process. See Table AP 2-1 for a checklist of factors that should be considered. You should also check your completed pages against your wireframes to make sure that you have followed the design plan and included all required components. You want to review the site reports available in Dreamweaver.

DETAILS

- ### Run site reports

  Dreamweaver is capable of running any type of report as frequently you want, as required by your project needs. The Reports command on the Site menu provides a list of reports, as shown in Figure AP 2-3, that you can generate for your Web site. You can generate reports for the current document, the entire local site, selected files in the site, or a selected folder. These reports are grouped by type. The first type of report includes three categories of workflow reports. **Workflow reports** are useful when working in a team environment. For instance, you can run a workflow report that enables you to see files that other designers are using or produce a report that will list all files that have been modified recently. You can also make a report that list **Design Notes**—notes directed to other content creators who are working on different parts of your site. In addition to workflow reports, there are five categories of **HTML reports**: Combinable Nested Font Tags, Missing Alt Text, Redundant Nested Tags, Removable Empty Tags, and Untitled Documents. The Missing Alt Text and the Untitled Documents reports are especially important for Web site accessibility. After you run a report, you can save it as an XML file in a database, spreadsheet, or template for subsequent use.

- ### Test pages

  Each Web page should be retested for design layout, using several types and versions of browsers, various screen resolutions, and different platforms. Some page elements such as fonts, colors, horizontal rules, and CSS div properties do not look the same in all browsers and operating systems. Be sure to test all external links to make sure they connect to valid, active Web sites. Few things are more frustrating to a user than clicking on a link that no longer works. Notice how long it takes each page to download, and consider trimming pages which download slowly. Figure AP 2-4 shows the Adobe BrowserLab online service, which can be used to test your CSS layouts across several of the major browsers. You can also use Live view for CSS inspection and debugging.

- ### Check links

  The Link Checker in the Results panel provides you with a way to check external and internal links in your Web site. Link Checker alerts you to any broken internal links and helps you repair them; although it does list external links, it does not verify their validity. You can either check the links on a single page, the entire Web site, or selected files or folders. In addition, the Link Checker alerts you to orphaned files. Even if you are not ready to link these files, routinely running a list of orphaned files will remind you of the work you must complete in preparation for linking them to the Web site. You can open the Link Checker through the Window menu or the Files panel. To use the Files panel, right-click a file (Win) or [control]-click a file (Mac), point to Check Links, then click Selected Files or Entire Local Site. Next click Window in the Application bar (Win) or Menu bar (Mac), point to Results, and then click Link Checker, or click Site in the Application bar (Win) or Menu bar (Mac), then click Check Links Sitewide. Figure AP 2-5 shows the options for using the Link Checker. You can fix a broken link in the Link Checker panel, or by using the Property inspector. To correct a broken link, use the Browse for File icon to browse to the file that is the correct destination.

FIGURE AP 2-3: Reports dialog box

Specify the scope of the report to run from this list

Select check box to run a workflow report

Select check box to run an HTML report

Report on list arrow

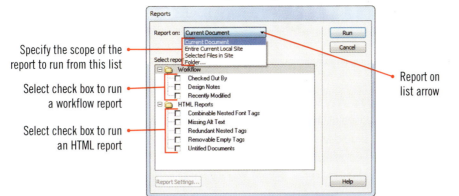

FIGURE AP 2-4: Adobe BrowserLab online service

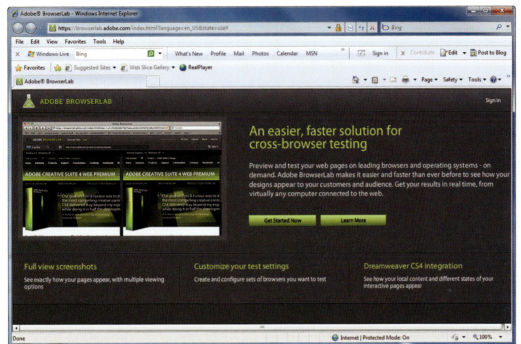

Adobe product screen shot reprinted with permission from Adobe Systems Incorporated—www.adobe.com

FIGURE AP 2-5: Link Checker options

Check links list arrow

Show options

Show list arrow

Using the Browser Compatibility check to manage styles

There are several tools available to assist you in defining, modifying, and checking CSS rules, such as the Code Navigator and Live view. Another is the Browser Compatibility check feature. This feature flags issues on a page that may present a problem when viewed in a particular browser. To use the Browser Compatibility check feature, open a Web page, the use the File, Check Page, Browser Compatibility command to locate issues that may be a problem. Any issues Dreamweaver finds are listed in the Browser Compatibility panel in the Results panel group with the line number and issue listed for each item. To modify the settings to add additional versions of browsers, click the arrow menu in the top left corner of the panel, then click Settings.

Evaluating and Presenting a Web site

Even if you create a great Web site, poor communication can put the project at risk. Ideally, a prototype of the Web site was approved at the beginning of the process. Before you present a Web site to a client as a finished product, you should answer a few key questions. If you are satisfied with your answers, it is time to present the project to your client. The method you choose will depend on the project, your client, and your preferred method of communication. You review a checklist of questions and when you are satisfied with the answers, you want to evaluate the options for presenting the work to your client.

DETAILS

- ### Are you ready to present your work?

  After running the battery of technical tests, you should answer the following questions:
  - Do all of your final design and development decisions reflect your client's goals and requirements and meet the needs of the intended audience?
  - Did you follow good Web development practices and check the entire site against current accessibility standards?
  - Did you check your pages against your wireframes as you developed them?
  - Did your final delivery date and budget meet the goals?

  If your answer to the final question is "no", then you need to determine the reason why before your presentation. If you find that you did spend more time on the site than you expected, determine if it was because you underestimated the amount of work it would take, ran into unforeseen technical problems, or because the client changed the requirements or increased the scope of the project as it went along. If you underestimated the project or ran into unexpected difficulties, you usually cannot expect the client to make up the difference without a prior agreement. Anytime there are budget and time considerations, it is best to communicate frequently with status updates during the project.

- ### How should you present your work?

  The best option for presenting the final project is to invite the client to your office and perform a full walkthrough of the site, if at all feasible. This offers your client a chance to ask questions. Alternately, consider publishing the site to a server and sending the client a link to view the completed site. Creating PDFs of the site and sending them to the client for approval is another possible method.

Design Matters

Using wireframes for planning, development, and presentation

You may have chosen to use low-fidelity wireframes, such as those created in Microsoft PowerPoint or Adobe Photoshop, or you may have used high-fidelity wireframes that are interactive and multi-dimensional, such as those created in OverSight, Protoshare, or Adobe Flash Catalyst, shown in Figure AP 2-6. Another popular method is BaseCamp, a professional Web-based project collaboration tool that focuses on collaboration and communication between you and your client. You should select your tool based on the size and complexity of the Web site, the budget, and your personal preferences. Used correctly, wireframes provide the basic framework of the site, the placement of the main page elements, and serve as a guide for all phases of development. They should be presented to the client for the initial project approval and used at the end of the project to document that the plan was executed as planned.

FIGURE AP 2-6: Adobe Flash Catalyst

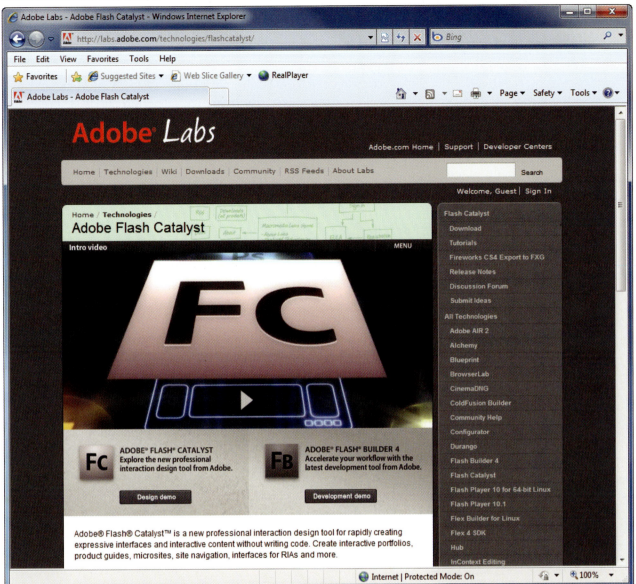

*Adobe product screen shot reprinted with permission from Adobe Systems Incorporated—*www. adobe.com

TABLE AP 2-1: End-User Considerations for Development and Design

page element	design considerations
Tables	Are table widths sized for viewing in various screen resolutions? Are they sized to print correctly? Do they include summaries or headings?
Colors	Will users be able to successfully navigate the Web site in case the colors do not render exactly as intended? Do any page elements rely on the use of color alone?
Text	Are the font sizes large enough for users to read? Is the contrast between the text and the page background strong?
Media Objects	Has the embedded code been provided that searches for the appropriate plug-ins and prompts missing plug-ins to download? Are there too many media objects that will slow the download time appreciably? Do all media objects have a purpose in presenting the page content?
Images	Are all images as small in file size as possible? Do they all include alternate text?
Accessibility	Will the site pass the W3C Priority 1 Checkpoints and the W3C Priority 2 POUR principles for making a Web site accessible?

Setting up Remote Access

Once your files are ready to publish, you must specify where Dreamweaver should place the files. Most Dreamweaver users begin first by creating a local site root folder to store all of their Web site files, called the **local site**. Next, they gain access to a remote site. A **remote site** is a folder on a Web server that is connected to the Internet with software for hosting Web sites, and is not directly connected to the computer housing the local site. Often the **ISP (Internet Service Provider)** will furnish users with space for publishing Web pages. This space then becomes the remote site. You want to review the processes available in Dreamweaver for setting up a remote site.

DETAILS

- ### Using the Site Setup dialog box

  When your pages are ready to publish, the files must be transferred from the local site to the remote site. In Dreamweaver, you use the Site Setup dialog box to enter the information about the remote server, such as the FTP address, root directory, username, and password. **FTP (File Transfer Protocol)** is the process of uploading and downloading files to and from a remote site. To open the Site Setup dialog box, use the Site, New Site; or Site, Manage Sites, Edit commands on the Application bar (Win) or Menu bar (Mac). To enter the server information, click Servers, then click the Add new Server button. The choices for remote access appear when you click the Connect using list arrow, as shown in Figure AP 2-7. After the remote site information is entered, you click the Put button in the Files panel to transfer the files.

- ### Setting up FTP

  Most users transfer files using FTP. If you select this file-transfer method, the Site Select dialog box will open, as shown in Figure AP 2-8. Some of the specific information, such as Username and Password, can be obtained from your ISP. The FTP Address is the address on the Internet where you will send your files. The Root Directory is your folder on the remote server where you will place your files.

STEPS

To set up remote access on an FTP site:

1. Click Site on the Application bar (Win) or Menu bar (Mac), then click Manage Sites

2. Click the Web site name in the Manage Sites dialog box, then click Edit

3. Click Servers in the Site Setup dialog box, click the Add new Server button ➕, type your server name in the server name text box, click the Connect using list arrow, then click FTP if necessary

4. Enter the FTP Address, Username, Password, Root Directory, and Web URL information in the dialog box

TROUBLE
If the connection is not successful, verify that you have the correct settings, then repeat Step 5.

5. Click Test
   The test button tests the connection between your computer and the server.

6. Click OK, click Save, then click Done
   The dialog boxes close.

To view a Web site on a remote server:

1. Click the View list arrow in the Files panel, then click Remote server

2. Click the Expand to show local and remote sites button 🗗
   The Remote site and the Local files panes display in the Files panel, as shown in Figure AP 2-9.

3. Click the Collapse to show only local or remote site button 🗗
   Your window returns to Local view.

FIGURE AP 2-7: Site Setup dialog box

Servers category

Connect using options

FIGURE AP 2-8: Site Setup dialog box server settings

Server name; yours will differ

Your ISP will provide this information

Test button

Root Directory provided by ISP

FIGURE AP 2-9: Viewing the Remote Server and Local Files

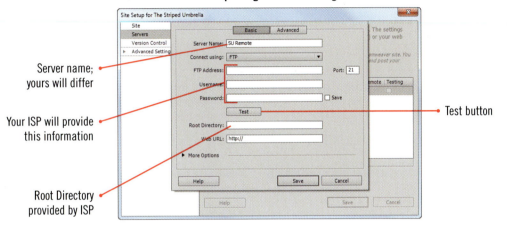

Collapse to show only local or remote site button

Choosing remote access options

Remote access choices include FTP, Local/Network, WebDAV, RDS, and Microsoft Visual SourceSafe. **Local/Network** refers to publishing a Web site on either the local drive (that is, your own hard drive) or a local network drive. **WebDAV (Web-based Distributed Authoring and Versioning)** is used with servers such as the Microsoft Internet Information Server (IIS) and Apache Web server. **RDS (Remote**

Development Services) is used with a remote folder running ColdFusion. Finally, **Microsoft Visual SourceSafe** is available under the Windows platform using Microsoft Visual SourceSafe Client. **Secure FTP (SFTP)** is an FTP option which lets you encrypt file transfers to protect your files, user names, and passwords.

Publishing Your Site

After setting up remote access and completing your Web site, you click the Put button on the Files panel to transfer a copy of your files to a remote server. This is similar process to the one used by FTP client programs. Transferring your files from your computer to a remote computer is called **uploading** or **publishing**. Transferring files from a remote computer to your computer is called **downloading**. To download a copy of your files click the Get button on the Files panel. To see both the remote and local versions of a site, you can expand the Files panel by clicking the Expand to show local and remote sites button. To collapse the Files panel, click the Collapse to show only local or remote site button. You want to review the processes available in Dreamweaver for publishing a Web site.

DETAILS

- ### Using Put and Get

  When you transfer dependent files; this transfers associated files, such as image files, in the Web site to the server. The following buttons, shown in Figure AP 2-10, are used for transferring files:

button	task
Put File(s) to (remote site name) button	Transfers files from the Local site to the Remote site; will connect to a remote host automatically once you've selected the files you want to transfer and clicked the Put File(s) button
Connects to remote host button	Connects to the remote host
Get File(s) from (remote site name) button	Transfers the files from the Remote site to the Local site.

- ### Synchronizing files

  The Synchronize command allows you to **synchronize** your files, transferring only the latest versions rather than all the Web site files. To synchronize your site, click Synchronize with (remote site name) button on the Files panel or click Site on the Application bar (Win) or Menu bar (Mac), then click Synchronize Sitewide. The Synchronize Files dialog box, shown in Figure AP 2-11, is used to specify which files to synchronize and the direction in which to synchronize them. If the files have not changed since the last transfer, Dreamweaver will notifies you that you do not need to synchronize. You can also use a remote SVN (Apache Subversion) repository to save and maintain current and previous versions of your files.

STEPS

To upload files for publication

1. Click the name of the file, folder, or site you want to publish, then click the Put Files(s) to (remote site name) button in the Files panel
2. Click Yes to include the dependent files if necessary

To synchronize files:

1. Click Site on the Application bar (Win) or Menu bar (Mac), then click Synchronize Sitewide
2. Click the Synchronize list arrow, then click Entire (Site name)
3. Click the Direction list arrow, then click Put newer files to remote
4. Click Preview, then click OK

FIGURE AP 2-10: Files panel

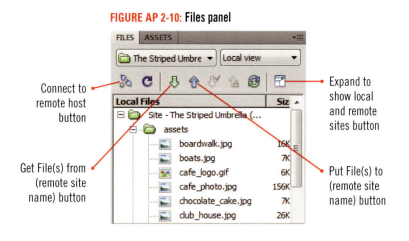

Connect to remote host button

Get File(s) from (remote site name) button

Expand to show local and remote sites button

Put File(s) to (remote site name) button

FIGURE AP 2-11: The Synchronize Files dialog box

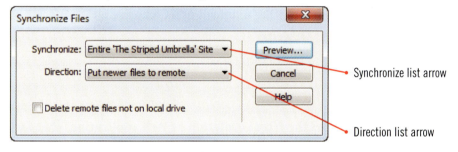

Synchronize list arrow

Direction list arrow

Cloaking files to exclude them from being uploaded to a server

There may be times when you want to exclude a particular file from being uploaded to a server. For instance, suppose you are not quite finished working on a particular Web page. You can exclude a file by cloaking it. **Cloaking** is the process of marking a file or files for exclusion when the commands Put, Get, Synchronize, Check In, and Check Out are used. Cloaked files can also be excluded from site-wide operations such as checking for links or updating a template or library item. You can also cloak a folder or specify a type of file to cloak throughout the site. The cloaking feature is enabled by default. To cloak a file, select the file, click the Files panel Options button, point to Site, point to Cloaking, and then click Cloak.

Managing a Web site with a team

When you work on a large Web site, chances are that many people will be involved in developing and keeping the site up to date. Different individuals will need to make changes or additions to different pages of the site by adding, changing, or deleting content. If everyone had access to the same pages at the same time, problems could arise. Fortunately, Dreamweaver's collaboration tools eliminate such problems. For example, the **Check Out** feature enables only one person at a time to work on a file. This ensures that content contributors cannot overwrite each other's pages. To access the Check Out feature, you must first enable it in the Remote Info settings of the Site Setup dialog box. To check out a file, select the file name in the Files panel, then click the Check Out File(s) button on the Files panel. Another file management tool is Subversion control. A remote SVN (Apache Subversion) repository is used to maintain current and historical versions of your Web site files. It is used in a team environment to move, copy, and delete shared files. You can protect files from being accessed using the svn:ignore property to create a list of files that are to be ignored in a directory.

Practice

Concepts Review

For current SAM information, including versions and content details, visit SAM Central (http://www.cengage.com/samcentral). If you have a SAM user profile, you may have access to hands-on instruction, practice, and assessment of the skills covered in this unit. Since various versions of SAM are supported throughout the life of this text, check with your instructor for the correct instructions and URL/Web site for accessing assignments.

Match each of the following terms with the statement that best describes it.

1. Check out feature
2. Link Checker
3. Upload
4. Cloak files
5. Synchronize
6. Download

a. To transfer files from your computer to a remote server.
b. To transfer files from a remote server to your computer.
c. A command that allows you to transfer only the latest versions of files.
d Allows a file to be used by only one user at a time.
e. Used to check for orphaned files and broken links.
f. To mark files for exclusion from several Commands, including Put, Get, Synchronize, check In, and check Out

Select the best answer from the following list of choices.

7. The process that involves requesting unbiased users who are not connected to the project to use to evaluate a site is called:
   a. a trial run.
   b. a test drive.
   c. a clinical trial.
   d. a site usability test.

8. What technology describes the recent evolution of Web applications that facilitate and promote information sharing among Internet users?
   a. Web 1.0 technology
   b. Web 2.0 technology
   c. Web 3.0 technology
   d. Virtual technology

9. A point of contact can include:
   a. A telephone number.
   b. An email address.
   c. A physical address.
   d. All of the above.

10. Which of the following is not an Html report?
    a. Untitled Documents.
    b. Missing Alt Tag.
    c. Design Notes.
    d. Combinable Nested Font Tags.

Data Files List

To complete the lessons and practice exercises in this book, students need to use Data Files that are supplied by Course Technology. Once they obtain the files, students select where to store the Web site files they create using the Data Files, such as to a hard disk drive, network server, or USB storage device.

Below is a list of the Data Files that are supplied and the unit or practice exercise to which the files correspond. For information on how to obtain Data Files, please refer to page *xvi* in the front of this book. The following list includes only Data Files that are supplied; it does not include the Web site files students create from scratch or the files students create by revising supplied files.

Unit	Location file is used in unit	Folder location for files	Files supplied
Unit A	Lessons (The Striped Umbrella site)	Unit A folder	dwa_1.html
		Unit A assets folder	pool.jpg
			su_banner.gif
	Skills Review (Blooms & Bulbs site)	Unit A folder	dwa_2.html
		Unit A assets folder	blooms_banner.jpg
			tulips.jpg
	Independent Challenge 1 (TripSmart site)	Unit A folder	dwa_3.html
		Unit A assets folder	tripsmart_banner.jpg
Unit B	Lessons (The Striped Umbrella site)	Unit B folder	dwb_1.html
		Unit B assets folder	su_banner.gif
	Skills Review (Blooms & Bulbs site)	Unit B folder	dwb_2.html
		Unit B assets folder	blooms_banner.jpg
	Independent Challenge 1 (Rapids Transit site)	Unit B folder	dwb_3.html
		Unit B assets folder	rt_banner.jpg
	Independent Challenge 2 (TripSmart site)	Unit B folder	dwb_4.html
		Unit B assets folder	tripsmart_banner.jpg
	Visual Workshop (Carolyne's Creations site)	Unit B folder	dwb_5.html
		Unit B assets folder	cc_banner.jpg
Unit C			No Data Files supplied

Unit	Location file is used in unit	Folder location for files	Files supplied
Unit D	Lessons (The Striped Umbrella site)	Unit D folder	dwd_1.html
			questions.doc
			spa.doc
		Unit D assets folder	sea_spa_logo.jpg
			su_banner.gif
	Skills Review (Blooms & Bulbs site)	Unit D folder	dwd_2.html
			gardening_tips.doc
		Unit D assets folder	blooms_banner.jpg
			butterfly.jpg
	Independent Challenge 1 (Rapids Transit site)	Unit D folder	dwd_3.html
		Unit D assets folder	rt_banner.jpg
	Independent Challenge 2 (TripSmart site)	Unit D folder	dwd_4.html
		Unit D assets folder	tripsmart_banner.jpg
	Visual Workshop (Carolyne's Creations site)	Unit D folder	dwd_5.html
		Unit D assets folder	cc_banner.jpg
			pie.jpg
Unit E	Lessons (The Striped Umbrella site)	Unit E folder	dwe_1.html
		Unit E assets folder	boardwalk.png
			club_house.jpg
			stripes_back.gif
			su_banner.gif
			umbrella_back.gif
	Skills Review (Blooms & Bulbs site)	Unit E folder	dwe_2.html
		Unit E assets folder	blooms_banner.jpg
			daisies.jpg
			rose_bloom.jpg
			rose_bud.jpg
			two_roses.jpg

Unit	Location file is used in unit	Folder location for files	Files supplied
	Independent Challenge 1 (Rapids Transit site)	Unit E folder	dwe_3.html
		Unit E assets folder	buster_tricks.jpg
			rt_banner.jpg
	Independent Challenge 2 (TripSmart site)	Unit E folder	dwe_4.html
		Unit E assets folder	bull_fighter.jpg
			stallion.jpg
			tripsmart_banner.jpg
	Visual Workshop (Carolyne's Creations site)	Unit E folder	dwe_5.html
		Unit E assets folder	cc_banner.jpg
			paella_pan.jpg
Unit F	**Lessons** (The Striped Umbrella site)	Unit F folder	dwf_1.html
		Unit F assets folder	heron_waiting_small.jpg
			su_banner.gif
			two_dolphins.jpg
	Skills Review (Blooms & Bulbs site)	Unit F folder	dwf_2.html
		Unit F assets folder	blooms_banner.jpg
			grass.jpg
			plants.jpg
			trees.jpg
	Independent Challenge 1 (Rapids Transit site)	Unit F folder	dwf_3.html
		Unit F assets folder	rt_banner.jpg
			young_paddler.jpg
	Independent Challenge 2 (TripSmart site)	Unit F folder	dwf_4.html
		Unit F assets folder	tripsmart_banner.jpg
	Visual Workshop (Carolyne's Creations site)	Unit F folder	dwf_5.html
			dwf_6.html
			dwf_7.html

Unit	Location file is used in unit	Folder location for files	Files supplied
		Unit F assets folder	cc_banner_with_text.jpg
			children_cooking.jpg
			cookies_oven.jpg
			dumplings1.jpg
			dumplings2.jpg
			dumplings3.jpg
Unit G	Lessons (The Striped Umbrella site)	Unit G assets folder	contestants_bak.jpg
	Skills Review (Blooms & Bulbs site)	Unit G assets folder	peaches_small.jpg
	Independent Challenge 2 (TripSmart site)	Unit G assets folder	sea_lions.jpg
	Visual Workshop (Carolyne's Creations site)	Unit G assets folder	cream_cheese_eggs.jpg
Unit H	Lessons (The Striped Umbrella site)	Unit H folder	dwh_1.html
		Unit H assets folder	cafe_logo.gif
			cafe_photo.jpg
			chocolate_cake.jpg
			su_banner.gif
	Skills Review (Blooms & Bulbs site)	Unit H folder	dwh_2.html
		Unit H assets folder	blooms_banner.jpg
			chives.jpg
			gardening_gloves.gif
	Independent Challenge 1 (Rapids Transit site)	Unit H folder	dwh_3.html
			rentals.doc
		Unit H assets folder	rt_banner.jpg
			rt_logo.gif
	Independent Challenge 2 (TripSmart site)	Unit H folder	dwh_4.html
		Unit H assets folder	hat.jpg
			pants.jpg
			tripsmart_banner.jpg
			vest.jpg

Unit	Location file is used in unit	Folder location for files	Files supplied
	Visual Workshop (Carolyne's Creations site)	**Unit H folder**	dwh_5.html
			menu_items.doc
		Unit H assets folder	cc_banner_with_text.jpg
			muffins.jpg
Unit I	**Lessons** (The Striped Umbrella site)	**Unit I folder**	dwi_1.html
			dwi_2.html
		Unit I assets folder	boats.jpg
			heron_small.jpg
			su_banner.gif
		Unit I SpryAssets folder	SpryMenuBar.js
			SpryMenuBardown.gif
			SpryMenuBarDownHover.gif
			SpryMenuBarHorizontal.css
			SpryMenuBarRight.gif
			SpryMenuBarRightHover.gif
	Skills Review (Blooms & Bulbs site)	**Unit I folder**	dwi_3.html
			dwi_4.html
			dwi_5.html
		Unit I assets folder	blooms_banner.jpg
			coleus.jpg
			ruby_grass.jpg
			water_lily.jpg
		Unit I SpryAssets folder	SpryMenuBar.js
			SpryMenuBardown.gif
			SpryMenuBarDownHover.gif
			SpryMenuBarHorizontal.css
			SpryMenuBarRight.gif
			SpryMenuBarRightHover.gif

Unit	Location file is used in unit	Folder location for files	Files supplied
Unit J	Lessons (The Striped Umbrella site)	Unit J folder	crabdance.swf
			dwj_1.html
			umbrella_anchor_movie.flv
		Unit J assets folder	one_dolphin.jpg
			two_dolphins.jpg
	Skills Review (Blooms & Bulbs site)	Unit J folder	garden_quote.swf
			hanging_baskets.flv
		Unit J assets folder	butterfly1.jpg
			butterfly2.jpg
	Independent Challenge 1 (Rapids Transit site)	Unit J folder	river_scenes.swf
	Independent Challenge 2 (TripSmart site)	Unit J folder	catalog.swf
			dwj_2.html
	Visual Workshop (Carolyne's Creations site)	Unit J folder	sugared_flowers.flv

Glossary

Absolute path A path containing an external link that references a Web page outside the current Web site, and includes the prefix *http://* and the URL of the Web page; *see also* URL.

Action A response to an event trigger that causes a change, such as text changing color or a form being processed.

Action property Specifies the application or script that will process form data.

Active panel A panel displayed as the front panel in an expanded panel group with the panel options displayed.

Add-on *See* plug-in.

Adobe Bridge An integrated file management tool that allows you to organize, search, and add meta tags to image files.

Adobe BrowserLab An Adobe online service for cross-browser and cross-platform compatibility testing.

Adobe Community Help A collection of materials that includes tutorials, published articles, or blogs, in addition to the regular Help content. All content is monitored and approved by the Adobe Community Expert program.

Adobe Flash A software program used for creating vector-based graphics and animations. *See also* vector-based graphic.

Adobe Flash Player A free program included with most browsers that allows you to view content created with Adobe Flash.

Advanced style A style used to format combinations of page elements; *also called* compound style.

AJAX (Asynchronous JavaScript and XML) A method for developing interactive Web pages that respond quickly to user input, such as clicking a map.

Alias (*Mac*) An icon that represents a program, folder, or file stored on your computer.

Align an image Position an image on a Web page in relation to other elements on the page.

Alphanumeric field A type of form field that will accept both numbers and letters or a combination of the two.

Alternate text Descriptive text that can be set to display in place of an image or while the image is downloading.

AP div A div that is assigned a fixed position on a page (absolute position); *also called* AP element.

AP element *See* AP div.

AP Elements panel The panel used to control the properties of all AP elements on a Web page.

Application bar (*Win*) A bar located at the top of the Dreamweaver workspace and includes menu names, a workspace switcher, and other program commands; *see also* Menu bar (*Mac*).

Assets folder A subfolder in which most of the files that are not Web pages, such as images, audio files, and video clips are stored.

Assets panel A panel that contains nine categories of assets, such as images, used in a Web site; clicking a category button will display a list of those assets.

AVI (Audio Visual Interleave) A digital video file format that can contain audio and video data.

Back-end processing The end of the form processing cycle when the data is processed.

Background color A color that fills the entire Web page, a table, or a cell.

Background image An image used in place of a background color to provide depth and visual interest.

Banner An image that generally appears across the top of a Web page and can incorporate information such as a company's logo and contact information.

Baseline The bottom of a line of text, not including descending portions of characters such as in *y* or *g*.

Behavior An action script that allows you to add dynamic content to your Web pages by allowing an object to respond to user input or as a result of a defined condition.

Blog A Web site containing regularly posted commentaries and opinions on various topics maintained and written by the Web site owner.

Body The part of a Web page that contains all of the page content users see in their browser window, such as text, graphics, and links.

Border An outline that surrounds an image, cell, or table, or CSS layout block.

Bread crumbs trail A list of links that provides a path from the initial page you opened in a Web site to the page that you are currently viewing.

Broken link A link that cannot find the intended destination file.

Browser *See* Web browser.

Browser Compatibility Check (BCC) A feature on the Adobe Web site that is used to check for problematic CSS features that may render differently in multiple browsers.

Browser Navigation toolbar A toolbar that contains navigation buttons you use when following links on your Web pages in Live view.

Buffer A temporary storage area on a hard drive that acts as a holding area for Flash content as it is being played.

Bullet A small image used to call attention to items in an unordered list.

Bulleted list A list of items that does not need to be placed in a specific order; *also called* unordered list.

Button On a form, a small rectangular object with a text label that usually has an action attached to it.

Camera Raw files File types used by many photographers that contain unprocessed data from a digital camera's sensor.

Cascading Style Sheet (CSS) Sets of formatting rules that create styles.

Cell A small box within a table that is used to hold text or images; cells are arranged horizontally in rows and vertically in columns.

Cell padding In a table, the distance between the cell content and the cell walls.

Cell spacing In a table, the distance between cells.

Cell wall In a table, the edge surrounding a cell.

Check box A classification of a form object that appears as a box that, when clicked by the user, has a check mark placed in it to indicate that it is selected.

Check Out A feature that enables only one person at a time to work on a file.

Child menu A submenu.

Class style A style that can be used to format any page element.

Client-side scripting A script that is processed on the user's computer.

Clip art collection A group of image files collected on CDs, DVDs, or downloaded from the Internet and sold with an index or directory of the files.

Cloaking The process of marking a file or files for exclusion.

Code and Design views A combination of Code view and Design view; each layout displays in a separate window within the Document window.

Code Navigator A small window that opens with code for the selected page element.

Code view The view that fills the Document window with the HTML code for the page and is primarily used when reading or directly editing the code.

Coder layout A layout in the Dreamweaver workspace in which the panels are docked on the left side of the screen and Code view is the default view.

Coding toolbar A toolbar used when you are working with HTML code; it can only be accessed in Code view.

Column A group of table cells arranged vertically.

Comment Helpful text describing portions of the HTML code, such as a JavaScript function.

Compound style *See* advanced style.

Computer server *See* server.

Copyright Protects the particular and tangible expression of an idea, but not the idea itself.

Cropping Removing part of an image, both visually (on the page) and physically (the file size).

CSS Advisor A part of the Adobe Web site that offers solutions for problems with CSS.

CSS Layout Box Model A way to view layout blocks in Design view with the padding and margins of a selected layout visible.

Data file A file created using a software program; for example, a letter, report, or Web page that you save on a drive so you can open and use it again later.

Debug To correct errors in HTML code.

Declaration Part of a Cascading Style Sheet; consists of a property and a value.

Default alignment For images, the automatic alignment with the text baseline.

Default base font Size 3 text without any formatting applied to it.

Default font color The color the browser uses to display text, links, and visited links if no other colors are assigned.

Default link color The color the browser uses to display links if no other color is assigned; the default link color is blue.

Default text color The color the browser uses to display text when another color is not specified.

Define a Web site Specify the site's local root folder location to help Dreamweaver keep track of the links among Web pages and supporting files and set other Web site preferences. Also referred to as setting up a site.

Definition list A list composed of terms that are displayed with a hanging indent and is often used with terms and definitions.

Delimiter A comma, tab, colon, semicolon, or similar character that separates tabular data in a text file.

Deliverables Products that will be provided to a client upon project completion, such as the creation of new pages or graphic elements.

Deprecated Features that are being phased out and will soon be invalid or obsolete, such as directory or menu lists.

Derivative work Work based on another preexisting work.

Description A short summary of Web site content; resides in the Head section.

Design notes Notes directed to other content creators who are working on different parts of your site.

Design view The view that shows a page in the entire Document window and is primarily used when designing and creating a Web page.

Designer layout A layout in the Dreamweaver workspace, in which panels are docked on the right side of the screen and Design view is the default view.

Distance A feature that shows you the distance between two guides when you hold down the control key and place the mouse pointer between the guides.

Div Page elements created with div tags that are used to position and style content.

Div tag An HTML tag that is used to format and position divs.

Document toolbar A toolbar that contains buttons for changing the current Web page view, previewing and debugging Web pages, and managing files.

Document window The large area under the document toolbar that encompasses most of the Dreamweaver workspace; Web pages that you open appear in this area.

Document-relative path A path referenced in relation to the Web page that is currently displayed.

Domain name An IP address expressed in letters instead of numbers, usually reflecting the name of the business, individual, or other organization represented by the Web site.

Download To transfer files from a remote computer to your computer.

Download time The amount of time it takes to download a file.

Drive A computer storage device designated by a drive letter (such as *C:*) and a drive name (such as *Local Disk*).

Drop zone The position on the screen where a panel that is being moved will be docked when you release the mouse button.

DSL (Digital Subscriber Line) A type of always-on Internet connection.

Dual Screen layout A layout that utilizes two monitors: one for the document window and Property inspector and one for the panels.

Dynamic content Content that changes either in response to certain conditions or through interaction with the user.

Dynamic image An image that is replaced with another image. *See also* Recordset.

Edit To insert, delete, or change page content, such as inserting a new image, adding a link, or correcting spelling errors.

Editable optional region In a template, a region that allows content contributors to both edit the content and choose to show or hide the content.

Editable region In a template, an area the template author creates that allows content contributors to insert text or images.

Embedded style A style whose code is stored in the head content of a Web page, rather than in a separate external file. *See also* internal style.

Event A reaction to an action that causes a behavior to start.

Expanded tables mode Displays a table with expanded table borders and temporary space between the cells to simplify working with individual cells.

Export data To save data that was created in Dreamweaver in a different file format so that other programs can read it.

External link A link that connects to a Web page in another Web site or to an e-mail address.

External style sheet A single file, separate from the Web page, that contains formatting code and can be attached to a Web page to quickly apply formatting to page content.

Facebook A social networking site that enables a user to set up a profile page in order to post and exchange information with others.

Fair use An exemption to copyright that allows limited reproduction of copyright-protected work for certain permissible purposes such as research and reporting.

Favorite An asset that you expect to use repeatedly while you work on a site and that is categorized separately in the Assets panel; also, the Dreamweaver Help feature that allows you to add topics to the Favorites window that you might want to view later without having to search again.

Field A form area into which users can insert a specific piece of data, such as their last name or address.

File field In a form, a field that lets users browse to and upload a file.

File hierarchy A tree-like structure that connects all the drives, folders, and files on your computer.

File management Organizing, saving, and finding files and folders on a computer.

File server *See* server.

File Transfer Protocol *See* FTP.

Files panel A file management tool similar to Windows Explorer or Finder, where Dreamweaver stores and manages your Web site files and folders.

Fixed layout A CSS layout that uses columns expressed in pixels that will not change sizes when viewed in different window sizes.

Flash movies Low-bandwidth animations and interactive elements created with the Adobe Flash program.

Flash Player *See* Adobe Flash Player.

Flash videos Videos that have been converted from a digital video format to an .flv file using Adobe Flash.

Focus group A marketing tool that gathers feedback from a specific group of people about a product, such as the impact of a television ad or the effectiveness of a Web site design.

Fold line The crease line on a newspaper when it is horizontally folded; the most important information goes above the fold line.

Folder A named location on a disk that helps you group related files together, similar to the way you might group papers in file folders in a file cabinet.

Font family A group of similar fonts used by Dreamweaver to format text, such as Arial, Helvetica, sans-serif.

Form A collection of input fields that allows one to obtain information from Web site users.

Form action attribute Part of a form tag that specifies how the form will be processed.

Form field A form area into which users can insert a specific piece of data.

Form object An individual component of a form that accepts an individual piece of information.

Format To adjust the appearance of page elements, such as resizing an image or changing the color of text.

Frameset A document that contains the instructions that tell a browser how to lay out a set of frames which show multiple documents on a single page.

Front-end processing The beginning of the processing cycle when the data is collected.

FTP (File Transfer Protocol) The technology used to upload and download files to and from a remote site.

Get method Specifies that the data collected in a form be sent to the server encoded into the URL of the Web page in the form action property.

GIF (Graphics Interchange Format) file A type of file format used for images placed on Web pages, is used for images with transparent backgrounds.

Global style A style used to apply common properties for certain page elements, such as text, links, or backgrounds.

Go to URLs Direct the browser to use a link to open a different window.

Google Video Chat A video and audio sharing application.

Graphic A picture or design element that adds visual interest to a page.

Graphic file A graphic in digital format.

Grid A set of horizontal and vertical lines resembling graph paper that fills the page.

Group selector A group of rules with common formatting properties that are grouped together to help reduce the size of style sheets.

GPS (Global Positioning System) A device used to track your position through a global satellite navigation system.

Guide A horizontal or vertical line that you drag onto a page from a ruler, used to position objects; guides are not visible in the browser.

Hard drive The main storage disk on a computer.

Head content Items such as the page title, keywords, and description that are contained in the Head section; *see also* description, head section, keyword, meta tag, *and* page title.

Head section The part of a Web page that is not visible in the browser window; *see also* head content.

Heading One of six different text styles that can be applied to text: Heading 1 (the largest size) through Heading 6 (the smallest size).

Height property (H) The height of an AP element expressed either in pixels or as a percentage of the page.

Hexadecimal value A numerical value that represents the amount of red, green, and blue in a color.

Hidden field On a form, an invisible field that stores user information.

History Panel A Dreamweaver panel that lists the steps that have been performed while editing and formatting a document.

Home page The first Web page that appears when you access a Web site.

Horizontal and vertical space Blank space above, below, and on the sides of an image that separates the image from the text or other elements on the page.

Hotspot A clickable area on an image that, when clicked, links to a different location on the page or to another Web page.

HTML (Hypertext Markup Language) A language Web developers use to create Web pages using tags surrounded by angle brackets; *see also* XHTML.

HTML div tag See div tag.

HTML form A Web page or a portion of a Web page that includes one or more form objects that allow a user to enter information and send it to a host Web server.

HTML reports Five reports that check files in a Web site: Combinable Nested Font Tags, Missing Alt Text, Redundant Nested Tags, Removable Empty Tags, and Untitled Documents.

HTML style A style used to redefine an HTML tag.

HTTP (Hypertext transfer protocol) The hypertext protocol that precedes absolute paths to external links.

Hyperlink *See* link.

Hypertext Markup Language *See* HTML.

Image map An image that has clickable areas defined on it that, when clicked, serve as links that take the viewer to other locations.

Import data To bring data created in another software program into Dreamweaver.

InContext Editing An online service that enables users to make changes to designated editable regions on a page while viewing it in a browser.

Index A directory, or list of files.

Inline style A style that uses code stored in the body content of a Web page. *See also* embedded style *and* internal style.

Insert panel A panel containing buttons organized by categories for creating or inserting objects such as images, forms, and videos.

Intellectual property A product resulting from human creativity.

Internal link A link to a Web page within the same Web site.

Internal style A style that uses code stored in the head content of a Web page. *See also* embedded style *and* inline style.

Internet Protocol *See* IP address.

Internet Service Provider *See* ISP.

Intranet An internal Web site without public access; companies often have intranets that only their employees can access.

IP (Internet Protocol) address An assigned series of four numbers, separated by periods, that indicates the address of a specific computer or other piece of hardware on the Internet or an internal computer network.

ISP (Internet Service Provider) A company that supplies Internet access.

Item Each link in a Spry menu bar.

JavaScript Code that adds interaction between the user and the Web page, such as rollovers or interactive forms.

JavaScript behavior An action script that allows you to add dynamic content to your Web pages.

JPEG (Joint Photographic Exports Group) file A file format used for images that appear on Web pages; many photographs are saved in JPEG format.

Keyword Word that provides information about the content of a Web site.

Left property (L) The distance between the left edge of an AP element and the left edge of the page or parent container, such as another div.

Licensing agreement Permission given by a copyright holder that conveys the right to use the copyright holder's work under certain conditions.

Line break Code that places text on a separate line without creating a new paragraph. You create a line break by pressing [Shift][Enter] (Win) or [shift][return] (Mac).

Line numbers Provide a point of reference when locating specific sections of code.

Link An image or text element on a Web page that users click to display another location on the page, another Web page on the same Web site, or a Web page on a different Web site; *also called* hyperlink.

Liquid layout A CSS layout that uses columns expressed as percents based on the browser window width, so they will change width according to the dimensions of the browser window.

List A form object that provides the user with a list or menu of choices to select. Lists display the choices in a scrolling menu.

Live view The view that displays an open document with its interactive elements active and functioning, as if you were viewing the document in a browser.

Local disk *See* drive.

Local site The folder location that contains all the files for a Web site.

Local site root folder A folder on your hard drive or other storage device that will hold all the files and folders for a Web site.

Local/Network The setting used in Dreamweaver to publish a Web site on either the local drive (that is, your own hard drive) or a local network drive.

Locked region An area on a page that only the template author has access to.

Low-bandwidth animations Animations that don't require a fast connection to work properly.

Mapped drive An icon representing a network drive, identified by a letter such as *J* or *K* and a name.

mailto: link An e-mail address on a Web page for users to contact the Web site's headquarters, a common point of contact.

Media objects Combinations of visual and audio effects and text used to create an interactive experience with a website.

Menu A form object displayed in a shortcut menu that provides the user with a list of options to select.

Menu bar (*Mac*) A bar located at the top of the Dreamweaver workspace that includes menu names, a workspace switcher, and other program commands; *see also* Application bar (*Win*).

Menu bar A set of text or graphical links used to navigate between pages in a Web site; *also called* navigation bar.

Merge cells To combine multiple adjacent cells into one cell.

Meta tags HTML code that includes information about the page such as keywords and descriptions.

Method property Specifies the protocol used to send form data to a Web server.

Micro blog A blog that only allows users to post short posts, such as Twitter.

Microsoft Visual SourceSafe A remote access option used on the Windows platform using Microsoft Visual SourceSafe Client.

MPEG (Motion Picture Experts Group) A video file format that compresses and stores digital video and audio data.

Multi-line text field In forms, a data entry area that is useful for entering text that may take several sentences to complete; *also called* text area field.

Multiple Document Interface (MDI) All the document windows and panels are positioned within one large application window.

Named anchor A specific location on a Web page that is represented by an icon and an assigned descriptive name.

Navigation bar *See* menu bar.

Nested AP div An AP div whose HTML code resides inside another AP div.

Nested table A table that is placed inside the cell of another table.

Nested template A template that is based on another template.

Network drive A remote drive connected to another computer that is not directly connected to your computer. For example, a local drive.

Nonbreaking space A space that appears in a fixed location to keep a line break from separating text into two lines or, in the case of table cells, to keep an empty cell from collapsing.

Non-Web-safe color A color that may not appear uniformly across platforms.

OnClick An event when the mouse is clicked on a page element that triggers an action.

OnLoad An event when a page is loaded in a browser window that triggers an action.

OnMouseOver An event that occurs when the mouse is placed over a page element that triggers an action.

Optional region In a template, an area that content contributors can choose to show or hide.

Ordered list A list of items that are placed in a specific order and is preceded by numbers or letters.

Orphaned file A file that is not linked to any page in the Web site.

Page title The title of a page that appears in the title bar in a browser when a Web page is viewed on the Internet.

Panel A small window that contains program controls.

Panel group A set of related panels that are grouped together; also called tab group.

Panel group title bar The dark gray colored bar at the top of each panel group.

Password field In a form, a field that displays asterisks or bullets when a user types in a password.

Path The name and physical location of a Web page file that opens when a link is clicked.

Plug-in A small computer program that works with a host application such as a Web browser to enable it to perform certain functions; *also called* add-on.

PNG (Portable Network Graphics) file A file format used for Web page images; capable of showing millions of colors, but is small in file size.

Podcast (Programming on Demand) Digital media files that are downloaded from Web pages.

Point of contact A place on a Web page that provides users a means of contacting a company if they have questions or problems.

Post method Specifies that the data be sent to the processing script as a binary or encrypted file.

Progressive download video A type of Web video which can be played while it is downloading to the user's computer. If the playback rate exceeds the download rate, a delay is experienced.

Properties panel *See* Property inspector.

Property inspector A Dreamweaver panel that displays the characteristics of the currently selected object on a Web page; *also called* Properties panel.

Pseudo class style A style that determines the appearance of a page element when certain conditions are met.

Public domain Images or text on a Web site that can be used by the public without restrictions or cost.

Publish a Web site To make a Web site available for viewing on the Internet or on an intranet.

Radio button An option button on a form that appears as a small empty circle that users click to select a choice.

Radio group Two or more radio buttons grouped together on a form.

RDS (Remote Development Services) A remote access option used with a remote folder running ColdFusion.

Recordset A database stored on a server that can contain image files for dynamic images. *See also* dynamic image.

Reference panel A panel that is used to find answers to coding questions, covering topics such as HTML, JavaScript, and accessibility.

Related Files toolbar The toolbar that displays the names of files related to the open and active file.

Relative path A path used with an internal link to reference a Web page or a graphic file within the Web site.

Relative positioning The placement of div tags in relation to other Web page elements.

Remote site The folder location on a Web server that is connected to the Internet with software for hosting Web sites, not directly connected to the computer housing the local site.

Repeating region In a template, a region that contains content that is used multiple times.

Repeating table A table with a predefined structure in a template that content contributors have access to.

Reset a form To erase the entries that have been previously entered in a form and set the values back to the default settings.

Rollover A screen element that changes in appearance as the pointer rests on it in a browser window.

Root-relative path A path referenced from a Web site's root folder.

Roundtrip HTML The Dreamweaver feature that allows HTML files created in other programs, such as Microsoft Expression Web, to be opened in Dreamweaver without adding additional coding, such as meta tags or spaces.

Row A group of table cells arranged horizontally.

Royalty-free graphic An image that you can purchase and use in your published Web pages without having to pay a royalty fee to the person that created it.

RSS (Really Simple Syndication) feed Regularly scheduled information downloads used by Web sites to distribute news stories, information, or announcements.

Rule A set of formatting attributes that defines styles in a Cascading Style Sheet.

Sans-serif font A block style character used frequently for headings, sub-headings, and Web pages.

Scope creep When impromptu changes or additions are made to a project without accounting for corresponding increases in the schedule or budget.

Screen reader A device used by the visually impaired to convert written text on a computer monitor to spoken words.

Seamless image A tiled image that is blurred at the edges so that it appears to be all one image, or made from a pattern that, when tiled, appears to be one image, such as a vertical stripe.

Selector The name or tags in Cascading Style Sheets to which style declarations are assigned.

Semantic markup Coding to emphasize meaning.

Semantic Web Refers to the way page content can be coded to emphasize the meaning to users.

Serif font A font with small extra strokes at the top and bottom of the characters; used frequently for paragraph text in printed materials.

Server A computer that is connected to other computers to provide file storage and processing services.

Server-side scripting A script that processes a form on the form's host Web server.

Server Behaviors panel The panel that is used to add, edit, and create server behaviors such as a login page.

Shortcut (*Win*) An icon that represents a software program, folder, or file stored on your computer system.

Single-line text field In a form, a data entry area that is useful for small pieces of data such as a name or telephone number.

Site map A listing of all of the pages in a Web site.

Site root folder A folder that stores all of the Web site files; *see also* Local site root folder.

Site usability test A process that involves obtaining Web site feedback from users who are not connected to the project.

Skin The bar at the bottom of a video with the control buttons.

Skype A video and audio communication service.

Smart object A Photoshop file with layers that contain image source information to allow an image to be modified while retaining the original data.

Snippets panel A panel that lets you create, insert, and store pieces of code, called snippets, for reuse.

Social networking Any Web-based service that facilitates social interaction among users.

Split cells To divide cells into multiple rows or columns.

Spry Open source code developed by Adobe to help designers quickly incorporate dynamic content on their Web pages; *also called* Spry framework for AJAX.

Spry effects Screen effects such as fading or enlarging page elements.

Spry framework for AJAX *See* Spry.

Spry menu bar A preset widget that creates a dynamic, user-friendly menu bar.

Spry widget A prebuilt component for adding interactivity to pages.

SpryAssets folder A folder that is automatically created in a site root folder when a spry effect is added to a page.

Standard mode A Dreamweaver mode that displays a table with no extra space added between the table cells.

Standard toolbar A toolbar that contains buttons for some frequently used commands on the File and Edit menus.

State On a menu bar, the condition of a menu item relative to the mouse pointer, such as Up, Down, Over, and Over While Down.

Status bar A bar that appears under the Dreamweaver window; the left side displays the tag selector, which shows the HTML tags being used at the insertion point location; the right side displays the window size and estimated download time for the page displayed.

Storyboard A small sketch that represents each page in a Web site; like a flowchart, shows the relationship of each page to the other pages in the site.

Streaming download video A Web video that begins playing before the entire file has been downloaded and uses buffers to gather the content as it downloads to ensure a smoother playback.

Style A named group of formatting characteristics.

Style Rendering Toolbar A toolbar that contains buttons that can be used to display a page using different media types.

Submit a form To send the information on a form to a host Web server for processing.

Swap Image behavior JavaScript code that directs the browser to display a different image when the mouse is rolled over an image on the page.

Swap Image Restore behavior JavaScript code that restores a swapped image back to the original image.

Synchronize To transfer the latest version of Web files to a server.

Tab group *See* panel group.

Table A grid of rows and columns that can be used to hold tabular data on a Web page.

Table header Text placed at the top or side of a table on a Web page and read by screen readers.

Tabular data Data arranged in columns and rows that are separated by a delimiter.

Tag An individual piece of HTML code that instructs the browser how each page element should be displayed.

Tag Editor A Dreamweaver panel that is used to insert or edit HTML code.

Tag selector A location on the status bar that displays HTML tags being used at the insertion point location.

Target The location on a Web page that the browser will display in full view when the user clicks an internal link.

Template A Web page that contains the basic layout for each page in a Web site.

Template author The person who creates a template.

Terms of use Rules that govern how a user may use a Web site's content.

Text area *See* multi-line text field.

Text field On a form, a box in which a user can enter text. *See also* single-line text field *and* multi-line text field.

Tiled image A small graphic that repeats across and down a Web page, appearing as individual squares or rectangles.

Timeline A JavaScript feature that will cause an AP element to appear to move along a path, or change size, visibility, or position.

Title bar A bar across the top of the Dreamweaver window that displays the name of the program, the name of the file, and the title of the open page enclosed in parentheses; also includes buttons for minimizing, resizing, and closing the window in the upper-left or upper-right corner, depending on which type of computer you are using.

Top property (T) The distance between the top edge of an AP element and the top edge of the page or AP element that contains it.

Trademark Protects an image, word, slogan, symbol, or design used to identify goods or services.

Transparent background A background composed of transparent pixels, rather than pixels of a color, resulting in images that blend easily on a Web page background.

Twitter A Web site where users post short messages, called "tweets."

Unordered list *See* bulleted list.

Up Image state The state of a page element when the user's mouse pointer is not on the element.

Upload To send a form or files to a host Web server.

URL (Uniform Resource Locator) The address for a Web page as an assigned series of numbers, separated by periods.

Vector-based graphic A scalable graphic built using mathematical formulas rather than pixels.

Vertical space *See* horizontal and vertical space.

Vidcast *See* vodcast.

Visited link A link that the user has previously clicked, or visited; the default color for a visited link is purple.

Visual Aid A page feature that appears in Design view but not in the browser, such as a table border.

Vodcast A video podcast; *also called* vidcast.

Web 2.0 The evolution of Web applications that facilitate and promote information sharing among internet users.

Web browser Software used to display pages on a Web site. The most popular Web browsers are Internet Explorer, Mozilla Firefox, Google Chrome, Opera, and Safari; *also called* browser.

Web cam A camera used for video communication on the Web.

Web design program A program for creating interactive Web pages with text, images, hyperlinks, animation, sounds, and video.

Web page A page of text in HTML format combined with images in various image formats.

Web server A computer that is connected to the Internet with a static IP address and software that enables it make files accessible to anyone on the internet or an intranet; *see also* IP address.

Web site A collection of related Web pages stored on a server that users can display using a Web browser.

WebDAV (Web-based Distributed Authoring and Versioning) A remote access option used with servers such as the Microsoft Internet Information Server (IIS) and apache Web server.

Web-safe color A color that will display consistently in all browsers, and on Macintosh, Windows, and Unix computers.

White space An area on a Web page that is not filled with text or graphics; not necessarily white.

Widget A piece of code that allows users to interact with the program interface.

Width property (W) The width of an AP element either in pixels or as a percentage of the page.

Wiki A site where a user can use simple editing tools to contribute and edit page content in the site.

Wikipedia An online encyclopedia where users can use simple editing tools to contribute and edit page content.

Wireframe A prototype of each page's content and relationship to other pages in a Web site.

Word wrap Keeps all code within the width of the Document window.

Workflow reports Reports that enable you to check the progress of a project, such as a report that will list all files that have been modified recently.

Workspace The Dreamweaver interface made up of the document window, the menu bar, toolbars, Property inspector, and panels.

Workspace switcher A drop-down menu on the Application bar (Win) or Menu bar (Mac) that allows you to quickly change the between different preset workspace screen arrangements.

WYSIWYG (What You See Is What You Get) A type of web design program (such as Dreamweaver) which shows the page as it will appear in a browser window.

XHTML (eXtensible HyperText Markup Language) The most recent standard for developing Web pages, based on HTML and XML; requires an end tag for every start tag; *see also* HTML.

YouTube A Web site where you can view or upload videos.

Z-index property The property used to specify the vertical stacking order of multiple AP divs on a page.

Index

hard return, 76
head content, **50**
header background color, 172
header row, 204
.header style, 172
Heading 2 format, 76
Heading 4 format, 76
headings, 54
   HTML code, 76
Head object, 50
head section, 50
Height (H) property, 170, **176**
help, context-specific, 14
Help, Dreamweaver Help command, 14
Help feature
   Adobe Community Help, 14, **19**
   topics and subtopics by category, 14
heron_small.jpg file, 236
heron_waiting_small image, 254, 256
heron_waiting_small.jpg file, 132
hexadecimal value, **52**
hidden fields, **222**
hidden toolbars, 6
History panel, **58**, 198
home image map, 148
Home item, 140
home page, **10**
   good first impression, 36
   links, 134
horizontal guide, 174
horizontal rule, 58, 60, 206, 234
horizontal space, **106**
horizontal symmetry, 63
hotspots, **148**–149
HR tag, 60
.htm file extension, 34
HTML code, 8, 10
   AP (absolutely positioned) div, 180
   body section, 180
   converting to XHTML-compliant code, 61
   headings, 76
   head section, 180
   ID, 164
   line numbers, **60**
   tags, **76**
   viewing, 60–61
   word wrap, **60**
HTML documents, 10
HTML errors, debugging, **61**
.html file extension, 2, 8, 34, 38, 60
HTML files, opening, 2
HTML form objects, 230
HTML (HyperText Markup Language), **2**, 61
HTML Property inspector, 54, 76, 81, 170
   Browse for File icon, 56, 134
   Class list arrow, 84, 86
   Class list box, 81, 86
   ...t box, 170
   ... arrow, 202
   ...tton, 54, 56
   ...ext box, 132, 133
   ... File icon, 138
   ...t arrow, 149

Unordered List button, 78
   Vertical alignment option, 203
HTML style, **80**
HTML tags and tables, 194
http (hypertext transfer protocol), **130**
hyperlinks, **12**, 56
Hypertext Markup Language. *See* HTML
   (Hypertext Markup Language)
hypertext transfer protocol. *See* http (hypertext
   transfer protocol)

I

icons and color, 8
ID property, 170
Illustrator image creation, 116
Image command, 202
image editors, 106
image files
   additional storage location, 115
   deleting from Web sites, 114
   managing, 115
image maps, **129**, **148**
images, 2, 12, 110
   aligning, **104**, 202
   alternate text, **108**
   borders, **106**
   centering, 164
   copying to Web site, 36
   copyright statement, 116
   correct source file location, 36
   creation, 116
   cropping, **106**, 107
   default alignment, **104**
   dynamic, **104**
   enhancing, 106
   file formats, 117
   finding, 116
   horizontal space, **106**
   hotspots, 148
   inserting, 102, 110, 202
   locating, 116
   original, 116
   public domain, 116
   resizing, 107
   resizing handles, 106
   transparent backgrounds, **116**
   vertical space, **106**
images folder, 32
Image Tag Accessibility Attributes dialog box,
   102, 109, 202
importing
   delimited files, 205
   Microsoft Office documents, 76
   tabular data, **205**
   text, 74
Import Tabular Data command, 194
Import Tabular Data dialog box, 205
indenting and outdenting text, 75
index, 116
index.html file, 34, 50, 56, 140, 146, 148, 168
   broken image, 36

e-mail link, 150
   external style sheet, 88
information bar, 254
inline styles, **80**
Input Tag Accessibility Attributes dialog box,
   226, 228, 230, 232
Insert, Form command, 224
Insert, Form submenu, 227
Insert, Horizontal Rule command, 58, 234
Insert, HTML, Horizontal Rule command, 206
Insert, Image command, 102
Insert, Image Objects, Fireworks HTML
   command, 141
Insert, Layout Objects, AP Div command, 174
Insert, Table command, 200
Insert, Table Objects command, 194
Insert bar, 2
Insert Date dialog box, 60
Insert Document dialog box, 76
Insert FLV dialog box, 260
Insert panel, **2**, **6**, 9, 202
   Button button, 232
   Checkbox, 230
   Common category, 3, 50, 56, 58, 60, 102,
      136, 194, 196, 202, 226, 252, 258
   Data category, 3
   Date object button, 60
   default button, 202
   Draw AP Div button, 174
   Expanded Tables mode button, 194
   Favorites category, 3
   FLV option, 260
   Form button, 224
   Forms category, 3, 224, 226–228, 230, 232
   Head list arrow, 50
   Horizontal rule, 58
   Images button, 102
   Images list arrow, 102, 202, 258
   InContext Editing category, 3
   Insert panel list arrow, 50, 56, 140
   Label button, 228
   Layout category, 3, 140, 174, 194, 196
   Media list arrow, 252, 260
   Named Anchor button, 136
   Radio Group button, 228
   Spry category, 3, 140
   Spry Menu Bar button, 140
   Standard mode button, 194
   SWF option, 252
   Table button, 194, 200, 226
   Table command, 196
   Textarea button, 227
   Text category, 3
   Text Field button, 226, 227
Insert Rows or Columns dialog box, 201
intellectual property, **118**
interactive elements, 250
interactive forms, 61
interactive games, 175
interactive menu bar, 140
interactive Web pages, 2
internal body_text style, 88